Recommended by **Teachers**
Trusted by **Toppers**

All in One

HOME SCIENCE
Class 12

EVERYTHING YOU NEED TO SCORE

- Simplified NCERT Theory
- NCERT & Other Important Questions
- CBQs; MCQs, A-R, Case Based
- Board Questions Upto 2025
- Sample Question Papers

CBSE Exams 2026

Author
Dr. Neetu Yadav

arihant
SUCCESS AND NOTHING LESS

arihant
SUCCESS AND NOTHING LESS

ARIHANT PRAKASHAN
(School Division Series)

卐 *ADMINISTRATIVE & PRODUCTION OFFICES*

Regd. Office
'Ramchhaya' 4577/15, Agarwal Road, Darya Ganj, New Delhi -110002
Tele: 011- 47630600, 43518550; Fax: 011- 23280316

卐 *Head Office*
Kalindi, TP Nagar, Meerut (UP) - 250002, Tel: 0121-7156203, 7156204

卐 *SALES & SUPPORT OFFICES*
Agra, Ahmedabad, Bengaluru, Bareilly, Chennai, Delhi, Guwahati, Hyderabad, Jaipur, Jhansi, Kolkata, Lucknow, Nagpur & Pune.

PO No : TXT-XX-XXXXXXX-X-XX

Published By Arihant Publications (India) Ltd.

For further information about the books published by Arihant, log on to www.arihantbooks.com or e-mail at info@arihantbooks.com

Follow us on

卐 *PRICE* ₹375.00

PRODUCTION TEAM

Publishing Managers
Mahendra Singh Rawat & Keshav Mohan

Cover Designer
Salman Shaikh

Inner Designer
Ankit Tyagi

Project Head
Monika Bhasin

Page Layouting
Chintoo Kumar

Proof Reader
Anurag Vashist, Pravesh Bhagrwal

Index *cum* Study Planner

Latest Course Structure

Paper: One **Time: 3 Hrs** **Max. Marks : 70**

No.	Units	Marks
I	Work, Livelihood and Career	05
II	Nutrition, Food Science and Technology	23
III	Human Development and Family Studies	10
IV	Fabric and Apparel	17
V	Resource Management	10
VI	Communication and Extension	05
	THEORY	70
	PRACTICAL	30
	GRAND TOTAL	**100**

UNIT I Work, Livelihood and Career

Ch. Work, Livelihood and Career

UNIT II Nutrition, Food Science and Technology

Ch. Clinical Nutrition and Dietetics

Ch. Public Nutrition and Health

Ch. Food Processing and Technology

Ch. Food Quality and Food Safety

UNIT III Human Development and Family Studies

Ch. Early Childhood Care and Education

Ch. Management of Support Services, Institutions and Programmes for Children, Youth and Elderly

UNIT IV Fabric and Apparel

Ch. Design for Fabric and Apparel

Ch. Fashion Design and Merchandising

Ch. Care and Maintenance of Fabrics in Institutions

UNIT V Resource Management

Ch. Hospitality Management

Ch. Consumer Education and Protection

UNIT VI Communication and Extension

Ch. Development Communication and Journalism

UNIT I WORK, LIVELIHOOD AND CAREER

Chapter : Work, Livelihood and Career

- Introduction
  - Work and meaningful work
  - Work, careers and livelihood
- Traditional Occupation in India
  - Agriculture
  - Handicrafts
  - Indian cuisine
  - Visual arts
- Work, Age and Gender
  - Gender issues in relation to work
  - Issues and concerns related to women and work
    - KGBV Scheme
    - Beti bachao, Beti Padhao Scheme
- Attitudes and Approaches to Work and Life Skills for livelihood
  - Attitudes and approaches to work
  - Life skills for livelihood
  - Essential soft skills at workplace

- Ergonomics
  - Definition and need for Ergonomics
  - Benefits of Ergonomics
- Entrepreneurship
  - Definition and characteristics

UNIT II NUTRITION, FOOD SCIENCE AND TECHNOLOGY

Chapter: Clinical Nutrition and Dietetics

- Introduction
  - Nutrition
  - Clinical Nutrition
- Significance
- Basic concepts
- Diet therapy
- Types of diets: Regular diet and Modified diets
  - Changes in consistency
  - Feeding routes
  - Prevention of chronic diseases
- Preparing for career
- Scope

Chapter: Public Nutrition and Health

- Introduction
- Significance
- Basic concept
  - Public health nutrition
  - Nutritional problems of India
- Protein energy malnutrition
- Micronutrient deficiencies
- Iron deficiency anemia
- Vitamin A deficiency
- Iodine deficiency disorders
- Strategies/Intervention to tackle nutritional problems
- Diet or food based strategies
- Nutrient based strategies
- Nutrition programmes operating in India
- ICDS
- Nutrient Deficiency Control Programmes
- Food Supplementation Programmes
- Food Security Programme
- Health Care
- Scope

Chapter: Food Processing and Technology

- Introduction
- Significance
- Basic concepts
  - Food science
  - Food processing
  - Food technology
  - Food manufacturing
- Development of food processing and technology
- Importance of food processing and preservation
- Classification of food on the basis of extent and type of processing
- Preparing for a career
- Scope

Chapter: Food Quality and Food Safety

- Introduction
- Significance
- Basic concepts
  - Food safety (Toxicity & Hazard)
  - Hazards (Physical, chemical and biological)
  - Food infection
  - Food poisoning
  - Food quality
- Food standards regulation in India-FSSA (2006)
- International organisation and agreements in the area of food standards, quality, research and trade
  - Codex Alimentarius Commission
  - International Organisation for Standardisation
  - World Trade Organisation

- Food Safety Management Systems
  - Good Manufacturing Practices (GMP)
  - Good Handling Practices (GHP)
  - Hazard Analysis Critical Control Points (HACCP)
- Scope

UNIT III HUMAN DEVELOPMENT AND FAMILY STUDIES

Chapter: Early Childhood Care and Education

- Significance
- Basic concepts
- Preparing for a career
- Scope

Chapter: Management of Support Services, Institutions and Programmes for Children, Youth and Elderly

- Significance
- Basic concepts
- Why are children vulnerable?
- Institutions, programmes and initiatives for children
  - ICDS
  - SOS Children's Village
  - Children's Homes run by the government
  - Adoption
- Why are youth vulnerable?
- Youth programmes in India
- Why are the elderly vulnerable?
- Some programmes for the elderly
- Preparing for a career
- Scope

UNIT IV FABRIC AND APPAREL

Chapter: Design for Fabric and Apparel

- Introduction
- Basic concepts (Design: Structural & Applied)
- Elements of design
  - Colour
  - Texture
  - Line
  - Shapes or form
- Principles of design
  - Proportion
  - Balance
  - Emphasis
  - Rhythm
  - Harmony
- Preparing for career
- Scope

Chapter: Fashion Design and Merchandising

- Introduction
- Significance
- Basic concepts
  - Fashion terminology –Fashion, fads, style, classic
- Fashion development
  - France-The centre of fashion
  - Fashion Evolution
- Fashion merchandising
- Fashion retail organisation
- Preparing for a career
- Scope

Chapter: Care and Maintenance of Fabrics in Institution

- Introduction
- Basic concepts
  - Washing equipment
  - Drying equipment
  - Ironing/pressing equipment
- Institutions
- Preparing for a career
- Scope

UNIT V RESOURCE MANAGEMENT

Chapter: Hospitality Management

- Introduction
- Significance
- Basic concepts
- Departments involved in hospitality management of an organisation
- Scope

Chapter: Consumer Education and Protection

- Introduction
- Significance of consumer education and protection
- Basic concepts
  - Consumer product
  - Consumer behaviour
  - Consumer forum
  - Consumer footfalls
  - Consumer problems
  - Consumer rights
  - Standardised marks (ISI, Wool Mark, Hall Mark, Silk Mark)
  - Protection councils
  - Consumer responsibilities
- Scope

UNIT VI COMMUNICATION AND EXTENSION

Chapter: Development Communication and Journalism

- Introduction
- Significance
- Basic concepts
  - Development
  - Development journalism
  - Development communication
- Methods of communication
  - Campaign
  - Radio and television
  - Print Media
  - Information and communication technologies
- Knowledge and skills required for a career in this field
- Scope and career avenues in development communication

PRACTICALS FOR CLASS XII

UNIT II NUTRITION, FOOD SCIENCE AND TECHNOLOGY

1. Modification of normal diet to soft diet for elderly person.
2. Development and preparation of supplementary foods for nutrition programme.
3. Planning a menu for a school canteen or mid-day meal in school for a week.
4. Design, prepare and evaluate a processed food product.
5. Qualitative test for food adulteration in: pure ghee, tea leaves, whole black pepper, turmeric powder, milk, asafoetida.

UNIT III HUMAN DEVELOPMENT AND FAMILY STUDIES

6. Preparation and use of any one teaching aid to communicate socially relevant messages for children/ adolescents /adults in the community.

   OR

   Preparation of any one toy for children (age appropriate) using locally available and indigenous material

UNIT IV FABRIC AND APPAREL

7. Preparation of any one article using applied textile design techniques; tie and dye/batik/block printing.
8. Remove different types of stains from white cotton cloth –Ball pen, curry, grease, ink, lipstick, tea and coffee.

UNIT V RESOURCE MANAGEMENT

9. Evaluate any one advertisement for any job position.
10. Develop a leaflet/pamphlet for consumer education and protection on any one of the following
    (a) Consumer Protection Act (CPA)
    (b) Consumer responsibilities
    (c) Consumer organisation
    (d) Consumer problem

PROJECT

ANY ONE OF THE FOLLOWING PROJECT MAY BE UNDERTAKEN AND EVALUATED

1. Study of an integrated community based, nutrition/health programme being implemented in own area, with reference to
   a) Programme objectives
   b) Focal group/Beneficiaries
   c) Modalities of implementation
2. Visit to the neighbouring areas and interview two adolescents and two adults regarding their perception of persons with special needs.
3. Profile any two person (child/adult) with special needs to find out their diet, clothing, activities,physical and psychological needs.
4. Planning any five messages for nutrition, health and life skills using different modes of communication for different focal groups.
5. Market survey any five processed foods with their packaging and label information.

SCHEME FOR PRACTICAL EXAMINATION — 30 Marks

1. Project (5 marks)
2. Modification of any one family meal for elderly person. Preparing any one of the modified dish. (5 marks)

   OR

   Development and preparation of any one supplementary food for pre-schooler (2-6 years) nutrition programme.

   OR

   Planning a menu for school canteen and preparing any one nutritious dish.
3. Identify adulterant using chemical test in any one of the following- pure ghee, tea leaves, whole black pepper, turmeric powder, milk, asafoetida. (2 marks)
4. Prepare a sample using applied textile design techniques tie and dye/batik/block printing. (4 marks)
5. Remove any one of the stain from white cotton cloth –Ball pen, curry, grease, ink, lipstick, tea, coffee. (2 marks)
6. Develop a leaflet/pamphlet for Consumer Education and Protection on any one of the following- (5 marks)
   (a) Consumer Protection Act (CPA)
   (b) Consumer responsibilities
   (c) Consumer organisation
   (d) Consumer problems
7. File (5 marks)
8. Viva (2 marks)

01 CHAPTER

Work, Livelihood and Career

A career is a vital aspect of life that fosters personal growth and adds value to one's existence. Choosing the right career path is essential as it should align with one's skills, interests and values that should contribute to the betterment of the society.

YOUR STUDY GOALS

YOUR PRACTICE GOAL

- Objective Type Questions (44 Qs ; MCQs, A-R, Matching, Case Based)
- Subjective Questions (20 VSAs, 9 SAs, 11 LAs)

1.1 Introduction

Choosing a career is a significant and often challenging decision. On one hand, there is a wide array of career paths to consider, and on the other, young individuals are still in the process of discovering their own aptitude and talent.

In some cases, their interests may be diverse and varied, making the decision even more difficult. To make an informed choice, it is crucial for youth to be exposed to different possibilities. The first step is to explore oneself—understanding one's own strengths, talents, personal preferences, needs and aspirations.

Once self-awareness is achieved, the next step is to explore various career options, aiming to align one's strengths with personal goals and contributions to society. Making the right choice will ultimately lead to both success and fulfillment.

Work and Meaningful Work

- **Work is a fundamental aspect of human life**, involving activities through which individuals may fulfill their necessities through interacting with the world, utilising their **unique skills and contributing to the society**. It is central to every culture, though each has its own values and perceptions about it. Essentially, work forms the core of daily life, providing both structure and purpose.
- Work[1] is more than just a way to earn a living; it significantly impacts one's **identity** and **self-esteem**.

1 Work It is an activity involving mental or physical effort to achieve a purpose or result.

- By engaging in work, individuals contribute to their **organisations**, improving **products, services** or **reputation** and enhancing their **communities.** Work provides **purpose** and **belonging** and affects the overall **quality of life**.
- Work basically constitutes bulk of daily life activities for all human beings. The type of work depends upon several factors like education, health, age, access to opportunities, globalisation, geographic location, financial returns, family background etc.

Importance of Work

Importance of work can be understood with the help of following points

- Work is performed to earn money, fulfill family needs for leisure and re-creation.
- It helps to develop personal identity and boosts self-esteem as well.
- Individuals through work may contribute to organisations by creating better products, improving reputation or increasing profits.
- Work impacts the quality of life in the surrounding world.
- It primarily enables the workers to earn a livelihood, but some may work for pleasure, intellectual stimulation or social contribution without pay. These unpaid workers can include volunteers and family members.
- Work involves contributions to oneself, family, employers, society, nation or the world, not just payment.
- Work can be viewed as a job and a means of making a living. It is a task or duty that entails a sense of obligation.
- Work is likened to "The oil that lubricates the machine of society".

Concept of Work

Work may be viewed as

- A job and a way to earn the livelihood.
- A task or duty that entails a sense of obligation.
- A means of security of livelihood through securing job and income. Dharma or duty, an expression of one's true self, an expression of one's unique talents that influences the quality of life of self and others around us.
- A part of spiritual practice. A vehicle of one's creations.
- A source of joy and fulfillment.
- Working and earning one's livelihood offers scope for hope, self-esteem and dignity.
- A symbol of status, power and control.
- A rewarding experience, a sort of mental or physical workout that can result in success.
- A means of self-development and self-actualisation by reflecting values and aspirations of an individual.

Meaningful Work

- **Meaningful work**[2] is characterised by its **usefulness** to **society** or others, the **engagement** it provides to one's **skills** and **creativity** and the **satisfaction** it brings. Such work fosters, positive, **professional relationships** and provides **recognition** and **rewards**.
- In a wider context, work provides opportunities that contribute towards the improvement of one's own life conditions. For an employee or self employed person, work should be best suits his/her personal attributes, talents or aptitude, competence and skills is very significant. Thus, it is necessary to choose that work which helps an individual to sustain his/her enthusiasm towards that work.

2 **Meaningful Work** Work that makes a difference and impacts society.

- Therefore, work life for anyone and everyone should be based on one's potential and aspirations. For a balanced approach towards building a career and entering a work life, following attributes are to be considered by an individual
  - Their special talents, traits and interests in relation to occupation.
  - Is the work they one choosing engaging and challenging.
  - Whether their chosen occupation provides a sense of usefulness to society or benefits their family.
  - To determine the jobs culture and atmosphere align with their personal growth and development .

Key Differences Between Job and Career

Aspect	Job	Career
Purpose and Scope	Focused on earning money to meet immediate needs. Often a short-term endeavor with specific tasks and responsibilities.	Involves a long-term pursuit of professional goals and personal growth. Includes a series of jobs or roles contributing to overall career development.
Focus	Narrow focus on tasks and compensation. May be part of a larger career but stands alone in its immediate purpose.	Broad focus on personal development, skill enhancement and long-term objectives. Encompasses a broader vision and long-term planning.
Growth and Advancement	Limited advancement beyond the specific role. Growth is confined to immediate responsibilities and tasks.	Provides opportunities for growth and advancement through various roles and experiences. Allows for upward mobility and professional development over time.
Investment in Skills	Minimal investment in education and training. Skills are often role-specific and may not require extensive specialisation.	Involves ongoing learning and skill development. Requires significant investment in education, specialised training and continuous professional development.
Personal Fulfillment	May or may not align with personal interests and passions. Primarily motivated by financial reasons.	Aligned with personal interests, passions and long-term goals. Offers a sense of purpose, fulfillment and achievement.

1.2 Ways to Choose Career

There are various ways through which careers are chosen.

- Some follow their parents' footsteps or careers chosen by their parents.
- A person's personal interests and passions should also be considered while choosing the career.
- A career should provide enjoyment, satisfaction and a sense of usefulness.
- Financial stability is important, but it should not be the sole focus.

Work, Careers and Livelihoods

- Work is defined as a set of activities with an intended set of outcomes. It is not always related to paid employment as it may include entrepreneurship, consulting, volunteerism, contract, social work towards the community welfare and other professional activities.
- **Webster dictionary** defines work as "The labour, task or duty that is one's accustomed means of livelihood or occupation chosen as one's life's work".
- **Livelihood** is defined as a means and occupation by which a person supports oneself to meet basic needs and sustain one's lifestyle. It also involves choice of occupation, career path and the design of work lifestyle.
- **Carrer**[3] is a personal journey that is different for everyone and changes over time. It is a lifelong process that involves balancing work both paid and upaid. Managing different roles in life, learning new skill and making changes when necessary to reason your own goals.

3 **Career** An occupation undertaken for a significant period with opportunities for progress.

- **Webster** dictionary defines career as "A field for or pursuit of consecutive progressive achievement especially in public, professional or business life". Thus, in a holistic sense one's work should nourish their body as well as their mind which further benefits self as well as others in the society.

Example to Explain the Difference Between Work, Livelihood[4] and Career

Three men were breaking stones with hammers. When asked what they were doing, their answers were different

- **The first man** answered, "My job is to break the stones into small pieces". (focuses on his employment.)
- **The second man** answered, "I feed my family by breaking stones into small pieces. So, this is my livelihood". (views his work as a means to sustain his livelihood.)
- **The third man** answered, "I am sculpting an idol on a stone with a hammer. My dream is to become a good sculptor one day". (sees his work as a step towards achieving his career goal and personal dream of becoming a sculptor.)

Perspectives of Work

- **Work as a Job and Livelihood**
  - Work is a source of income enabling desired outcomes.
  - Example Performing a job to support one's family.
  - Satisfaction comes from income generation that meets family needs.
- **Work as a Career**
  - Work is viewed as a path to professional escalation.
  - Focus on higher posts, status, pay and responsibility.
  - Refers to the progression of someone's professional life.
  - A considerable amount of time and energy is dedicated to work.
  - Satisfaction arises from continuous advancements and achievements.
- **Work as a Calling**
  - Satisfaction is derived from the work itself.
  - Work as a call, inprised by an inner drive or higher aim in life.

Quick Test 1

1. When does work become meaningful?
2. Which perspective derives satisfaction from work in a person?
3. What sense and feeling are must for choosing a correct career path?
4. Which life management concept is unique and dynamic in approach?
5. What enables the worker to earn a livelihood?

1.3 Traditional Occupations in India

Unlike many other countries, **India** has a **rich and diverse heritage** of art and culture. Even though there are many different **cultures** and **communities** across the country, there is a **uniting** cultural thread that has lasted over time.

- This article looks at some **traditional jobs** that have been sustained by the **Indian society** over the years.

4 **Livelihood** It means of securing the necessities of life.

Agriculture

- **Agriculture** has long been the backbone of **India's economy**, with approximately **70 per cent** of the population engaged in or reliant up on **agricultural activities.** Historically, agriculture contributed a significant portion to the **national income**, though earlier periods saw insufficient **food grain production,** leading to **imports.**
- However, with the advent of the **Green Revolution** and successive. **Five-Year Plans,** Indian agriculture has experienced significant advancements, achieving **self-sufficiency** in food grain production and even it became an **exporter.**
- India now leads in the production of
  - Tea
  - Milk
  - Ginger
  - Black pepper
  - Spices
  - Groundnut
  - Coconuts
  - Turmeric
  - Cashew
  - Fruits & Vegetable
- India's Key **Cash Crops**[5] like coffee, tea, cardamon and rubber are highly sought after both domestically and internationally, contributing valueable foreign exchange.
- **Fishing** has also been a traditional occupation, bolstered by India's extensive **coastline.** The diverse **fish varieties** found along the coast make fishing a crucial livelihood for those in **coastal regions.**
- Agriculture remains the primary source of **employment** in **rural India.** A significant portion of the farming population consists of **peasant families** with less than **one hectare** of cultivable land, while **small farmer families** manage between **one and two hectares. Agricultural labourers,** many of whom work on a **daily wage** or a **share of the crop,** face challenges such as **seasonal unemployment**[6] and **lower wages,** particularly for **women.**

Handicrafts

- **Handicrafts** represent a time-honored tradition in **India's rural communities.** These crafts are created using only manual skills and **traditional techniques,** without the aid of modern machinery.
- In recent years, handcrafted items have gained popularity as **symbols of fashion** and **luxury,** with increasing demand in **global markets.** This growing interest has made handicrafts an important **source of income** for many rural **artisans.**
- India's rich **cultural heritage** is clearly reflected in its wide variety of handicrafts. Each handmade piece not only displayes the artists skills but also represents the culture of the region it comes from.
- The knowledge and skills involved in traditional handicrafts are typically passed down through generations within families. Crafting techniques are often taught from parents to children, maintaining a continuity of tradition for ivory craft, pottery, sholapitha craft, embroideries, rugs and carpets etc.

▲ *Stone Sculpture*

Other Traditional Occuptions

- In India, many **traditional occupations**[7], such as salt making, palm juice extraction, mining, brick and tile making, handloom weaving and leather crafting, are hereditary. These professions not only sustain livelihoods but also preserve the cultural and artisanal heritage of the country.

---

5 **Cash Crops** Crops that are grown in large quantity for industrial use and export to the other countries.

6 **Seasonal Unemployment** When people are unemployed at particular times of the year when demand for labour is lower than usual.

7 **Traditional Occupations** Occupations practiced by successive generations, rooted in customs and focused on subsistence economies, predating colonisation and the industrial revolution.

- Other inter-generation traditional occupations are priests, sweepers, ledder workers.

▲ *Shola Craft (Odisha)*

▲ *Channapatna Dolls (Karnataka)*

- **Weaving** is the process of making textiles by interlacing fiber threads. Weaving is a cottage industry[8] in India. Each state has typical wover fabrics, embroideries and traditional costumers which are suitable for the region-specific climate and life style, regions, villages and communities throughout India have unique weaving traditions with distinct customs and patterns.

▲ *Embroidery and Textiles of India*

Indian Cuisine

- In India each region is famous for its traditional cuisines comprised of vast variety of local foods cooked with indigenous ingredients and spices. India is also known for its delicious cuisine which has emerged as a source of livelihood for street vendors to five-star hotels.
- Traditional foods give an exquisite vision of India's rich cultural heritage. Many popular traditional dishes, spice mixes and masalas are in great demand in other countries of the world.

Visual Arts

- **Indian art** encompasses a wide range of forms, including **painting, sculpture, pottery** and **textile arts** like **woven silk.** For thousands of years, a diverse array of **visual arts** has been practiced in India.
- Artists and artisans historically received support from two major sources: large **Hindu temples** and various **Princely States**. Much of the visual art was created for **religious purposes.**
- Distinct **regional architectural styles** showcase the influence of various religions such as **Islam, Sikhism, Jainism, Christianity** and **Hinduism.** The art from different periods is evident in places of worship, mausoleums (burial sites) and palaces, featuring diverse sculptures and images. These works were often skillfully carved in stone, cast in bronze or silver, modeled in clay or wood, or vividly painted.

▲ *Warli Painting of Maharashtra*

▲ *Bamboo craft of Assam*

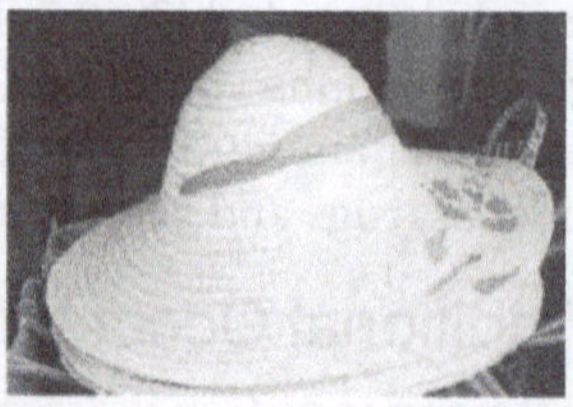

▲ *Coconut craft of Kerala*

8 **Cottage Industry** A business or manufacturing activity carried on in people's homes.

1.4 Threatening the Survival of Handicrafts and Indigenous Art

Handicrafts and traditional art are facing numerous challenges that threaten their survival and highlight the urgent need for their revival and preservation. These challenges have led to a decline in popularity and poor income for artisans. The primary issues include

- **Mass-produced Goods** Cheaper mass-produced items reduce demand for handcrafted goods.
- **Decreased Appreciation** There is a diminishing appreciation for fine arts.
- **Environmental Degradation** The shrinking of forests, depletion of resources and general environmental harm impact raw material availability.
- **Socio-economic Issues** Illiteracy and widespread socio-economic disadvantages affect artisans' livelihoods.
- **Slow Land Reforms** Progress in land reforms has been inadequate.
- **Finance and Marketing** There are insufficient or inefficient financial and marketing services.

Revival and Sustaining Traditional Occupations

To revitalise Indian handicrafts and indigenous art, interventions are needed in the following areas

- **Design Innovations** Introducing new design ideas.
- **Eco-friendly Materials** Using sustainable raw materials.
- **Training Facilities** Establishing training centers for skill development.
- **Intellectual Property Rights** Protecting artisans' **intellectual property**[9].
- **Preservation Strategies** Implementing methods to preserve and enhance traditional techniques.
- **Packaging** Improving packaging to appeal to modern markets.
- **Conservation of Knowledge** Preserving traditional knowledge and skills.

1.5 Work, Age and Gender

The impact of **age and gender**[10] on an individual's **work life** extends beyond just their professional responsibilities; it also influences their **personal well-being** and **social perspectives**. How work affects children, women and the elderly can vary significantly and engaging in tasks unsuited to their **physical** or **psychological needs** can have adverse effects on their health and development.

Gender Issues in Relation to Work

- The gender roles and behaviours has been evolved with time and resulted into a notion of continuity with change. For instance, traditional role of men as a bread winner of the family and role of women as a homemaker has been changed with time.
- Indian women have been engaged in production and in societies even in marketing related activities since ages. Working women in rural areas are involved in agriculture and animal husbandry while in urban areas, they get engaged in construction activities and domestic labour, in order to support their families economically.
- Sex and gender, men and women differ from each other, ranging from biological to socio-cultural differences. However, India's **Supreme Court** has recognised transgender people as a third gender who are also referred to as **transexual,** cross dresses etc.

---

9 Intellectual Property Legal protections for creations of the human mind, such as inventions, designs and artistic works.

10 Age and Gender Age refers to different stages in one's life cycle; gender refers to socially constructed roles for women, girls, men and boys.

- The terms **sex** and **gender** are often used synonymously but they are two very different terms with different meanings. 'Sex' refers to the biological categorisation based on genetics, reproductive organs whereas **gender** is based on the **social identity**.
- The external manifestation of sex is through the primary sexual organs and this difference is due to XX and XY or someother chromosomes. In terms of gender, the social and cultural practices determine within the society how an individual is supposed to act throughout their life.

Need for Empowerment of Women

- Traditionally, the role of women in Indian society, women play a crucial role in every stage of life.
- They shape families, which build communities and in turn, contribute to the nation. Overlooking their contributions undermines the very foundation of society.
- **Empowering women** means valuing their domestic work as much as paid jobs. Despite their crucial role in managing households, their efforts are often undervalued and seen as more responsibilities rather than significant economic activities.
- Women, as **sisters, wives, mothers** and **daughters**, dedicate themselves to their families' needs, including nutrition, education and overall well-being. Their domestic roles should be recognised and appreciated alongside their economic contributions.
- In rural areas, women work tirelessly from dawn to dusk, handling tasks such as fetching water, preparing meals, working in fields and caring for livestock. Many migrate to cities due to unemployment, poverty and other challenges, often taking up jobs as **construction workers** or **domestic help**.
- Urbanisation has brought positive changes. With increased literacy, women are now entering professions traditionally dominated by men, such as the military, aviation, banking and entrepreneurship. They are improving their families' lives and gaining personal independence.
- However, female workforce participation in India remains low at just **27 per cent**, despite rising literacy rates. Many women face constraints from domestic responsibilities and societal norms that limit their job opportunities. Addressing these challenges and fully recognising women's contributions is crucial for building a more equitable and thriving society.

Issues and Concerns Related to Women and Their Work

- Women constitute nearly half of India's population, yet their participation in the workforce remains significantly lower than it could be. According to a World Bank report, increasing female participation in the labour market could boost India's economic growth. Several key issues contribute to the low levels of women in the workforce
  - Opportunities for women in the labour market have declined due to demand for skilled workers.
  - Need to increase training facilities to develop women's skills and safeguard their interests.
  - Men are viewed as primary earners, while women are considered supplementary.
  - Women as sole income generators do not receive equal standing in the market.
- Concerns in modern India include
  - Stress and adverse health effects.
  - Security and safety at workplaces without gender discrimination.
  - Maternity benefits.
  - Social support for child care first responsibilities.

Organised Efforts for Empowerment of Women

- Shri Mahila Griha Udyog Lijjat Papad is an organisation of, by and for women.
- Objective: Provide employment to women for a decent and dignified livelihood.
- Founded in 1959 with 7 members.
- Registered in 1966 under the Bombay Public Trust and Societies Registration Act.
- Recognised by Khadi and Village Industries Commissions (KVIC) as a village industry.
- Awarded Best Village Industry.
- Provides self-employment to about 45,000 members across India.
- Annual sales turnover of ₹ 1,600 crores, including exports to many countries.
- Aims to promote women's self-reliance.

Quick Test 2

1. Mention any four cash crops.
2. In what way does the long coastline benefit the traditional occupation in India?
3. What do you understand by weaving?
4. Which two main patrons have supported the artists and artisans, historically?
5. How does depletion of forests posses a challenge to the artisans?

1.6 Constitutional Rights, Acts and Government Initiatives for Women

The Right to Equality

- The Indian Constitution guarantees equality for both men and women across all spheres of life.
- It ensures that all individuals receive equal protection under the law, prohibiting discrimination based on race, caste, religion, sex or place of birth.
- Equal opportunities are guaranteed in employment within government sectors.
- The Constitution mandates humane working conditions for women and protection from workplace exploitation.
- It supports educational and economic advancement for women through various incentives.

- **Artical 16(1)** of the Constitution guarantees equality of opportunities for all citizens in matter of employment and oppointment to any office under the state.

Legislative Protections for Women

Several acts have been enacted to uphold the Constitutional rights of women

- The Factories Act, 1948
- The Plantation Labour Act, 1951
- The Mines Act, 1952
- The Employees' State Insurance Act, 1948
- The Maternity Benefit Act, 1961
- **The Equal Remuneration Act, 1976** This act mandates equal pay for equal work and has led to the development of a National Plan of Action (NPA) for women by the Department of Social Welfare.

State Initiatives for Women

- Many state initiatives were taken to improve the conditions of women in employment or in need of employment. Some of them are women's cells were created in the Ministry of Labour to look upon the problems of women workers.
- The Equal Remuneration Act for equal wages for the same work or of similar nature also came into force.

- A National Plan of Action (NPA) for women was taken up by the Department of Social Welfare to implement the Equal Remuneration Act.
- A working group on women's employment was Constituted by the Planning Commission for enhancing the employment opportunities for rural women
- Working group also review the labour laws on women's work and their participation in economic and productive activities. A Steering Committee was established to build the data base on women's work, particularly in the rural areas. This was also formed by the Planning Commission of India.

- In the earlier decades, the programmes for women were based on the welfare approach, which moved towards equality of opportunity and then finally towards the development approach. There is need to change our attitude and approaches towards the gender issues related to work that are prevalent in the society.

Women Entrepreneur

- **Kiran Mazumdar Shaw** is an eminent woman entrepreneur and biotechnologist.
- Chairperson and Managing Director of Biocon India Ltd.
- Started her professional career as a trainee brewer at Carlton & United Beverages.
- Founded Biocon India Ltd. in 1978.
- Transformed Biocon into an integrated bio-pharmaceutical company with strategic research initiatives.
- Received numerous prestigious awards, including
  - ET Business Woman of the Year
  - Leading Exporter
  - Technology Pioneer
  - Best Woman Entrepreneur
- Honoured with Padma Shri in 1989 and Padma Bhushan in 2005.
- Recognised as a model entrepreneur and successful technocrat with global understanding.

Schemes of Government

The Government of India has initiated several women empowerment schemes to facilitate education among the girls. Two such schemes are given bellow

Kasturba Gandhi Balika Vidyalaya (KGBV) Scheme

- This scheme was initiated by the Government of India under the **Sarva Shiksha Abhiyaan (SSA)**. Presently, it is subsumed under Samagrashiksha, an overaching scheme and the scheme for care, protection and development of women. KGBV started as a scheme for bringing never-enrolled and dropout girls from rural, remote and disadvantaged sections of the society into school education till elementary level in residential schools.
- Aimed at enrolling never-enrolled and dropout girls from rural, remote and disadvantaged sections into school education at the elementary level.
- Provides residential schooling for enrolled girls.
- Girls entitled to study a Bridge Course to prepare for entry level.
- Entry level in KGBV is Class VI.
- KGBVs opened in backward blocks of each district.
- Supports the implementation of the **Right to Education** (RTE) law passed by the Government of India.
- RTE (2009) provides free and compulsory education to children, enforced as a Fundamental Right under Article 21-A.
- Established in backward blocks across districts to facilitate this education.

Beti Bachao, Beti Padhao Scheme

The Beti Bachao, Beti Padhao (BBBP) scheme is a collaborative initiative involving the Ministry of Women and Child Development, Ministry of Health and Family Welfare and Ministry of Human Resource Development. Launched on 22nd January 2015, in 100 districts with low girl-child sex ratios, the scheme aims to protect and empower girls. India faces a declining female-to-male ratio, with only 918 girls per 1000 boys as per the 2011 census. The country ranks 41st out of 195 globally in terms of sex ratio, lagging behind 40 other nations.

Objectives of the Scheme

- Provide a better and safe environment for the girl child to grow.
- Improve the child sex ratio (number of girls per 1,000 boys aged 0-6 years).
- Prevent gender-biased, sex-selective elimination.
- Ensure survival and protection of the girl child.
- Promote gender equality and women's empowerment.
- Encourage education and participation of the girl child.
- Curb child marriages and dowry practices.
- Break gender stereotypes in Indian society.

1.7 Attitudes and Approaches to Work and Life Skills for Livelihood

A work life demands from an individual the possession of certain skills as well as the positive **attitudes and approaches to work**[11]. These help an individual grow professionally as well as personally.

Attitudes and Approaches to Work It usually looks as if skills and experience are the most important characteristics of an employee, but attitude plays just as big of a role. Thus, how we behave at work often depends on how we feel about being there, how an individual handles the situations, complexities and demands of the job and various tasks involved within that job.

Important Aspects of Attitude Towards Work

- Level of employee satisfaction or dissatisfaction is crucial to determine **quality of work life.**
- Satisfaction can be affected by comparisons (e.g., salary comparisons without considering responsibilities, qualifications, output, sincerity and dedication).
- Greater satisfaction occurs when individuals consider both positive and negative aspects of their job.
- A considerable amount of time is spent at the office; thus, healthy routines are necessary (e.g., healthy eating, balanced diets, proper sleep, proactive leisure time).
- Work is often perceived as an obligation, leading to a lack of enjoyment.
- Viewing work as a source of energy, fulfillment and learning ensures job satisfaction.
- Enjoyment of jobs, willingness to face challenges and a positive outlook contribute to job satisfaction.
- Opportunities for career progress and utilising skills and knowledge enhance personal happiness and quality of working life.

Quick Test 3

1 What is the key difference between 'sex' and 'gender'?
2 When did the Supreme Court identify as the third gender?
3 Which article of the Constitution provide for the equal employment opportunity?
4 Mention any one challenge faced by the women in India.
5 Mention any two organised efforts for women in India.

11 **Attitudes and Approaches to Work** Work attitudes are feelings we have towards different aspects of the work environment.

Life Skills for Livelihood

Life skills are essential **abilities** that empower individuals to navigate and thrive in the complexities of everyday life.

According to the **World Health Organisation**, life skills encompass **thinking, coping** and **social abilities** that enhance our interactions with others and our environment. They also contribute to greater **personal resilience** in challenging situations.

Here are ten core life skills identified by expert

(i) Self-Awareness
(ii) Communication
(iii) Decision-Making
(iv) Coping with Emotions
(v) Empathy
(vi) Inter-personal Skills
(vii) Problem Solving
(viii) Critical Thinking
(ix) Coping with Stress
(x) Creative Thinking

Importance of Life Skills

- According to the World Health Organisation, life skills includes thinking, coping and social skills.
- Life skills enhance interaction with others and the environment.
- They contribute to greater individual resilience in adversity.
- Important throughout the life span for healthy behavior, especially in challenging situations.
- Promote and protect life, health and well-being in all situations.
- Enable personal and social changes that promote health and development within communities.
- Adequate knowledge, attitudes and values aid in developing healthy life skills and preventing negative health behavior.

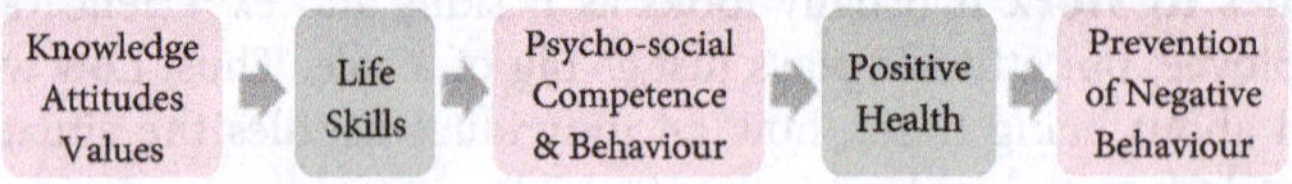

- Life skills are competencies and behaviors that cannot be taught in a classroom, they are attained through experiences.
- Personal and social skills enable individuals to handle situations confidently and competently within their families and society.

Improving One's Own Work Life

- Improving work life is crucial for the organisation.
- Individuals should consciously work to improve their own work life to ensure job satisfaction and to maximise the output as well.

  Some general tips to improve the quality of work life are
  - Develop healthy personal habits by caring for one's body, mind and spirit.
  - Be empathetic and compassionate towards peers and seniors.
  - Acknowledge that all individuals at work are interdependent on each other personally, professionally and psychologically.
  - Enhance team cohesion.
  - Being loyal to the organisation and professionally ethical.

Essential Soft Skills for Workplace Success

Soft skills, often referred to as **behavioural skills,** are crucial personality traits and habits that complement technical expertise. Achieving career success requires more than just academic qualifications; practical skills and effective behaviour play a significant role.

Some Essential soft skills important at the workplace are

- **Working Productively** Effective work habits and attitudes are applied. This requires sufficient knowledge, skills, expertise and experience. It influenced by enthusiasm, zeal and dynamism. Hence, involvement and a sense of belonging to the organisation increase productivity.
- **Learning Effectively** Necessary skills include reading, writing, computing and using learning tools.
- **Communicating Clearly** Communication conveys information, ideas and opinions through writing, speaking and listening.
- **Working Co-operatively** Every individual must show co-operation is needed to complete tasks, solve problems, resolve conflicts and provide support. This helpsin cultivates a sense of belonging within the organisation.
- **Thinking Critically and Creatively** Creative thinking devises new ways to carry out tasks and solve problems involves analytical thinking, critical evaluation and innovation.
- **Other Required Skills** It includes concentration, alertness, presence of mind, tactfulness and empathy, abilities to train, delegate, foresee and multi-task are also important.

1.8 Ergonomics

- Ergonomics is derived from two Greek words- **ergon,** meaning work and **nomos,** meaning laws or natural principles. It is a branch of engineering science that focuses on optimising the interaction between workers and their work environment using principles from biological sciences.
- It may be called as, **Human Factors Engineering (HFE).** It basically involves the application of human biological science with engineering science to maximise the mutual adjustment of human work.

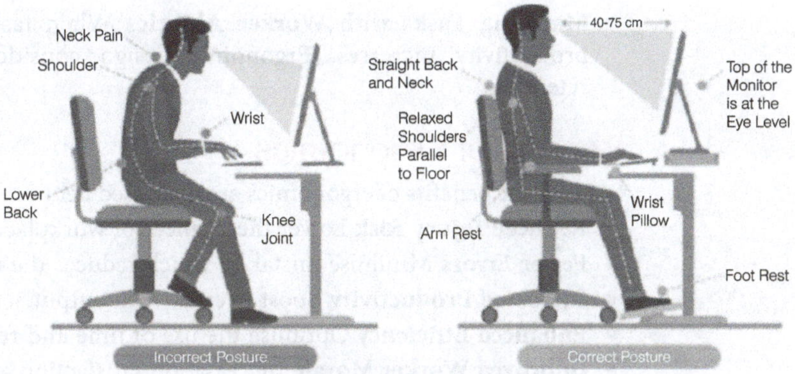

▲ *Ergonomics at work*

Main Objectives of Ergonomics

Workplace Customisation	Tailor workspaces to meet the specific needs of workers, enhancing their comfort and efficiency.
Enhanced Productivity	Improve worker efficiency while minimising physical strain and discomfort.
Health and Safety	Ensure the work environment promotes health and reduces the risk of injury.

For example, if a worker operates a machine with various controls, the levers and buttons should be positioned so that they are easily reachable without causing strain. Similarly, if the machine has a screen, it should be placed about one to two feet from the worker's eyes to prevent eye strain and should feature an anti-glare surface.

- **Improved Worker Morale** Increase job satisfaction and motivation.
- **Lower Absenteeism** Decrease time off due to health issues, stress or injuries.

Ergonomists consider aspects related to worker capacity (both physiological and psychological), task demands comprised of nature, complexity, force required, duration, posture and the work environment. Ergonomics is set on the following **four pillars**

(i) Anthropometry i.e. body size and measurements
(ii) Biomechanics i.e. musculoskeletal activities and forces exerted
(iii) Physiology
(iv) Industrial psychology

Need for Ergonomics

There is a need for ergonomics at the workplace for several reasons

- **Improving Safety and Health** To improve the safety and health of workers by reduces severity of workplace injuries. It also helps in reducing the possibility of accidents due to human error.
- **Enhancing Job Effectiveness** It helps in Increasing productivity, reduces errors as well as by eliminates or reduces injuries.
- **Improving Job Satisfaction** Provides comfortable working conditions, leading to higher job satisfaction. Employee satisfaction through comfortable working conditions.
- **Importance of Ergonomics** To imporve the productivity, efective implementation of Ergonomics Principles is necessary. For example, a chair that does not conform to ergonomic safety specifications can cause back pain. Ergonomic principles require adjustable chair height and support for user comfort.
- **Valuing Employees** Employees are the most important asset of an organisation. There is a need to create a safe and productive environment is essential for every workplace.
- **Matching Tasks with Worker Abilities** When tasks match worker abilities, errors decrease and productivity increases. Ergonomic design considerations influence employee productivity and retention.

Benefits of Ergonomics

Some of the benefits of ergonomics are discussed below

- **Reduced Injury Risk** Lower the chances of workplace injuries and accidents.
- **Fewer Errors** Minimise mistakes, which reduces the need for rework.
- **Increased Productivity** Boost overall work output.
- **Enhanced Efficiency** Optimise the use of time and resources.
- **Improved Worker Morale** Increase job satisfaction and motivation.
- **Lower Absenteeism** Decrease time off due to health issues, stress or injuries.

1.9 Entrepreneurship

Entrepreneurship refers to the process of creating and managing a new and innovative business, product or service. It involves turning novel ideas into successful business models.

- The term **Entrepreneurship** originates from the French word entrepreneur, meaning **to undertake**. Entrepreneurship is crucial for driving innovation, productivity and competitive effectiveness. When an individual recognises their potential and starts a new venture to experiment with it, this is considered entrepreneurship.
- An entrepreneur is defined as someone who has the ability and desire to establish, administer and succeed in a venture along with risk entitled to it. The entrepreneurs are often known as a source of new ideas or innovators, risk takers who bring new ideas in the market by replacing old with a new invention. India has many brilliant examples of entrepreneurs like JRD Tata, Kiran Mazumdar Shaw, Azim Premji, Shiv Nadar to name a few.

Characteristics of Entrepreneurs

There are some personal attributes required by an entrepreneur to take up the challenges of an enterprise. An entrepreneur must have

- The willingness to work hard towards goals. Knowledge and skills for planning and implementation of goals in an effective manner.
- The management skills related to finances, materials, personnel and time.
- The courage to take up calculated risks for the smooth functioning of the business.
- The ability and preparedness to handle a number of tasks simultaneously.
- The ability to learn and acquire the necessary skills for the tasks allotted.
- The ability to deal with tough issues and find the appropriate solutions in a fixed timeframe.
- The ability to cope up with set-backs, challenges and failures.
- The ability to develop partnerships and able networking that would help an enterprise grow on a large-scale.
- The ability to negotiate, strategise and prioritise along with good communication skills.
- An entrepreneur must be realistic towards the enterprise goals and not expect easy solutions.
- They must be flexible in approach and handle the situation of crises at an optimum level.

Social Entrepreneurship

- Social entrepreneurs focus on solving societal problems using entrepreneurial principles. They aim to bring about positive social change by addressing issues affecting disadvantaged communities.
- These entrepreneurs often work in sectors like education, health, environment and economic development.
- Social entrepreneurs measure success by the impact they make on society, often operating through non-profit organisations or civic groups.
- Prominent social entrepreneurs like Mahatma Gandhi, Vinoba Bhave and Florence Nightingale have significantly contributed to societal progress by addressing issues like child marriage, caste discrimination, gender inequality and domestic violence.

Quick Test 4

1. How do interactions with others affect perception at work?
2. How can you develop life skills?
3. What are soft skills and why are they important for work performance? Mention any one reason.
4. What two branches of science are combined in Ergonomics?
5. What qualities should an entrepreneur have for smooth business operations?

Mind Map

WORK, LIVELIHOOD AND CAREER

1 Work and Meaningful Work

Self-Development
- **Meaningful Work** Useful to society, engages skills, brings satisfaction, fosters growth.

Job Vs. Career
- **Job** Short-term, focused on immediate tasks and money.
- **Career** Long-term, growth-focused, personal fulfillment, skill development.
- **Work** Central to life; fulfills needs, uses skills, contributes to society.
- **Importance** Earns money, boosts identity/self-esteem, improves organisations and society.
- **Concepts** Livelihood, duty, self-expression, joy, dignity.

2 Ways to Choose a Career

Choosing a Career
- Based on family, interests, satisfaction and financial stability.

Work, Livelihood, Career
- **Work** Activities (paid/unpaid).
- **Livelihood** Occupation supporting needs.
- **Career** Lifelong growth and skill development.

For examples
- **Job** Task-focused.
- **Livelihood** Supports family.
- **Career** Long-term goals.
- **Work Perspectives** Job and Income.
- **Career** Growth and status.
- **Calling** Inner fulfillment.

3 Traditional Occupations in India

- **Agriculture** Key crops (e.g., tea, milk, spices).
- **Handicrafts** Manual arts (pottery, weaving).
- **Other Occupations** Salt making, mining, weaving, priests.
- **Cuisine** Regional foods as livelihood.
- **Visual Arts** Painting, sculpture, textiles.

4 Threats to Handicrafts and Indigenous Art

- **Mass Production** Cheaper goods reduce demand.
- **Decreased Appreciation** Diminishing interest in fine arts.
- **Environmental Issues** Resource depletion impacts raw materials.
- **Socio-economic** Illiteracy and poverty affect artisans.
- **Slow Land Reforms** Inadequate progress.
- **Finance and Marketing** Lack of support services.

Revival Strategies
- **Design Innovations** New creative ideas.
- **Eco-friendly Materials** Sustainable resources.
- **Training** Skill development centers.
- **IP Protection** Safeguarding artisan rights.
- **Preservation** Traditional techniques and knowledge.

5 Work, Age and Gender

- **Gender Roles** Evolving roles; women working in rural (agriculture) and urban areas (construction/domestic work).
- **Sex Vs. Gender** Sex = biological, Gender = social identity.
- **Empowerment of Women** Recognise unpaid domestic work and equal value for economic contributions.
- **Women's Work Issues** Low workforce participation (27%), limited opportunities, societal constraints, need for skill development.
- **Concerns** Stress, health, workplace safety, maternity benefits, child care support.
- **For examples** Shri Mahila Griha Udyog Lijjat Papad – Empowering women through self-employment, 45,000 members, ₹1,600 crores turnover.

6 Constitutional Rights and Government Initiatives for Women

- **Right to Equality** Equal rights, protection, and opportunities in employment.
- **Key Acts** Factories Act, Maternity Benefit Act, Equal Remuneration Act - Protect women's rights at work.
- **State Initiatives** Equal wages, women's cells, rural employment.
- **Women Entrepreneurs** Kiran Mazumdar Shaw – Biocon founder, awarded Padma Shri and Padma Bhushan.

Government Schemes
- **KGBV** Education for rural girls.
- **Beti Bachao, Beti Padhao** Empower girls, improve sex ratio, prevent child marriage.

7 Attitudes and Life Skills for Livelihood

- **Work Attitude** Positive attitude, job satisfaction, and a balanced perspective enhance work quality.
- **Life Skills** Core skills like self-awareness, communication, and problem-solving improve resilience and social interactions.
- **Improving Work Life** Focus on healthy habits, empathy, teamwork and professionalism.
- **Soft Skills** Essential for career growth, including communication, creativity, critical thinking and co-operation.

8 Ergonomics

- It is a branch of engineering science.
- It Focuses on interaction between works and work environment.
- Improve works efficience while minimising physical stain and discomfort.
- It ensure the work environment promotes health and reduces the risk of injury.

Need for Ergonomics
- Improving safety and health.
- Enchaining job effectiveness.
- Importance of ergonomics.
- Improving job satisfaction.
- Valuing employees.

9 Entrepreneurship

- **Entrepreneurship** is about creating and managing innovative businesses, with entrepreneurs driving change and taking risks. They need skills like hard work, management, risk-taking and resilience.
- **Social Entrepreneurship** aims to solve social issues through business principles, focusing on positive societal impact. Social entrepreneurs like Mahatma Gandhi work to address problems such as inequality and discrimination.

NCERT Folder

1. What are the different ways in which work can be perceived?

Ans. Following are the three ways in which work can be perceived

(i) **Work as Job or Livelihood** When the main objective of the work is to earn money and sustain the needs of life. For example, performing a job to support one's family or one's own needs. In this case, the person seeks satisfaction from the money earned in exchange of the job done.

(ii) **Work as Career** When the main objective of the work is lifelong progression, learning and upgrading oneself with new skills. It requires patience and time devotion. One may perform several jobs of their interest to gain more experience and become a professional. In this case, the person seeks satisfaction from their growth during their lifetime.

(iii) **Work as a Calling** When the main objective of the work is beyond earning money, to derive inner-satisfaction, pleasure and peace. For example, helping the needy, joining organisations that do social good without being paid, etc. in this case, the person seeks satisfaction by contributing for the betterment of the society or world at large.

2. Differentiate between Job and Career. **Diksha App**

Ans. For answer refer to text under the heading 'Key Differences Between Job and Career' on page no. 3.

3. What is meant by meaningful work?

Or **What do you undestand by meaningful work.** **Diksha App**

Ans. Meaningful work refers to work that is not only fulfilling on a personal level but also brings a positive impact to society or others. It is characterised by several key attributes

- **Utility** The work benefits society or contributes to the well-being of others. It holds value beyond personal gain, offering tangible benefits to the community or the world at large.
- **Engagement** Meaningful work actively involves one's skills, creativity and judgment. It provides an opportunity to apply one's talents and fosters a sense of challenge and intellectual stimulation.
- **Satisfaction** Such work brings a deep sense of enjoyment and fulfillment. It aligns with personal values, leading to emotional rewards and a sense of accomplishment.
- **Purpose** Meaningful work contributes to both personal growth and the betterment of the community. It is driven by a sense of purpose, offering individuals the chance to make a meaningful difference.

4. What do you understand by the terms gender and sex?

Ans. **Gender** refers to the socially constructed characteristics of women and men – such as norms, roles and relationships of and between groups of women and men. Gender determines what is expected, allowed and valued in a woman or a man in a given context. Different societies and cultures may therefore have different understandings of what is 'masculine' or 'feminine'.

Sex refers to the different to the biological aspects of males and females as determined by their anatomy, which is produced by their chromosomes, hormones and their interactions. Sex is something that is assigned at birth.

5. Who are homemakers? What is their contribution in the economy of the family?

Ans. A homemaker is a person who manages all aspects of a family household. In most cases, the term refers to a person who does not work outside of the home.

The duties of a homemaker can include taking care of children, cleaning, cooking, managing the family schedule of activities and running family errands.

The said role is usually taken up by the females in an Indian society and for this role, they receive no money wage. Due to this reason, they are not considered to be contributors to the economy. However, opposite is true.

Homemakers play a vital role in a family's economic growth. The care for everybody and nourishes everyone in the family so that other members can work hard outside the home for the family's and at large nation's economic growth. Thus, homemakers directly or indirectly are playing a vital role in the economic development of country.

6. How will the women get recognition in the family and the society?

Ans. Women are the pioneers of nation. The woman performs the role of wife, partner, organiser, administrator, director, re-creator, economist, mother, disciplinarian, teacher, health officer, artist etc. in the family at the same time. Women are the key to sustainable development and quality of life in the family.

Hence, for making the women recognisable in society and the family, the work needs to be done at the basic level. People need to change their thinking, which can only be done through education. Education is the most important instrument for human resource development. It enables women to respond to opportunities, to challenge their traditional roles and to change their life circumstances.

Other than these, modern economic life has helped in empowering women by enabling them to leave the narrow sphere of the family circle and work side by side for the enrichment of society. Government is also taking steps to empower women and to give them equal respect and status in the society.

7. How are women guaranteed equality in India?

Ans. Some of the ways which guaranteed equality to women in India are discussed below

The Constitution of India under Article 16 (1) ensures equality to both men and women including equal opportunity for all citizens in matters relating to employment or appointment to any office under the state. It also forbids discrimination in respect of any employment or office on grounds of caste, creed, colour, race or sex.

- The Constitution also holds that women workers should be provided with just and humane conditions of work, protection from any kind of exploitation, given support and encouragement in their educational and economic pursuits.
- The Indian Constitution empowers the state to make special provisions for women and children. Some of them are Factories Act, of 1948, The Plantation of Labour Act, 1951, The Mines Act of 1952, etc. which provides protection to women in various industrial sectors, Employees State Insurance Act (ESI Act) and the Maternity Benefit Act, 1961.

8. What are the government initiatives in favour of women?

Or **Explain the Constitutional Rights and Acts taken up in India for women.**

Ans. The government initiatives taken in the favour of women are discussed below

- Women's cells were created in the Ministry of Labour to look upon the problems of women workers.
- The Equal Remuneration Act for equal wages for the same work or of similar nature also came into force.
- A National Plan of Action (NPA) for women was taken up by the Department of Social Welfare to implement the Equal Remuneration Act.
- A working group on women's employment was Constituted by the Planning Commission for enhancing the employment opportunities for women of rural areas.
- Working group also review the labour laws on women's work and their participation in economic and productive activities.
- A Steering Committee was established to build the data base on women's work, particularly in the rural areas. This was also formed by the Planning Commission of India.
- Kasturba Gandhi Balika Vidyalaya (KGBV) is a scheme which was initiated by the Government of India under the Sarva Shiksha Abhiyaan for bringing never-enrolled and dropout girls from rural, remote and disadvantaged sections of the society into school education till elementary level.
- Beti Bachao, Beti Padhao scheme is a campaign launched by PM Narendra Modi to promote awareness regarding girl's education and combat the declining Child Sex ratio. This scheme also carries provisions for awards and recognitions.

9. Explain the term 'Life skill'.

Ans. Life skills refer to the abilities for adaptive and positive behaviour that enable individuals to deal effectively with the demands and challenges of everyday life. In other words, life skills are a large group of psychosocial and interpersonal skills, which can help people

- to make informed decisions,
- to communicate effectively and
- to develop coping and self management skills that may help an individual to lead a healthy and productive life.

Exam Pattern Questions

Objective Type Questions

Multiple Choice Questions

1. .... is an activity that all beings perform on a day to day basis.

(a) Meaningful work (b) Work
(c) Career (d) Job

2. Work can be viewed as ....

(a) a spiritual practice (b) a medium to earn money
(c) a duty to be fulfilled (d) All of these

3. Puppets are traditional handicraft of which state? **CBSE 2023**

(a) Punjab (b) Uttar Pradesh
(c) Rajasthan (d) Goa

4. Select the traditional handicraft of Odisha. **CBSE 2025**

(a) Channapatna dolls (b) Shola craft
(c) Bamboo craft (d) Warli painting

5. Following are the popular traditional handicrafts of India. Which option is incorrect? **CBSE SQP, 2021**

(a) Coconut Craft-Kerala
(b) Warli Painting-Maharashtra
(c) Shola Craft-Karnataka
(d) Bamboo Craft-Assam

6. .... is socially constructed in nature.

(a) Ethnicity (b) Gender
(c) Sex (d) Nationality

7. The Factories Act, 1984 makes sure that there is facility of .... on the work premises. **CBSE SQP Term I, 2021**

(a) canteen (b) shade
(c) créche (d) first aid

8. Which of the following statement is incorrect regarding the 'Kasturba Gandhi Balika Vidyalaya' scheme?

(a) It was initiated under Sarva Shiksha Abhiyaan.
(b) This scheme will be helpful in implementing RTE Act.
(c) This scheme also carries provisions for awards and recognitions.
(d) KGBV's were opened in the backward blocks of each district.

9. She is the Chairperson and Managing Director of Biocon India Ltd. She started her career as a trainee brewer in Carlson and United Beverages. In 2005, she was honoured with Padma Bhushan. Identify the personality. **CBSE SQP, Competency Based Que, 2021**

(a) Ms. Kiran Mazumdar Shaw
(b) Ms. Kusum Mazumdar Shaw
(c) Ms. Kiran Mazumdar Shah
(d) Ms. Kalyani Mazumdar Shaw

10. An individual experience of job satisfaction or dissatisfaction is influenced by ....

(a) their attitude (b) their work
(c) their perspective (d) their interaction

11. Ergonomics is needed at the work place because ....

(a) it helps in reducing errors as well as by eliminating or reducing injuries.
(b) it helps in improving job effectiveness by improving job satisfaction.
(c) it helps in improving job effectiveness by increasing productivity.
(d) All of the above

12. Which of the following is not an objective of Ergonomics?

(a) Optimum work capacity
(b) Increase in errors
(c) Increase in productivity
(d) Comfortable working conditions

13. Which is not amongst the four pillars of ergonomics? **CBSE SQP, 2021**

Or **Which of the following pillar of ergonomics is based on musculoskeletal activities.** **Diksha App**

(a) Biometrics (b) Anthropometry
(c) Physiology (d) Industrial psychology

14. Entrepreneurship can take place in ....

(a) small businesses (b) large businesses
(c) wide variety of contexts (d) social enterprises only

15. Nitya owns a garment company and took risky decisions in her work very day. Nitya is an/a .... **Competency Based Que**

(a) entrepreneur (b) wage employed person
(c) labourer (d) unskilled worker

16. Which of the following personal attributes should be there for social entrepreneurship? **CBSE 2024 C**

(a) Work in comfort zone
(b) Work only for health care
(c) Work for neglected and disadvantaged groups
(d) Work for financial gains

17. Section 48 of which of the following Act states that crèches should be maintained if more than thirty women are employed in an industry or factory? CBSE 2025

(a) The Plantations Labour Act
(b) The Maternity Benefit Act
(c) The Factories Act
(d) The Mines Act

18. Which of the following is the main aim of social entrepreneur? CBSE SQP, 2024

(a) Changing the pattern of design of a product/commodity.
(b) Achieving large scale benefits through entrepreneurship for a specific group.
(c) Attempting new technological methods for producing a commodity.
(d) Attaining full employment and self-reliance for women workers.

19. Besides a good salary, an employer can ensure job satisfaction in his employees by .... and ....

(a) good salary, enjoyment
(b) parties, incentives
(c) training, feedback
(d) training, vigorous workload

20. KGBV scheme provides school education in residential schools up to which class? CBSE 2024 C

(a) Class 5 (b) Class 12 (c) Class 6 (d) Class 10

21. 'Beti Bachao, Beti Padhao' scheme was started by the Government of India with which of the following objectives? CBSE 2024

(a) To enrol girls in a bridge course to prepare them for admission to a school.
(b) To promote gender biased selection process.
(c) To ensure survival protection and education of the girl child.
(d) To provide employment to all.

22. Use of ...... is important for designing tools, machines and workstations to reduce stress and health problems of the workers at the workplace. CBSE 2024

(a) entrepreneurship (b) ergonomics
(c) anthropometry (d) physiology

23. The objective of the equal remuneration act is .... CBSE SQP 2023

(a) equal wages for the same work
(b) different working hours
(c) equality among men and women in every field
(d) special facilities for women

24. Women cells have been created in Ministry of .... to look at the problems of women workers.

(a) Education
(b) Home Affairs
(c) Women and Child Development
(d) Labour and Employment

25. Abilities that enable people to behave in healthy ways, particularly in situations that challenge them are known as ....

(a) Attitudes (b) Life skills
(c) Values (d) Physical labour

26. Select the correct pair CBSE 2024

(a) Warli painting-Maharashtra
(b) Channapatna dolls-Kerala
(c) Shola craft-Gujarat
(d) Bamboo craft - Punjab

27. Select the correct pair CBSE 2024 C

(a) Woman Entrepreneur - Kiran Mazumdar Shaw
(b) Shri Mahila Griha Udyog Lijjat Papad - JRD Tata
(c) Cash Crops - Less economic importance
(d) Section 16(1) - Factories Act

28. When the chair height and stand is adjusted according to the height and body measurements.

(a) Ergonomics (b) Economics
(c) Employment (d) Job

29. Life skills are important because they ....

(a) enhancing people's interactions with others.
(b) help people to behave in healthy ways.
(c) can be taught in the classroom easily.
(d) Both (a) and (b)

30. Which type of crops is produced by Indian farmers for sale in urban market? Diksha App

(a) Food crops
(b) Cash crops
(c) Plantation crops
(d) Horticulture crops

31. After graduation Reena got the job in MNC but she is finding it difficult to cope with her working life. Here are few tips to improve work life.

I. Be empathetic
II. Thinking in monotonous way
III. Encourage partnership
IV. Be rigid CBSE SQP Term I, 2021; Competency Based Que

Choose the correct option.

(a) I and II (b) II and IV
(c) I and III (d) II and III

32. Which of the following are considered essential soft skills at the workplace?

I. Learning effectively
II. Working co-operatively
III. Working overtime
IV. Communicating unprofessionally

Choose the correct option.

(a) I and II (b) II and III
(c) III and IV (d) I and III

33. **Match the Following.**

List I	List II
A. Agriculture	1. Found in different places of worship and mausoleums.
B. Handicrafts	2. Vision of India's rich cultural heritage.
C. Indian Cuisine	3. A means of livelihood for the rural folk.
D. Visual Arts	4. Practiced for subsistence and market.

Codes

	A	B	C	D
(a)	1	3	2	4
(b)	2	1	4	3
(c)	3	4	1	2
(d)	4	3	2	1

34. **Match the concepts in List I with their descriptions in List II.**

List I	List II
A. Meaningful work empowerment and satisfaction	1. Provides increased levels of commitment
B. Job	2. Short-term or temporary
C. Career	3. Fulfill passions and professional goals
D. Traditional Occupation in India.	4. Includes activities like weaving pottery making and jewellery

Codes

	A	B	C	D
(a)	1	2	3	4
(b)	2	3	1	4
(c)	3	1	3	4
(d)	4	1	3	2

35. **Match the terms in List I with their definitions in List II.**

List I	List II
A. Agriculture	1. A means by which a person supports oneself and sustains lifestyle
B. Handicrafts	2. Involves subsistence and market crops
C. Dharma talents	3. Duty or responsibility reflecting one's true self and unique
D. Livelihood	4. Involves activities like weaving pottery making and jewellery making

Codes

	A	B	C	D
(a)	2	4	3	1
(b)	1	3	2	4
(c)	4	1	2	3
(d)	3	2	1	4

Assertion-Reason Questions

Directions (Q. Nos. 36-37) In the questions given below, there are two statements marked as Assertion (A) and Reason (R). Read the statements and choose the correct option.

Codes

(a) Both A and R are true and R is the correct explanation of A.

(b) Both A and R are true, but R is not the correct explanation of A.

(c) A is true, but R is false.

(d) A is false, but R is true.

36. **Assertion** (A) Meaningful work is useful to society or to other, is done responsibly and is enjoyable to the worker.

Reason (R) It is important to choose something to sustain the individual's enthusiasm to cary on his/her work. **CBSE SQP Term I, 2021**

37. **Assertion** (A) A National Plan of Action for women was taken up by the department of social welfare.

Reason (R) It was set to implement the equal remuneration act. **CBSE SQP Term I, 2021**

Picture Based

38. **Identify the craft.**

(a) Channapatna dolls (b) Bamboo craft

(c) Shola craft (d) Coconut craft

39. **Identify the painting and name the state where it is popular.** **CBSE 2021 C**

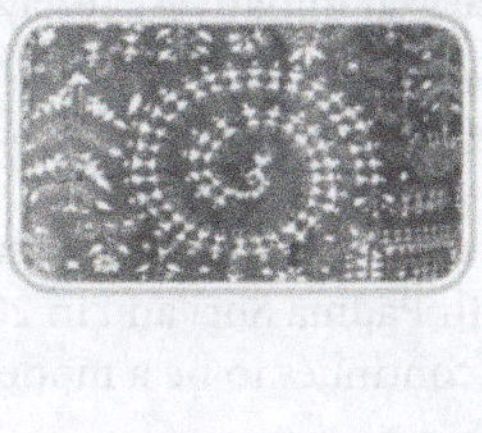

40. **Identify the craft.** CBSE 2021 C

(a) Shola craft (b) Coconut craft
(c) Bamboo craft (d) Warli craft

41. **Identify the craft involved in manufacture of the object in the illustrations.** CBSE SQP 2023, CBSE 2023

(a) Coconut (b) Puppetry
(c) Bamboo (d) Shola

42. **Identify the handicraft in the given picture craft and name the state in which it is popular.** CBSE SQP, 2021

Case Based Objective Type Questions

43. **Read the given passage and answer the following questions.**

Woman Entrepreneur

Kiran Mazumdar Shaw (a biotechnologist), the Chairperson and Managing Director of Biocon India Ltd., is an eminent woman entrepreneur. She started her professional career as a trainee brewer in Carlton & United Beverages and in 1978 formed her own company, Biocon India Ltd. Under her leadership, Biocon has transformed to an integrated bio-pharmaceutical company with strategic research initiatives. Today Biocon is India's pioneering enterprise. Kiran Mazumdar Shaw received many prestigious awards such as ET Business Woman of the Year, Leading Exporter, Technology Pioneer and Best Woman Entrepreneur. In 1989 she was honoured with Padma Shri and in 2005 with Padma Bhushan. She continues to be a model entrepreneur.

(i) **Match the following information regarding the life of women entrepreneur Kiran Mazumdar Shaw.**

	List I		List II
A.	Beginning of Professional Career	1.	Padma Bhushan
B.	Bio-Pharmaceutical Company	2.	Trainee Brewer
C.	Award in 1989	3.	Padma Shri
D.	Award in 2005	4.	Biocon India, Ltd.

Codes

	A	B	C	D		A	B	C	D
(a)	3	2	1	4	(b)	1	4	2	3
(c)	2	4	3	1	(d)	4	2	3	1

(ii) **Choose the correct pair**
(a) Kiran Mazumdar Shaw - Chairperson of Biocon India Ltd.
(b) Kiran Mazumdar Shaw - Chairperson of Carlton & United Beverages
(c) Kiran Mazumdar Shaw - Chairperson of Infosys
(d) Kiran Mazumdar Shaw - Chairperson of Wipro

(iii) **Assertion** (A) Kiran Mazumdar Shaw transformed Biocon into an integrated bio-pharmaceutical company with strategic research initiatives.

Reason (R) Kiran Mazumdar Shaw started her career as a trainee brewer in Carlton & United Beverages.

Codes
(a) Both A and R are true and R is the correct explanation of A.
(b) Both A and R are true, but R is not the correct explanation of A.
(c) A is true, but R is false.
(d) A is false, but R is true.

(iv) **Assertion** (A) Kiran Mazumdar Shaw received the Padma Bhushan in 1989.

Reason (R) She was awarded the Padma Shri in 1989 and the Padma Bhushan in 2005 for her contributions to biotechnology.

Codes
(a) Both A and R are true and R is the correct explanation of A.
(b) Both A and R are true, but R is not the correct explanation of A.
(c) A is true, but R is false.
(d) A is false, but R is true.

44. **Read the given passage and answer the following questions.**

Life skills enable people to act in ways that can contribute to personal and social changes for the promotion of their own health and development, as well as that of the communities in which they live. They are needed by individuals to function effectively and constructively in society.

They include personal and social skills and help the person to function confidently and competently in their families and in society. Life skills are competencies and actual behaviours which cannot be taught in a classroom; rather experiential learning helps people to acquire them.

(i) The life skills approach encompasses and balances all the three components, namely knowledge, ... and skills.

(a) competence (b) attitude
(c) interaction (d) thinking

(ii) Life skills are competencies and actual behaviour held by an individual which are attained with the help of .... and ....

I. individual learning II. classroom learning
III. experiential learning IV. social learning

Choose the correct option

(a) I and II (b) II and III
(c) III and IV (d) I and IV

(iii) Identify the correct pair from the options given below

(a) Life skills - Classroom-based learning
(b) Life skills - Experiential learning
(c) Life skills - Theoretical understanding
(d) Life skills - Passive learning

(iv) **Assertion** (A) Life skills include personal and social competencies that help individuals function confidently in society.

Reason (R) Experiential learning helps individuals acquire these life skills more effectively than traditional classroom learning.

Codes

(a) Both A and R are true and R is the correct explanation of A.
(b) Both A and R are true, but R is not the correct explanation of A.
(c) A is true, but R is false.
(d) A is false, but R is true.

Answers

1. (b) Work
2. (d) All of these
3. (c) Rajasthan
5. (c) Shola Craft-Karnataka
4. (b) Shola craft
6. (b) Gender
7. (c) créche
8. (c) This scheme also carries provisions for awards and recognitions.
9. (a) Ms. Kiran Mazumdar Shaw
10. (a) their attitude
11. (b) it helps in improving job effectiveness by improving job satisfaction.
12. (b) Increase in errors
13. (a) Biometrics
14. (c) wide variety of contexts
15. (a) entrepreneur
16. (c) Work for neglected and disadvantaged groups
17. (c) The Factories Act
18. (b) Achieving large scale benefits through entrepreneurship for a specific group.
19. (c) training, feedback
20. (b) Class 12
21. (c) To ensure survival, protection and education of the girl child.
22. (b) Ergonomics
23. (a) equal wages for the same work
24. (d) Labour and Employment
25. (b) Life skills
26. (a) Warli painting-Maharashtra
27. (a) Woman Entrepreneur - Kiran Mazumdar Shaw
28. (a) Ergonomics
29. (d) Both (a) and (b)
30. (b) Cash crops
31. (c) I and III
32. (a) I and II
33. (d) 4 3 2 1
34. (a) 1 2 3 4
35. (a) 2 4 3 1
36. (b) Both A and R are true, but R is not the correct explanation of A.
37. (a) Both A and R are true and R is the correct explanation of A.
38. (a) Channapatna dolls
39. These are 'Warli painting' which is popular in the state of Maharashtra.
40. (b) Coconut craft
41. (c) Bamboo
42. The given craft is 'Shola craft' of Odisha.
43. (i) (c) 2 4 3 1
    (ii) (a) Kiran Mazumdar Shaw - Chairperson of Biocon India Ltd.
    (iii) (b) Both A and R are true, but R is not the correct explanation of A.
    (iv) (b) Both A and R are true, but R is not the correct explanation of A.
44. (i) (b) attitude
    (ii) (c) III and IV
    (iii) (b) Life skills - Experiential learning
    (iv) (a) Both A and R are true and R is the correct explanation of A.

Subjective Questions

Very Short Answer Type Questions

1. Define the term livelihood.

Ans. It is defined as a means and occupation by which a person supports oneself to meet basic needs and sustain one's lifestyle.

2. Name any one traditional handicraft each of Assam and Kerala. CBSE 2024 C

Ans. • Assam-Bamboo craft • Kerala-Coconut craft

3. Write down the theme of 'Beti Bachao, Beti Padhao' scheme.

Ans. The theme of this scheme is to push the Indian society towards offering girl-child a better and safe environment to grow in.

4. What is life skills as per WHO (World Health Organisation)?

Ans. According to WHO, life skills are thinking, coping and social skills.

5. Who is mean by entrepreneur and entrepreneurship?

Ans. An entrepreneur is a person who undertakes the creation of changes in an enterprise or business. It is the act of creating a new and innovative enterprise or product or service.

6. What aspects should be considered by an individual while building his career and entering work life?

Ans. Following aspects should be considered by an individual while building his career and entering work life

- Their special talents, traits and interests in relation to occupation.
- If the work that they are going to choose is stimulating and challenging.
- If the occupation selected by them gives the sense of being useful to society or family.
- If the ethos and environment of the job are suitable to them and their development.

7. What do you mean by traditional occupations? Name some traditional occupations of India.

Ans. Traditional occupations can be described as occupations practiced by successive generations, rooted in customs and practices and focused on subsistence economies, pre-dating colonisation and the industrial revolution. They are often combined with traditional modes of practicing occupations. Handicrafts, agriculture, visual arts, weaving are some of the traditional occupations in India.

8. Where can one find visual arts in India? What are they inspired from?

Ans. Majority of visual arts can be found in temples and mausoleums in India.

These are mainly inspired from different religions found in India.

9. Mention any two challenges faced by handicrafts industry. In what two ways is the government trying to help revive this industry? CBSE 2021 C

Ans. Two challenges faced by handicrafts industry are

(i) Traditional handicrafts are on a verge of dying because of mass produced goods.

(ii) Illiteracy and general socio-economic backwardness of artisans result in less or no expansion of their handicraft business.

Two ways in which government is trying to help revive this industry are

(i) Organising fairs like Surajkund and World Trade Fair.

(ii) Providing skills development training.

10. Why are women in India still powerless?

Ans. Despite contributing significantly to the Indian economy and occupying senior positions in offices, women in India are still powerless. This is because they are still denied of their independence and freedom to take their decision on their own.

11. What are the main objectives of 'Kasturba Gandhi Balika Vidyalaya' scheme and 'Beti Bachao, Beti Padhao' scheme?

Ans. The main objective of Kasturba Gandhi Balika Vidyalaya scheme was to bring never-enrolled and dropout girls from rural, remote and disadvantaged sections of the society into school education till elementary level in residential schools and Beti Bachao, Beti Padhao scheme was to encourage education and participation of the girl child.

12. How can employees achieve greater satisfaction from their jobs? What is the possible reason for dissatisfaction?

Ans. Employees achieve greater satisfaction from their jobs when they scrutinise both positive and negative aspects of their jobs without comparing with others.

The possible reason for dissatisfaction is comparing one's job with that of others without taking into account the work responsibilities, the qualifications required, the work output, sincerity and dedication of the other person.

13. "Life skills are applied across the life span". Write down the importance of life skills for an individual with reference to the statement. **Competency Based Que**

Ans. The importance of life skills can be understood with the help of following points

- Life skills help to enhance people's interactions with others and with the environment and which may give rise to greater individual recovering capacity in situations of adversity.
- Life skills enable people to behave in healthy ways especially in challenging situations. They help to promote and protect life, health and well-being in all situations.

14. What do you understand by soft skills? Why are they important for career?

Ans. Soft skills are not job-specific skills. They are the characteristics required by individual to perform and achieve better in their lives. Soft skills are an essential part of improving one's ability to work with others and can have a positive influence on furthering one's career. These skills make it easier to form relationships with people, create trust and dependability and lead teams.

15. Mention some of the benefits of entrepreneurship.

Ans. Following are the benefits of entrepreneurship

- Rewarding career
- Work-life balance
- Leadership experience
- Work from anywhere
- Company control
- Flexible schedule
- Building a beneficial network
- Pride and satisfaction

16. Write any four personal attributes which should be possessed by an entrepreneur. **CBSE SQP, 2020**

Ans. Four personal attributes which should be possessed by an entrepreneur are

(i) Willingness to work hard.
(ii) Knowledge and skills for planning and implementation.
(iii) Having the courage to take calculated risks.
(iv) Ability and preparedness to handle many tasks simultaneously.

17. Your younger brother is very confused regarding which career to choose. Mention four factors he should consider while taking career related decision. **Competency Based Que**

Ans. Four factors that my younger brother can consider while making a career related decision are

(i) His own personal interests and passion.
(ii) The career which would give him satisfaction.
(iii) His own aptitude.
(iv) Sense of usefulness other than financial stability.

18. Renu has recently joined new company but she is finding it difficult to adjust with her colleagues. Suggest her any four essential soft skills she must adopt at her workplace. **Competency Based Que; CBSE 2023**

Ans. Four essential soft skills adopted by Renu at her workplace are as follows

(i) Working productively and effective work habits.
(ii) Thinking critically and creatively.
(iii) Communicating clearly.
(iv) Working co-operatively.

19. List four pillars on which the science of ergonomics is set. **CBSE 2023**

Ans. Ergonomics is set on the following four pillars

(i) Anthropometry i.e. body size and measurements
(ii) Biomechanics i.e. musculoskeletal activities and forces exerted
(iii) Physiology
(iv) Industrial psychology

20. Why are social entrepreneurs called 'social catalysts'? Write any two characteristics of an entrepreneur. **CBSE 2023**

Ans. Social entrepreneurs are called 'social catalysts because they aims to achieve large scale benefits through entrepreneurship for a specific group or to society at large.

The two characteristics of an entrepreneur are

(i) The willingness to work hard towards goals.
(ii) Knowledge and skills for planning and implementation of goals in an effective manner.

Short Answer Type Questions

1. "Traditional occupations are the chief source of livelihood in India". Discuss any three traditional occupations with reference to India.

Ans. Some of the traditional occupations prevalent in India are discussed below

- **Agriculture** It is the largest source of livelihood for rural people of India who approximately constitutes 70 per cent of the total population.
- **Handicrafts** It has been one of the traditional occupations in villages of India. Nowadays, Indian arts and crafts are popular in the international market and this has become a means of livelihood for the rural folk.
- **Indian Cuisine** Each region of India is famous for its typical or traditional cuisines comprised of local foods cooked with indigenous ingsredients and spices.

2. (i) State two factors that are responsible for the gradual erosion of traditional art. **CBSE SQP 2024**

(ii) Why do you think there is an urgent need to revive and sustain this traditional art and craft forms?

(iii) List two steps taken by the government to sustain and promote the traditional art and craft.

Ans. (i) Two factors that are responsible for the gradual erosion of traditional art are

(a) Low sources of income (b) Illiteracy

(ii) Reason of need to revive and sustain this traditional art and craft forms are

(a) For revival and sustaining of the indigenous knowledge.

(b) For revival of skills which are fast losing ground.

(iii) Two steps taken by the government to sustain and promote the traditional art and craft are

(a) **Design Innovations** It modernise and promote traditional crafts.

(b) **Preservation and Refinement Strategies** It aims to protect and enhance the quality of these art forms.

3. Convince your friend to do work by giving four importance of work. Competency Based Que; Diksha App

Ans. Here are four important reasons for friend to consider the value of work

(i) **Personal Growth and Development** Engaging in work challenges us to learn new skills, develop resilience and expand our capabilities. It fosters personal growth, helping us evolve into more competent and confident individuals.

(ii) **Financial Independence** Work provides a source of income, which is essential for meeting our basic needs and achieving personal goals. Financial stability empowers us to make choices that improve our quality of life.

(iii) **Social Connections and Networking** Through work, we build relationships with colleagues and clients, fostering a sense of community and collaboration. These connections can lead to new opportunities and support networks.

(iv) **Contributing to Society** Work allows us to contribute positively to our communities and the economy. By fulfilling our roles, we help drive social change and progress, making a meaningful impact in the world around us.

4. Discuss the Kasturba Gandhi Balika Vidalaya scheme initiated under Government of India.

Ans. For answer refer to text under the heading 'Kasturba Gandhi Balika Vidalaya (KGBV) scheme on page no. 10 and 11.

5. Sumera lived in a remote village and was never sent to school. Now her parents want to admit her in a residential school. Suggest the name of the scheme by the Government of India meant for such girls. Explain any two other features of this scheme. CBSE 2025

Ans. The **Kasturba Gandhi Balika Vidyalaya (KGBV)** scheme is suitable for Sumera. It provides residential schools for girls from disadvantaged backgrounds in areas with low female literacy.

Two features of this scheme are

- It offers free education up to 8th standard, including hostel facilities.
- It focuses on girls from Scheduled Castes, Scheduled Tribes, Other Backward Classes and minority communities, ensuring equal opportunities for education and empowerment.

6. Discuss the role of an entrepreneur in an enterprise.

Ans. A lot of hard work goes into starting and eventually expanding an enterprise. This hard work starts with the entrepreneur and trickles down the entire organisation.

Following roles tell how an entrepreneur is vital to the enterprise

- **Initiating and Leading Business Activities** Initiating and growing a business to its maturity is a traditional role for entrepreneurs.
- **Risk Taker** In an enterprise, the entrepreneur, being the owner, is the biggest risk taker. He is the one who finds the capital to back up his idea and also the person who is accountable in the face of the failure of that particular idea.
- **Financer** The entrepreneur mobilises the resources required to start and run a business, i.e. human workforce, finances, raw materials, machineries, etc.
- **Creating Jobs** When an entrepreneur sets up or expands a business, they decide which employees they need to hire.

7. Define Ergonomics and write its objective.

Or **What is the meaning of word Ergonomics.** Diksha App

Ans. Ergonomics is a branch of science that aims to learn about human abilities and limitations, and then apply this learning to improve people's interaction with products, systems and environments. It is the process of designing or arranging workplaces, products and systems so that they fit the people who use them.

Some of the objectives of ergonomics are

- Ergonomics aims to improve workspaces and environment to minimise injury or harm to improve productivity and output of workers.
- If the technologies change it ensures that tools that workers access for workers to work are designed for individual's body, size or strength.

8. Enlist three each benefits and need of ergonomics.

Ans. The following benefits of ergonomics are Diksha App

(i) **Improved Productivity** Ergonomically designed workspaces reduce fatigue and discomfort, allowing workers to perform tasks more efficiently and with greater focus.

(ii) **Reduced Risk of Injury** Ergonomics minimises physical strain and awkward postures, reducing the likelihood of musculoskeletal injuries like back pain, carpal tunnel syndrome and neck strain.

(iii) **Enhanced Employee Satisfaction** Comfortable work environments lead to higher employee morale and job satisfaction, which can contribute to reduced turnover and absenteeism.

The following need for ergonomics are

(i) **Prevention of Workplace Injuries** Ergonomics is essential to prevent injuries caused by repetitive tasks, poor posture, and improper lifting techniques in the workplace.

(ii) **Improved Work Quality** When employees work in ergonomic conditions, they are less distracted by discomfort, leading to higher-quality output and fewer errors.

(iii) **Cost Savings for Organisations** Implementing ergonomic solutions reduces health care and compensation costs associated with workplace injuries, leading to financial savings for organisations.

9. Jacob wants to set up a suitable workplace for his employees in his own manufacturing company. Advise him to use ergonomics in designing workplaces by giving the definition of ergonomics and its two benefits. **CBSE 2025**

Ans. Ergonomics is the science of designing workplaces and tools to fit the workers, ensuring comfort and efficiency. Jacob should use ergonomics to create a better work environment in his manufacturing company.

Two benefits of ergonomics are

(i) It reduces the risk of physical strain, injuries and fatigue and promotes better employee health.

(ii) It increases efficiency and productivity by creating a comfortable and focused workspace. A well-designed ergonomic workplace can positively impact both the employees and the company as a whole.

Long Answer Type Questions

1. How work contributes in the life of an individual? Discuss.

Ans. Work contributes in the life of an individual in many forms like

- It helps in boosting self-confidence as well as financial gain for an individual.
- An individual contributes to an organisation by creating better products or better reputation or greater profits for the organisation.
- It has an impact on the quality of life in the world around us.
- It helps as a means of self-development and self-actualisation by reflecting values and aspirations of an individual.
- It entails a task or duty that entails a sense of obligation.

Mostly in all cases, work enables the worker to earn a livelihood. But in some cases workers work for their own pleasure, intellectual stimulation, contribution towards the society, etc. knowing the fact that they wouldn't be paid for that work. These workers are basically volunteers, family members etc.

2. Explain about any three initiatives taken by Government of India to provide equality to women at workplace. **Diksha App**

Ans. (i) **The equal Remuneration Act** This act was enforced to ensure equal wages for women performing the same or similar work as men. It addresses wage disparities based on gender ensuring that women receive fair compensation for their labour creating a more equitable work environment.

(ii) **The maternity Benefit Act 1961** The maternity benefit act protects the rights of working women by providing maternity leave and ensuring that they are not discriminated against due to pregnancy. It grants women paid leave during childbirth and ensures job security upon their return, supporting them in balancing work and family responsibilities.

(iii) **Beti Bachao, Beti Padhao Scheme** This initiative aims to prevent gender-biased sex selection and improve the status of the girl child in society. By encouraging education and participation of girls, it helps in breaking gender stereotypes and promotes the empowerment of women giveing them equal opportunities in various spheres, including the workplace.

3. Your uncle is not happy with this work life. Suggest him about any ten ways of improving work life. **Competency Based Que; Diksha App**

Ans. Here are ten suggestions for improving work life that can share with uncle

(i) **Cultivate Healthy Habits** Encourage him to prioritise physical and mental well-being by adopting a balanced diet, exercising regularly and getting sufficient sleep. This holistic approach can significantly enhance his ability to handle workplace challenges.

(ii) **Practice Empathy and Compassion** Building supportive relationships with colleagues can foster a positive work environment. Practicing empathy allows for better understanding and co-operation among team members.

(iii) **Foster Teamwork** Collaborating with others not only drives collective success but also promotes learning and achievement of common goals. Emphasising teamwork can lead to a more satisfying work experience.

(iv) **Manage Stress Effectively** Suggest engaging in stress-relief activities like listening to music, practicing yoga, or spending time in nature. These activities can help maintain mental balance and improve overall job satisfaction.

(v) **Maintain Loyalty and Commitment** Demonstrating loyalty to the workplace fosters trust and creates a cohesive environment. A committed employee often experiences greater job satisfaction.

(vi) **Support Mutual Growth** Encourage him to assist colleagues and create a culture of mutual benefit. Helping each other can lead to improved teamwork and a more productive atmosphere.

(vii) **Embrace Core Abilities** Developing skills such as flexibility and problem-solving can enhance his ability to navigate workplace dynamics and overcome challenges.

(viii) **Learn from Life's Lessons** Encourage viewing daily challenges as opportunities for growth. Reflecting on experiences can build resilience and improve professional effectiveness.

(ix) **Be a Responsible Citizen** Contributing positively to the community can enhance personal fulfillment and create a sense of belonging, impacting work life positively.

(x) **Respond Wisely to Situations** Advise him to approach situations thoughtfully rather than reacting impulsively. Taking time to evaluate feedback or criticism can lead to constructive outcomes.

4. Discuss in detail about the attitudes and approaches possessed by an individual in work life.

Ans. An individual can possess both positive and negative attitudes and approaches to work in following ways

- A positive attitude involves rationally scrutinising the positive and negative aspects of one's job and accepting with happiness and a challenge to grow further. This increases job satisfaction and loyalty to the organisation one is working for.
- A positive attitude lets one relax, remember, focus and absorb information as one learns. They're ready to welcome new experiences and recognise many different kinds of learning opportunities. And when they can see opportunities, hope increases.
- A negative attitude can lead to job dissatisfaction when one compares their salary with other employees without thinking about their work pressure, output, capabilities etc.
- A negative attitude makes the work boring and an obligation to be fulfilled. It hinders in grabbing new opportunities in life thereby, making an individual stagnant at their position.

5. "Skills help an individual grow professionally as well as personally". Discuss. Competency Based Que

Ans. For answer refer to text under the headings 'Life Skills for Livelihood' and 'Essential Soft Skills for Workplace Success' on page no. 12 and 13.

6. Explain the concept of ergonomics in detail.

Ans. For answer refer to text under the heading 'Ergonomics' on page no. 13 and 14.

7. Your friend is social entrepreneur give its two objectives and four targets group whose need are fulfilled.

Competency Based Que; Diksha App

Ans. The following objectives of social entrepreneurship are

(i) **Address Societal Issues** Social entrepreneurs aim to tackle pressing social challenges, such as poverty, education inequality and environmental degradation, by developing innovative solutions that benefit communities.

(ii) **Create Sustainable Change** Their goal is to create long-lasting improvements in the lives of individuals and communities, ensuring that solutions are sustainable and scalable over time.

Target groups whose needs are fulfilled

(i) **Disadvantaged Communities** Social entrepreneurs focus on helping marginalised groups, such as low-income families, by providing access to essential resources and services that improve their quality of life.

(ii) **Women and Girls** Many social ventures target the empowerment of women and girls by promoting education, health services and economic opportunities that enable them to thrive.

(iii) **Youth** Initiatives often aim to equip young people with skills, education and resources necessary for their personal and professional development, addressing issues like unemployment and under-education.

(vi) **Elderly Population** Social entrepreneurs also work to support the elderly by creating services that enhance their well-being, such as health care, companionship programes and opportunities for engagement in community activities.

8. 'Several women empowerment schemes were initiated by the Government of India'. Discuss 'Beti Bachao, Beti Padhao' scheme with reference to the given statement.

Ans. For answer refer to text under the heading 'Schemes of Government' on page no. 10 and 11.

9. Guide Mr. Verma about any eight attributes for becoming successful entrepreneurs.

Competency Based Que; Diksha App

Ans. To become a successful entrepreneur, Mr. Verma should focus on developing the following eight key attributes

(i) **Visionary Thinking** Successful entrepreneurs have a clear vision of what they want to achieve. They can see opportunities where others see challenges and can plan for the future.

(ii) **Risk-Taking Ability** Entrepreneurs need to be comfortable with taking calculated risks. This means assessing potential failures and rewards and moving forward with confidence.

(iii) **Innovativeness** Entrepreneurs must be creative problem solvers who can think outside the box and continuously innovate their products, services or processes to stay ahead of the competition.

(iv) **Resilience** The entrepreneurial journey is filled with ups and downs. Being resilient and having the ability to bounce back from failures is critical to long-term success.

(v) **Leadership Skills** Strong leadership is essential to guide a team, inspire others and make difficult decisions. Entrepreneurs must lead by example and create a positive, motivating work environment.

(vi) **Networking Skills** Building strong relationships with mentors, industry professionals and peers is important for growth. Entrepreneurs need to develop networking skills to gain advice, partnerships and market insights.

(vii) **Financial Acumen** Understanding finances, managing cash flow and making smart investments are vital for the survival and growth of any business. Entrepreneurs must be able to manage resources efficiently.

(viii) **Adaptability and Flexibility** Markets change rapidly, and entrepreneurs must be able to pivot their business strategies when necessary to stay relevant. Adaptability is key to dealing with unforeseen challenges.

10. Riya is working in a manufacturing organisation. Her manager is not available today, so she has to handle several projects at once. Suggest some ways how she should handle the situation. **Competency Based Que**

Ans. Soft skills are required to handle the given situation. Soft skills are the skills that are not job-specific skills but general character traits required by a person. They are necessary to excel in professional as well as personal life.

Following are the suggestions which can help Riya in managing the situation

- She should prioritise the projects first according to their importance. The most urgent project should be done followed by less important projects.
- Time management skills come into play here. Riya should know how to manage time and calculate the time required by each project. Possible timeline should be assigned to each project.
- She should assign the tasks to the employees according to the skills required in each project. She should select such employees who are proficient in the required skills.
- She has to then monitor her employees and the tasks given to them. She herself has to check each project before sending them for submission.
- She should have the ability to multi-task the projects.

11. Pranav is an entrepreneur. His business is going well but a situation came when nothing is going as planned. **Competency Based Que**

(i) What do you understand by entrepreneurship?

(ii) Which characteristics of an entrepreneur come into play in such a situation?

(iii) What is social entrepreneurship ? What is the main aim of this type of entrepreneurship?

Ans. (i) Entrepreneurship is the act of creating a new and innovative enterprise, product or service. The function of entrepreneurs is to change the pattern of a production or design of a product through innovations, invention or even attempting new technological methods or modification for producing a new commodity or producing an old one in a new way.

(ii) When a situation comes when nothing goes according to the plan following characteristics of an entrepreneur come into play

(a) **Leadership Skills** Leadership is not only about managing others, but also about being a strong example to other people in the organisation. A great leader is the one who can demonstrate the ability to look after and inspire the employees, who always motivates them to work hard.

(b) **Communication Skills** Good communication skills are a key requirement to an entrepreneur. The way an entrepreneur communicates with their employees affects the attitudes of the employees towards their work. Clear communication leads to positive outcomes.

(c) **Problem Solving Skills** An entrepreneur should have problem solving skills. He/She should know the possible problems that could arise in an enterprise and should be ready with back-up solutions to them.

(iii) Social entrepreneurship that focuses on doing social good is called social entrepreneurship. The social entrepreneur aims to achieve large scale benefits through entrepreneurship for a specific group or to society at large. Generally, the social entrepreneur works for the benefit of the underserved, neglected, disadvantaged groups or individuals who do not have the financial resources to achieve the benefit by themselves.

SELF ASSESSMENT TEST

Objective Type Questions

1. Which of the following statement is incorrect regarding work?
   (a) It helps in boosting self-confidence
   (b) It has an impact on the quality of life in the world around us
   (c) It can be considered a form of essential activities
   (d) None of the above
2. Which of the following perspective of work aptly suits the statement,"Amit gets job satisfaction from continuing amusement and achievements"?
   (a) Work as a job (b) Work as a career
   (c) Work as a calling (d) None of these
3. As per the Indian Constitution women workers must be provided with ....
   (a) just and humane conditions of work
   (b) protection from any kind of exploitation
   (c) given support and encouragement in their educational and economic pursuits
   (d) All of the above
4. Choose the correct pair
   (a) Anthropometry-Psychology (b) Biomechanies-Body size
   (c) Work environment-Humidity (d) Worker capacity-Posture

Very Short Answer Type Questions

5. How do the 'age' and 'sex' of members of any workforce influence the personal and professional lives?
6. Who are 'trans sexuals'? By what other name the SC has directed to call them?
7. Mention any two state initiatives taken up by the government for women.

Short Answer Type Questions

8. How do you think soft skills are helpful in one's professional and personal growth?
9. A healthy environment is a positive work environment. Write any four ways by which a teacher can create healthy environment in her class.
10. Write any four personal attribute which should be possessed by enterpreneur.
11. Write any two reason for extinction of Indian Traditional Occupations?

Long Answer Type Questions

12. Career is something that lasts a lifetime. Explain what is career, while choosing a career, which points should be considered? How can a career be satisfying? **Competency Based Que**
13. Good workplace design results in healthy, fit and engaged work force. Identity the principle involved in designing a good work place. What are its benefits?
14. Who do you think the following quote is suitable for "If opportunity doesn't work, build a door– Milton Berle". Explain the skills required by that individual. **Competency Based Que**

02 CHAPTER

Clinical Nutrition and Dietetics

Nutrition is the science of food, nutrients and other substances as well as their digestion, absorption and utilisation by the body. Optimum nutrition is essential for providing immunity and recovery from various diseases. That is why nutrition is concerned with the social, phychological and economic aspects of food and eating.

▼ YOUR STUDY GOALS

▼ YOUR PRACTICE GOAL

- Objective Type Questions (31 Qs ; MCQs, A-R, Matching, Case Based)
- Subjective Questions (13 VSAs, 5 SAs, 8 LAs)

2.1 Nutrition

Consequences of inadequate intakes of nutrients are

- One may have difficulty in maintaining immunity defenses.
- Healing process of wounds may get slow.
- One may have difficulty in utilising medications.
- Supporting organs of body may not function properly.

Role of Nutrition in Disease Management

Nutrition has a very important role during disease states

- It helps in management and treatment of diseases.
- In some diseases, nutrition supports the medical treatment or it is a part of the treatment.
- They play an important role in prognosis (diagnosis), recovery and duration of hospitalisation.
- The overall nutritional status of an individual can be disrupted by illnesses and diseases.
- Various health problems can occur due to poor nutritional status and existing problems can become worse. Thus, health and nutrition are inter-linked.

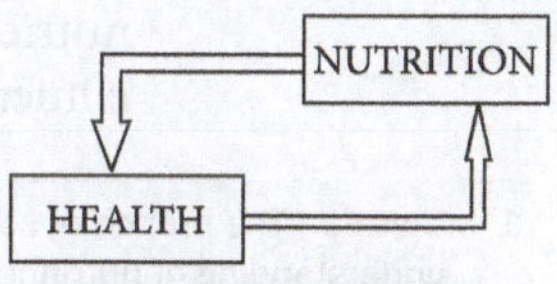

Health and Nutrition are interlinked intimately

2.2 Clinical Nutrition

- **Clinical Nutrition** is the discipline that deals with the prevention, diagnosis and management of nutritional and metabolic changes related to acute and chronic diseases and conditions caused by a lack or micro-nutrients or nutritional deficiencies.
- Clinical nutrition also known as **Medical Nutrition Therapy**.
- This field plays a crucial role in patient care by tailoring nutritional interventions to support recovery and improve health outcomes in individuals with chronic conditions.
- **Dietician**[1] It is an expert in diet and nutrition.

Significance of Clinical Nutrition

- Nutritional care has gained significant importance globally, driven by advancements in understanding metabolic disturbances and nutritional assessments in both chronic and acute diseases.
- Health problems can negatively impact nutritional status in several ways
  - Impairment of an individual's ability to eat and/or swallow.
  - Interference with digestion, absorption, metabolism and excretion.
  - Dysfunction of organs, tissues or body systems.
- The function of any organ, tissue or system can be affected by diseases, potentially leading to minor issues or escalating to acute, major or chronic illnesses.
- Trained dietitians, medical nutrition therapists and clinical nutritionists play a critical role in ensuring adequate nutrition for patients, by following a systematic logical approach to the nutritional care process, focusing on each patient's unique needs with a holistic perspective.
- Patients are the primary focus of clinical nutritionists, ensuring individualised care.

Evolving Field of Clinical Nutritions

- The prevalence of **non-communicable diseases**, such as obesity, heart disease, hypertension and diabetes is rising, affecting both young and adults.
- India is recognised as the **Diabetic Capital** of the world, highlighting the urgent need for effective nutritional care.
- Elderly individuals require special attention to maintain their nutritional status due to weakening of physiological systems.
- **Therapeutic**[2] nutritionists aid in improving nutritional status, preventing diseases, promoting good health and providing support during various health challenges.
- The significance of clinical nutrition has increased due to
  - New scientific knowledge regarding physiological and metabolic disturbances in chronic and acute diseases. Development and adoption of innovative nutritional assessment methods.
  - Use of newer techniques and supplements for patient nourishment.

Future of Clinical Nutrition

- Advances in the food and pharmaceutical industries have emphasised the importance of various nutrients and substances, including **nutraceuticals**[3] and **phytochemicals**[4], contributing to the growth of clinical nutrition.

---

1 **Dietitian** The branch of science concerned with the diet and its effects on health, especially with the practical application of a scientific understanding of nutrition.

2 **Therapeutic** The branch of medicine concerned with the treatment of disease and the action of remedial agents.

3 **Nutraceuticals** The term 'nutraceutical' is a combination of the words 'nutrition' and 'pharmaceutical'. It includes foods, food ingredients or dietary supplements that may have health benefits.

4 **Phytochemicals** Chemical compounds found in plants that may help protect humans from disease.

- Researchers are investigating the role of individual nutrients in gene expression, metabolic regulation and disease prevention and treatment, with antioxidants like beta-carotene, selenium and vitamins E and C showing protective roles.

Foods for Special Dietary Uses

- According to the FSSAI, foods for special dietary uses, functional foods, nutraceuticals or health supplements are specially processed or formulated to meet specific dietary requirements.
- These foods are designed for particular physical or physiological conditions or specific diseases and disorders. These foods have different composition as comperred to normal foods.
- These foods may contain one or more of the following ingredients
  - Plants or botanicals or their parts, in forms such as powder, concentrate or extracts (water, ethyl alcohol or hydro-alcoholic).
  - Minerals, vitamins, proteins, metals, their compounds, amino acids (not exceeding the re-commended daily allowance for Indians) or enzymes (within permissible limits).
  - Substances derived from animal origin.
  - Dietary substances intended to supplement the diet by increasing total dietary intake.
- **Medical foods** Specifically manufactured for individuals with particular needs and are regulated for use only with a doctor's prescription.
- These products are intended for the dietary management of specific diseases or conditions, such as gluten-free biscuits or low-sodium salt.
- **Phytochemical or bioactive compounds** Non-nutrient constituents found in foods that exhibit physiological or biological activity and can influence health.

2.3 Basic Concepts of Clinical Nutrition

Role of a Clinical Nutritionist

A dietitian or medical nutrition therapist is a person who is trained in managing nutrition during diseases. They play a major role in preventing or curing a disease state. These roles are

- They provide advice and translate technical information into dietary guidelines.
- They provide advice to patients, give prescription to healthy individuals at different stages of the life cycle i.e. pregnancy, infancy and childhood up to old age (womb to the tomb) in order to help them maintain good nutritional status and to remain healthy.

Diet Therapy

- Diet therapy is a branch of dietetics focused on using foods for therapeutic purposes. It involves altering or adopting diets to prevent or treat diseases and promote optimal health.
- Various health conditions that may require diet therapy include: Diarrhea, Vomiting, Pancreatic disorders, Metabolic syndrome, Liver disorders.
- A well-qualified dietitian is essential for implementing effective diet therapy for these conditions.
- Patients preparing for surgery need specific pre and post-operative nutritional support.
- Clinical nutrition and dietetics provide dietary prescriptions based on the nutritional needs of patients with different diseases.
- The primary goal of diet therapy is to promote a balanced selection of foods essential for good health.

Objectives of Diet Therapy

Following are the objective of diet therapy

- To maintain a good nutritional status.
- To correct nutrient deficiencies which may have occurred due to the disease.
- To adjust the food intake to the body's ability to metabolise the nutrients during the disease.
- To modify the existing diet in order to manage the disease condition.
- To prevent short-term and long-term complications in case of chronic diseases.
- To educate and counsel patient regarding the need of adherence to the prescribed diet.

Quick Test 1

1. How does a person's nutritional status help before and after illness?
2. Why poor nutrition is not considered good for health?
3. What does clinical nutrition primarily emphasise?
4. What therapies are used to improve the overall health of patients?
5. What plays an important role in enhancing immunity?

Role of Dietitian and Nutrition Care During Illness

The most important role of a dietitian is during illness, where they consider how the illness affects food acceptance and absorption capacity.

Factors that dietitians take into account include

- Nutritional stress
- Psychological stress
- The effect of illness on food acceptance
- Acceptability of modified therapeutic diets

Nutritional care during illness involves several key activities

- Collecting, organising and assessing data related to the health and nutritional status of individuals, groups and communities.
- Diagnosing nutritional problems.
- Reviewing and analysing a patient's nutritional needs to make suitable dietary re-commendations.
- Developing and implementing nutrition care plans while monitoring, following up and evaluating these plans, making corrective measures as needed.
- Calculating the nutritional value of planned food/meals.
- Prescribing **therapeutic diets**[5] and special nutrition support, along with feeding regimens.

Role of a Dietitian

- A study of clinical nutrition and dietetics equips professionals to plan diets that meet nutritional requirements at various life stages.
- Dietitians modify diets based on disease conditions, taking into account physical state, occupation, cultural and ethnic backgrounds, socio-economic status, treatment regimens and individual preferences.
- They design diets for athletes, sports persons and individuals in specialised environments, such as space, submarines and for defense personnel and industrial workers.

5 **Therapeutic diets** A meal plan that controls the intake of certain foods or nutrients.

- Dietitians promote the health and well-being of patients in hospitals, out-patient clinics and institutional settings.
- They manage food services in various institutional environments, including old age homes, schools and orphanages.
- Dietitians assist patients in managing chronic diseases like diabetes and heart disease, aiming to prevent complications and enhance quality of life.
- They work to improve community health, promote holistic care and contribute to better survival and recovery rates.

Nutritional Assessment

It is the process of determining the nutritional status of an individual or group. Dietitians can evaluate nutritional status through several methods

- Assessing dietary intake and personal or familial history of diseases.
- Measuring physical growth using **anthropometric measurements**, which provide quantitative data on body composition.
- Identifying potential nutritional deficiencies or risks of future deficiencies.

- While it is the physician's duty to address a patient's medical needs, dietitians play a crucial role based on the doctor's diagnosis and nutritional assessment.
- Dietitians prescribe diets, ensure food provision in hospitals according to dietary restrictions and provide dietary counseling to patients even in Out-Patient Department (OPD).
- Physicians rely on dietitians or medical nutrition therapists for the implementation of diet prescriptions.
- This collaboration has made clinical nutrition an integral part of mainstream treatment, highlighting its importance in health care.
- When planning a modified or therapeutic diet, several factors are taken into consideration
  - The patient's food patterns and frequency of food intake.
  - The diagnosis of the disease and the medical prescription provided by the doctor.
  - The patient's health status and physical condition, including their ability to eat, chew, swallow and their digestion and absorption capacity.
  - The patient's lifestyle patterns, including physical activity, cultural or ethnic practices and religious beliefs.

Quick Test 2

1. How has clinical nutrition evolved and been incorporated into mainstream health care?
2. What types of diets are planned in clinical nutrition?
3. What detailed information is needed to assess a patient's nutritional status?
4. What is one factor considered while planning a diet for a patient?
5. Mention the factors that a dietitian must consider when providing nutritional care during illness?

2.4 Types of Diets in Nutritional Care

A nutritional care plan consists of adequate intake of all nutrients as per the requirements based on age, sex, physiological state, occupation and health status of an individual. Diets are generally divided into two types that are as follows

(i) **Regular Normal or Standard Diet** A regular diet is a healthy meal plan that includes a variety of healthy foods from all the food groups to meet the needs of healthy individuals. However, in the hospitals a regular diet would be low in fried fatty foods, sweets, spices and condiments.

(ii) **Modified Diets** A diet that is altered by changing food consistency or nutrient content or by including or eliminating specific foods is called modified or therapeutic diet.

Modification in Consistency of Diet

To meet the medical needs of a patient, a diet can be modified in following ways

Diets of Altered Consistency

- Therapeutic diets are modified in consistency and texture to meet specific nutritional needs.
- Some individuals may require a clear liquid diet, while others may need a fully liquid diet or soft diet, depending on their medical condition.

Liquid Diet

- It consists of foods served in liquid or strained form at room temperature, also known as full fluid diets. These include foods which are free from fiber and nutritionally adequate, easily absorbed if the gastro-intestinal tract is functioning normally. Recommended for individuals who cannot chew or swallow normally. e.g coconut water, fruit juice, soup, milk and buttermilk.
  The two major types of liquid diets includes are

  (i) **Clear Liquid Diet** It is nutritionally inadequate, intended for short-term use (1-2 days). These diets are prescribed after surgery but may not meet all nutritional requirements. For examples, water, strained fruit juices, coconut water, lime juice, rice water, strained vegetable or meat soup and tea or coffee without milk or cream.

  (ii) **Full Liquid Diet** It provides liquid or semi-liquid foods and fluids at room temperature. It is suitable for post-operative patients and those with gastro-intestinal illnesses. For examples, foods include beverages, cream soups, vegetable soups, dal soups, strained fruit juices and lassi/buttermilk.

Soft Diet

- It provides soft whole foods that are lightly seasoned and similar to a regular diet.
- The foods are soft in consistency, easy to chew and made from simple, easily digestible ingredients.
- Excludes harsh fibre and gas-forming foods. Re-commended during acute infections, certain gastro-intestinal disorders and early recovery phases post-surgery. e.g khichdi and sago kheer.
- **Mechanical Soft Diet** Modifications for older adults who have chewing difficulties. Includes soft, mashed and pureed foods that are easily digestible. Excludes harsh fibre, high fat and spicy foods to give the digestive system rest.

Feeding Routes

- To provide adequate nutrition, oral feeding (by mouth) is typically recommended. When oral feeding is not possible, alternative feeding methods such as enteral or tube feeding and parenteral or intravenous feeding may be used.

Tube Feeding

It involves delivering a nutritionally complete diet through a tube. The diet is administered through the nose into the stomach, as long as the gastro-intestinal tract is functional and the person can digest and absorb food.

Intravenous Feeding

Nourishes the patient with special solutions given through a drip into a vein. This method includes fluids that contain water, glucose, amino acids, minerals and vitamins, administered through peripheral and central veins.

Prevention of Chronic Diseases

- Diet, nutrition and a healthy lifestyle are crucial for individuals with diseases.
- Healthy dietary practices can help control and delay the onset of chronic diseases.
- Urban populations often consume foods high in fat, sugar, refined cereals and sodium, while being low in fibre and micro-nutrients and high in animal protein.
- This increased intake of unhealthy foods, combined with low or no physical activity, contributes to various lifestyle diseases, including, heart disorders, obesity, colon cancer, diabetes, liver and kidney dysfunction.
- For example, rising sugar and fat consumption, along with decreased fibre intake and reduced physical activity, significantly contribute to obesity and diabetes.
- Preventive measures include adopting healthy lifestyle changes and seeking advice from clinical nutritionists on appropriate food choices and diet counseling.
- Dietitians can provide counseling to various groups, such as school and college students, to promote better dietary habits.

Quick Test 3

1. Which diet can be altered by changing food consistency or nutrient content?
2. What is the diet that includes soft, mashed and pureed forms of food?
3. In which type of feeding are patients nourished with special solutions?
4. What health risks have resulted from dietary changes among urban people?
5. In which condition is sodium restricted?

2.5 Preparing for a Career

To pursue a career in clinical nutrition and dietitian, an individual should have

- Passed 10+2 level followed by completion of a B.Sc. degree in Home Science or B.Sc. with a specialisation in nutrition/food technology.
- If a person wants to be a dietitian, they must complete their Post Graduate Diploma in Dietetics with an internship to be a registered dietitian.
- A person who has attained a B.Sc. degree in Home Science, Life Sciences, Biochemistry, Microbiology or Biotechnology can pursue this career at the postgraduate diploma level.
- An M.Sc. in Food Science and Nutrition or Dietetics helps a person to specialise in this field and they are preferred in many places of employment.
- A dietitian, after completing their university education, can further pursue and qualify to obtain the credential of a **Registered Dietitian**.

- Thus, if a person chooses a career in teaching and research, a number of opportunities are available in universities, colleges and research institutions.
- In order to attain a teaching post, it is necessary to clear the National or State Eligibility Tests conducted by the University Grants Commission (UGC).
- To pursue a career in academics or research, it is advisable for students to complete their Ph.D. in this field.

Essential Requirements for a Career as a Clinical Nutritionist/Dietitian

The essential requirements which should be possessed by the professional clinical nutritionist are discussed below

- He/She must have knowledge of physiological changes in disease conditions, changes in RDA's or nutrient requirements in illness and types of **dietary modifications**[6] required by the patient, as well as traditional and ethnic cuisines.
- He/She must have the skills in assessing the nutritional status of patients using clinical and biochemical criteria, diet planning customised to the requirements of individual patients and specific disease conditions, recommending and administering diets to patients, communication for diet counseling, adapting to cultural milieu, food taboos and overcoming myths.
- He/She must have knowledge of both theoretical and practical subject areas of nutrition, food science, food composition, clinical nutrition and dietetics or medical nutrition management.
- The clinical nutritionist must possess an understanding of basic biological and physical sciences, including biology, physiology and biochemistry. As food safety is critical in institutional settings, he/she must have knowledge of microbiology and food microbiology and safety, food quality and assurance, food laws and regulations and the use of physics, as well as maintenance of various equipments used in food preparation, storage and service.
- They must have knowledge of food service management, including the quantity of food production, which is important. They can also have a basic understanding of book-keeping and accounts; record-keeping and management are also important.
- Disease changes both mind and body, which has a major impact on the physiological and mental state of a person. A dietitian must possess sound knowledge of psychology, sociology, education and counseling that will help him/her to become a good counselor.
- An additional understanding of **epidemiology**[7] and patterns of prevalence and incidence of nutritional disorders and diseases, skills in surveying patient populations, laboratory research using biochemical parameters and skills in conducting experimental designs with patients will help to find out the usefulness of various diets, drugs and nutritional supplements.

2.6 Scope of Clinical Nutrition and Dietetics

- There is a vast scope and satisfying career potential in clinical nutrition and dietetics.
- Career opportunities include roles as a dietitian, diet counselor, researcher or corporate consultant.
- Professionals can engage in teaching or research within the field.
- Opportunities exist in the food industry, particularly in research and development, production of medical foods, nutraceuticals, tube feeds and various nutritional support formulations.
- Individuals interested in improving food's role in controlling, preventing and treating disease can pursue a career in Clinical Nutrition and Dietetics.

6 **Dietary modifications** It refers to changes made during food preparation, processing and consumption to increase the absorption of micro-nutrients and reduce mirco-nutrients deficiencies.

7 **Epidemiology** The branch of medicine which deals with the incidence, distribution and possible control of diseases and other factors relating to health.

- The expanding scope of research addresses physiological and psychosocial changes caused by disease conditions.
- Nutritional considerations in preventing, treating and curing various diseases are increasingly recognised.
- Research in this field has led to the development of drugs, nutritional supplements, rehabilitation programmes in community settings, dietary guidelines and nutrition education.
- Clinical nutritionists can play a significant role in public policy by designing and implementing preventive and promotive nutrition programmes to address nutritional deficiency disorders.
- Possible positions include dietitian in hospitals or clinics, researcher in medical research establishments or nutrition supplements and food service manager or provider in hospitals.

Career Avenues

Career avenues for dietitians are given below

- Dietitians with consultants/physicians, in health clubs or gymnasiums.
- Dietitians in hospitals including specialty departments, a key member to provide nutrition support in the health care team.
- Freelance Dietitian
- Dietitians in catering services for hospitals, schools, industrial canteens etc.
- Entrepreneurs who develop and supply specialty foods for specific health purposes.
- Teaching and Academics
- Research including Clinical Research
- Nutrition marketing
- Technical writing

Quick Test 4

1. What is the minimum qualification to become a dietitian?
2. Which postgraduate degree specialises in clinical nutrition?
3. Name two skills required for a clinical nutritionist.
4. Why is microbiology important for a clinical nutritionist?
5. Mention two career options for dietitians.

Mind Map

CLINICAL NUTRITION AND DIETETICS

1 Nutrition

Consequences of Inadequate Nutrient Intake
- Weak immunity and poor defense.
- Slow wound healing.
- Difficulty in utilising medications.
- Improper functioning of body organs.

Role of Nutrition in Disease Management
- Aids in managing and treating diseases.
- Supports medical treatments or is part of the treatment.
- Impacts diagnosis, recovery and hospitalisation duration.
- Poor nutritional status worsens health problems.

2 Clinical Nutrition

- **Definition** Focuses on preventing and managing nutritional issues related to diseases.
- **Role** Supports patient recovery, improves health outcomes, and customise care for chronic conditions.
- **Significance** Addresses issues in eating, digestion, and organ function due to disease; involves individualised care.
- **Trends** Rising non-communicable diseases (e.g., diabetes, heart disease) and special care for the elderly.
- **Future** Growth in nutraceuticals and advanced nutrition techniques.

3 Basic Concepts of Clinical Nutrition

Role of Clinical Nutritionist
- Provide dietary advice for health at all life stages.
- Translate medical info into practical dietary guidelines.

Diet Therapy
- Use food to treat diseases like diarrhea, liver disorders, etc.
- Requires professional dietitians for effective treatment.

Objectives of Diet Therapy
- Maintain nutrition, correct deficiencies, adjust food intake for metabolic needs.
- Prevent complications and educate patients on diet adherence.

Role in Illness
- Assess how illness affects food absorption and acceptance.
- Develop and monitor nutrition care plans.

Nutritional Assessment
- Evaluate dietary intake, physical growth, and risks of deficiencies.
- Collaborate with doctors to implement dietary.

4 Types of Diets in Nutritional Care

- **Regular Diet** Balanced diet for healthy individuals.
- **Modified Diet**
  - **Liquid Diet** Clear (short-term) and Full (nutritionally complete).
  - **Soft Diet** Easy-to-chew, for recovery.
- **Mechanical Soft Diet** Mashed/pureed foods for chewing issues.
- **Feeding Methods**
  - **Oral Feeding** Preferred.
  - **Tube/IV Feeding** When oral intake isn't possible.
- **Chronic Disease Prevention** Healthy diet prevents diseases like obesity, diabetes, heart disease.
- Diet, nutrition and a healthy lifestyle are crucial for individual. **For example** Rising sugar and fat consumption.

5 Career in Clinical Nutrition and Dietetics

- **Skills** Knowledge in disease-related dietary needs. Expertise in nutritional assessment, counseling and food safety. Understanding food science, psychology and food service management.
- **Opportunities** Careers in hospitals, clinics, food industries, research and teaching.

Education
- B.Sc. in Home Science/Nutrition/Food technology.
- Post Graduate Diploma in Dietetics + Internship.
- M.Sc. for specialisation, Ph.D. for academics.
- Duality to abstain the credentials of a registered dietitian.
- Necessary to clear the National Eligiblity Tests conduct by the UGC.

6 Clinical Nutrition and Dietetics

- **Career Roles** Dietitian, Counselor, Researcher, Consultant, Entrepreneur.
- **Key Areas** Nutritional Support, Disease Prevention, Food Industry.
- **Specialisations** Teaching, Marketing.
- Technical Writing.
- **Research** Supplements, Dietary Guidelines.
- **Growth Potential** Expanding field with diverse opportunities.

7 Careen Avenues

- Freelance dietitian.
- Nutrition marketing.
- Technical writing.
- Teaching and academics.
- Dictations in catering service.

NCERT Folder

Intext Questions

1. Scientists have found connection between diet and disease. For example in a clinical study of 20,000 men, consuming fish once a week was linked to a 52 per cent reduction in the risk of sudden death from heart attack. Fish is high in omega-3 fatty acids, which are essential components of cells and can protect the heart from abnormal heart rhythm. In another clinical study of more than 42,000 women, those who ate lots of fruits, vegetables, whole grains, low-fat dairy products and only lean meats lived longer. High intake of fruits, vegetables and legum. What can you conclude about?

(i) Role of the diet in disease causation.

(ii) Role of the diet in disease prevention. (Pg. no. 39)

Ans. (i) The changes in diet patterns and over consumption of any food product in diet may cause the following diseases,

(a) The over consumption of sugar and fat along with decrease in fibre consumption, may lead to obesity and diabetes.

(b) Increase in sodium content and decrease in potassium intake, rich fruits, vegetables may increase the risk of hypertension (high blood pressure).

(c) Scientists have also found that consuming fish may reduce the risk of sudden death from heart attack.

(ii) Diet and good nutrition can control and delay the age of onset of chronic diseases. Healthy diet patterns like fruits, vegetables, whole grains and legs with enough fibre may lead to disease prevention.

Exercise

1. What is the significance of the study of clinical nutrition and dietetics? **Diksha App**

Ans. Clinical nutrition and dietetics have gained wide clinical and scientific interest in the recent times. The significance of clinical nutrition and dietetics is due to the following reasons

- The main aim of clinical nutrition is to maintain a healthy energy balance, while also providing sufficient amounts of nutrients such as protein, vitamins and minerals to patients/individuals.
- Trained dietitians/medical nutrition therapists are required to give advice about diet and nutrition to the individual as well as the community.
- Newer methods of nutritional assessment are being developed and adopted.
- Newer techniques and supplements for nourishing the patient/individual are being used.
- With advances in the food and pharmaceutical industry, the role of various nutrients and other substances such as nutraceuticals, phytochemicals/bioactive substances has been emphasised and helped in the growth of the discipline of clinical nutrition.
- Researchers and scientists are discovering the role of individual nutrients ranging from a role in gene expression, metabolic regulation also in the prevention and treatment of disease. For example, antioxidants like beta-carotene and Vitamin C, particularly from food, plays an important role in providing protection.

2. What are the types of diets and how you can modify diet. **Diksha App**

***Or* What are the types of dietary modifications that a medical nutrition therapist may make?**

Ans. Following dietary modifications may be made by a medical nutrition therapist

- Change in consistency of foods, such as liquid diet, soft diet, balance diet.
- Increase or decrease in energy value of the diet such as low calorie diet for weight reduction, high calorie diet for burns.
- Increase or decrease in specific nutrients or type of food consumed, such as sodium restricted diet, lactose restricted diet, high fibre diet, high potassium diet.
- Omission of specific foods such as allergy diets, gluten free diet.
- Adjustment in the ratio and balance of proteins, fats and carbohydrate such as diabetic diet, renal diet and cholesterol lowering diets.
- Change in frequency of meals, feeding intervals, rearrangement of the number and frequency of the meals such as diet for peptic ulcer disease.
- Special plan for patients when route of feeding is altered.

3. Why do we need dietary changes to prevent chronic diseases? How are they linked with lifestyle?

Or **Prevention of Chronic disease.** **Diksha App**

Ans. Chronic diseases are the diseases which last for a long time when occurred. These include diabetes, heart diseases, obesity etc. These can occur in people having familial history of such diseases and due to inadequate or poor dietary intake. This includes high intake of refined sugars, processed foods, foods high in sodium and fat, foods rich in animal protein, low in fibre etc. Chronic diseases are largely preventable as diet is a modifiable factor.

So, we should modify our diets accordingly. One can include a diet low in fat, sodium and sugar to prevent high blood pressure, obesity, diabetes and heart diseases. Inclusion of fresh fruits and vegetables provides anti-oxidants and micro-nutrients which help in delaying the onset of chronic diseases.

Chronic diseases are linked with lifestyle as poor diet coupled with poor or no physical activity leads to various metabolic changes inside the body, thus, resulting in chronic diseases. Including physical activity in everyday routine and making healthy food choices can greatly decrease the risk of chronic diseases.

4. What are the roles performed by a dietitian? How does the dietitian form a team in patient care with other health care professionals?

Ans. A dietitian is an expert in dietetics, dealing with human nutritional care. Following roles are performed by a dietitian in order to promote good health among patients/individuals.

- They collect, organise and assess data related to health and nutritional status of individuals, groups and communities.
- They review and analyse patient's nutritional needs and goals to make appropriate dietary recommendations.
- They develop and implement nutrition care plans and monitor, follow up and evaluate the suggested plans and take corrective measures wherever required.
- They prescribe therapeutic diets and special nutrition support and feeding regimens.
- They oversee the preparation of special diets, special nutrition formulas for patients who are critically or terminally ill and require special feeding through oral, enteral or parenteral routes.
- They planning and prepare basic menus and assist in supervising food service personnel in preparing menus and serving of meals.

The dietitians form a team in patient care with other health care professionals by prescribing the food required by the patient for speedy recovery. The dietitian has to prescribe food keeping in mind the disease, medicines and physical condition of the patient. The medicines and other treatments work well when the nutritional status of the patient is maintained. Thus, both physicians and dietitians are dependent on each other.

5. How can we prepare for a career in clinical nutrition and dietetics?

Ans. One can prepare for a career in clinical nutrition and dietetics by following the steps given below

- To prepare for a career in dietetics and clinical nutrition one has to pass 10+2 level followed by Bachelors in Home Science with Specialisation in Nutrition. This can be followed by either a Postgraduate Diploma in Nutrition or Masters in Food and Nutrition.
- An individual may study further and pursue a Ph.D. in nutrition. They may also pursue further and qualify to obtain the credential of a 'Registered Dietitian'.
- Other than above qualifications, one should have a knowledge of physiological changes in disease conditions, changes in RDAs/nutrient requirements in illness and types of dietary modifications required, traditional and ethnic cuisines.
- Skills in assessing nutritional status of patients using clinical and biochemical criteria, diet planning customised to requirements of individual patients and specific disease conditions and much more.

6. How does illness/disease affect nutritional status of a person?

Ans. Various health problems and illnesses can negatively affect an individual's nutritional status in the following ways

- Illness and disease can result in nutrient imbalances even in a person who previously had good nutritional status.
- All infections no matter how mild decrease nutrient intakes and increase nutrient losses.
- Impairment of an individual's ability to eat and/or swallow.
- Impairment of processes of digestion, absorption, metabolism as well as excretion.
- Dysfunction of any organ/tissue/system of the body.

Exam Pattern Questions

Objective Type Questions

Multiple Choice Questions

1. Which of the following statement is incorrect about the nutrition?

(a) It deals with the social, psychological and economic aspects of food and eating process.
(b) Health and nutrition are not linked to each other.
(c) Nutrition helps to complement the treatment process.
(d) It is essential for providing immunity and protection from infections.

2. In recent times, Clinical Nutrition is known as ....
Diksha App

(a) Psychological Nutrition Therapy
(b) Nutritional Management
(c) Medical Nutrition Therapy
(d) Dietetics

3. Which method is adopted by the professional clinical nutritionist?

(a) He/She uses a logical approach to handle the nutrition care process by focussing on each person's needs.
(b) He/She addresses the patients in an individualistic and holistic manner.
(c) He/She focuses on nutritional management of patients with established disease.
(d) All of the above

4. Identify the new constituent present in food which was found by researchers that have physiological or biological activity and influence health.
CBSE SQP, 2020, Diksha App

(a) Nutraceuticals
(b) Medical foods
(c) Antioxidants
(d) Phytochemicals

5. What is India known as?

(a) Diabetic capital of the world
(b) Hypertensive capital of the world
(c) Diabetic country
(d) None of the above

6. A branch of dietetics concerned with use of foods for therapeutic purpose

(a) Nutrition (b) Clinical nutrition
(c) Diet therapy (d) Dietary changes

7. .... is an art and a science. **Diksha App**

(a) Psychology (b) Counseling
(c) Listening (d) Meditation

8. While assessing nutritional status of a patient which factor is not considered by the clinical nutritionist?
CBSE SQP Term I, 2021-22

(a) Anthropometric measurements
(b) Detailed information on diet and medication histories
(c) Relating the information on laboratory and physical measurements
(d) Diet survey

9. Diet therapy is favourable in conditions of ....

(a) nutritional deficiencies (b) psychological stress
(c) nutritional stress (d) None of these

10. Nutritional Assessment helps to access ....

(a) anthropometric measurements are adopted.
(b) potential nutritional deficiencies and risk of future deficiencies are identified.
(c) medication histories of the patient are obtained through this assessment.
(d) All of the above

11. Which of the following is not an objective of diet therapy?
CBSE SQP Term I, 2021

(a) Modification of existing diet
(b) Knowledge of traditional cuisine
(c) Prevention of complications
(d) Correction of nutritional deficiency

12. Important job profile of a dietitian along with the knowledge and understanding of basic science is ....
Diksha App

(a) knowledge of Microbiology
(b) record keeping
(c) presribing medicines
(d) counseling patients

13. Find the incorrect statement from the following.
CBSE 2024 C

(a) In recent times, clinical nutrition field is also known as medical nutrition therapy.
(b) Healthy lifestyle can delay the age of onset of chronic diseases.
(c) Mechanical, soft diet is not easily digestible diet.
(d) Intravenous feeding means that the patient is nourished with special solutions which are given through a trip in a vein.

14. .... are regulated health care professionals licensed to assess, diagnose and treat nutritional problems. **Diksha App**

(a) Doctors (b) Nurses
(c) Dietitian (d) Physicians

15. After surgery of stomach your grandfather is unconscious, which mode of feeding would be preferred for him and why? **CBSE SQP Term I, 2021**

(a) Oral feeding and easy to chew
(b) Tube feeding and easy to digest
(c) Intravenous feeding and to get nourishment
(d) Nasogastric feeding and nutrition

16. Which type of diets should be prescribed by the dietician to your grandfather who is suffering from kidney and chewing problem respectively? **CBSE SQP Term I, 2021**

(a) Low protein diet and mechanical soft diet
(b) High protein diet and mechanical soft diet
(c) Low fibre diet and liquid diet
(d) High fibre diet and regular diet

17. When a patient is nourished with special solution which are given through a drip in a vein is known as .... **Diksha App**

(a) oral feeding (b) tube feeding
(c) intravenous feeding (d) nasogastric feeding

18. Diet which includes soft, mashed and pureed foods for the elderly with problems in chewing is known as ....

(a) soft diet (b) mechanical soft diet
(c) liquid diet (d) clear liquid diet

19. The increase in sugar and fat consumption, along with the decrease in fibre consumption results in the cause of .... **Diksha App**

(a) hypertension (b) typhoid
(c) obesity and diabetes (d) tuberculosis

20. Clinical nutritionists have career opportunities in fields like .... **Diksha App**

(a) food industry (b) teacher
(c) researcher (d) All of these

21. Which of the following option is most suitable for a career in the field of clinical nutrition? **CBSE 2025**

(a) Quality control manager (b) Specialist in HACCP
(c) Diet consultant (d) Sensory evaluator

22. Your sister has completed her diploma in clinical nutrition and dietetics. Choose from the following options which are available to her to start her career? **Competency Based Que**

(a) School Counsellor
(b) Research and Development and Nutraceuticals
(c) ECCE
(d) In Agriculture Industry

23. Career avenues for dietitians are given below **CBSE SQP 2023**

I. Doctor II. Nutrition Marketing
III. Technical Writer IV. Editor

Choose the correct option.

(a) I and II (b) II and III (c) III and IV (d) I and IV

24. India is often referred as the identify two possible causes of a chronic disease such as diabetes. **CBSE 2024**

I. Taking diet prescribed by medical nutrition therapist
II. Less physical activity
III. Increase in sugar and fat consumption
IV. Increase in fibre consumption

Choose the correct option from the following

(a) I and II (b) II and IV
(c) II and III (d) III and IV

25. Match the following **CBSE SQP 2023**

List-I	List-II
A. Clear liquid diet	1. Gluten free biscuits
B. Full liquid diet	2. Strained fruit juices
C. Soft diet	3. Vegetable soups
D. Medical foods	4. Khichdi

Codes

	A	B	C	D		A	B	C	D
(a)	2	3	4	1	(b)	3	4	2	1
(c)	2	1	4	3	(d)	1	2	3	4

Assertion-Reason Questions

Directions (Q. Nos. 26-27) In the questions given below, there are two statements marked as Assertion (A) and Reason (R). Read the statements and choose the correct option.

Codes

(a) Both A and R are true and R is the correct explanation of A.
(b) Both A and R are true, but R is not the correct explanation of A.
(c) A is true, but R is false.
(d) A is false, but R is true.

26. **Assertion** (A) Nutritional status and support, prior to and after illness, play an important role in prognosis, recovery and even duration of hospitalisation.

Reason (R) Nutritional care has gained importance worldwide, more so in recent times.

27. **Assertion** (A) A medical nutrition therapist is a health professional that diagnosis and treats the dietary and nutritional problems of a person.

Reason (R) Medical nutrition therapist plans diet at gym, hostels, aircraft, five star hotels, etc.

Case Based Questions

28. **Read the given passage and answer the following questions.**

What are the consequences of these dietary changes? Broadly speaking, such changes have been associated with increased incidence of chronic diseases such as obesity, cancer of the colon, diabetes, cardiovascular disease and hypertension. For example, the increase in sugar and fat consumption, along with the decrease in fibre consumption and less physical activity, play a role in causing of obesity and diseases. It has also been found that high consumption of highly salted convenience foods, processed foods with high sodium content, decreased intake of potassium-rich fruits, vegetables, grains and legumes, possibly low calcium intakes, less physical activity as well as stress are associated with increased risk of hypertension.

(i) **Select the correct pair of diet-related change and its associated disease**

(a) Increase in sugar intake : Hypertension
(b) Decrease in fibre intake : Obesity
(c) High salt intake : Diabetes
(d) Low calcium intake : Cardiovascular disease

(ii) **Match the following in List I with List II.**

List I (Dietary Factor)	List II (Associated Disease)
A. Increase in sugar and fat consumption	1. Hypertension
B. High sodium content in processed foods	2. Diabetes
C. Decrease in fibre consumption	3. Colon cancer
D. Low intake of potassium-rich fruits	4. Obesity

Codes

	A	B	C	D		A	B	C	D
(a)	2	4	3	1	(b)	3	4	2	1
(c)	2	1	4	3	(d)	4	2	3	1

(iii) **Assertion** (A) High consumption of sodium-rich processed foods increases the risk of hypertension.

Reason (R) Sodium causes fluid retention, which increases blood pressure.

Codes

(a) Both A and R are true and R is the correct explanation of A.
(b) Both A and R are true, but R is not the correct explanation of A.
(c) A is true, but R is false.
(d) A is false, but R is true.

(iv) **Assertion** (A) A decrease in physical activity and fibre consumption increases the risk of obesity.

Reason (R) Fibre aids in digestion and increases satiety, reducing overall caloric intake.

Codes

(a) Both A and R are true and R is the correct explanation of A.
(b) Both A and R are true, but R is not the correct explanation of A.
(c) A is true, but R is false.
(d) A is false, but R is true.

29. **Read the given passage and answer the following questions.** **CBSE SQP 2024**

The medical nutrition therapist takes into account the food pattern and frequency of intake of different types of food, diagnosis of disease and prescription given by the doctor, the health status and physical condition including ability to eat, chew, swallow, digest and absorb the food eaten, feeling of hunger, physical activity and life style, dietary and other supplements consumed, cultural/ethnic practices and religious beliefs.

(i) **In the context of medical nutrition therapy choose the correct pair.** **Competency Based Que**

(a) Antioxidants : Low sodium salt
(b) Nutraceuticals : Beta-carotene
(c) Medical foods : Lactose free milk
(d) Phyto chemicals : Amla powder

(ii) **Match type of diets given in List I with the examples in List II.** **Competency Based Que**

List I (Type of Diets)	List II (Examples)
A. Mechanical soft diet	1. Buttermilk
B. Liquid diet	2. Sago kheer
C. Soft diet	3. Strained soup
D. Clear liquid diet	4. Pureed apple

Codes

	A	B	C	D
(a)	1	2	3	4
(b)	4	3	2	1
(c)	3	4	2	1
(d)	4	1	2	3

(iii) **Given below are two statements labelled as Assertion (A) and Reason (R).** **Competency Based Que**

Assertion (A) Intravenous feeds are preferred over tube feeds.

Reason (R) In intravenous feeds the patients are nourished with the special solutions that are given through a drip in the vein.

Codes

(a) Both A and R are true and R is the correct explanation of A.
(b) Both A and R are true, but R is not the correct explanation of A.
(c) A is true, but R is false.
(d) A is false, but R is true.

(iv) Given below are two statements labelled as Assertion (A) and Reason (R). Competency Based Que

Assertion (A) High consumption of convenience and processed foods increases the incidence of Hypertension.

Reason (R) It is attributed to the presence of high sodium content.

Codes

(a) Both A and R are true and R is the correct explanation of A.
(b) Both A and R are true, but R is not the correct explanation of A.
(c) A is true, but R is false.
(d) A is false, but R is true.

30. Read the given passage and answer the following questions.

Nutrition is the science of food, nutrients and other substances as well as their digestion, absorption and utilisation by the body. Optimum nutrition is an important for providing immunity and protection from infection and to promote recovery from a variety of illnesses as well as managing chronic diseases. Nutrition and health are intimately interlinked. Health problems, illness/disease and their treatment can affect nutritional status in a variety of ways such as

- by impairing a person's ability to eat and/or swallow,
- by interfering with digestion, absorption and metabolism. The specialised area of nutrition which deals with nutritional management during illness is clinical nutrition, more recently called medical nutrition therapy. The professional who delivers this service is referred to as dietitian/medical nutrition therapist/clinical nutritionist. CBSE 2023

(i) Which of the following are features of optimum nutrition?

I. Providing protection from disease
II. Ensuring abundance of food
III. Promoting recovery from illness
IV. Promoting socio-economic health
V. Managing chronic disease

Choose the correct option.

(a) I, II and III (b) I, III and V
(c) II, III and IV (d) III, IV and V

(ii) Which of the following parameters not considered while taking anthropometric measurements?

(a) Waist circumference
(b) Height
(c) Haemoglobin level
(d) Weight

(iii) Which of the following is not an objective of diet therapy?

(a) Formulation of the diet to meet the needs of the patient.
(b) Modification of the existing diets to ameliorate (ractify) the disease condition.
(c) Prevention of short-term and long-term complications in case of chronic diseases.
(d) Educating and prescribing medicines to the patients.

(iv) Illness can influence the nutritional status of an individual by

I. providing alternate therapy
II. impairment in a person's ability to eat and swallow
III. promoting holistic recovery
IV. problem with digestion, absorption
V. interference with proper metabolism

Choose the correct option.

(a) I, II and III (b) I, III and V
(c) II, IV and V (d) III, IV and V

31. Read the given passage and answer the following questions.

Health and nutrition are intimately interlinked. In some diseases, nutrition plays a major role in its management and treatment and for some it compliments the medical treatment. Nutritional status and support prior to and after illness, plays an important role in determining prognosis, recovery and even duration of hospitalisation. Nutritional assessment is required to obtain information on the patients. Nutritional status and nutritional needs. A dietician can help a nutrition care plan by analysing the nutritional requirements in the state of disease and also provide appropriate diet, counselling and guidance. CBSE 2024

(i) Which of the following is an incorrect pair?

(a) Soft diet : Semi-solid foods
(b) Liquid diet : Fluids high in fibre and fats
(c) Regular diet : Normal foods, all food groups included
(d) Mechanical soft diet : Mashed and pureed foods

(ii) Which of the following statements is correct with respect to Clinical Nutrition and Dietetics?

(a) It is also called Public Nutrition Therapy.
(b) It is the specialised area of nutrition which deals with nutrition during illness.
(c) It addresses the problems of the community at large.
(d) It improves the sanitary condition of rural households.

(iii) Given below are two statements labelled as Assertion (A) and Reason (R).

Assertion (A) In tube feeding, nutritionally complete feeds are delivered to a patient through a tube.

Reason (R) Oral feeding means that the patient is nourished with special solutions which are given through a drip in a vein.

Codes

(a) Both A and R are true and R is the correct explanation of A.
(b) Both A and R are true, but R is not the correct explanation of A.
(c) A is true, but R is false.
(d) A is false, but R is true.

(iv) Given below are two statements labelled as Assertion (A) and Reason (R).

Assertion (A) Fish is high in Omega-3 fatty acids which are essential components of cells.

Reason (R) They can protect the heart from abnormal heart rhythm.

Codes

(a) Both A and R are true and R is the correct explanation of A.
(b) Both A and R are true, but R is not the correct explanation of A.
(c) A is true, but R is false.
(d) A is false, but R is true.

Answers

1. (b) Health and nutrition are not linked to each other.
2. (c) Medical Nutrition Therapy
3. (d) All of the above
4. (d) Phytochemicals
5. (a) Diabetic capital of the world
6. (b) Clinical nutrition
7. (b) Counseling
8. (c) Relating the information on laboratory and physical measurements
9. (a) nutritional deficiencies
10. (d) All of the above
11. (b) Knowledge of traditional cuisine
12. (d) counseling patients
13. (c) Mechanical, soft diet is not easily digestible diet.
14. (c) Dietitian
15. (c) Intravenous feeding and to get nourishment
16. (b) High protein diet and mechanical soft diet
17. (c) intravenous feeding
18. (b) mechanical soft diet
19. (c) obesity and diabetes
20. (d) All of these
21. (c) Diet consultant
22. (b) Research and Development and Nutraceuticals
23. (a) I and II
24. (c) II and III
25. (a) 2 3 4 1
26. (b) Both A and R are true, but R is not the correct explanation of A.
27. (c) A is true, but R is false.
28. (i) (b) Decrease in fibre intake : Obesity
    (ii) (c) 2 1 4 3
    (iii) (a) Both A and R are true and R is the correct explanation of A.
    (iv) (a) Both A and R are true and R is the correct explanation of A.
29. (i) (b) (c) Medical foods : Lactose free milk
    (ii) (d) 4 1 2 3
    (iii) (d) A is false, but R is true.
    (iv) (a) Both A and R are true and R is the correct explanation of A.
30. (i) (b) I, III and V
    (ii) (c) Haemoblobin level
    (iii) (d) Educating and prescribing medicines to the patients.
    (iv) (c) II, IV and V
31. (i) (b) Liquid diet : Fluids high in fibre and fats
    (ii) (b) It is the specialised area of nutrition which deals with nutrition during illness.
    (iii) (c) A is true, but R is false.
    (iv) (a) Both A and R are true and R is the correct explanation of A.

Subjective Questions

Very Short Answer Type Questions

1. What is nutrition? Diksha App

Ans. Nutrition is the science of food, nutrients and other substances as well as their digestion, absorption and utilisation by the body. Nutrition is also concerned with the social, psychological and economic aspects of food and eating.

2. Why nutrition is essential for an individual?

Ans. Nutrition is essential for an individual as it provides immunity and protection from diseases.

3. Write the importance of good nutrition.

Or **How is health related to Nutrition?** Diksha App

Ans. Good nutrition is importance to promote recovery from illness and managing chronic diseases. It provides immunity and protection from infections.

4. Discuss clinical nutrition as a discipline.

Or **What is clinical nutrition?** Diksha App

Ans. Clinical nutrition is a discipline that deals with the prevention, diagnosis and management of nutritional and metabolic changes related to acute and chronic diseases and conditions caused by a lack or excess of energy and nutrients.

Thus, any nutritional measure, preventive or curative, targeting individual patients is clinical nutrition.

5. What is the primary role of dietitian?

Ans. The primary role of a dietitian is to maintain the nutritional status of the patient/individual and promote good health.

6. Why nutritional assessment is required?

Ans. It is required to obtain information on the patient's nutritional status as well as the nutrient needs.

7. Which organised activities are adopted in the nutritional care during illness of the patient?

Or **You are a clinical therapist in a hospital. Which four activities would you adopt for nutritional care of patients?** Competency Based Que; CBSE 2021 C

Ans. As a clinical therapist in hospital following four activities can be adopted for nutritional care of patients

(i) Collecting, organising and assessing data relating to health and nutritional status of a patient.

(ii) Reviewing patient's nutritional needs to make appropriate dietry recommendation.

(iii) Develop and implement nutrition care plans.

(iv) Prescribe therapeutic diets and special nutrition support.

8. What to you mean by normal or a regular diet? CBSE 2014 C

Ans. A regular diet is a healthy meal plan that includes a variety of healthy foods from all the food groups to meet the needs of healthy individuals. However, in the hospitals a regular diet would be low in fried fatty foods, sweets, spices and condiments.

9. Why do we consider a therapeutic diet to be a modification of normal diet?

Ans. We consider a therapeutic diet to be a modification of normal diet because it has been tailored to suit the changing nutritional requirements of a patients/individual and is used to improve specific health/disease conditions.

10. Which four methods are used by a dietitian/clinical nutritionist to assess the nutritional statues of a patient? CBSE 2023

Ans. There are a few simple ways by which a dietitian can know your nutritional status

(i) By determining dietary intake, personal and familial history of diseases, etc.

(ii) By measuring physical growth i.e., anthropometric measurements.

(iii) By recognising potential nutritional deficiencies of future deficiencies.

(iv) By daignosising nutritional problems.

11. Your mother is admitted in the hospital for a surgery. Her gastro-intestinal tract is functioning properly, but she is not able to take food by mouth. Which feeding route should be adopted in this situation? Write any one advantage of the method. Competency Based Que; CBSE 2023

Ans. If my mother is not able to take the food by mouth, tube feeding is the best method to feed her. In tube feeding, nutritionally complete diet is given to the patients through a tube. One advantage of this method is that it is nutritionally adequate i.e, it is able to meet the nutritional requirements of the patient.

12. What type of diet would a dietician advice for an old person who has recently undergone a surgery? Name any two foods which he can take. CBSE 2023 C

Ans. An old person is advised to take the two type of diet after surgery

(i) clear liquid diet (ii) high protein diet

Strained juices and lentils are the two foods that can be taken.

13. Which four career avenues are available to a person who is trained in the field of Clinical Nutrition and Dietetics?

Ans. Career avenues for dietitians are given below

(i) Dietitians with consultants/physicians, in health clubs or gymnasiums.

(ii) Freelance Dietitian

(iii) Research including Clinical Research

(iv) Nutrition marketing

Short Answer Type Questions

1. Enlist any four objectives of diet therapy. CBSE 2024

Or **What are the objectives of diet therapy.** Diksha App

Ans. The objectives of diet therapy are

(i) Formulation of the diet to meet the needs of the patient taking into consideration her or his food habits.

(ii) Modification of the existing diets to ameliorate (make better) the disease condition and to keep it under control.

(iii) Correction of nutritional deficiencies.

(iv) Prevention of short-term and long-term complications in case of chronic diseases.

(v) Education and counselling of the patient regarding the need to adhere to the prescribed diet.

2. Nutritional assessment is an important aspect. With reference to the given statement discuss what does this process consist of? Competency Based Que; Diksha App

Ans. Nutritional assessment is required to obtain information on the patient's nutritional status and nutrient needs. It involves

- Obtaining detailed information on health, diet, personal and medication histories.
- Anthropometric measurements (Anthropometric measurements are a series of quantitative measurements of the muscle, bone and adipose tissue used to assess the composition of the body. The core elements of anthropometry are height, weight, body mass index (BMI), body circumferences (waist, hip, and limbs) and skinfold thickness.)
- Relating the information on laboratory and physical measurements with the above and the physician's diagnosis.
- Interpreting all of the above to identify potential nutritional deficiencies and risk of future deficiencies.

3. What are the factors considered by a dietician regarding the effect of illness on food acceptance and utilisation by the patient?

Ans. Following factors are considered by a dietitian regarding the effect of illness on food acceptance and utilisation by the patient

- Plan the diets to meet the nutritional requirements at various stages of life appropriately.
- Plan diets for athletes or sportspersons and for individuals working in space or working in submarines, defence personnel, industrial workers, etc.
- Promote health and well-being of patients admitted to the hospital or in outpatient clinics as well as in institutional settings.
- Manage food services in a variety of institutional settings like old age homes, schools, orphanages, etc.

4. (i) What do you understand by modified diets?

(ii) Based on changes in consistency, what are the three types of diets? Give one example of each diet. CBSE 2023

Ans. (i) A diet that is altered by changing food consistency or nutrient content or by including or eliminating specific foods is called modified or therapeutic diet.

(ii) On the basis of changes in consistency the three types of diet are

(a) **Liquid Diet** It consists of foods that can be served in liquid or strained form at room temperature for example, fruit juice, coconut water.

(b) **Full Liquid Diet** It provides food and fluids that are liquid or semi-liquid at room temperature for example, vegetable soups, dal soups.

(c) **Soft Diet** It provides soft whole food that is lightly seasoned and is similar to regular diet for example, khichdi.

5. How does the study of clinical nutrition and dietetics help medical professional?

Ans. The study enables professionals to

- Plan diets appropriately to meet the nutritional requirements at various stages of the life cycle.
- Modify diets in various disease conditions, keeping in mind the physical state, occupation, cultural, ethnic and socio-economic background, the treatment regimen and the individual's likes and dislikes.
- Plan diets for athletes/sports persons, for individuals in special situations such as nutrition in space, persons working in sub-marines, defense personnel, industrial workers, etc.
- Promote health and well-being of patients admitted to hospital or in outpatient clinics as well as in institutional settings.
- Manage food services in a variety of institutional settings such as old age homes, schools, orphanages etc.

- Help patients with chronic diseases such as diabetes and heart disease in management, to prevent complications and improve quality of life.
- Promote better health in the community and better efficacy (ability to produce desired result) of services in health care institutions/ establishments in terms of better patient care management, holistic care and contribute to better survival and recovery.

Long Answer Type Questions

1. Give a brief description about the following term.
(i) Nutraceuticals **Diksha App**
(ii) Medical foods
(iii) Phytochemicals/Bioactive substances

Or **What are the Medical foods? Give any one example.** **CBSE 2024 C**

Ans. (i) **Nutraceuticals** Nutraceuticals refer to food products that provide health benefits beyond basic nutrition. They can be derived from food sources and include isolated nutrients, dietary supplements and fortified foods. Nutraceuticals are often used to promote health, prevent chronic diseases or support the treatment of health conditions. For example, omega-3 fatty acids, probiotics and vitamins. They are not classified as drugs but can play a significant role in enhancing overall health and wellness.

(ii) **Medical Foods** Medical foods are specially formulated products designed for the dietary management of specific medical conditions and diseases. They are intended for patients who have unique nutritional needs that cannot be met through normal diet alone. Medical foods are typically prescribed by health care professionals and are regulated by the FDA. For example, products for individuals with metabolic disorders, such as phenylketonuria (PKU) or specialised formulas for patients with certain gastro-intestinal conditions.

(iii) **Phytochemicals/Bioactive Substances** Phytochemicals, also known as bioactive substances, are natural compounds found in plants that contribute to their color, flavor and disease resistance. These compounds have been shown to provide various health benefits, including antioxidant, anti-inflammatory and immune-boosting properties. Common examples include flavonoids, carotenoids and polyphenols. While not essential nutrients, phytochemicals can play a significant role in disease prevention and overall health when consumed as part of a balanced diet.

2. The professional clinical nutritionist uses a logical approach to handle the nutrition care process. With reference to the given statement discuss the role played by a professional nutritionist.

Ans. Professional clinical nutritionist plays following role in planning nutritional diet for individuals

- They plan the diet to meet the nutritional requirement of the individual at various stages of life.
- They modify diet according to various disease conditions considering the physical state, occupation, socio-economic background and treatment regimen.
- They plan diet for athletes or sports persons and the individuals working in space, submarines or for the defence personnel, industrial workers.
- They also promote health and well-being of patients admitted to the hospitals.
- They also promote better health in the community and better efficacy of services in health care institutions.
- They help patients in managing chronic diseases such as diabetes and heart disease and to prevent complications and improve quality of life.

Thus, in this way the professional clinical nutritionist uses logical approach to handle the nutrition care process.

3. There is a need of modifications in food consistency which are ranged into different types. Discuss the types of modifications in food consistency in detail. **CBSE 2025**

Or **Describe any two ways of feeding a patient.**

Ans. The different type of modifications in food consistency are discuss below

(i) **Diets of Altered Consistency** Some individuals may require a clear liquid diet, while others a fully liquid diet or soft diet based on their medical condition.

(a) **Liquid diet** consists of foods that can be served in liquid or strained form at room temperature. They are usually prescribed in post-operatively i.e. after surgery when the patient is unable to tolerate solid foods. It is also used for individuals with acute infections or digestive problems, to replace fluids lost by vomiting or diarrhea.

(b) **Soft diet** as the name suggests provides soft whole food that is lightly seasoned and is similar to the regular diet. The foods included in this type of diet are soft in consistency, easy to chew and made of simple, easily digestible foods.

It does not contain harsh fibre or strong flavours. It is given during acute infections, certain gastro intestinal disorders and to individuals who are in the early phase of recovery following a surgery.

(ii) **Altered Feeding Routes** To provide adequate nutrition, normally oral feeding (by mouth) is recommended. Sometimes oral feeding is not possible, under such circumstances special feeding methods such as enteral or tube feeding and parenteral or intravenous feeding is recommended.

(a) **Tube feeding** is provision of liquid formula diet delivered via nasogastric feeding tube. The feeds provided are nutritionally adequate and preferred if the gastrointestinal tract of the patient is functional and is able to digest and absorb nutrients.

(b) **Intravenous feeding** In intravenous feeding, the patient is nourished with special solutions which are given through a drip in a vein. It includes fluids containing water, glucose, amino acids, minerals, vitamins given through the peripheral and central veins.

4. What are the essential requirements which should be possessed by the professional clinical nutritionist?

Ans. The essential requirements for a professional clinical nutritionist are

- Knowledge of physiological changes in disease conditions, nutrient requirements in illness, and dietary modifications needed for patients.
- Skills in assessing nutritional status, customising diet plans for individual patients, and providing diet counseling while adapting to cultural and food-related preferences.
- Knowledge of nutrition, food science, clinical nutrition, dietetics and medical nutrition management.
- Understanding of basic biological and physical sciences, including biology, physiology, biochemistry and microbiology.
- Knowledge of food safety, food quality, food laws, regulations and food service management.
- Understanding of psychology, sociology, education, and counseling to support patients effectively.
- Knowledge of epidemiology, nutritional disorders and research skills to assess the effectiveness of diets and nutritional interventions.

5. Discuss the scope of Clinical Nutrition and Dietetics in detail. **Diksha App**

Ans. Clinical Nutrition and Dietetics offers rich scope and potential for a satisfying career as a dietitian, diet counsellor, teacher, researcher or corporate consultant.

The primary career possibilities in this field include becoming a dietitian, diet counselor or clinical nutritionist engaged in research and/or teaching.

Besides this, clinical nutritionists also have career opportunities in the food industry, research and development (R&D) and production of medical foods, nutraceuticals, tube feeds, various types of nutritional support formulations or functional foods.

You could expect jobs as a dietitian in hospitals/clinics with consultants, teacher/faculty in a university or college, researcher in medical research establishments and nutrition research laboratories, consultant in companies developing therapeutic foods and supplements, food service manager/provider in hospitals etc. You can also work as a freelancer.

6. Your mother is admitted in the hospital for a surgery. Her gastro-intestinal tract is functioning properly but she is not able to take food by mouth. **Competency Based Que**

(i) Which feeding route should be adopted in this situation? Discuss.

(ii) State one difference between the two types of feeding routes.

(iii) Discuss in brief the ways in which diet can be modified to meet the medical needs of a patient.

Ans. (i) In this situation, tube feeding should be adopted. In tube feeding, nutritionally complete diet is given to the patients through a tube. Diet is delivered through the nose into the stomach as long as the gastro-intestional tract is functional and the person is able to digest and absorb food.

(ii) The difference between two types of feeding route

For answer refer to Q.No. 3(ii) of Long Answer Type Question.

(iii) To meet the medical needs of a patient, a diet can be modified

For answer refer to Q.No. 3(i) of Long Answer Type Question.

7. Which type of diet should be given to a person who has dentures? Give any two examples of this diet. CBSE 2025

Ans. A person with dentures should have a soft and easy-to-chew diet to avoid discomfort. The two examples of this diet are

- **Mashed Foods** Examples include mashed potatoes, cooked vegetables or pureed fruits.
- **Soft Dairy** Items like yogurt, paneer (cottage cheese), or milk-based puddings are suitable for easy consumption.

8. As a dietician in a hospital explain about the qualities that one must adopt to become good dietician. Competency Based Que

Ans. To become a good dietitian in a hospital setting, it's essential to cultivate a range of qualities that will enhance patient care and promote effective dietary practices. Here are the key qualities to adopt

(i) **Strong Knowledge Base** A solid understanding of nutrition, dietetics and related health sciences is crucial. Stay updated with the latest research, dietary guidelines and clinical practices.

(ii) **Effective Communication Skills** Clearly convey dietary recommendations and nutritional information to patients, families and health care teams. Understand patients' concerns, preferences and needs by actively listening and engaging in conversation.

(iii) **Empathy and Compassion** Show genuine concern for patient's well-being, respecting their emotional and psychological states. It establish trust and connection with patients, making them feel comfortable discussing their dietary needs.

(iv) **Analytical and Problem-Solving Skills** Skillfully evaluate patients' nutritional status and dietary habits. It develop tailored nutrition plans that address individual health issues and preferences.

(v) **Attention to Detail** It ensure precise documentation, meal planning and dietary adjustments. Regularly assess and adjust nutrition plans based on patient progress and feedback.

(vi) **Teamwork and Collaboration** Collaborate effectively with doctors, nurses and other healthcare professionals to provide comprehensive care. Share relevant nutrition information within the health care team to support patient management.

(vii) **Cultural Sensitivity** Understand and respect cultural differences in dietary practices and preferences. It create dietary plans that honor patients' cultural backgrounds and traditions.

(viii) **Motivational Skills** In inspire and motivate patients to make healthy dietary changes through positive reinforcement and support. It help patients set realistic and achievable dietary goals.

(ix) **Adaptability and Flexibility** Be willing to adjust nutrition plans and approaches as needed based on evolving patient needs and circumstances. Adapt strategies to overcome barriers that patients may face in following dietary recommendations.

(x) **Professionalism and Ethics** Maintain patient confidentiality and adhere to ethical standards in all interactions. Uphold professional conduct and provide evidence-based, unbiased dietary advice.

(xi) **Counseling Skills** Provide effective counseling to support patients in making sustainable dietary changes. Work collaboratively with patients to develop practical dietary plans that fit their lifestyles.

SELF ASSESSMENT TEST

Objective Type Questions

1. What does the term 'OPD' stand for?
   (a) Open department (b) Open display
   (c) Open primary disease (d) Open prevention of disease
2. Which of the following is not a non-communicable disease?
   (a) Diabetes (b) Hypertension
   (c) HIV/AIDS (d) Obesity
3. Which of the following statement is incorrect regarding the mechanical soft diet?
   (a) It restricts fat, fibre, spices or seasonings in the food.
   (b) High-fibre foods such as whole grains and cereals are given.
   (c) Foods may be blended, pureed, ground or finely chopped.
   (d) All foods are allowed that can be made easier to chew and swallow by using machines.
4. Which of the following is a disadvantage of Liquid Diet?
   (a) Nutrients are easily absorbed in this diet.
   (b) It is difficult to manage nutritional requirements.
   (c) It is difficult to continue this diet for long period.
   (d) Both (b) and (c)

Very Short Answer Type Questions

5. How do therapeutic nutritionists help in dealing with various health challenges?
6. What is a clear liquid diet?
7. What are the basic feeding routes? **Diksha App**
8. Explain the concept of Diet Therapy.
9. 'Clinical nutrition has evolved into a practice that is incorporated in mainstream medical treatment'. Justify this statement.

Short Answer Type Questions

10. How have dietary changes contributed in increased prevalence of chronic diseases?
11. Explain the concept of Nutritional Assessment in detail.
12. Enlist any four objectives of Diet Therapy.

Long Answer Type Questions

13. What do you mean by nutrition and how is nutrition linked with good health ? Asses the role of nutrition in disease management.
14. What is the significance of the study of clinical nutrition and dietetics? **Diksha App**
15. How does the study of clinical nutrition and dietetics help medical professionals? **Diksha App**

03

CHAPTER

Good amount of nutrition is the foundation and cornerstone of health. In this context, the concept of Public health becomes important. Public health is the collective efforts by the society for the improvement of the overall health. It aims to achieve optimal nutrition by avoiding both the over-nutrition as well as under-nutrition.

Public Nutrition and Health

YOUR STUDY GOALS

YOUR PRACTICE GOAL

- Objective Type Questions (34 Qs ; MCQs, A-R, Matching, Case Based)
- Subjective Questions (16 VSAs, 8 SAs, 8 LAs)

3.1 Introduction

- The concept of nutrition is vast and extensive because good nutrition not only means maintaining a **nutritional status**[1], but it also implies to grow and enjoy good health as well.
- The World Health Organisation (WHO) defines health as, "A state of complete physical, mental and social well-being and not merely an absence of disease and the ability to lead a socially and economically productive life".
- In this context, the idea of **public nutrition**[2] is gaining importance. Public nutrition is concerned with improving nutritional problems of the population in both the developing and developed countries all over the world.

Significance of Public Health and Nutrition

- A healthy lifestyle, with nutrition at its core, is crucial for overall health and disease prevention. **Malnutrition**[3], resulting from imbalances in nutrient intake, can manifest as under-nutrition or over-nutrition. It contributes to nearly 50 per cent of deaths in children under 5 globally.

1 **Nutritional Status** It is the condition of the body as a result of the intake, absorption and use of nutrition, as well as the influence of disease-related factors.
2 **Public Nutrition** It is part of the study of nutrition that deals with the nature, causes and consequences of nutrition problems in society.
3 **Malnutrition** It is a lack or excess intake of one or more nutrients and/or faulty utilisation of nutrients in our body resulting in imbalance in the body.

- In India, malnutrition is exacerbated by shifting dietary patterns and sedentary lifestyles, leading to increased obesity, hypertension, heart disease and diabetes. Urban children are missing out on physical activities, and unhealthy food choices are on the rise, while the consumption of whole grains, vegetables and fruits is declining.
- Alarming statistics in India show that one-fifth of newborns have low birth weight, 50 per cent of children from low socio-economic backgrounds experience **under-nutrition**[4] and micro-nutrient deficiencies are widespread. Poor nutrition also impacts immunity, increasing susceptibility to diseases like HIV/AIDS, tuberculosis and malaria.
- Malnutrition not only affects health but also hampers economic productivity, causing significant financial losses. There is an urgent need for trained public health professionals, including nutritionists, to address these challenges and improve societal well-being.

3.2 Basic Concepts

Public Health Nutrition

- **Public Health Nutrition** focuses on promoting good health through preventing nutrition-related illnesses in populations. It involves developing government policies and programmes aimed at addressing nutritional issues. Understanding the causes of nutrition-related diseases is a key component of this field.
- A multi-disciplinary approach is utilised, incorporating insights from various fields to tackle public health challenges. The foundation of public health nutrition is built on both biological and social sciences. This field is distinct from clinical nutrition and dietetics, as it prioritises community well-being over individual health.
- Public nutrition encompasses knowledge from nutritional, biological, behavioural, social and managerial sciences. It can be seen as both an art and a science, focusing on health promotion and disease prevention through organised societal efforts. The ultimate goal is to prolong life and enhance the quality of life for communities through effective nutrition strategies.

Community

A community is a specific group of people that share common characteristics. For example, common language, exposed to similar conditions, common lifestyle or the same health problem.

Nutritional Problems

Any professional to look into the public nutrition should consider nutritional problems first. There are several factors related to nutritional problem that includes

- Nutritional problems stem from various interrelated factors, not just food availability.
- Poverty is the major underlying cause of many nutritional issues.
- Lack of access to basic amenities, such as sanitation and clean drinking water, significantly contributes to these problems.
- Rural households often lack proper sanitation facilities, impacting health and nutrition.
- Limited access to safe drinking water results in lost workdays and economic losses.
- Economic factors play a crucial role, including the availability of financial resources for individuals.
- Agricultural policies affect the production and pricing of food, influencing nutrition.
- Access to health care facilities is essential for addressing nutritional problems.

4 **Under-nutrition** It means the condition of health of a person that results due to the lack of one or more nutrients.

Nutritional Problems in India

- Nutritional imbalance occurs when nutrients are consumed below required levels or not utilised properly by the body.
- There are two main types of nutrient deficiencies: macro-nutrient deficiency and micro-nutrient deficiency.
- **Macro-nutrients** are needed in large quantities and include nutrients like energy and protein.
- Deficiencies in macro-nutrients can lead to conditions such as protein-energy malnutrition.
- It is important to have knowledge aboue the nutritional problem in our country.

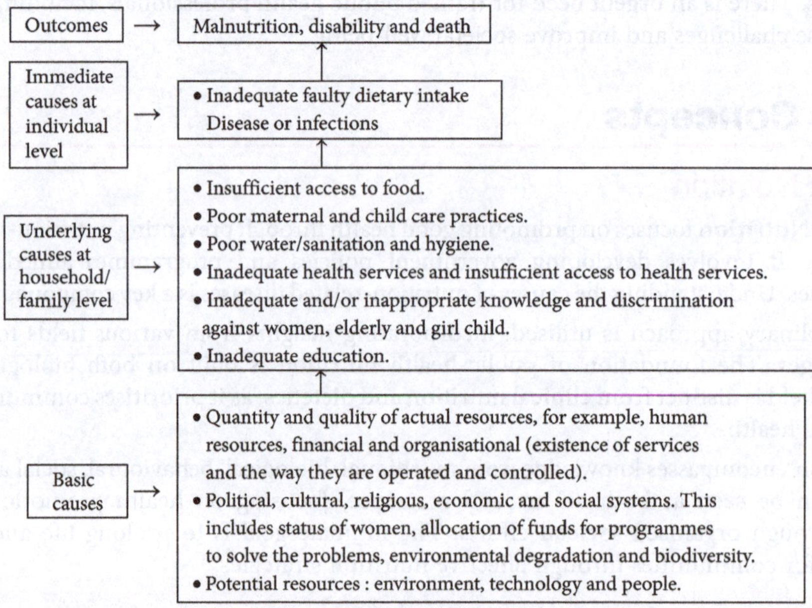

▲ *Factors Related to Under-nutrition*

Protein Energy Malnutrition (PEM)

- Protein-energy malnutrition (PEM) is a major nutritional problem in many countries, including developing and industrialised ones. It results from inadequate food intake, particularly insufficient energy and protein. Children are at the highest risk for PEM, Although it can also affect adults, especially the elderly or those with infectious diseases like TB and HIV/AIDS. Assessment of PEM is done through anthropometric measurements, such as head and chest circumferences, height and weight.
- **Underweight** indicates low weight for age.
- **Short Stature Stunting** refers to low height for age.
- **Wasting** is characterised by low weight for height.
- There are two main types of protein-energy malnutrition
  - **Marasmus,** which is caused by a deficiency of both energy and proteins.
  - **Kwashiorkor,** which results from a deficiency of proteins alone.

Differences between Marasmus and Kwashiorkor include

Differences	Marasmus	Kwashiorkor
Causes	Deficiency of both energy and proteins	Deficiency of proteins alone
Age group	Before 12 months of age	Young children between 1-3 years of age
Signs and Symptoms	▪ Loose and wrinkled skin due to loss of fat beneath the skin ▪ Shrunken abdomen ▪ Hunger ▪ Diarrhoea (often) 	▪ Oedema/swelling due to water accumulation in the body especially on face, arms and legs ▪ Pot belly, loss of appetite ▪ Skin rash which tends to peel off ▪ Liver enlargement 

Micro-nutrient Deficiency

- Micro-nutrients, such as iron, Vitamin D and Vitamin A, are required in smaller quantities but are essential for vital bodily functions. Diets deficient in energy and protein often lack adequate amounts of other nutrients, including minerals and vitamins. The term **hidden hunger** refers to deficiencies in micro-nutrients.
- **Deficiencies of iron**, Vitamin A, iodine and zinc are major public health concerns. There is increasing worry about deficiencies in Vitamin B12, folic acid, calcium, Vitamin D and riboflavin. Addressing these micro-nutrient deficiencies is crucial for improving overall health and preventing associated diseases.
- Some of the micro-nutriens deficiencies are discussed below

Iron Deficiency Anaemia (IDA)

- Anaemia is a widespread issue in both developing and developed countries. It is characterised by low levels of haemoglobin in the blood, which is essential for oxygen transport throughout the body.
- Iron deficiency in the diet is a common cause of decreased haemoglobin levels.
- Anaemia is particularly prevalent among women of reproductive age, pregnant and lactating women, adolescent girls and school-aged children. Symptoms of anaemia can vary based on the severity of haemoglobin reduction and may include general body weakness, tiredness and breathlessness.
- Additional symptoms include loss of appetite, paleness of the tongue and the whites of the eyes, brittle and spoon-shaped nails and decreased work capacity add cognitive functions (attention span).

Vitamin A Deficiency (VAD)

- Vitamin A is essential for maintaining normal vision, skin health, growth and immune function. A lack of Vitamin A in the diet results in Vitamin A deficiency (VAD).
- Symptoms of VAD can start with night blindness, which is the inability to see in low light conditions. If untreated, night blindness can progress to complete blindness. Other symptoms include dryness of the white portion of the eye.
- Individuals with VAD have an increased susceptibility to infections, particularly in the respiratory system. There exists a vicious cycle between infections and Vitamin A deficiency, worsening health outcomes.

- Vitamin A deficiency is a leading cause of childhood blindness worldwide.

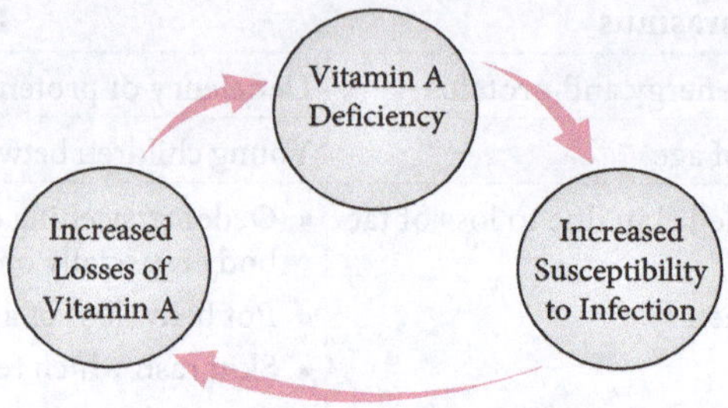

▲ *Vicious Cycle of Vitamin A Deficiency and Infection*

Iodine Deficiency Disorder (IDD)

- Iodine is essential for normal physical and mental growth and development. Iodine Deficiency Disorders (IDD) largely result from inadequate iodine in the soil. IDD is most prevalent in regions such as the Himalayan belt, Jammu and Kashmir, Andhra Pradesh, Maharashtra, Madhya Pradesh, Karnataka and Kerala. IDD encompasses a range of disabling conditions affecting health from fetal life to adulthood.
- Iodine deficiency leads to reduced production of thyroid hormones by the **thyroid gland**. The most common manifestation of IDD in adults is **goitre**, which is the enlargement of the thyroid gland.
- In young children, IDD can result in cretinism, a severe form of growth and developmental impairment. Iodine deficiency during pregnancy poses significant risks for both the mother and the child. Adverse effects can include mental retardation and congenital abnormalities in the fetus. Approximately 13 per cent of the world's population is affected by iodine deficiency, with 30 per cent at risk.

Quick Test 1

1. How does WHO define health?
2. What do you understand about the dual burden of malnutrition?
3. Mention any one consequence of deficiency in macro-nutrients.
4. What does stunting refer to?

3.3 Strategies/Intervention to Tackle Nutritional Problems

- There are multiple determinants contribute to nutritional problems, necessitating a multi-disciplinary approach for effective solutions. The Indian Government is actively working to address nutritional issues through various initiatives.
- POSHAN Abhiyaan, launched in March 2018 in Jhunjhunu, Rajasthan, aims to combat stunting, under-nutrition, low birth weight, and anaemia in young children, adolescent girls and women of reproductive age. This initiative is a multi-ministerial convergence mission with the goal of achieving a malnutrition-free India by 2022.
- The Ministry of Women and Child Development (MWCD) is implementing POSHAN Abhiyan in 315 districts will be covered in the first year, 235 district in the second year and remaining districts will be covered in the third year.

- POSHAN Abhiyaan serves as an apex body to monitor, supervise, set targets and guide nutrition-related interventions across ministries.
- Some **direct short-term** interventions include
  - Integrated Child Development Services (ICDS) to support vulnerable groups.
  - Fortification of essential foods, such as iodised salt.
  - Promotion of low-cost nutritious foods using locally available materials, particularly involving women.
  - Control of micro-nutrient deficiencies, focusing on iron, Vitamin A, folic acid and iodine among children and women.
- **Indirect policy instruments** involve long-term strategies for achieving national goals through structural changes, such as
  - Ensuring food security by improving food availability.
  - Enhancing dietary patterns by making nutritionally rich foods accessible.
  - Poverty alleviation efforts for both rural and urban poor through employment generation and public distribution systems.
  - Implementing land reforms, improving health and family welfare and preventing food adulteration.
  - Promoting media involvement, basic nutrition knowledge and monitoring nutrition programmes.
  - Improving women's status, education, literacy and community participation.
- Various strategies can be employed to combat public nutrition problems, broadly classified into different categories.

Diet or Food-Based Strategies

- They are preventive and comprehensive strategies utilise food to address nutritional deficiencies. These strategies aim to prevent micro-nutrient deficiencies by enhancing the availability and consumption of micro-nutrient-rich foods.
- Important food-based approaches include
  - Dietary diversification and modification.
  - Horticulture interventions, such as home gardening.
  - Nutrition and health education.
  - Food fortification.
- Benefits of these strategies include
  - Sustainability, providing long-term benefits.
  - Cost-effectiveness and adaptability to various cultural and dietary traditions.
  - Reduced risk of overdose or toxicity, unlike nutrient-based or medicinal approaches.

Nutrient-based or Medicinal Strategies

- The primary focus of this approach is on vulnerable groups who are at risk of or currently experiencing deficiencies. Nutrient supplements are provided specifically to these at-risk populations.
- In India, this approach is commonly applied for Vitamin A, iron and folic acid supplementation. These programmes can be expensive to implement, leading to potential coverage issues. Different nutrients target specific key groups, highlighting the need for tailored interventions based on nutrient requirements.

Different Interventions for Tackling Malnutrition

Intervention	Appropriate for	Advantages	Challenges/Disadvantages
Medicinal or Nutrient Based Strategies			
Nutrient Supplementation	▪ Therapeutic treatment ▪ Prevention Programmes for specific nutrient and specific target groups	▪ Timely ▪ Sustainability	▪ More costly than other measures ▪ Narrow scope of coverage
Food Based or Diet Based Strategies			
Fortification (fortifying food with nutrients)	Prevention (Universal/For all)	▪ Highly cost-effective ▪ Wide coverage sustainable	▪ Requires research participation of food industry ▪ Does not lead to awareness in the population about the importance of nutrition and nutrients ▪ Does not lead to long term dietary/behavioural changes
Dietary Diversification	Prevention (Universal/For all)	▪ Highly cost-effective ▪ Wide coverage sustainable ▪ Provides many micro-nutrients simultaneously ▪ Improves food security	▪ Requires changes in eating behaviour ▪ Requires economic development to be feasible ▪ Requires change in agricultural policies

Nutrition Programmes Operating in India

India has several nutrition intervention programmes under different government ministries. These programmes are already in place and working for the social welfare of people. Some of the nutrition programmes operating in India are discussed below

Integrated Child Development Services (ICDS)

This is an outreach programme for early childhood care and development covering pregnant and lactating women and infants and young children upto 6 years of age. The programme's main aim is to provide nutrition, health and educational services to children through the early childhood period so that their proper physical, mental and social development is ensured.

Nutrient Deficiency Control Programmes

- **National Prophylaxis Programme for Prevention of Nutritional Blindness** This programme aims preventing blindness due to Vitamin A deficiency. The services provided under this programme include: promoting consumption of Vitamin A rich foods and providing massive doses of Vitamin A orally to children between 6 months to 5 years of age.
- **National Nutritional Anaemia Control Programme (NNACP)** This programme aims at significantly decreasing the prevalence and incidence of anaemia in young children and women. The services provided through this programme are: promotion of regular consumption of foods rich in iron, providing iron and folic acid supplements and treatment of severe anaemic cases.
- **National Iodine Deficiency Disorder Control Programme (NIDDCP)** The aim of this programme is to decrease the prevalence of Iodine Deficiency Disorder (IDD) in our country by providing iodine in the common salt (iodised salt). The services provided are: assessing the extent of the problem, arranging production/supply of iodised salt and taking quality control measures in order to ensure supply of standard quality of iodised salt to the consumer.

Food Supplementation Programmes

These programmes were started to eradicate the problems of nutritional disorders from the country. Currently major nutrition supplement programmes in India are

- **Mid-Day Meal Programme (MDM)** It is one such programme started by Government of India. The main aim of MDM programme is to provide supplementary meal to primary school children between 6 to 11 years of age belonging to backward classes, Scheduled Caste and Scheduled Tribes on priority. This in turn to increase school attendance.
- **Special Nutrition Programme (SNP)** The main aim of this programme is to improve the nutritional status of pre-school children, pregnant and lactating mothers of poor socio-economic groups. The major activities under this programme are to provide supplementary nutrition, healthcare services and supplying Vitamin A solution and iron and folic acid tablets.

Other Nutritional Programmes

- **Applied Nutrition Programme (ANP)** Its objective is to make people concern about nutritional needs and to increase production of nutritious foods.
- **Wheat based Supplementary Nutrition Programmes (WSNP)** Its objective is to provide nutrition through **wheat based** supplementary nutrition.
- **Balvadi Nutrition Programme (BNP)** Its aim is to supply about one-third of the caloric and half of the protein requirements of the pre-school children.

Food Security Programmes

To improve the food security among marginalised sections of the society and vulnerable groups, government has promoted provision of subsidised grain through Public Distribution System (PDS). Other than this, schemes like **Antyodaya Anna Yojana, Annapurna Scheme and National Food for Work Programmes** have also been initiated.

Self-Employment and Wage Employment Schemes

These are social safety net programmes to benefit the marginalised sections of the society. Some schemes and wage employment programmes under this are

- Integrated Rural Development Programme
- Jawahar Rozgar Yojana
- Sampoorna Grameen Rozgar Yojana
- Pradhan Mantri Kaushal Vikas Yojana
- Mahatma Gandhi National Rural Employment Guarantee Act (MGNREGA)

3.4 Health Care

Health is a Fundamental Right of every human being. The government is responsible for providing adequate health care to citizens. Health care encompasses various services aimed at promoting, maintaining, monitoring or restoring health. The health care system in India operates at three levels

- **Primary Level**
  - First level of contact for individuals, families or communities.
  - Services are typically provided through Primary Health Centres (PHCs).
  - Care is comprehensive and handled by general physicians without the need for specialists.
- **Secondary Level**
  - Resolves more complex health problems through district hospitals and **community health**[5] centres.
  - Community health centres serve as the first referral level.
  - Involves specialists such as cardiologists, dermatologists and urologists.

5 **Community Health** It is a medical specialty that focuses on the physical and mental well-being of the people in a specific geographic region.

- **Tertiary Level**
  - Highest level of health care dealing with complex health issues not resolved at the first two levels.
  - Requires advanced medical procedures like major surgeries, transplants and long-term management for diseases.
  - Includes medical college hospitals, regional hospitals, specialised hospitals and All-India Institutes of Medical Sciences.

3.5 Scope of Public Health

Role of Public Nutritionist

Public health tends to counter threats to the general health of a social circle on the basis of the analysis of population health. The scope of public health service has become exceedingly broad in nature. The public nutritionist is well trained and equipped in key areas of health promotion and prevention. Some of the key areas include

- Nutritional science
- Nutritional assessment
- Nutritional care
- Food science
- Educational methods
- Use of mass media
- Programme management
- Nutritional needs in health and disease throughout the life cycle

Thus, he/she works in the following situations or areas that show the vast scope of public health. These areas are

- Become a part of outreach programmes undertaken by hospitals for prevention, promotion and education.
- Become a part of the National Integrated Child Development Services at different levels based on qualifications and expertise.
- Become a part at the government level as consultants, advisors or in policy-making committees.
- In all developmental programmes of government, voluntary organisations and international organisations like UNICEF, OXFAM, DFID, FAO, WHO, USAID, GAIN, Micro-nutrient Initiative, IFPRI and others. They are also part of numerous national and regional organisations.

Career Avenues

There are several career avenues available for a public health nutritionist like in teaching, research, entrepreneurship, industries as a part of their welfare or corporate social responsibilities, with agencies involved in developing communication and educational packages for those who are skilled in their training. Some other career options include

- Community nutritionist in PSM departments of hospitals.
- They can be indulged in nutrition programmes of the government like ICDS, Food and Nutrition Board.
- They can be a part of voluntary organisations at the regional, national and international level as nutritionists.
- They can work as consultants.

Quick Test 2

1 What disease is caused by a deficiency of protein?
2 What substances are responsible for vital functions in the human body?
3 What deficiency is the most common cause of childhood blindness?
4 Which programme aids in prevention of blindness?
5 Which nutrient supplement programme is undertaken for pre-school level children?

Mind Map

PUBLIC NUTRITION AND HEALTH

1 Public Health and Nutrition

Key Points
- **Malnutrition** Leads to undernutrition, overnutrition and nutrient deficiencies.
- **India's Challenges** Poor diet, sedentary lifestyle and hidden hunger.
- **Economic Impact** Malnutrition causes productivity loss and harms GDP.
- **Need for Professionals** Trained nutritionists are essential for improving public health.

- **Nutrition** Essential for growth, health and well-being.
- **WHO Health Definition** Focuses on physical, mental and social well-being.
- **Public Nutrition** Aims to solve global nutritional issues.

2 Basic Concepts

Nutritional Problems
- **Causes** Poverty, poor sanitation, lack of clean water, economic factors.
- **Types**
  Macronutrient Deficiency Protein-Energy Malnutrition (e.g., Marasmus, Kwashiorkor).
  Micronutrient Deficiency Iron, Vitamin A, Iodine (e.g., anemia, night blindness, goitre).

Nutritional Issues in India
- Iron Deficiency Anemia, Vitamin A Deficiency, Iodine Deficiency Disorder are major concerns.

Public Health Nutrition
- **Focus** Preventing nutrition-related diseases, promoting health through policies and programmes.
- **Approach** Multi-disciplinary, community focused, distinct from clinical nutrition.
- **Community** Specific group of people share common characteristics like common language, lifestyle.

3 Strategies to Tackle Nutritional Problems

Food-Based Strategies
- **Diet Diversification** Horticulture, nutrition education.

Nutrient-Based Strategies
- **Supplements** Iron, Vitamin A, folic acid for vulnerable groups.

Key Programs
- ICDS, MDM, SNP, PDS, Antyodaya Yojana
- **Employment Schemes** MGNREGA, Skill Development.

Government Initiatives
- **POSHAN Abhiyaan** Address malnutrition, stunting, anemia.

Direct Interventions
- **ICDS** Early childhood care, nutrition support.
- **Food Fortification** Iodised salt, nutritious foods.

Indirect Interventions
- **Food Security** Improve food access.
- **Poverty Alleviation** Employment schemes, public distribution.

4 Health Care Levels in India

- **Primary Level** Basic care via Primary Health Centres (PHCs), general physicians.
- **Secondary Level** Complex issues treated at district hospitals and community health centres with specialists.
- **Tertiary Level** Advanced care at specialised hospitals and medical colleges for complex conditions.

5 Scope of Public Health Nutrition

Career Avenues
- Community nutritionist, government programmes
- Voluntary organisations
- Consultants
- Entrepreneurs

- **Key Areas**
  Nutritional science, assessment, care, food science, health promotion and programme management.
- **Roles**
  Outreach programmes, ICDS, government policy, large-scale feeding programmes, school health and CSR projects.

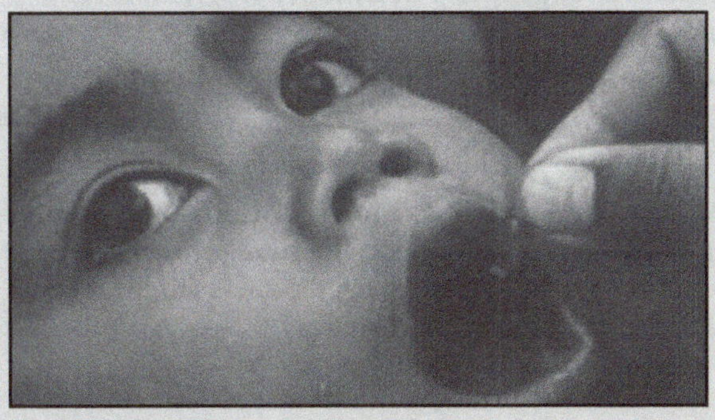

Iron and Folic acid drops

Counselling with Mothers

NCERT Folder

1. Explain the terms: Stunting, Low Birth Weight Baby, IDD, Wasting, Double Burden of Malnutrition, Marasmus, Kwashiorkor, Community.

Ans. (i) **Stunting** Stunting is said to be present when the child has low height for age. It results in short stature and once set in, cannot be corrected.

(ii) **Low Birth Weight Baby** When an infant is born with body weight less than 2500g or 2.5kg.

(iii) **IDD** Iodine Deficiency Disorder cause due to deficiency or absence of iodine in the diet. It leads to dysfunction of thyroid gland and results in goitre (enlargement of thyroid gland) in adults and cretinism in children. Cretinism has adverse effects on children. It negatively affects their mental and cognitive development.

(iv) **Wasting** Wasting is said to be present when the child has low weight for height. It results in growth retardation and permanent damaging effects, if not corrected in time. It also lowers the immunity of a child further making them susceptible to various infections.

(v) **Double Burden of Malnutrition** Malnutrition has two forms: under-nutrition and over-nutrition. This means that some people are suffering from deficiency of macro and micro-nutrients and at the same time some other are taking nutrients in amounts more than required by the body. Thus, co-existence of under-nutrition and over-nutriton is called double burden of malnutrition.

(vi) **Marasmus** It is a type of protein-energy malnutrition in which both energy and protein are lacking in the diet. It occurs in infants below 12 months of age. It is characterised by loose and wrinkled skin due to loss of fat beneath the skin, shrunken abdomen. It results in low immunity thus, making them prone to infections. Diarrhea is often seen in such infants.

(vii) **Kwashiorkor** It is a type of protein-energy malnutrition in which protein is deficient in the diet of the child. It occurs in children between 1 to 3 years of age. It is characterised by oedema/ swelling due to water accumulation in the body especially on face, arms and legs, pot belly, loss of appetite, skin rash which tends to peel off. It also causes lower immunity.

(viii) **Community** A community is a specific group of people that share common characteristics, e.g. a common language, exposed to similar conditions, common lifestyle or the same health problem.

2. Discuss the various strategies that can be adopted to combat public nutrition problems.

Ans. Two types of strategies can be adopted to combat public nutritional problems: short term strategies and long term strategies.

Some direct short term interventions are

- Fortification of essential foods (e.g. salt fortified with iodine, rice fortified with iron, etc.)
- Production and popularisation of low cost nutritious foods from indigenous and locally available raw material by involving women in this activity.
- Control of various micro-nutrient deficiencies among vulnerable groups through nutrient supplementation either in liquid form or in tablet form.

Some long term strategies are

- Ensuring food security i.e. improving availability of food.
- Improvement in dietary patterns by ensuring availability of nutritionally rich foods through dietary diversification and modification, change in dietary pattern and food choices, horticulture interventions e.g., home gardening, nutrition and health education.
- Poverty alleviation for rural and urban poor through employment generation schemes and public distribution system, implementing land reforms, improving health and family welfare, prevention of food adulteration, involvement of media, monitoring of nutrition programmes, improvement of status of women, education and literacy and community participation.

3. What is Public Health Nutrition?

Ans. Public Health Nutrition is the field that focuses on the promotion of good health through nutrition and the primary prevention of nutrition related illness in the population. It also focuses on understanding the causes of nutrition related situations and problems and finding solution and approaches to combat these problems.

4. What are the common nutritional problems India is facing?

Or **Explain about any five nutritional programmes of India.** **Diksha App**

Or **Write the full form of PEM and describe it briefly.** **CBSE 2025**

Ans. The common nutritional problems found in India are

Protein Energy Malnutrition (PEM) PEM can occur at any age, but it mainly affects the young children. It results due to lack of energy and proteins in the diet or lack of proteins alone in the diet.

It results in growth retardation in children. If not corrected, it can have permanent damaging effects in the adult life of a child or can be fatal.

PEM is assessed by evaluating the anthropometric measurements like head and chest circumferences, height, weight, etc.

Protein energy malnutrition is of two types Marasmus and Kwashiorkor.

Micro-nutrient Deficiency Micro-nutrients are those nutrients (Vitamin D, A, iron) which are required in small quantities in human body but perform vital functions in the body. Their deficiency can cause following disorders in our body.

(i) **Iron Deficiency Anaemia** (IDA) Anaemia means low level of haemoglobin in the blood. Haemoglobin is the red pigment in the blood and it helps in carrying oxygen to different parts of the body. Haemoglobin level decreases when iron is deficient in the diet. It is mostly prevalent in women of reproductive age, adolescent girls, pregnant and lactating women and school-aged children.

(ii) **Vitamin A Deficiency** (VAD) Vitamin A is required for maintenance of vision, skin, growth and immunity. The lack of Vitamin A in the diet leads to Vitamin A deficiency.

(iii) **Iodine Deficiency Disorder** (IDD) Iodine is required for the normal functioning of metabolic processes in the body and physical and mental development of an individual. IDD is present largely due to its deficiency in soil. Therefore, IDD is a spectrum of disabling conditions that adversely affect the human health, from fetal life to adulthood. It occurs due to deficiency of iodine in the diet.

5. What are the consequences of IDA and IDD?

Ans. The consequences of IDA i.e. Iron Deficiency Anaemia are discussed below

- Some of the visible affects of IDA includes paleness of conjunctiva of eyes, tongue and nail beds and soft palate. Among the children, cognitive functions like the attention span, memory, concentration are affected adversely.
- Iron deficiency anaemia may lead to a rapid or irregular heartbeat. In infants and children, severe iron deficiency can lead to anaemia as well as delayed growth and development.
- Additionally, iron deficiency anaemia is associated with an increased susceptibility to infections.

The consequences of IDD i.e. Iodine Deficiency Disorders are discussed below

- The deficiency of iodine led to insufficient amount of thyroid hormone which is synthesised by the thyroid gland. Thus, iodine deficiency can lead to enlargement of the thyroid known as goitre, hypothyroidism and intellectual disabilities in infants and children whose mothers were iodine deficient during pregnancy.
- Other complications which are caused due to this deficiency includes heart diseases and related disorders, mental health issues such as depression, damage to body's peripheral nerves, etc.

6. What is the scope of public health nutrition? List some of the career choices in this area.

Ans. Public health tends to counter threats to the general health of a social circle on the basis of the analysis of population health. The scope of public health service has become exceedingly broad in nature.

The public nutritionist is well trained and equipped in key areas of health promotion and prevention.

He/She works in the following situations or areas that show the vast scope of public health.

These areas are

- Becomes a part of outreach programmes undertaken by hospitals for prevention, promotion and education.
- Becomes a part of the National Integrated Child Development Services at different levels based on qualifications and expertise.
- Becomes a part at the government level as consultants, advisors or in policy-making committees.
- In all developmental programmes of government, voluntary organisations and international organisations like UNICEF, OXFAM, DFID, FAO, WHO, USAID, GAIN, Micro-nutrient Initiative, IFPRI and others. They are also part of numerous national and regional organisations.
- They can be involved with organisations who undertake large scale feeding programmes for various target groups such as young children, adolescents, pregnant and lactating mothers, elderly, challenged individuals.

Exam Pattern Questions

Objective Type Questions

Multiple Choice Questions

1. What are the two main foundations of public health as a discipline that makes it multidisciplinary in nature?

(a) Social Sciences (b) Biological Sciences
(c) Both (a) and (b) (d) None of these

2. Which of the following factors affects the nutritional requirements of the people?

(a) Agricultural Policies (b) Economic Factors
(c) Political Will (d) All of these

3. What is Public Health Nutrition concerned with?

I. Promotion of good health at individual level
II. Promotion of good health at population level
III. Prevention of community- related nutritional illnesses/problems
IV. Prevention of individual nutrition- related illnesses/ problems
V. Planning and implementing strategies for holistic nutrition

Choose the correct option

(a) I, III, IV (b) I, II, IV (c) II, III, V (d) II, IV, V

4. Professionals who deal with the nutritional management of illness of an individual are referred to as CBSE 2023

I. Clinical Nutritionist
II. Public Health Nutritionist
III. Medical Representative
IV. Medical Nutrition Therapist
V. Dietitian

Choose the correct option

(a) I, II, III (b) I, III, IV (c) I, III, V (d) I, IV, V

5. What is under-nutrition?

(a) Deficiency of energy and protein
(b) Deficiency of macro and micro-nutrients
(c) Deficiency of micro-nutrients
(d) Inadequate weight in accordance with age

6. Micro-nutrient deficiency is called .... CBSE 2023

(a) Goitre (b) Anemia
(c) Hidden hunger (d) Obesity

7. Which of the following is short term strategy to combat malnutrition? CBSE SQP 2024

(a) Ensuring food security
(b) Control of micro-nutrient deficiencies
(c) Employment generation schemes
(d) Prevention of food adulteration

8. IDD is common in which of the following state of India. Diksha App

(a) Uttar Pradesh (b) Punjab
(c) Kerala (d) Bihar

9. Infants and young children having iodine deficiency from birth suffers from a condition known as ....

(a) Hyperthyroidism (b) Cretinism
(c) Goitre (d) All of these

10. Your brother has not gained height since past five years and hence is the shortest boy in his class. His condition is known as .... CBSE C 2021

(a) Stunting (b) Wasting
(c) Underweight (d) Obesity

11. Your sister is very tall but her weight is below average. Her condition is known as .... CBSE C 2021

(a) Stunting (b) Wasting
(c) Underweight (d) Obesity

12. Which of the following conditions results when an individual's body weight is less than adequate weight for his/her age? CBSE 2023

(a) Overweight (b) Underweight
(c) Wasting (d) Stunting

13. When the height of the child is less than adequate for age, this is termed as............ .

(a) Underweight (b) Stunting
(c) Wasting (d) Obesity

14. Annapurna Scheme is under which nutrition programme operating in India? CBSE 2025

(a) Nutrient Deficiency Control Programmes
(b) Food Supplementation Programmes
(c) ICDS
(d) Food Safety Programmes

15. The disease caused by protein deficiency is .... Diksha App

(a) Goitre (b) Night Blindness
(c) Marasmus (d) Kwashiorkor

16. Low birth weight babies weigh less than .... Diksha App

(a) 3000 gms (b) 2500 gms
(c) 3500 gms (d) 4000 gms

17. **Which of the following are symptoms of marasmums?**

I. Loose skin **II. Pot belly**
III. Hunger **IV. Liver enlargement**

Choose the correct option.

(a) I and II (b) II and III
(c) III and IV (d) I and III

18. **POSHAN Abhiyaan was launched in March, 2018 at which of the following places?** **CBSE 2024**

(a) Panipat, Haryana
(b) Jhunjhunu, Rajasthan
(c) Kanyakumari, Tamil Nadu
(d) Mysuru, Karnataka

19. **Identify a short term strategy to combat public nutritional problems.**

(a) Dietary diversification (b) Nutrient supplementation
(c) Ensuring food security (d) Alleviation of poverty

20. **Choose the correct food supplementation programme from the following.**

(a) Integrated Child Development Services (ICDS) Scheme
(b) Mid-Day Meal (MDM) Programme
(c) Public Distribution System (PDS)
(d) Both (a) and (b)

21. **The mission in Public Health Nutrition is to prevent............ .** **Diksha App**

(a) under-nutrition
(b) malnutrition
(c) under-nutrition and malnutrition
(d) over-nutrition

22. **Which of the following is a Food Supplementation Programme?** **CBSE 2024**

(a) National Nutritional Anaemia Prophylaxis Programme
(b) National Food for Work Programme
(c) Annapurna Scheme
(d) Mid-Day Meal Programme

23. **Which nutrient deficiency is targeted by National Prophylaxis Programme for Prevention of Blindness?**

(a) Vitamin A (b) Iron **CBSE 2025**
(c) Iodine (c) Protien

24. **Why it is difficult to conduct supplementation programmes in India?**

(a) Because it is a short term strategy
(b) Because these programmes are expensive
(c) Because these programmes are time-saving
(d) Because these programmes are promoted on a larger basis

25. **All India Institutes of Medical Sciences provide which level of health care services in India?** **CBSE 2025**

(a) Primary (b) Tertiary
(c) Secondary (d) Intermediary

26. **In India, health care is provided at three levels. Which of the following is not correctly matched?** **CBSE SQP Term I, 2021**

(a) Primary level-PHC (b) Secondary level-CHC
(c) Tertiary level-CHC (d) Tertiary level-AIIMS

27. **Which of the following is not an example of tertiary health care?** **CBSE 2023**

(a) All India Institute of Medical Sciences
(b) Primary Health Centre
(c) Medical College Hospital
(d) Specialised Hospitals

28. **Choose an international organisation that works to improve public health and nutrition.**

(a) Oxfam
(b) Public Health Foundation of India
(c) Indian Council of Medical Research
(d) Foundation for Mother and Child Health

29. **A community nutritionist can work in following organisation.** **Diksha App**

(a) USAID (b) OXFORD (c) DND (d) GAN

30. **Match the following**

	List-I (Deficiencies)		**List-II** (Problems)
A.	Iodine Deficiency	1.	Marasmus
B.	Vitamin A Deficiency	2.	Anaemia
C.	Iron Deficiency	3.	Night Blindness
D.	Protein Energy Deficiency	4.	Goitre

	A	B	C	D		A	B	C	D
(a)	1	2	3	4	(b)	2	3	4	1
(c)	4	3	2	1	(d)	3	4	1	2

Assertion-Reason Questions

Directions (Q. Nos. 31-32) In the questions given below, there are two statements marked as Assertion (A) and Reason (R). Read the statements and choose the correct option.

Codes

(a) Both A and R are true and R is the correct explanation of A.
(b) Both A and R are true, but R is not the correct explanation of A.
(c) A is true, but R is false.
(d) A is false, but R is true.

31. **Assertion** (A) Food fortification is done by adding the nutrient that is lacking in the food stuffs to ensure that minimum dietary requirements are met. **CBSE SQP Term I, 2021**

Reason (R) India has progressed from an agro-deficit to an agro-surplus country creating need for storage and processing of agricultural and horticultural produce.

32. **Assertion** (A) Nutrient based approach is very effective strategy to overcome nutritional deficiencies.

Reason (R) It has wide coverage and is inexpensive .

Picture Based Question

33. Identify the types of malnutrition given in the image.

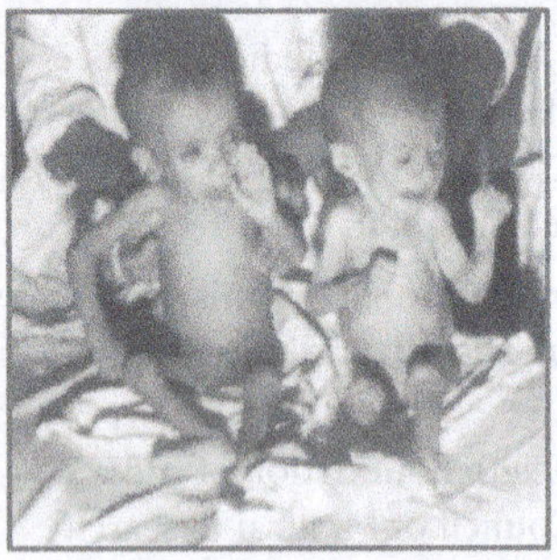

(a) Marasmus (b) Kwashiorkor
(c) Goitre (d) Cretinism

34. Identify the nutritional deficiency given in the image.

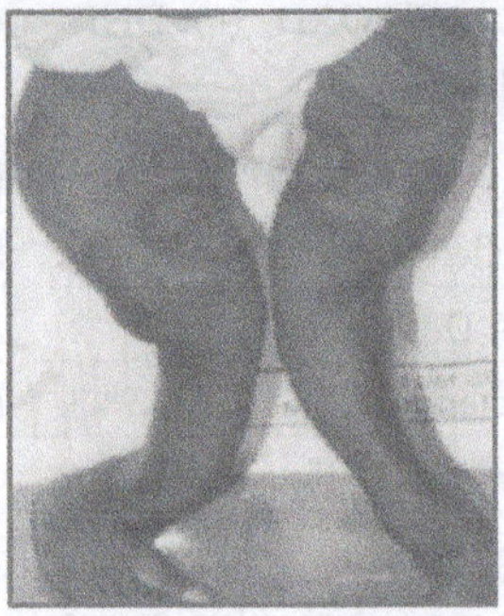

(a) Protein energy malnutrition (b) Deficiency of energy
(c) Micro-nutrient deficiency (d) None of these

Case Based Questions

35. Read the given passage and answer the following questions. **CBSE SQP 2020**

Malnutrition is the underlying cause of at least 50 per cent of deaths of children under 5 years of age. The statistics for nutrition-related problems in our country reveal an alarming situation.

- Almost one-third of the infants born in India are low birth weight babies. Low birth weight may have adverse effects throughout their growing years and may have adverse implications even in adult life. Low birth weight may even lead to child mortality.
- There is widespread prevalence of growth retardation among pre-schoolers (from socio-economically disadvantaged families) and almost half the children suffer from mild and moderate under-nutrition.
- A large proportion of children (and adults) suffers from micro-nutrient deficiencies in varying degrees of severity. The micro-nutrients of most concern are iron, zinc, Vitamin A, iodine, folic acid, B12.

(i) Which of the following correctly pairs a nutritional issue with its consequence?

(a) Micro-nutrient deficiencies - Impaired cognitive development
(b) Over-nutrition - Low birth weight
(c) Malnutrition - Increased height
(d) Vitamin A deficiency - Improved vision

(ii) Match the following nutritional issues with their impacts.

List I (Nutritional Issue)		List II (Impact)	
A.	Low Birth Weight	1.	Impaired physical growth
B.	Growth Retardation	2.	Increased risk of infections
C.	Micro-nutrient Deficiencies	3.	Long-term developmental issues

	A	B	C		A	B	C
(a)	2	1	3	(b)	2	3	1
(c)	3	1	2	(d)	1	2	3

(iii) Assertion (A) Malnutrition contributes to 50 per cent of deaths in children under 5 years of age.

Reason (R) Proper nutrition can significantly reduce child mortality rates.

Codes

(a) Both A and R are true and R is the correct explanation of A.
(b) Both A and R are true, but R is not the correct explanation of A.
(c) A is true, but R is false.
(d) A is false, but R is true.

(iv) Assertion (A) Many children in India suffer from growth retardation.

Reason (R) Socio-economic factors significantly influence nutritional status.

Codes

(a) Both A and R are true and R is the correct explanation of A.
(b) Both A and R are true, but R is not the correct explanation of A.
(c) A is true, but R is false.
(d) A is false, but R is true.

36. Read the given passage and answer the following questions. **CBSE SQP Term I, 2021**

Public Health Nutrition is the field of study that is concerned with promotion of good health through prevention of nutrition related illnesses/problems in the population and the government policies and programmes that are aimed at solving these problems. Public Health nutritionists/professionals use large scale, organised and multidisciplinary approaches to solve the problems that affect the population, i.e., large number of people for whom group action is necessary. Therefore, this field is multi-disciplinary in nature and is built on the foundation of biological and social sciences. It differs from other fields of nutrition, for example clinical nutrition and dietetics, because the professionals are required to address problems of community/public, specially the vulnerable groups.

(i) Public Health Nutrition is concerned with the promotion of good health through the prevention of

(a) Individual nutritional preferences
(b) Nutrition-related illnesses/problems
(c) Over-nutrition
(d) Food marketing

(ii) Professionals in Public Health Nutrition use which of the following approaches?

I. Organised and large scale
II. Individualised and specific
III. Multi-disciplinary
IV. Isolated interventions

Choose the correct option

(a) I, II, IV (b) I, III, II
(c) II, III, IV (d) I, III, IV

(iii) Public Health Nutrition differs from clinical nutrition and dietetics primarily because it focuses on

(a) Individual health issues
(b) Nutritional preferences of individuals
(c) Problems of the community/public
(d) Dietary restrictions

(iv) Which of the following groups is primarily targeted by Public Health Nutrition?

(a) Health professionals (b) Vulnerable groups
(c) Food industry workers (d) Urban populations

37. Read the given passage and answer the following questions. **CBSE SQP Term I, 2021**

In any society, nutritional problems are not just linked to food but to a variety of interacting/ interrelated factors at various levels. While poverty is often the underlying cause, the situation becomes worse when a substantial proportion of families do not have access to basic amenities.
Rural households have less access to toilets.
Poor sanitation results in loss of work days and further economic loss. Further, considerable proportion of the population does not have safe drinking water.

(i) What is the mission of Public Health Nutrition?

(a) To prevent over-nutrition and to maintain optimal nutritional status of individual and family.
(b) To prevent under-nutrition and to maintain optimal nutritional status of individuals.
(c) To prevent under-nutrition and over-nutrition problem of society.
(d) To prevent both under-nutrition and over-nutrition and to maintain optimal nutritional status of the population.

(ii) Following are nutrition programmes and their examples operating in India. Select the incorrect option.

(a) Food Supplementation Programme - Mid-Day Meal
(b) Food Security Programme - Public Distribution System
(c) ICDS-Annapurna Scheme
(d) Nutrient Deficiency Control Programme- National Prophylaxis Programme

(iii) To tackle with nutritional problems POSHAN Abhiyaan was started. Following interventions were initiated

I. Food fortification
II. Ensuring food security
III. Poverty alleviation
IV. Production of low cost nutritious food

Which of these are direct short term interventions to tackle nutritional problems?

(a) I and II
(b) II and III
(c) I and IV
(d) II and IV

(iv) Given below are two statements labelled as Assertion (A) and reason (R).

Assertion (A) Deficiency of iodine results in insufficient amount of thyroid hormone which is synthesised by the thyroid gland.

Reason (R) IDD is an ecological phenomenon, largely due to deficiency of iodine in the soil.

Codes

(a) Both A and R are true and R is the correct explanation of A.
(b) Both A and R are true, but R is not the correct explanation of A.
(c) A is true, but R is false.
(d) A is false, but R is true.

Answers

1. (c) Both (a) and (b)
2. (d) All of these
3. (c) II, III, V
4. (d) I, IV, V
5. (b) Deficiency of macro and micro-nutrients
6. (c) Hidden hunger
7. (b) Control of micro-nutrient deficiencies
8. (b) Punjab
9. (b) Cretinism
10. (a) Stunting
11. (b) Wasting
12. (b) Underweight
13. (b) Stunting
14. (d) Food Safety Programmes
15. (d) Kwashiorkor
16. (b) 2500 gms
17. (d) I and III
18. (b) Jhunjhunu, Rajasthan
19. (b) Nutrient supplementation
20. (d) Both (a) and (b)
21. (c) under-nutrition and malnutrition
22. (d) Mid-day Meal Programme
23. (a) Vitamin A
24. (b) Because these programmes are expensive
25. (c) Tertiary level-CHC
26. (b) Tertiary
27. (b) Primary Health Centre
28. (a) Oxfam
29. (a) USAID
30. (c) 4 3 2 1
31. (b) Both A and R are true, but R is not the correct explanation of A.
32. (c) A is true, but R is false.
33. (a) Marasmus
34. (c) Micro-nutrient deficiency
35. (i) (a) Micro-nutrient Deficiencies - Impaired cognitive development
    (ii) (c) 3 1 2
    (iii) (a) Both A and R are true, but R is not the correct explanation of A.
    (iv) (a) Both A and R are true, but the R is not the correct explanation of A.
36. (i) (b) Nutrition-related illnesses/problems
    (ii) (b) I, III, II
    (iii) (c) Problems of the community/public
    (iv) (b) Vulnerable groups
37. (i) (d) To prevent both under-nutrition and over-nutrition and to maintain optimal nutritional status of the population.
    (ii) (c) ICDS-Annapurna Scheme
    (iii) (c) I and IV
    (iv) (b) Both A and R are true, but R is not the correct explanation of A.

Subjective Questions

Very Short Answer Type Questions

1. How is public health different from public nutrition? **Diksha app**

Ans. **Public Health** It refers to the collective action taken by society to protect and promote the health of the whole populations.

Public Nutrition It is combined field of art and science of promoting health and preventing diseases or certain conditions, prolonging life through organised action of society.

2. Describe the mission of Public Health Nutrition.

Ans. The mission in public health nutrition is to

- Prevent both under-nutrition and over-nutrition.
- Maintain optimal nutritional status of the population.

3. Write down the factors responsible for nutritional problems in India.

Or **'Nutritional problems are not just linked to food, but to a variety of interrelated factors at various levels'. Justify the statement by giving any four factors related to under-nutrition at individual or family levels.** **CBSE 2024 C**

Ans. There are several factors related to nutritional problems that include

(i) Economic factors i.e. availability of financial resources to the people.

(ii) Agricultural policies that includes production and price of food stuffs.

(iii) Healthcare facilities availability and access among the people.

(iv) Government policies, political will and socio-cultural factors also affect the nutritional requirements.

4. "Public health plays an important role in the developing countries as well as the developed countries". Discuss the significance of public health with reference to the given statement.

Ans. Public health plays an important role in developing countries as well as the developed countries because

- Public health is diverse and takes into account the health of the whole population, rather than focusing on health at an individual level.
- Public health ensures everyone is aware of health hazards through educational programmes, campaigns and through influencing government policies.

5. Indicate two each functions of Iodine and consequences of its deficiency for a pregnant woman. **Diksha App**

Ans. Two functions of Iodine are

(i) Required for normal mental and physical growth and development.

(ii) Required for synthesis of thyroxin hormone from thyroid gland

Two consequences of Iodine deficiency for a pregnant woman

(i) Mental retardation in the foetus.

(ii) Congenital abnormalities of the foetus.

6. Mention four consequences of under-nutrition.

Ans. Four consequences of under nutrition are

(i) Low weight (ii) Weakness

(iii) Poor appetite (iv) Delayed mental development

7. Mention four symptoms of Vitamin A deficiency. **Diksha App**

Ans. Four symptoms of Vitamin A deficiency are

(i) Night blindness which progresses to complete blindness if corrective measures are not taken.

(ii) Less resistance to infection

(iii) Growth may be adversely affected

(iv) Dry skin

8. Give four causes of malnutrition. **Diksha App**

Ans. Four causes of malnutrition are

(i) Inadequate faulty dietary intake individual

(ii) Disease

(iii) Poor sanitation and hygiene

(iv) Inadequate maternal and child care practices

9. List two each reasons and consequences of over-nutrition. **Diksha App**

Ans. Two reasons of over-nutrition are

(i) Sedentary life style

(ii) Reduced intake of fibre rich food products.

Two consequences of over-nutrition are

(i) Overweight/obesity

(ii) Diseases like hypertension, heart disease, diabetes, etc.

10. What do you understand by the term food-based strategy? Enlist any two food-based strategies you may adopt to tackle public nutrition problems. **CBSE SQP 2023**

Ans. Food based strategies are the preventive and comprehensive strategies that use food as a tool to overcome nutritional deficiencies.

Two food-based strategies to tackle public nutritional problems are

(i) Fortification of essential foods (salt fortified with iodine).

(ii) Production and popularisation of low cost nutritious foods from indigenous and locally available raw material.

11. Compare two advantages and disadvantages of food/diet based approach used to combat public nutrition problems.

Ans. The two advantages of food/diet based approach are

(i) They are highly cost effective.

(ii) They provide many micro-nutrients simultaneously.

The two disadvantages of food/diet based approach are

(i) They require change in eating behaviour of the community.

(ii) They require change in agricultural policies.

12. Discuss the Integrated Child Development Services Programme.

Ans. This is an outreach programme for early childhood care and development. The programme's main aim is to provide nutrition, health and educational services to children through the early childhood period so that their proper physical, mental and social development is ensured. It covers all vulnerable children in the age group of 0-6 years and all pregnant and lactating mothers.

13. State any two indirect long term strategies of NNP. **Diksha App**

Ans. Two indirect long term strategies of NNP are

(i) Ensuring food security i.e., improving availability of food.

(ii) Improving the dietary patterns by ensuring availability of nutritionally rich foods.

14. "Tertiary level is the highest level of health care in India". With reference to the given statement discuss the importance of tertiary level.

Ans. It is true that tertiary level is the highest level of health care in our country. It basically deals with more complex health problems which can't be resolved at the first two levels. The individuals may require advanced medical procedures like major surgeries, transplants, replacements and long-term medical aid management for diseases like cancer or neurological disorders.

The institutions which are part of this are medical college hospitals, regional hospitals, specialised hospitals and All-India Institutes of Medical Sciences.

15. What do you understand by the term Hidden Hunger? Name any two conditions classified under Hidden Hunger. **CBSE SQP 2023**

Ans. Hidden Hunger refers to micro-nutrient deficiencies of varying severity that can be seen in a large proportion of children and adults.

Two conditions classified under Hidden Hunger are

(i) Deficiency of Vitamins

(ii) Anemia

16. Advise your friend about any four career avenues for public nutritionist. **Diksha App**

Ans. Four career avenues for public nutritionist are

(i) Community nutritionist in PSM departments (department of preventive and social medicine) of hospitals.

(ii) Nutrition programmes of the government e.g., ICDS, Food and Nutrition Board.

(iii) In voluntary organisations (regional, national and international) as nutritionists.

(iv) Nutritionists or counselors for schools, industries, etc.

Short Answer Type Questions

1. "Public health nutrition is a multi-disciplinary field". With reference to the given statement discuss the concept of public health nutrition in detail.

Ans. Public health nutrition is concerned with promotion of good health through prevention of nutrition-related problems in the population and the government policies and programmes that are focussed to solve these problems.

To deal with the problems that affect the population, public health professionals adopt.

- Multi-disciplinary
- Organised and
- A large scale approach

Thus, public health nutrition is a multi-disciplinary field which is built on the basis of biological and social sciences. As a specialised body of knowledge, Public nutrition is derived from the nutritional, biological, behavioural, social and managerial sciences.

2. "Adequate nutrition is essential for human development". With reference to the given statement discuss the nutritional challenge of Protein Energy Malnutrition in detail.

Ans. Nutritional Challenge of Protein Energy Malnutrition (PEM)

Protein Energy Malnutrition (PEM) is a significant nutritional challenge affecting both developing and industrialised countries. It arises from insufficient intake of energy and proteins, with children being the most vulnerable, although adults, especially the elderly or those suffering from infectious diseases like TB and HIV/AIDS, can also be affected.

PEM is commonly assessed using anthropometric measurements, including head and chest circumferences, height and weight. Key indicators of PEM include underweight (low weight for age) stunting (low height for age), and wasting (low weight for height).

There are two primary forms of PEM

(i) **Marasmus** Caused by a deficiency of both energy and proteins, typically affecting children under 12 months. Symptoms include loose, wrinkled skin, a shrunken abdomen, and general emaciation.

(ii) **Kwashiorkor** Resulting from protein deficiency alone, typically affecting children aged 1-3 years. It is characterised by edema (swelling, especially in the face, arms and legs), a pot belly, skin rashes and often liver enlargement.

3. Why a person with low hemoglobin level complains of fatigue? Also give two symptoms of anemia. **Diksha App**

Ans. A person with low hemoglobin level complains of fatigue because

(i) Hemoglobin is required for carrying oxygen in the body.

(ii) When hemoglobin level is low any physical exertion will lead to shortness of breath (breathlessness on slight exertion).

Two symptoms of anemia are

(i) General pallor

(ii) Paleness of conjunctiva of eyes, tongue

4. A doctor has diagnosed a fall in heamoglobin level of an adolescent girl. Which nutritional deficiency disorder does it indicate?
List any two other symptoms which may be seen in her in this disorder. **CBSE 2025**

Ans. A fall in haemoglobin levels of an adolescent girl indicates anaemia deficiency disorder. Two other symptoms of this disorder are fatigue (feeling tired all the time) and pale skin. It commonly results from a lack of iron in the diet.

5. Discuss the long term strategies adopted in India to tackle nutritional problems.

Ans. In India, there are indirect policy instruments which include long term strategies for the achievement of national goals through institutional or structural changes like

- Ensuring food security which is basically improving the availability of food among the people.
- Improvement in dietary patterns by ensuring the availability of nutritionally rich foods.
- Poverty alleviation for rural and urban poor through employment generation schemes and public distribution system, implementing land reforms, improving health and family welfare, prevention of food adulteration, involvement of media, monitoring of nutrition programmes, education and literacy, etc.
- Change in dietary behaviour horticulture inventions e.g. home gardening, nutrition and health education.

6. (i) Enlist any two short- term interventions of POSHAN Abhiyaan which was launched in March, 2018.

Or **Poshan Abhiyaan moniters and reviews the implementation of strategies to address the nutritional problems'. Justify this statement by giving any two short term interventions.** **CBSE 2025**

(ii) Mention any four nutritional programmes operating in our country, other than POSHAN Abhiyaan. **CBSE 2023**

Ans. (i) The two short-term interventions of POSHAN Abhiyaan which was launched in March 2018 are

(a) Integrated Child Development Services (ICDS) to cover all vulnerable children in the age group of 0-6 years and all pregnant and lactating mothers.

(b) Fortification of essential foods (salt fortified with iodine).

(ii) The four nutritional programmes operating in our country, other than POSHAN Abhiyaan are

(a) Mid-Day Meal Programme

(b) Public Distribution System

(c) National Iodine Deficiency Disorder Control Programme

(d) National Nutritional Anemia Prophylaxis programme

7. Differentiate between underweight and wasting. **CBSE 2025**

Ans. The difference between underweight and wasting are

Underweight	Wasting
It means having a low weight for age, reflecting a general state of undernutrition.	It means having a low weight for height, often caused by acute malnutrition or recent weight loss.
It reflects long-term health issues.	It indicates severe weight loss.

8. Give target groups and to each advantages and challenges faced in nutrient based approach to combat public nutrition. **Diksha App**

Or **Discuss target groups and to each advantages and challenges faced in diet based approach of including fortified food to combat public nutrition.** **Diksha App**

Ans. Different Interventions for Tackling Malnutrition

Intervention	Appropriate for	Advantages	Challenges/ Disadvantages
Medicinal or Nutrient Based			
Nutrient Supplementation	Therapeutic treatment Prevention programmes for specific nutrient and specific target groups	Timely, Sustain-ability	More costly than other measures Narrow scope of coverage
Food Based or Diet Based Strategies			
Fortification (fortifying food with nutrients)	Prevention (Universal /For all)	Highly cost effective Wide coverage Sustainable	Requires research Participation of food industry Does not lead to awareness in the population about the importance of nutrition and nutrients Does not lead to long-term dietary/ behavioral changes
Dietary Diversification	Prevention (Universal /For all)	Highly cost effective Wide coverage Sustainable Provides many micro-nutrients simultaneously Improves food security	Requires changes in eating behaviour Requires economic development to be feasible Requires change in agricultural policies

9. Write down any two nutrition programmes operating in India.

(i) What is meant by micro-nutrient deficiencies? Which is the other term used to refer to micro-nutrient deficiency? **CBSE 2024 C**

(ii) **Name anyone micro-nutrient deficiency prevalent in India. Also state any two major symptoms seen in these patients.**

Ans. (i) Micro-nutrient deficiencies are certain deficiencies which occurred due to the lack of micro-nutrients such as iron, vitamin D and vitamin A. The other term used to refer to micro-nutrient deficiency is 'hidden hunger'.

(ii) iron deficiency anaemia is very prevalent in India. The two symptoms of this deficiency are as follows

(a) paleness (b) loss of appetite

10. NNP was launched to tackle Nutritional problems. Enumerate its four direct short term interventions. Diksha App

Ans. Direct short term interventions of NNP are

(i) Integrated Child Development Services (ICDS) to cover all vulnerable children in the age group of 0-6 years, adolescent girls, all pregnant and lactating mothers and all women (18-40 years of age).

(ii) Fortification of essential foods (salt fortified with iodine).

(iii) Production and popularisation of low cost nutritious foods from indigenous and locally available raw material by involving women in this activity.

(iv) Control of micro-nutrient deficiencies (iron, vitamin A folic acid and iodine) among vulnerable groups (children, pregnant women and nursing mothers) by supplementing these nutrients, distributing free tablets, etc. The mission in public health nutrition is to prevent under-nutrition, malnutrition and over-nutrition.

Long Answer Type Questions

1. "The field of public health nutrition is muliti-disciplinary in nature and is built on the foundations of biological and social sciences".

(i) Explain the statement by highlighting four knowledge and skills required by the Public Health Nutritionists. CBSE SQP 2024

(iii) Give four career avenues for Public Health Nutritionists.

Ans. (i) The field of public health nutrition is indeed multi-disciplinary, integrating knowledge from both biological and social sciences to address nutritional issues effectively. The Public Health Nutritionists requires knowledge and skills, these are

(a) **Nutritional Science** Understanding the principles of nutrition, including the role of nutrients and their effects on health.

(b) **Nutritional Needs Throughout the Life Cycle** Knowledge of how nutritional requirements vary from infancy to old age.

(c) **Nutritional Assessment** Skills in evaluting dietary intake, health status and nutritional needs of individuals and populations.

(d) **Nutritional Care** Ability to develop and implement dietary plans and interventions to address specific health conditions and improve overall well-being.

(ii) Four career avenues for Public Health Nutritionists are

(a) **Community Nutritionist** Working in public health departments of hospitals to promote and manage nutrition programmes.

(b) **Government Nutrition Programmes** Involvement in national initiatives like ICDS and the Food and Nutrition Board.

(c) **Voluntary Organisations** Serving as nutritionists in regional, national and international non-profits.

(d) **Consultancy** Offering expert advice on nutrition and dietary management to various clients.

2. Discuss the following approaches to combat nutritional problems.

(i) Nutrient supplementation

(ii) Food fortification

(iii) Diet-based approach

Ans. (i) **Nutrient Supplementation** These are prevention programmes for specific nutrient deficiencies and target specific groups. They provide a therapeutic treatment. It is particularly used for Vitamin A, iron and folic acid in India.

However, these programmes are often expensive and there may be problems of coverage.

(ii) **Food Fortification** It is the deliberate addition of specific micro-nutrients to some commonly consumed foods to combat the micro-nutrient deficiencies among a particular population. It is a highly cost effective method and has a wide coverage. However, there are some disadvantages of it also.

- It requires research and participation of food industry.
- It does not lead to awareness in the population about the importance of nutrition and nutrients.
- It does not lead to long term dietary/behavioural changes.

(iii) **Diet-Based Approach** These are the preventive and comprehensive strategies that use food as a tool to overcome nutritional deficiencies. Through these strategies micro-nutrient deficiencies can be prevented by increasing the availability and consumption of micro-nutrient-rich foods.

Some important food-based approaches include dietary diversification and modification, horticulture interventions e.g. home gardening, nutrition and health education, food fortification.

Although it is a good strategy, still has the following disadvantages

- It requires changes in eating behaviour.
- It requires economic development to be feasible.
- It requires change in agricultural policies.

3. As a health worker, you noticed that most of the children in the village have pale yellowish skin. **CBSE 2021 C**

(i) What do you think they are suffering from?

(ii) Mention any three additional consequences on their health, if they are not given timely treatment.

(iii) Make their parents aware of nutriation-based and diet-based strategies so that they can improve the health of their children.

(iv) What two government programmes are operational in our country, for such children?

Ans. (i) The children are suffering from iron deficiency anaemia.

(ii) Iron deficiency anaemia may lead to

(a) delayed growth and development.

(b) increased susceptibilty to infections.

(c) Adverse effects on cognitive functions like reduced attention span, reduced memory span, reduced concentration.

(iii) Parents of such children should be aware of short term and long term approaches i.e. nutrient-based and diet-based respectively.

(a) In nutrient based approach, iron is given orally in the form of tablets.

(b) In diet based approach eating behaviour needs to be changed by modifying and diversifying the diet.

This can be done by including iron rich foods such as green leafy vegetables, meal and meat products, etc.

(iv) The two government programmes that are operational in our country for such children are

(a) National Nutritional Anaemia Control Programme

(b) POSHAN Abhiyaan

4. "The health care system of India is divided into three levels". With reference to given statement discuss the healthcare system of India in detail.

Or **Elaborate on health care system of India.** **Diksha App**

(i) 'India is facing the double burden of malnutrition'. Justify this statement by giving two reasons.

(ii) Indian health care services help to promote, maintain, monitor or restore health of people. Discuss how these health services are provided to people at different levels. **CBSE 2024**

Ans. (i) The dual burden of malnutrition implies that the over-nutrition as well as under-nutrition. India is facing this double burden of malnutrition because of the following reasons

(a) Shifting in dietary patterns and lifestyle, for example, sedentary lifestyles have become more common with decreased physical activity and reliance on motorised transportation.

(b) The shift towards unhealthy foods like processed foods, fast foods and sugary beverages have led to the non-communicable diseases like obesity, hypertension and diabetes.

(ii) Health is a Fundamental Right of every human being. Therefore, Indian Government has been providing adequate health care to its citizens through the robust health care system which operates at three levels. These levels are explained below

(a) **Primary level** It is the first level of contact for individuals, families or communities. It provides typically primary healthcare services which can be taken through Primary Health Centre is (PHCs). At this level comprehensive care is taken place by general physicians without the need for specialists.

(b) **Secondary level** At this level, complex problems can be resolved through district hospitals and Community Health Centres. It involves various specialists like cardiologist, dermatologist and urologist.

(c) **Tertiary level** It is the highest level of the health care system which deals with complex health issues that cannot be resolved at the first two levels. It requires advanced medical procedure like major surgeries, transplant and long term management for diseases. It also includes medical college hospitals, regional hospitals, specialise hospitals and AIIMS.

5. You recently went to a village in Madhya Pradesh for an educational campaign started by your NGO. You witnessed the problem of goitre in adults there. **Competency Based Que**

(i) **What kind of deficiency causes goitre in adults and cretinism in children? Where is it most prevalent?**
(ii) **State the adverse effects of this deficiency.**
(iii) **Which specific nutrition programme is being run in India for this?**

Ans. (i) Iodine Deficiency Disorder (IDD) causes goitre (enlargement of thyroid gland) in adults and cretinism in young children. It is most prevalent in the Himalayan belt, Jammu and Kashmir, Andhra Pradesh, Maharashtra, Madhya Pradesh, Karnataka and Kerala.
(ii) Iodine deficiency during pregnancy is harmful both for the mother and child. The several adverse effects specially resulting in mental retardation and congenital abnormalities of the fetus.
(iii) National Iodine Deficiency Disorder Control Programme (NIDDCP) is being run in India. The aim of this programme is to decrease the prevalence of Iodine Deficiency Disorder (IDD) in our country by providing iodine in the common salt (iodised salt). The services provided are: assessing the extent of the problem, arranging production/supply of iodised salt and taking quality control measures in order to ensure supply of standard quality of iodised salt to the consumer.

6. Describe three basic causes and two underlying causes at household level contributing to under-nutrition in our country. CBSE SQP 2023

Ans. Three basic causes at household level contributing to under-nutrition in our country are
(i) Economic factors i.e. availability of financial resources to the people as well as agricultural policies that includes production and price of food stuffs.
(ii) Availability of healthcare facilities and access among the people. Nutritional problems are not only due to problems related to food, but they involve several inter-related factors which have a role to play.
(iii) Government policies, political will and socio-cultural factors that affect the nutritional requirements. It includes status of women, allocation of funds for programmes to solve the problems of environmental degradation and biodiversity.

Two underlying causes at household or family level contributing to under-nutrition in our country are
(i) Inadequate access to toilets and sanitised conditions and unavailability of safe drinking water. Although, poverty is the major and underlying cause of nutritional problems, other issues such as lack of access to basic amenities and stress conditions are also equally contributing.
(ii) Low quality of child and maternal health practices and lack of awareness and education among the population of the country.

7. Discuss the role of a Public Health Nutritionist.

Ans. A Public Health Nutritionist/professional is an expert who works in this field, providing education and resources related to nutrition. Following roles are performed by a Public Health Nutritionist

- They focus on general trends of how the public eats, then find ways to educate the community about how to improve their dietary choices.
- Public Health Nutritionists are responsible for identifying the source of nutrition issues in a community and finding ways to address them.
- Their main goal is to improve the health and nutrition of the overall population, creating a culture of positive, well-informed eating habits.
- They develop programmes to improve access to healthy food, improve nutrition in schools and support healthy eating in the workplace.

8. Explain about any five nutritional programmes of India.

Ans. Five nutritional programmes of India are as follows
(i) National Prophylaxis Programme for Prevention of Nutritional Blindness aims at preventing blindness due to vitamin A rich foods and providing massive doses of vitamin A orally to children between 6 months to 5 years of age.
(ii) National Nutrition Anaemia Control Programme aims to significantly decrease the prevalence and incidence of anaemia in young children and women. The services provided through this programme are promotion of regular consumption of foods rich in iron.
(iii) National Iron Deficiency Disorder Control Programme aims to decrease the prevalence of Iodine Deficiency Disorder (IDD) by providing iodine in the common salt.
(iv) Mid-Day Meal Programme is a food supplementation programme launched by Government of India. The main aim of MDM programme is to provide meal, to primary school children between the age of 6-11 years belonging to backward classes and Scheduled Caste. This in turn to increase the school attendance.
(v) Self-employment and Veg-employment schemes or food security programmes which aim at improving the food security among marginalised sections of the society in vulnerable groups. Under these schemes, the government distributes subsidised grains through the Public Distribution System.

SELF ASSESSMENT TEST

Objective Type Questions

1. Which age group is the most affected by the disease called marasmus?
   (a) Below 12 months of age. (b) Below 24 months of age.
   (c) Between 12 and 24 months. (d) Between 6 months and 2 years.
2. Which of the following is not a micro-nutrient?
   (a) Riboflavin (b) Folic acid (c) Protein (d) Vitamin A
3. What challenges can be faced during the dietary diversification?
   (a) It requires changes in eating behaviour (b) It does not require any change in agricultural policy.
   (c) It requires economic development to be feasible. (d) Both (a) and (c)
4. Identify the group which is not covered in the Special Nutrition Programme.
   (a) Lactating mothers (b) Pre-school children (c) Elderly people (d) Pregnant women
5. What is included in the secondary level of health care?
   (a) Cardiologists (b) Dermatologists (c) Urologists (d) All of these

Very Short Answer Type Questions

6. What is PEM and which method is used to assess PEM?
7. Which disease is caused by Vitamin A deficiency and what other susceptibility is linked with VAD?
8. Mention any one indirect policy instrument that involves long-term strategy for nutrition under POSHAN Abhiyaan.

Short Answer Type Questions

9. Differentiate between the nutrient supplementation and food fortification. Mention any one advantage of each.
10. What are the different organisations under which a nutritionist can work for?

Long Answer Type Questions

11. What is the significance of public health and nutrition?
12. (i) Amit is a nutritionist and he has been assigned a role for taking care of the nutritional requirements for the newborn babies. He has to prepare the diet chart for the children to prevent them from protein energy, malnutrition diseases. In this context, differentiate between the diseases of Marasmus and Kwashiorkor. **Competency Based Que**
    (ii) Preeti has been assigned as a medical therapist under government programme. She has to prepare some policy related chart to prevent micro-nutrient deficiency using the diet or food based strategy. In this context, what approaches and factors she should consider for the successful implementation of diet or food base strategy. **Competency Based Que**

04

CHAPTER

Food, a vital part of our lives, needs to be safe, nutritious and delicious. Food processing and technology help us achieve this by transforming raw ingredients into wholesome and convenient products. This chapter explores the fascinating world of food processing, from traditional methods to modern techniques.

Food Processing and Technology

4.1 Introduction

- **Food processing**[1] makes raw foodstuffs suitable for consumption, cooking or storage. It includes basic preparation, alteration of food products e.g., preserving fruits/vegetables, preservation and packaging techniques.
- The various reasons for food processing
  - To increases shelf-life e.g., sun-drying grains after harvest.
  - To improves digestibility and palatability, ensures a continuous supply of food.
  - To make food edible e.g., processing wheat into flour for chapattis, breads, cereals, pasta.
  - To provides convenience with ready-to-eat foods, canned dishes, and preserved fruits/vegetables.
  - To aim for cost-effective production.
  - To enable preservation of traditional foods like papads, murabbas and pickles.

1 **Food Processing** The branch of manufacturing where raw materials are transformed into intermediate food, stuffs or edible products through the application of scientific knowledge and technology.

- Increasing industrialisation, transportation and communication have diversified **consumer needs.**
- Growing demand for fresh and organic foods, as well as safer and healthier options.
- Consumers expect **high-quality foods** that retain nutrients and have specific functional properties.
- Desire for foods with desirable taste, texture and consistency while being **shelf-stable.**
- Opportunities for scientists to develop processing methods that meet evolving consumer requirements.

Ready-to-Eat Foods

- Ready-to-eat food refers to pre-cooked and pre-packed meals that require minimal or no further preparation or cooking e.g., biscuits, bread, pickles, papads, ready-to-eat curries and various meal items and snacks.
- These foods are manufactured using a variety of processes and technologies.
- Some products still rely on simple traditional methods for preparation.
- Newer processes and technologies are utilised to produce processed foods in bulk.

4.2 Significance of Food Processing

- India has progressed from an **agro-deficit** country to an **agro-surplus** country. This shift has created a need for storage and processing of agricultural and horticultural produce.
- The Indian food industry has emerged as a major producer of processed foods.
- It ranks fifth in terms of size and contributes nearly **6 per cent of GDP.**
- Along with changes in lifestyle, has heightened demand for various products.
- This demand makes research for newer technologies necessary.

Food Fortification

- Simple diets based on staple foods like cereals that lack certain nutrients, leading to nutrient deficiencies. Food fortification addresses this issue by deliberately adding required nutrients to commonly consumed items. Examples of food fortification include
  - Iodisation of salt to prevent iodine deficiency disorder.
  - Addition of iron to rice.
  - Fortification of milk and oils with Vitamins A and D.
- FSSAI has established standards for fortification of staple foods like salt, wheat flour, milk and oats. Increased prevalence of diseases like diabetes and heart disease has prompted scientists to modify nutrient content in foods.
- Examples of modifications include
  - Reducing calorie content in processed foods with artificial sweeteners.
  - Replacing fat in ice creams with treated proteins to maintain texture while lowering energy value.
- Changing consumer perceptions have led to higher demand for foods free of chemicals, pesticides and preservatives.
- Consumers seek natural flavour, appearance and longer shelf-life in products. This emphasises the growing importance of food processing and technology as a discipline.

4.3 Basic Concepts

Some of the basic concepts related to food processing and technology are discussed below

Food Science

- **Food Science**[2] involves the application of basic sciences like **chemistry, physics, culinary arts, agronomics** and **microbiology**. It is a broad discipline focused on all technical aspects of food, from harvesting or slaughtering to cooking and consumption.
- Food scientists utilise knowledge from biology, physical sciences and engineering.
- They study and analyse the composition of foods and changes during harvest, processing and storage.
- Food scientists investigate causes of spoilage and the principles underlying food processing.
- They also explore physico-chemical aspects of food to understand its nature and properties.

Food Processing

- Food processing encompasses methods and techniques that convert raw ingredients into finished and semi-finished products.
- This process necessitates high-quality raw materials from plant and/or animal sources.
- The aim is to create attractive, marketable food products with often long shelf-life.

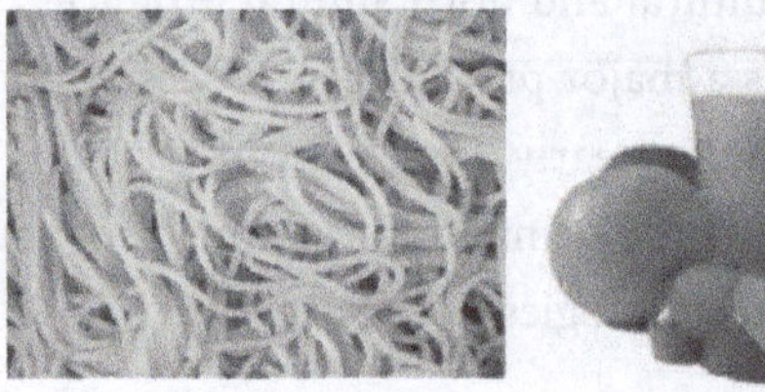

▲ *Food Processing*

Food Technology

- Technology is the science and application of scientific, socio-economic knowledge and legal rules for production.
- Food technology utilises knowledge from **food science** and **food engineering** to produce a variety of foods.
- It applies food science to the selection, storage, **preservation**[3], processing, packaging and distribution of safe and nutritious foods.
- The focus is on producing wholesome, desirable, affordable and convenient foods.
- **Food technology**[4] promotes sustainability, avoids waste and aims to save, and utilise all food produced.

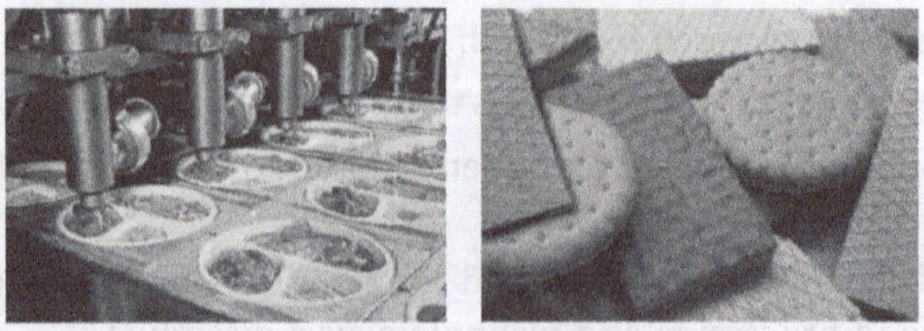

▲ *Food Technology*

2 **Food Science** The study of the physical, biological and chemical makeup of food; the causes of food deterioration and the concepts underlying food processing.

3 **Preservation** The procedure by which food is treated and handled to stop or slow down food spoilage, loss of quality, edibility or nutritional value and thus allow for longer food storage.

4 **Food Technology** A branch of food science that deals with the production, preservation, quality control and research and development of the food products.

Food Manufacturing

- Food manufacturing is defined as the mass production of food products using principles of food technology.
- It aims to meet the diverse needs of a growing population.
- Food manufacturing is one of the largest manufacturing industries today.

Quick Test 1

1. In earlier times, why were foods processed?
2. What is the contribution of the food industry to India's GDP?
3. What is the main purpose of food fortification?
4. What is the largest manufacturing industry today?

4.4 Development of Food Processing and Technology

Food technologists aim to provide both safer and fresher food using new techniques. Today, in the 21st century, food technologists face challenges related to health and the changing needs of consumers.

For decades, research in the field of food technology has been conducted. Some of the developments in food processing techniques are discussed below

- **Canning** The development of the canning process by **Nicolas Appert** was a decisive event that emerged in 1810. The process of canning had a major impact on food preservation techniques.
- **Spoilage** Louis Pasteur's research in 1864 was based on the spoilage[5] of wine and his description of how to avoid spoilage was an early attempt to put food technology on a scientific basis. He also conducted research on the production of alcohol, vinegar, wines, beer and the souring of milk.
- **Pasteurisation** Louis Pasteur developed the process of pasteurisation, which is defined as the process of treating milk to destroy disease-producing organisms. This method was a significant advancement in ensuring microbiological safety of food.
- In the initial years, food technology served military needs. However, in the 20th century, due to world wars, exploration of space and the rising demand for various products from consumers, food technology grew. For example, products like instant soups and ready-to-cook meals were developed to fulfill the needs of working women.
- Further developments in this industry focus on nutritional concerns. Changes in food preferences and choices led people to incorporate food items from different regions and countries into their diets, increasing the demand for seasonal foods year-round.
- Food technology has provided a vast variety of safe and convenient food items to consumers. This field is expanding and developing in developing countries. It has been helpful in improving food security and has opened up access to employment at all levels.

Importance of Food Processing and Preservation

The importance of food processing can be understood with the help of the following points

- Different food processing methods are adopted to convert bulky, perishable and inedible food materials into more useful, concentrated, shelf-stable and palatable foods. The changes in the products often help to reduce preparation time for the cook.
- Processing of food helps to add value to the resultant product by increasing storability, portability, palatability and convenience.

5 **Spoilage** A process or change which renders a product undesirable or unacceptable for consumption.

- Professionals must know about the general characteristics of raw food materials, principles of food preservation, processing factors that influence quality, packaging, water and waste management, good manufacturing processes and sanitation procedures.

Food Spoilage

- There is a need for food processing as foods are subject to **physical, chemical** and **biological** deterioration. Food deterioration can be witnessed in the form of spoilage, development of off-flavours, deterioration of textures, discoloration and loss of nutritional value in varying degrees, reducing aesthetic appeal and rendering it unfit for consumption.
- There are several factors responsible for food deterioration such as
  - Infestation by insects or pests.
  - Inappropriate temperatures used for processing or storage.
  - Excessive exposure to light and other radiations, oxygen and moisture.
  - Micro-organisms (like fungus and bacteria) or chemical pesticides are responsible for food contamination.
  - Naturally present enzymes[6] can degrade the quality of food.
  - Physical and chemical changes in certain constituents of food from plant or animal sources can alter food quality.

Thus, there is a need for food processing and preservation so that edible items can be preserved appropriately. There are several methods by which food is preserved from spoiling after harvesting or slaughtering. Some of the oldest methods of preservation include

- Sun drying
- Salting or pickling
- Roasting
- Controlled fermentation
- Candying
- Smoking
- Baking and using spices as preservatives for longer duration.

- These techniques of preservation are still used, but with the advent of the industrial revolution, new methods have been developed and adopted.

Classes of Foods Based on Perishability

Foods can be classified on the basis of perishability

- Perishable foods are foods that spoil quickly within one or two days. For example, milk, curds, fish and meat.
- Semi-perishable foods can last for 1-2 weeks. For example, fruits and vegetables. Root crops like onions and potatoes last for 2-4 weeks.
- Non-perishable foods are those that generally last for one year. For example, grains like rice, wheat, pulses and dals, oilseeds.

Need of Food Processing

- Food processing incorporates and unifies characteristics of different classes of food and principles of food science, chemistry, food microbiology, nutrition, sensory analysis and statistics.
- It includes good manufacturing practices as per regulations.
- Food processing operations are designed to extend the shelf-life of food products.
- Concepts related to food processing focus on reducing or eliminating microbial activity and factors that lead to spoilage.
- Principal micro-organisms responsible for food spoilage include bacteria, fungi, yeasts and moulds.
- Factors leading to microbial growth include nutrient availability, moisture, pH level, oxygen levels and the presence of inhibiting substances like antibiotics.

6 **Enzymes** A specific class of protein molecules that act as biological catalysts to accelerate chemical reactions.

- Enzyme activity in foods depends on pH and temperature.
- For example, oxidative enzymes in fresh fruits and vegetables use oxygen to metabolise, reducing shelf-life.
- Basic concepts in food processing methods to prevent spoilage include
  - Application of heat
  - Removal of water moisture
  - Lowering temperature during storage
  - Reduction in pH level
  - Controlling availability of oxygen.

High Risk Food

Bacteria prefer protein-rich foods, e.g., meat, fish, poultry, eggs and dairy products. These are known as High Risk Foods. Bacteria grow at any temperature between 5-60°C. This temperature range is known as the Danger Zone.

4.5 Classifications of Processed Food on the Basis of Extent and Type of Processing

Processed foods can be classified based on how much they are processed and the type of processing involved. Here's a breakdown

- **Minimally Processed Foods**
  - These foods are processed as little as possible to keep them fresh.
  - For examples include, cleaning, trimming, shelling, cutting, slicing and storing at low temperatures (like refrigeration).
- **Preserved Foods**
  - These foods maintain their original characteristics and are preserved to extend shelf-life.
  - For examples include, frozen peas, frozen vegetables and canned fruits and vegetables.
- **Manufactured Foods**
  - In these foods, the original characteristics are altered, often using preservatives.
  - For examples include, jams, pickles and squashes.
- **Formulated Foods**
  - These are made by mixing and processing various ingredients to create shelf-stable products.
  - For examples include, bread, biscuits, ice creams and cakes.
- **Food Derivatives**
  - This category includes components extracted from raw foods through purification processes.
  - For examples include, sugar from sugarcane and oil from oilseeds. Some derivatives may undergo further processing, like hydrogenated oils.
- **Functional Foods**
  - These foods offer health benefits beyond basic nutrition.
  - For examples include, foods with probiotics that support digestive health.
- **Medical Foods**
  - Designed for the dietary management of specific health conditions with special nutritional needs.
  - For examples include, low-sodium salt and lactose-free milk for lactose intolerance.

Skill Required by Professionals

Professionals in food processing and technology need a variety of knowledge and skills across three main stages : Food as a Material, Food Product Development and Recipe Development. Here's a breakdown

Food as a Material	Food Product Development	Recipe Development
Seasonal availability of food stuffs	Knowledge of food preparation and cooking skills for large scale food production	Expertise in cooking
Nature and properties of food	Knowledge of product specifications and testing it	Knowledge of nature and properties of food
Nutritional content and its analysis	Observing and measuring quality control as per specifications	Uses of ingredients, measuring and weighing them accurately
Cost of foodstuff	Assessment by sensory methods (by testing and testing produced foods)	Designing, analysing and adapting a basic recipe
Influence of chemical pesticides, time, moisture, temperature and additives	Industrial practices and manufacturing systems and their control	Food handling skills
Assessment of the quality of raw foods and ingredients for quality production of food	Labelling and packaging of marketable product	Food production following hygiene and safety norms
Food hygiene and food safety	Hazard Analysis and Critical Control Point (HACCP)	Handling tools and equipment accurately
Knowledge of Information Technology for contemporary food production		Innovations in product design and preparation according to consumer perceptions
		Use of Information Technology for contemporary production

4.6 Preparing for a Career

- In the food industry, individuals can work in processing, research and development, focusing on
  - modifying existing food products
  - ensuring food safety
  - monitoring food quality
  - improving quality control procedures
- Specialisations may include branches like beverages, dairy products, seafood, etc.

  To be a professional in this area, one must have the following knowledge and skills
- Food science, food chemistry, microbiology, food processing, safety or quality assurance, good manufacturing practices and nutrition.
- Ability to analyse raw and cooked or manufactured foods for composition, quality and safety.
- Knowledge of food ingredients and their uses in large-scale food production.
- Understanding of product specifications and **food product development**[7].
- Skills in sensory evaluation and assessing acceptability.
- Familiarity with industrial practices, systems control, distribution channels and consumer purchasing patterns.
- Knowledge of food packaging and labeling.

7 **Food Product Development** A series of stages that a business goes through, whether a home-based company or corporate business, to bring a new food product or innovation to the consumer market.

- Ability to use information technology to support product design and conduct sensory evaluations.
- Skills in food preparation and cooking.
- Capacity to design, analyse and adapt recipes based on a design brief.

Career options in this field include

- After 10+2, pursuing short-term certificate, craft and diploma courses at various institutes, including the **Central Food Technological Research Institute (CFTRI) in Mysore.**
- Courses suitable for self-employment or placements in small-scale food preservation and processing units.
- Bachelor's and Master's degrees, along with research qualifications, providing comprehensive grounding for jobs in large-scale food industries, research, training and entrepreneurship.
- Many universities in India and abroad offer graduate and postgraduate degrees in food processing and technology.
- Institutes also provide postgraduate courses focusing on specialised aspects of food processing and technology like National Institute of Food Technology and Entrepreneurship Management (NIFTEM) at Sonipat.

4.7 Scope of Food Processing and Technology

The scope of food processing and technology can be understood with the help of the following points

- Food technologists work mainly in food industries, in quality control departments, hotels, hospitals, labelling and packaging industries, soft drink industries, dairy, confectionery, processing of grains, etc.
- Their knowledge and expertise in their field are useful for various departments such as purchase and storage, processing or manufacture, quality monitoring and management, safety assessment, as well as in research and development.
- One can pursue or take a path as an entrepreneur in the food processing industry. Due to globalisation and foreign investments, many foreign companies and multinational companies are investing in India in production, research and development, educational and outsourcing facilities. This has increased the scope for food technologists in Indian as well as international organisations.
- The food processing industry also provides an opportunity for the export of products.
- On the other hand, employment exchanges will also be strengthened and upgraded.

Career Avenues

Career avenues related to the food processing and technology industry are

- Production Managers
- Marketing and Sales Personnel
- Quality Assurance
- Project Financing
- Teaching and Research
- Consultancy
- Project Implementation
- Sensory Evaluation
- Research and Development, Product Development
- Project Appraisal
- Entrepreneurship Development
- Technical Marketing of Products

Self-Employment Avenues

- In India, food processing has traditionally been a household or cottage scale activity.
- Historically, despite a lack of basic training in food processing, products like pickles and papads were still prepared and sold locally.

- With advancements in agriculture, horticulture and pisciculture, the production of raw materials has significantly improved.
- A self-employment venture in food technology can range from technology-intensive and investment-heavy projects to low-tech, low-investment units (For example, salted peanuts, pickles).

Initiatives of Government

- The government is providing incentives and support for entrepreneurs through finances, training, infrastructure and marketing facilities.
- Women entrepreneurs receive additional financial support from various banks.
- State Governments offer space for individuals interested in starting their own businesses.
- The food industry in India is valued at 61 billion US dollars, ranking fifth in size and contributing nearly 6 per cent to GDP.
- Approximately 13 per cent of Indian exports involve the food industry, which represents 6 per cent of total industrial investment in the country.
- This investment is expected to grow at a rate of 20 per cent, with processed foods accounting for 25 per cent of that growth.
- Key segments in the food processing industry include
  - Milk and milk products
  - Snack foods
  - Bakery products
  - Fruit and vegetable products
  - Beverages
  - Food processing machines and equipment
- Rising exports in this sector are expected to further boost employment opportunities.

Quick Test 2

1. Who developed the canning process in 1810?
2. Who developed the process of pasteurisation?
3. What types of food use trimming and shelling processes?
4. Can you give an example of functional foods?
5. What opportunities does the food processing industry provide for products?

Mind Map

FOODS PROCESSING AND TECHNOLOGY

1 Food Processing

Trends
- Industrialisation, transportation, and communication diversify consumer needs.
- Demand for fresh, organic, healthier and nutrient-retaining foods.
- Focus on taste, texture and shelf stability.

Ready-to-Eat Foods
- Pre-cooked, pre-packed meals needing little/no preparation.
- **For examples** Biscuits, bread, pickles, snacks.
- Traditional and modern manufacturing methods used.

Purpose
- Makes raw food safe for consumption, cooking, or storage.
- Includes preservation, preparation and packaging.

Reasons for Processing
- Increases shelf-life (e.g., sun-drying).
- Makes food edible (e.g., wheat → flour).
- Cost-effective production.
- Improves digestibility and taste.
- Provides convenience (ready-to-eat).
- Preserves traditional foods.

2 Food Processing and Significance

Food Fortification
- **Issue** Nutrient deficiencies in staple diets.
  For examples Iodised salt (iodine), Iron in rice.

Health Modifications
For examples Artificial sweeteners (lower calories), Protein in ice cream (lower fat).

India's Progress
- Shift from agro-deficit to agro-surplus.
- Increased need for food storage and processing.

Indian Food Industry
- Major producer of processed foods.
- Contributes 6% of GDP.
- Growing demand due to lifestyle changes.

3 Basic Concepts

Food Science
- Applies chemistry, physics, microbiology to food.
- Studies composition, spoilage and processing changes.

Food Processing
- Converts raw ingredients into finished products.
- Requires high-quality raw materials and creates long shelf-life foods.

Food Technology
- Uses scientific knowledge for food production.
- Focus on safe, nutritious, affordable foods.
- Promotes sustainability and reduces waste.

Food Manufacturing
- Mass production using food technology.
- Meets needs of a growing population.
- One of the largest industries.

4 Development and Importance of Food Processing

- **Canning (1810)** Key in food preservation.
- **Pasteur (1864)** Developed pasteurisation for safety.
- **Modern Needs** Ready meals, health focus, year-round availability.

Food Spoilage
- Caused by physical, chemical and biological factors.
- Micro-organisms, enzymes, and improper storage lead to spoilage.

Preservation Methods
- **Traditional** Sun-drying, salting, smoking.
- **Modern** Industrial methods for better shelf-life.

Classes of Foods
- **Perishable** Milk, meat (1-2 days).
- **Semi-perishable** Fruits, vegetables (1-4 weeks).
- **Non-perishable** Grains, pulses (up to 1 year).

Need for Processing
- Extends shelf-life, reduces spoilage and eliminates microbes.

Microbial Growth
- **Factors** Moisture, pH, oxygen, nutrients.
- **Danger Zone** 5-60°C (ideal for bacteria growth).

5 Processed Foods and Skills Required

Processed Food Classification
- **Minimally Processed** Fresh foods (e.g., cleaned, cut, refrigerated).
- **Preserved** Retain original traits (e.g., frozen peas, canned vegetables).
- **Manufactured** Altered with preservatives (e.g., jams, pickles).
- **Formulated** Mixed ingredients for shelf stability (e.g., bread, ice cream).
- **Food Derivatives** Extracted components (e.g., sugar, oil).
- **Functional** Health-benefiting foods (e.g., probiotics).
- **Medical** For specific health needs (e.g., lactose-free milk).

Skills Needed
- **Food as a Material** Knowledge of food properties, handling and hygiene.
- **Product Development** Testing, quality control and industrial practices.
- **Recipe Development** Design, ingredient use, cost management and safety.

6 Career in Food Industry

Career Areas
- Processing, Research & Development food safety, quality control.
- **Specialisation** Beverages, dairy, seafood.

Required Skills
- Knowledge in food science, microbiology, processing, safety and nutrition.
- Food analysis, ingredients use, product development, sensory evaluation.
- Packaging, labeling, and IT for design support.

Career Options
- **After 10+2** Certificates, diplomas (e.g., CFTRI).
- **Self-Employment** Small-scale food processing.
- **Degrees** Bachelor's/Master's for industry, research and entrepreneurship.

Institutes
- CFTRI, NIFTEM, and other universities offering related courses.

7 Scope of Food Processing and Technology

Career Avenue
- Production Manager
- Quality Assurance
- Consultancy
- Sensory Evaluation
- Project Appraisal
- Marketing and sales managers
- Research & Development, Product Development

Self-Employment
- Traditional industries (e.g., pickles) and low/high-investment ventures.

Government Support
- Financial incentives, training and infrastructure support.
- Special support for women entrepreneurs.

NCERT Folder

1. Explain the following terms. CBSE Diksha

(i) Food Science **(ii) Food Processing**
(iii) Food Technology **(iv) Food Manufacturing**
(v) Food Spoilage

Ans. (i) **Food Science** It is a broad discipline concerned with all the technical aspects of food, beginning with harvesting or slaughtering and ending with cooking and consumption. It is being done by using biological, physical science and engineering knowledge.

(ii) **Food Processing** It is the set of methods and techniques used to transform raw ingredients into finished and semi-finished products. Food processing requires good quality raw materials from either plant and/or animal source to be converted into attractive, marketable and often long shelf-life food products.

(iii) **Food Technology** It is the science and application of scientific, as well as socio-economic knowledge and legal rules for production. Food technology uses knowledge of food science and food engineering to produce varied foods.

(iv) **Food Manufacturing** It is the mass production of food products using principles of food technology to meet the diverse needs of the growing population. Food manufacturing is one of the largest manufacturing industries in the present times.

(v) **Food Spoilage** Food spoilage is the process in which food deteriorates to the point that it is not edible for humans or its quality of edibility is reduced.

2. Explain briefly the significance of food technology. How has it affected the life of modern housewives, specially working women?

Or **Food processing industry plays a significant role in many ways. Discuss the significance of food processing industry.**

Ans. The significance of food technology are

- It offers an opportunity to form a sustainable livelihood and economic development for every section of the society.
- Food technology has provided a vast variety of safe and convenient food items to the consumers.
- It enhances consumer choices and allows food from other parts of the world to be a part of local market.

Food technology has been of great help to both housewives as well as working women in following ways

- With the help of food technology, one can get the best quality of food with suitable packing which helps in storing them for a reasonable time.
- It preserves the nutritive quality of food and prolongs the shelf-life by preventing them from spoilage due to microbes and other spoilage agents.
- Availability of ready-to-eat meals such as soups, pastas etc., have helped in managing food choices for working women.

3. List some of the old methods of food preservation followed at home giving examples and their viability in present times.

Ans. Some of the oldest methods of preservation include

- Sun drying
- Controlled fermentation
- Salting or pickling
- Candying
- Roasting
- Smoking
- Baking and using spices as preservatives for longer duration

These techniques of preservation are still used but with the advent of Industrial Revolution, new methods have been developed and adopted. For example, typical pickling agents include vinegar and vegetable oil, especially olive oil but also many other oils. Pickling can preserve perishable foods for months. Anti-microbial herbs and spices, such as mustard seed, garlic, cinnamon or cloves, are often added. If the food contains sufficient moisture, pickling brine may be produced simply by adding dry salt. Natural fermentation at room temperature, by lactic acid bacteria, produces the required acidity.

4. Give a brief account of development of food preservation to its present status.

Or **Discuss some of the developments in food processing techniques in the earlier times.**

Ans. For answer refer to text under the heading 'Development of Food Processing and Technology' on page no. 81.

5. As a prospective food technologist what knowledge and skills does the industry require you to have?

Ans. As a prosective food technologist require following skills and knowledge

- Food science, food chemistry, microbiology, food processing, safety, quality assurance, good manufacturing practices and nutrition.
- Analysis of raw and cooked/manufactured foods for composition, quality and safety.
- Food ingredients, their uses in food preparations and food production on a large scale.
- Product specifications and food product development.
- Sensory evaluation and acceptability.
- Industrial practices, systems control, distribution channels, consumer purchase patterns.

6. Keeping the concept of health and wellness in mind, explain with examples how food scientists are trying to enhance the food values in processed and packaged foods. Competency Based Que

Ans. Food scientists are trying to enhance the food values in processed and packaged foods in the following manner

- Food fortification is done by deliberately adding the required nutrients that food stuffs or condiments lack so that minimum dietary requirements are met. For instance, iodised salt, folic acid is added to the flour so that required nutrients could be ensured.
- The increased prevalence of diseases like diabetes and heart problems as well as the concern for wellness, has led the scientists to develop or alter the nutrient content of foods. For example, calorie content of processed food is reduced by the usage of artificial sweeteners.
- Due to change in consumer's perceptions about food, the demands for food free of chemicals, pesticides and preservatives with a longer shelf-life, natural flavour and appearance are increasing.

7. Explain the following briefly.

(i) Why do we need to process and preserve food?

(ii) What causes food spoilage and renders it unfit for human consumption?

(iii) Food spoilage is generally caused by bacteria. What are the four conditions that bacteria need to grow and multiply?

(iv) What is done in food processing to extend shelf-life?

(v) After the completion of 10+2 examination, what is the professional scope in the field of food processing and technology?

Or **Your sister wants to pursue her career in the food industry. Guide her about two courses she should do after 10+2.** Diksha App

Ans. (i) We need to process and preserve food because

- Processing of food helps to add value to the resultant product by increasing storability, portability, palatability and convenience.
- Food preservation is necessary as it is a process of treating and handling food in such a way as to stop or greatly slow down spoilage and prevent food borne illness while maintaining nutritional value, texture and flavour.

(ii) Several factors responsible for food spoilage are

- Infestion by pest and insects
- Inappropriate temperatures used for processing or storage
- Excessive exposure to light and other radiations, oxygen and moisture.
- Micro-organisms (e.g., fungus, bacteria, moulds, etc.) or chemical pesticides are responsible for food spoilage.
- Naturally present enzymes can degrade the quality of food.
- Physical and chemical changes in certain constituents of food from plant or animal sources can alter the food quality.

(iii) The four conditions that bacteria need to grow and multiply include

- nutrient availability
- moisture
- oxygen
- pH level

(iv) To extend the shelf-life of food, several methods of preservation are used such as

- sun drying
- controlled fermentation
- salting or pickling
- candying
- roasting
- smoking
- baking
- using spices as preservatives for longer duration.

Other than these, following methods are used to prevent the food spoilage

- Application of heat
- Removal of water moisture
- Lowering of temperature during the storage
- Reduction in pH level
- Controlling the availability of oxygen

(v) The professional scope in the field of food processing and technology after 10+2 is

- One can pursue a short term certificate, food craft and diploma courses at various institutes in different states as well as at the Central Food Technological Research Institute (CFTRI), Mysore. Such courses which are suitable for self-employment as well as for the placement in small scale units of food preservation and processing.
- Bachelor's and Master's degrees as well as the research qualifications provide an individual with most comprehensive grounding for jobs in food industry in large scale units so that they can take up research and training as well as entrepreneurship in this field.
- Many universities in India and abroad offer postgraduate courses in specialised aspects of food processing and technology like National Institute of Food Technology and Entrepreneurship Management (NIFTEM), Sonipat, Haryana.

Exam Pattern Questions

Objective Type Questions

Multiple Choice Questions

1. Which of the following is an advantage of food processing?
(a) Availability of seasonal food throughout the year
(b) Removal of toxins and preserving food for longer
(c) Adds extra nutrients to some food items
(d) All of the above

2. Which factors have increased the demand of readymade foods in India? CBSE 2025
I. Deficit in agriculture
II. To decrease the nutritive value of diet
III. Catering to the needs of working women
IV. Changes in lifestyle
Choose the correct option from the following
(a) I and II (b) II and III
(c) III and IV (d) I and IV

3. The set of methods and techniques used to transform raw ingredients into semi-finished and finished products is .... CBSE SQP 2024
(a) Food Science
(b) Food Manufacturing
(c) Food Processing
(d) Food Technology

4. Conversion of oil to vanaspati is an example of .... Diksha App
(a) manufactured food (b) formulated food
(c) preserved food (d) food derivatives

5. Which of the following act as biological catalysts to accelerate chemical reactions in food? CBSE SQP Term I, 2021
(a) Pesticides (b) Exposure to light
(c) Enzymes (d) Moisture

6. Which of the following method was a significant advancement in ensuring microbiological safety of food in 1864?
(a) Canning (b) Pasteurisation
(c) Fermentation (d) Pickling

7. Sun drying is the oldest method of food preservation. Which principle of food preservation is involved in it? CBSE SQP Term I, 2021
(a) Lowering of temperature
(b) Reduction of pH
(c) Removal of water
(d) Controlling the availability of oxygen

8. Which processes are used in minimally processed foods to retain the quality of fresh foods? CBSE 2025
(a) Shelling
(b) Storage at low refrigeration temperature
(c) Hydrogenation
(d) Baking at high temperature

9. In the 21st century, food technologists are developing foods according to the health and other needs of the consumers. Choose the option which is an example of such food.
(a) Pickle (b) Lactose free milk
(c) Papad (d) Grains

10. Food items are being processed for various reasons. Based on the given statement, choose the reason(s) from the following to process foods.
(a) To increase the shelf-life of food
(b) To develop new products
(c) To improve digestibility and palatability
(d) All of the above

11. When is food said to be spoilt? CBSE SQP Term I, 2021
I. Poor presentation
II. Change in consistency
III. Change in texture and flavour
IV. Unhealthy meal
Choose the correct option.
(a) I and III (b) II and III
(c) III and IV (d) II and IV

12. Which of the following factor(s) is/are responsible for food deterioration?
(a) Micro-organisms
(b) Physical and Chemical conditions
(c) Nutritional level
(d) Both (a) and (b)

13. Bacteria multiply quickly in the food temperature danger zone. What is the temperature range of this? Diksha App
Or **Identify the Danger Zone temperature range at which bacteria grow on food stuffs.** CBSE 2025
(a) 5 – 60°C (b) 5 – 60°F (c) 15 – 100°C (d) 15 – 100°F

14. Find the incorrect statement from the following CBSE 2024

(a) Canning was developed by Nicolas Appert.
(b) Food fortification is removing of nutrients from the food stuffs.
(c) Lactose-free milk is an example of medical food.
(d) Temperature range between 5°C-60°C is known as danger zone.

15. The mass production of food products using principles of food technology is .... Diksha App

(a) Food Technology
(b) Food Manufacturing
(c) Food Science
(d) Food Processing

16. The basic concepts in food processing methods to prevent the food spoilage are

I. Application of heat
II. Increase in pH level
III. Increasing the temperature during storage
IV. Removal of water moisture

Choose the correct option.

(a) I and IV (b) II and III
(c) I and II (d) I and III

17. To become professional at food industry, you need knowledge of .... Diksha App

(a) Mathematics (b) Chemistry
(c) Microbiology (d) Biology

18. The examples of low investment unit of food industry is .... Diksha App

(a) salted peanuts
(b) pickles
(c) drinking water Pouches
(d) All of the above

19. Ramesh wants to start new industry of cheese manufacturing. What knowledge and skills he requires for this? CBSE SQP Term I, 2021

I. Assessment by sensory methods
II. Labelling and packaging of marketable product
III. Seasonal availability of food stuff
IV. Food handling skills

Choose the correct option.

(a) I and II (b) I and IV
(c) III and IV (d) II and III

20. Identify the food derivatives from the following CBSE 2024 C

I. Canned fruits and vegetables
II. Sugar from sugarcane
III. Marmalades and squashes
IV. Oil to vanaspati ghee

Choose the correct option from the following

(a) II and IV (b) I and II
(c) III and IV (d) II and III

21. Louis Pasteur conducted research on which of the following food items. CBSE 2024 C

I. Soup II. Water
III. Vinegar IV. Milk

Choose the correct option from the following

(a) I and III (b) II and IV
(c) I and II (d) III and IV

22. Match the following. CBSE SQP Term I, 2021

List I	List II
A. Manufactured food	1. Sugar from sugarcane
B. Derivative food	2. Bread
C. Formulated food	3. Enzymes used in food industry
D. Synthetic food	4. Papad

Codes

	A	B	C	D		A	B	C	D
(a)	4	1	2	3	(b)	2	1	4	3
(c)	4	1	3	2	(d)	3	2	4	1

23. Frozen peas are an example of .... CBSE SQP 2024

(a) functional food (b) formulated food
(c) preserved food (d) minimally processed food

Assertion-Reason Question

24. Given below are two statements labelled as Assertion (A) and Reason (R). Read the statements and choose the correct option.

Assertion (A) Milk and curd spoil quickly within one or two days.

Reason (R) They are perishable foods.

Codes

(a) Both A and R are true and R is the correct explanation of A.
(b) Both A and R are true, but R is not the correct explanation of A.
(c) A is true, but R is false.
(d) A is false, but R is true.

Case Based Question

25. Read the given passage and answer the following questions.

The Indian food industry with a size of 61 billion US dollars, ranks fifth in terms of size, contributes nearly 6 per cent of GDP, 13 per cent of Indian exports and involves 6 per cent of total industrial investment in the country. Besides, it is estimated to grow at the rate of 20 per cent of which processed food segment accounts for 25 per cent. Key segments of this industry are milk and milk products, snack foods, bakery products, fruit and vegetable products, beverages (alcoholic and non-alcoholic), fish and meat processing, food processing machines and allied equipment. Exports are rising and this boosts employment avenues.

(i) The set of methods and techniques which converts raw ingredients into finished and semi-finished products. Choose the procedure involved in the given statement

(a) Food Technology (b) Food Science
(c) Food Processing (d) Food Manufacturing

(ii) What are the key segments popular in the food industry?

(a) Bakery products (b) Beverages
(c) Milk and milk products (d) All of these

(iii) How is government providing support to entrepreneurs in the field of food processing and technology?

I. By providing finances
II. By providing space
III. By providing information
IV. By giving labour

Choose the correct option.

(a) I and III (b) II and IV
(c) I and II (d) III and IV

(iv) Given below are two statements labelled as Assertion (A) and Reason (R).

Assertion (A) There is an sample scope for food technologists in India.

Reason (R) Many foreign countries and MNCs are setting up their production, R&D, educational facilities in India.

Codes

(a) Both A and R are true and R is the correct explanation of A.
(b) Both A and R are true, but R is not the correct explanation of A.
(c) A is true, but R is false.
(d) A is false, but R is true.

26. Read the given passage and answer the following questions.

With globalisation, Indian shares have opened up to foreign investments and technologies. As a result, many foreign companies and multinational companies are setting up their production, R&D, educational and outsourcing facilities in our country. Thus there is sample scope for food technologists/scientists in Indian as well as foreign organisations. Also, food processing industry provides good opportunity for export of products. Employment exchanges will also be strengthened and upgraded.

(i) There have been food processing activities in India since the beginning. Which of the following is example of this?

(a) Pickles (b) Coke
(c) Pastry (d) Cake

(ii) What is the region for improvement in production of raw materials?

(a) Growth in agriculture and horticulture
(b) Industrial growth
(c) Increase in production
(d) Technology advancement

(iii) How does the government give encouragement and support to those people who want to set up their own enterprise?

I. By providing finances
II. By training
III. By not providing marketing facilities
IV. By advertising

Choose the correct option

(a) I and III (b) I and IV
(c) II and III (d) I and II

(iv) Which of the following statement is incorrect?

(a) Many banks do not provide financial support for women entrepreneurs.
(b) State Government contribute by providing space to entrepreneurs.
(c) A self employment venture in food technology may be highly technology-oriented and investment-intensive.
(d) India has progressed from an agro-deficit to an agro-surplus country.

27. Read the passage carefully and answer the following questions **CBSE 2024**

Food industry is involved in processing/manufacture, research and development (modifying existing food products, developing new products, researching consumer markets and developing new technologies), ensuring food safety and monitoring food quality, improving quality control procedures, costing to ensure profitable production and regulatory affairs. They may specialise in a particular branch of food technology such as beverages, dairy products, meat and poultry, sea food, fats and oils, stabilisers/preservatives/colours, food grains and additives.

(i) Which of the following is an incorrect pair?

(a) Food fortification – Iodised salt, Vitamin A, D added to oil
(b) Non-perishable – Milk, green leafy vegetables
(c) Perishable – Paneer, curd
(d) Semi-perishable – Onion, potato

(ii) **Which is a distinct field involving the application of basic sciences such as chemistry, physics, culinary arts, agronomics and microbiology?**

(a) Food Science (b) Food Processing
(c) Food Technology (d) Food Manufacturing

(iii) **Given below are two statements labelled as Assertion (A) and Reason (R).**

Assertion (A) India has progressed from an agro-deficit to an agro-surplus country, creating a need for storage and processing of agricultural produce.

Reason (R) Now-a-days, food processing technologies do not use simple traditional methods at all.

Codes

(a) Both A and R are true and R is the correct explanation of A.
(b) Both A and R are true, but R is not the correct explanation of A.
(c) A is true, but R is false.
(d) A is false, but R is true.

(iv) **Given below are two statements labelled as Assertion (A) and Reason (R).**

Assertion (A) Instant soup mixes and ready to cook meals were developed cater to the needs of working women.

Reason (R) Processed food products often reduce preparation time for cook.

Codes

(a) Both A and R are true and R is the correct explanation of A.
(b) Both A and R are true, but R is not the correct explanation of A.
(c) A is true, but R is false.
(d) A is false, but R is true.

Answers

1. (d) All of the above
2. (c) III and IV
3. (c) Food Processing
4. (d) food derivatives
5. (c) Enzymes
6. (b) Pasteurisation
7. (c) Removal of water
8. (b) Storage at low refrigeration temperature
9. (b) Lactose free milk
10. (d) All of the above
11. (b) II and III
12. (d) Both (a) and (b)
13. (a) 5-60°C
14. (b) Food fortification is removing of nutrients from the food stuffs.
15. (d) Food Processing
16. (a) I and IV
17. (c) Microbiology
18. (d) All of the above
19. (b) I and IV
20. (a) II and IV
21. (d) III and IV
22. (a) 4 1 2 3
23. (c) preserved food
24. (a) Both A and R are true and R is the correct explanation of A.
25. (i) (c) Food Processing
(ii) (d) All of these
(iii) (a) I and III
(iv) (a) Both A and R are true and R is the correct explanation of A.
26. (i) (a) Pickles
(ii) (a) Growth in agriculture and horticulture
(iii) (d) I and II
(iv) (a) Many banks do not provide financial support for women entrepreneurs.
27. (i) (b) Non-perishable-Milk, green leafy vegetables
(ii) (a) Food Science
(iii) (b) Both A and R are true, but R is not the correct explanation of A.
(iv) (b) Both A and R are true, but R is not the correct explanation of A.

Subjective Questions

Very Short Answer Type Questions

1. During earlier times, food processing methods were used for what reasons?

Ans. In the earlier period, food items were processed to improve their digestibility, palatability and to maintain a continuous supply.

2. How are the demands and expectations of the consumers met by the food scientists?

Ans. Food scientists try to develop methods and techniques of food processing in a manner that the food products are able to meet the requirements of the consumers.

3. On what aspects, consumer's expectations are based? Discuss.

Ans. The expectations of consumers are based on the following aspects

- Better-quality foods with retention of nutrients.
- Specific functional properties and taste or texture or consistency.
- Being shelf-stable and easy to pack, store and transport.

4. By whom are standards for fortification of staple foods like salt, milk, oils laid down in India? **CBSE 2024**

Ans. Standards for fortification of staple foods like salt, milk, oils are laid down by FSSAI in India.

5. "Technology is the science and application of scientific, socio-economic knowledge and legal rules for production".

With reference to the given statement explain the concept of food technology. **Competency Based Que**

Ans. Food technology is the application of food science to the selection, storage, preservation, processing, packaging, distribution of safe, nutritious, wholesome, desirable as well as affordable, convenient foods. It has another important aspect that it avoids wastage and utilises all the food produced. Food technology uses the knowledge of food science and food engineering to produce varied foods.

6. Why is food fortification performed?

Ans. Food fortification is done by deliberately adding the required nutrients that food stuffs or condiments lack so that minimum dietary requirements are met.

7. Name any two high risk foods. **CBSE 2021 C**

Ans. Two high risk foods are

(i) Milk and milk products

(ii) Meat, fish and poultry

8. Classify food on the basis of its shelf-life. **CBSE Diksha App**

Ans. Based on shelf-life, foods can be classified into three main categories

(i) **Perishable Foods** These foods have a short shelf-life, typically spoiling within one to two days.

For example, milk, curds, fish, meat, fresh fruits and vegetables.

(ii) **Semi-Perishable Foods** These foods can last longer, generally from one to two weeks.

For example, fresh fruits and vegetables, root crops like onions and potatoes (which can last 2-4 weeks).

(iii) **Non-Perishable Foods** These foods have a long shelf-life, often lasting for a year or more.

For example, grains (rice, wheat), pulses (dals), oilseeds, canned goods and dried foods.

9. "Food spoilage is caused due to various factors".

With reference to the given statement explain the basic concepts in food processing methods to prevent the food spoilage.

Or **Enumerate four factors which can lead to food deterioration or spoilage.** **CBSE SQP 2024**

Ans. The basic concepts in food processing methods to prevent the food spoilage are as follows (any four)

(i) Application of heat

(ii) Removal of water moisture

(iii) Lowering of temperature during the storage

(iv) Reduction in pH level

(v) Controlling the availability of oxygen

10. What is pasteurisation ? Give its one advantages. **Diksha App**

Ans. Pasteurisation is a process developed by Louis Pasteur that involves treating milk (and other liquids) to destroy disease-producing organisms and extend shelf-life. This method significantly enhances the microbiological safety of food, making it safer for consumption.

One advantage of pasteurisation is that it effectively reduces the risk of food-borne illnesses by eliminating harmful bacteria without significantly affecting the nutritional value of the food.

11. "Processed food is classified on the basis of extent and type of processing".

With reference to the given statement describes manufactured foods in brief.

Ans. In processed food products, the original characteristics of the raw products are lost and some basic methods of preservation are adopted. It often uses various ingredients like salt, sugar, oil or chemical preservatives. It includes food products like jams, pickles, squashes, etc.

Short Answer Type Questions

1. What do you mean by food fortification? Give an example of. **CBSE Diksha App**

Or **What is meant by food fortification? Give its two examples.** **CBSE 2025**

Ans. Food fortification refers to the deliberate addition of essential nutrients to commonly consumed foods to prevent nutrient deficiencies in the population. For example, iodisation of salt is a common example, where iodine is added to prevent iodine deficiency disorders.

The following advantages are

- **Extended Shelf-Life** Food processing methods help to convert perishable items into shelf-stable products, reducing spoilage and waste.
- **Improved Nutritional Value** Processing can enhance the nutritional profile of foods, such as through fortification, where essential nutrients are added to staple foods.
- **Increased Convenience** Ready-to-eat and processed foods save time and effort in meal preparation, making them more convenient for consumers with busy lifestyles.
- **Enhanced Palatability and Variety** Processing adds flavours textures and forms to foods, increasing their appeal and allowing for a wider variety of food choices.

2. A student is curious to learn about the major developments in food processing and technology that occurred before the 20th century. In this context, name two researchers who made a significant contribution in those times. Also name the process developed by each one of them. **CBSE 2025**

Ans. Two researchers who made significant contributions to food processing before the 20th century are

(i) **Nicolas Appert** He developed the process of canning in 1809 to preserve food.

(ii) **Louis Pasteur** He introduced pasteurisation in 1862 to ensure food safety.

3. Indicate four traditional methods of food processing. **Diksha App**

Or **Mention any four traditional methods by which food is preserved from spooling after harvesting or slaughtering.** **CBSE SQP 2024**

Ans. The following traditional methods of food processing are

(i) **Sun Drying** This method involves exposing food to sunlight to remove moisture, which helps in preservation by preventing microbial growth.

(ii) **Controlled Fermentation** Fermentation is a process where micro-organisms like bacteria and yeast convert sugars into acids or alcohol, enhancing flavour and extending shelf-life (e.g., yogurt, sauerkraut).

(iii) **Salting or Pickling** This method uses salt or acidic solutions to preserve food, drawing out moisture and creating an environment that inhibits spoilage (e.g., pickled vegetables).

(iv) **Smoking** Smoking involves exposing food to smoke from burning or smoldering materials (usually wood), which imparts flavour and helps in preservation by reducing moisture and adding antimicrobial properties.

4. Enumerate any four principles of food processing.

Ans. The four principles of food processing are

(i) **Extension of Shelf-Life** Food processing operations are designed to enhance the longevity of food products by minimising spoilage and maintaining quality.

(ii) **Reduction of Microbial Activity** Processing techniques focus on reducing or eliminating the growth of micro-organisms, such as bacteria, fungi and molds, which are responsible for food spoilage.

(iii) **Control of Enzyme Activity** Managing enzyme activity through temperature and pH control is crucial, as certain enzymes can accelerate spoilage and reduce the shelf-life of food.

(iv) **Application of Preservation Techniques** Common methods such as heat application, moisture removal, temperature reduction, pH adjustment and oxygen control are fundamental to preventing spoilage and ensuring food safety.

5. List four reasons of microbial growth. **CBSE Diksha App**

Ans. The four reasons of microbial growth are

(i) **Moisture** Micro-organisms thrive in moist environments, making high humidity or water content in food ideal for their growth.

(ii) **Nutrient Availability** The presence of organic matter and nutrients in food provides a rich source of sustenance for microbes.

(iii) **Temperature** Many microbes grow best within specific temperature ranges, often between 20°C and 40°C (68°F to 104°F), which are common in food storage environments.

(iv) **pH Levels** Microbial growth is influenced by pH; most bacteria prefer neutral pH levels (around 6.5 to 7.5), while fungi can tolerate more acidic conditions, enabling their growth in various foods.

6. Differentiate between functional foods and medical foods.

Ans. The difference between functional foods and medical foods are

Functional Foods	Medical Foods
Functional foods are foods that have a potentially positive effect on health beyond basic nutrition.	Medical foods are generally intended for the dietary management of a disease that have distinctive nutritional needs.
Example of functional foods is probiotics.	For examples of medical foods are low-sodium salt, lactose-free milk.

7. Differentiate between manufactured foods and formulated foods. Give one example each. **CBSE 2023**

Ans. In manufactured food products, the original characteristics of the raw products are lost and some basic methods of preservation are adopted. They often use various ingredients like salt, sugar, oil or chemical preservatives. It includes food products like jams, pickles, squashes, etc. Whereas formulated food products, are prepared by mixing and processing of individual ingredients that resulted into relatively shelf-stable food products like bread, biscuits, ice-creams, cakes, etc.

8. Food has been preserved using various methods since pre-historic times **CBSE 2024**

(i) Make a list four old methods of food preservation, which are still being used today.

(ii) Name any one institute in India offering specialised courses in food processing and technology.

Ans. (i) For answer refer to Q.No. 3 of NCERT Folder.

(ii) IIT Kharagpur offers specialised courses in Food Processing and Technology.

9. When food is at the first stage 'a material', which skills and knowledge are required by professionals?

Ans. When food is at first stage, skill and knowledge which are required by professional are

- Seasonal availability of food stuffs.
- Nature and properties of food.
- Nutritional content and its analysis.
- Cost of food stuff.
- Influence of chemical pesticides, time, moisture, temperature and additives.
- Assessment of the quality of raw foods and ingredients for quality production of food.
- Food hygiene and food safety.
- Knowledge of Information Technology for contemporary food production.

10. Professionals who develop recipes are involved in food processing and technology need to have a wide range of knowledge and skills. Elaborate on eight knowledge and skills need to develop recipe. **Competency Based Que; Diksha App**

Ans. Here are eight essential knowledge and skills needed for professionals involved in recipe development within food processing and technology

(i) **Cooking Techniques** Mastery of various cooking methods (e.g., baking, boiling, sautéing) is crucial for developing recipes that achieve the desired taste and texture.

(ii) **Ingredient Knowledge** Understanding the properties and functions of different ingredients (e.g., emulsifiers, leavening agents) allows for effective ingredient selection and substitution.

(iii) **Nutritional Analysis** Ability to analyse the nutritional content of recipes ensures that products meet dietary requirements and health guidelines, making them appealing to health-conscious consumers.

(iv) **Sensory Assessment** Skills in evaluating the taste, texture, aroma and appearance of food help in refining recipes to enhance consumer acceptance and enjoyment.

(v) **Recipe Design and Adaptation** Proficiency in designing, analysing and modifying recipes enables professionals to create innovative dishes that cater to specific dietary needs or market trends.

(vi) **Food Safety Knowledge** Understanding food safety standards and regulations ensures that recipes comply with hygiene practices and safety norms during preparation and storage.

(vii) **Information Technology** Familiarity with software tools for recipe development and nutritional analysis aids in streamlining processes, documentation and product formulation.

(viii) **Innovation and Creativity** The ability to think creatively allows for the development of unique recipes and food products that stand out in a competitive market, appealing to diverse consumer preferences.

11. What are formulated food? Indicate two examples of it. **Diksha App**

Ans. Formulated foods are products created by mixing and processing various ingredients to achieve specific textures, flavours and shelf stability. These foods often undergo formulation to enhance taste, nutritional value or convenience.

Two examples of formulated foods are

(i) **Bread** Made from a mixture of flour, water, yeast and other ingredients to create a stable and versatile product.

(ii) **Ice Cream** A blend of cream, sugar, flavorings and stabilisers that is churned to achieve a creamy texture and extended shelf-life.

Long Answer Type Questions

1. Your mother faces problem of food spoilage during rainy season. Tell her about any eight possible causes of food spoilage. **Competency Based Que; Diksha App**

Ans. Here are eight possible causes of food spoilage, especially relevant during the rainy season

(i) **High Humidity** Increased moisture in the air can lead to mold growth and bacterial contamination, accelerating spoilage.

(ii) **Inadequate Storage** If food is not stored in airtight containers or proper refrigeration, it becomes more susceptible to spoilage from moisture and pests.

(iii) **Temperature Fluctuations** Warm and humid conditions can promote the growth of micro-organisms, especially if food is stored in environments without consistent temperature control.

(iv) **Microbial Growth** The rainy season can create ideal conditions for bacteria and fungi, which thrive in moist environments, leading to quicker spoilage.

(v) **Pest Infestation** Increased humidity may attract pests such as ants, cockroaches and rodents, which can contaminate food.

(vi) **Poor Handling Practices** Improper washing or handling of food can introduce contaminants that lead to spoilage, particularly if hygiene is compromised.

(vii) **Chemical Reactions** Moisture can cause chemical reactions in food, such as oxidation, which can lead to off-flavours and loss of quality.

(viii) **Enzymatic Activity** Naturally occurring enzymes in fruits and vegetables may be activated by moisture and warmth, causing degradation and spoilage.

2. What do you understand by the following foods? Give one example of each. **CBSE 2021 C, Diksha App**

(i) Formulated foods (ii) Synthetic foods
(iii) Food derivatives (iv) Medical foods
(v) Manufactured foods

Ans. (i) **Formulated Foods** These are products prepared by mixing and processing of individual ingredients to result in relatively shelf-stable food products such as bread, biscuits, ice cream, cakes, kulfi.

(ii) **Synthetic Foods** Synthetic foods can be defined as food substances or products that are produced artificially rather than through natural processes. Also referred to as artificial foods, these generally imitate the characteristics of natural foods including appearance, texture and taste and are typically manufactured under controlled laboratory conditions. For examples, of these sources include soybeans, sunflower seeds, sesame, oil cake, green vegetables.

(iii) **Food Derivatives** In industry, components of foods may be obtained from the raw product through purification, e.g. sugar from sugarcane or oil from oil seeds. In some cases, the derivative or the component may be processed further, e.g. conversion of oil to vanaspati (the process is called hydrogenation).

(iv) **Medical Food** These are used in dietary management of diseases, for example, low sodium salt, lactose-free milk for persons with lactose intolerance.

(v) **Manufactured Food** In such products, the original characteristics of the raw products are lost and some basic methods of preservation are used, often using various ingredients such as salt, sugar, oil or even chemical preservatives. For example, pickles, jams, marmalades, squashes, papads, wadis.

3. Your friend wants to start a career in the food processing industry and need your advice on how to begin. **Competency Based Que; CBSE SQP 2023**

(i) Let him know about the knowledge and skills that he should possess before starting.

(ii) State some courses that he can opt to pursue a career in this field.

(iii) What is the scope of food processing and technology?

Or **Discuss briefly the significance of food processing and technology as a discipline.** **CBSE 2024**

Or **During COVID, Seema has done online diploma on Food Product Development.**
If she wants to start Food Processing Unit, what four skills she may require to do so?
Competency Based Que; CBSE SQP 2023

Or **Your brother wants to join food industry. Discuss about any ten areas of which knowledge and skills he must process before joining the food industry.**
Competency Based Que; Diksha App

Ans. (i) The knowledge and skills that he should possess before starting a career in the food processing industry are

- Food science, food chemistry, microbiology, food processing, safety or quality assurance, good manufacturing practices and nutrition.
- Analysis of raw and cooked or manufactured foods for composition, quality and safety.
- Food ingredients, their uses in food preparations and food production on a large scale basis.
- Product specifications and food product development.

(ii) Some courses that he can opt to pursue a career in this field are

- After 10+2 he/she can pursue a short-term certificate, craft and diploma courses at various institutes in different states as well as at the Central Food Technological Research Institute (CFTRI), Mysore.
- Many universities in India and abroad offer graduate and post-graduate degrees in this field of discipline.

(iii) The scope/significance of food processing and technology can be understood with the help of following points

- This field is based on the application of science and technology to the processing, utilisation, preservation, packaging and distribution of food and food products. It also encompasses a diverse range of specialisations for the individuals.
- Food technologists work mainly in food industries, in quality control departments, hotels, hospitals, labeling and packaging industries, soft drink industries, dairy, confectionery, processing of grains, etc.

4. Advice your junior fellow student about any four career avenues related to food industry.

Competency Based Que; Diksha App

Ans. Four career avenues related to food industry are

(i) **Quality Assurance** In this role, you will ensure that food products meet safety and quality standards. This involves monitoring production processes, conducting inspections and implementing quality control measures to maintain product integrity.

(ii) **Research and Development (R&D)** As an R&D professional, you will focus on creating and improving food products. This includes developing new recipes, enhancing nutritional content and innovating processing techniques to meet consumer demands.

(iii) **Production Management** In production management, you'll oversee the manufacturing process of food products. This includes planning, co-ordinating production schedules, managing resources and ensuring efficient operations while adhering to safety and quality standards.

(iv) **Marketing and Sales Personnel** This role involves promoting food products to consumers and retailers. You will develop marketing strategies, conduct market research and build relationships with clients to drive sales and increase brand visibility in the competitive food industry.

SELF ASSESSMENT TEST

Objective Type Questions

1. What kinds of demand are evident among the consumers nowadays?
   (a) Increased demands for convenient foods
   (b) Safer and Healthier foods
   (c) High sodium processed foods
   (d) Both (a) and (b)
2. Which of the following aspect is correct with respect to food storage or preservation?
   (a) Each food type has a potential storage life.
   (b) High temperature is required for food storage.
   (c) Light a form of energy can upgrade the value of food.
   (d) High moisture content is beneficial for food storage.
3. In this category, components of foods may be obtained from the raw product through purification process. This is called ....
   (a) formulated foods
   (b) food derivatives
   (c) manufactured foods
   (d) functional foods
4. The process of conversion of oil to vanaspati is called as ....
   (a) Hydrogenation
   (b) Fortification
   (c) Preserved Food
   (d) Supplementation

Very Short Answer Type Questions

5. Explain with the help of an example how food scientists are dealing with changes in customer's demands.
6. Why is there a need of food processing?
7. How food technology as a field of discipline is helpful for the people?
8. Which temperature range is called the Danger Zone for growing of bacteria?

Short Answer Type Questions

9. How globalisation has enriched the scope of food technologists? Discuss.
10. How Indian food industry is playing a dominant role? Discuss.

Long Answer Type Questions

11. Write a short note on the scope of food processing industry.
12. Give a brief classification of food on the basis of extent and type of processing in detail.
13. "Food processing and preservation are important aspects for a food product". With reference to the given statement discuss the importance of food processing and preservation.
14. How an individual can prepare for a career in food processing and technology? Discuss in detail.
15. Write a short note on self employment avenues available in India for food processing industry.

05

CHAPTER

Food safety and hygiene are crucial for public health, especially in urbanised areas with complex food supply chains. Effective food processing, handling and transportation are essential to prevent food-borne illnesses. Regulations and international standards play a vital role in ensuring the safety and quality of food products.

Food Quality and Food Safety

YOUR STUDY GOALS

YOUR PRACTICE GOAL

- Objective Type Questions (27 Qs ; MCQs, A-R, Case Based)
- Subjective Questions (17 VSAs, 13 SAs, 10 Las)

5.1 Introduction

- Food is the main determinant of health, nutritional status and productivity of an individual. It is essential that the food consumed is wholesome and safe. Unsafe food can cause many food-borne diseases. The food-borne illness is a major public health concern globally.
- Food-borne illnesses[1] are a preventable and underreported public health problem.
- In India, the **National Family Health Survey** (2015-2016) reported that over 9 lakh children under five suffered from acute diarrhea.
- **Food-borne illnesses** can cause mortality and significantly increase health care costs in the following ways
  - Damaging trade and tourism.
  - Leading to loss of earnings.
  - Leading to unemployment and litigation.
  - Impeding economic growth.
- In this context food quality[2] and safety have gained global significance.

1 Food-Borne Illness Illness caused by consuming unsafe foods or beverages.

2 Food Quality The term food quality represents the sum of all properties and attributes of a food item that are acceptable to the customer.

Significance of Food Safety and Quality

- Food safety and quality are important at the home level but most important in large-scale food production and processing.
- In earlier times, food processing was done at home. Nowadays, advancements in technology and processing have increased the variety of processed food products.
- Larger per capita incomes and better purchasing power have contributed to this rise.
- Increased consumer demand has led to more functional foods being manufactured. There is a need to maintain and assess the safety of such foods.
- The quality of food, including raw and processed items, is a public health concern and must be addressed properly.

5.2 Basic Concepts

Factors responsible for the rising importance of food quality are

- With rising commercial settings, food is handled by multiple hands thus, more chances of contamination.
- Quality of processed, packaged, raw food stuffs like spices, condiments, oilseeds is a major public health concern.
- Risk assessment between the long process of production and distribution to the public is important.
- Nearly half of the known food-borne pathogens have been discovered during the past 25-30 years. Food-borne microbial diseases have been increased due to microbial adaptations, antibiotic resistance and international travelling.
- India is a signatory to the WTO non-tariff agreement which has provided greater access to world markets. Therefore, it is essential for every country to protect the safety and quality of foods for safety, import and export.
- Rising pollution in atmosphere, soil and water due to excessive use of pesticides and other reasons are also one of the reason for ensuring food safety.
- Use of additive like preservatives, colour, ends, flavouring agents and other substances like stabilisers have been a cause of concern.

Some basic concepts related to food quality and safety are discussed below

Food Safety

Food safety[3] refers to handling, preparing and storing food to reduce the risk of food-borne illnesses. It assures that food will not cause harm when prepared and/or eaten according to its intended use. Understanding food safety is enhanced by defining two concepts: toxicity and **hazard**[4].

- Toxicity is the capacity of a substance to produce harm or injury under any conditions.
- A hazard is a biological, chemical or physical agent in food that can cause adverse health effects.
- Hazards represent the relative probability that harm will occur when substances are not used as prescribed.
- Hazards can be categorised into **biological, chemical and physical,** causing harmful effects on health.

3 **Food safety** Food safety refers to routines in the preparation, handling and storage of food meant to prevent food-borne illness and injury.

4 **Hazards** Any substance in a food with the potential to cause adverse health effects.

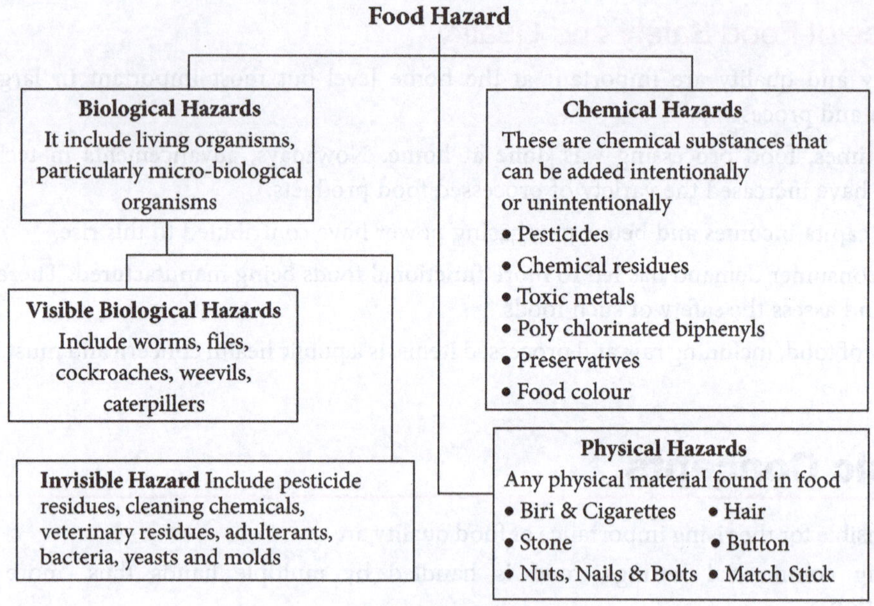

▲ *Food Hazard*

Food Infection/ Food Poisoning

- Food poisoning is caused by the ingestion of live pathogenic organism.
- Infectious organisms, including bacteria, viruses and parasites or their toxins, are the most common causes of food poisoning. These organisms multiply in the body and cause disease. For example, Salmonella exists in the intestinal tract of animals and is found in raw milk and eggs.
- Food may also become infected by Salmonella if an infected food handler does not wash hands with soap after using the bathroom and before touching food.
- Salmonella can reproduce very quickly, doubling their number every 20 minutes.
- Symptoms of Salmonella infection include diarrhea, fever and abdominal cramps.

Food Intoxication

- Intoxication occurs when food poisoning micro-organisms produce a toxin that triggers sickness when ingested. Some bacteria produce harmful toxins that can remain in food even if the pathogen has been killed.
- Organisms produce toxins when the food has not been kept at the correct temperatures, either too hot or too cold. These toxins cannot be detected by smell, appearance or taste, meaning foods that smell and look good may not be safe.
- For example, staphylococcus aureus and similar micro-organisms exist in air, dust and water.
- They can also be present in the nasal passage, throat, and on the skin and hair of about 50 per cent of healthy individuals.
- People carrying this organism can contaminate food if they touch their body while handling food.
- Diarrhea is one of the symptoms associated with this contamination.
- Parasites can also cause infestation, such as tapeworm infestations from undercooked pork.
- Additionally, food can be infested by pests and insects, including rodents and flies.

Microbial Food-Borne Pathogens

- Among various hazards, **biological hazards** are a significant cause of food-borne illnesses.
- Despite numerous efforts in food safety, microbial food-borne pathogens remain a serious concern. New pathogens continue to emerge and evolve. Factors significant in the emergence of pathogens include
  - Human hosts
  - Animal hosts
  - Pathogen's interaction with humans
  - The pathogen itself
  - The environment in which food is produced, processed, handled and stored
- Genetic exchanges or mutations in organisms can create new strains with the potential to cause disease.
- New pathogens may emerge due to changes in eating habits, climate, mass production, food processing and increased globalisation of the food supply. These factors allow pathogens to spread to new populations or geographic areas.
- Changes in host susceptibility due to malnutrition, age and other conditions can facilitate the emergence of new infections in vulnerable populations. For example, Norovirus, Rotavirus and Hepatitis E account for about 70 per cent of cases.
- It is believed that new pathogens will continue to evolve, highlighting the need to develop methods to isolate, control and detect their presence in food items.
- In the context of food safety, understanding the terms contamination and adulteration is important.

Contamination and Adulteration

- **Contamination** It is the presence of harmful or objectionable foreign substances in food such as chemicals, micro-organisms, dilutants before/during or after processing or storage.
- **Adulteration** It is the process in which the quality of food is lowered either by the addition of inferior quality material or by extraction of valuable ingredients. It not only includes the intentional addition or substitution of substances but also biological and chemical contamination during the period of growth, storage, processing, transport and distribution of the food products. It is also responsible for lowering or degradation of the quality of food products.
- **Adulterants** are those substances which are used for making the food products unsafe for human consumption.

Food Quality

- It refers to attributes that influence a product's value to consumers. This consists of both negative attributes spoilage, contamination, adulteration, food safety hazards and positive attributes texture, colour, flavour of the food. It is a holistic concept that includes factors like nutritional traits and sensorial properties (colour, texture, shape, appearance, taste, flavour, odour).
- Social considerations and safety are also included, with safety being a primary attribute and a precursor of quality. To ensure that foods are safe and of good quality, various governments and international bodies have established food standards that manufacturers are expected to follow.
- All food service providers should adhere to good manufacturing practices to ensure food safety.

  Some salient points to maintain food quality include
  - Quality of raw materials and water
  - Cleanliness of premises, personnel, equipment, food preparation, storage and serving areas
  - Storage of food at appropriate temperatures
  - Food hygiene
  - Good service practices

Quick Test 1

1 What can pose global health threats and endanger people's lives?
2 Which agreement is signed between India and the World Trade Organisation?
3 Food-borne pathogens are an example of biological hazards.
4 Write one factor that is significant in the emergence of pathogens.

5.3 Food Standards

Food standard[5] is a set of criteria that a food must meet if it is to be suitable for human consumption, such as source, composition, appearance, freshness, permissible additives, etc. They are as follows

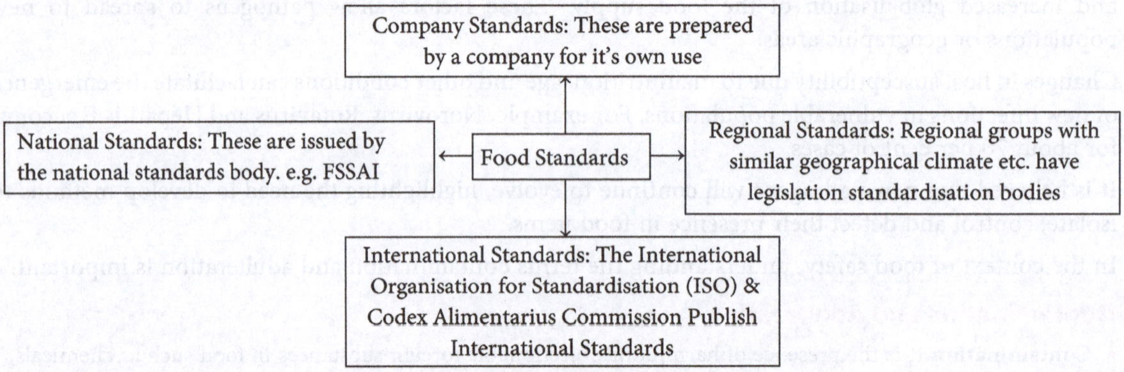

▲ *Levels of Food Standards*

Food Standards and Regulations in India

- In India, food standards rules are framed by the Central Government.
- The Food Safety and Standards Authority of India (FSSAI) is an autonomous body responsible for framing food regulations.
- FSSAI covers limits for additives, contaminants, pesticides, food labeling and more.
- Various acts have been enacted regarding Food Standards Regulations in India.

Prevention of Food Adulteration Act, 1954 (PFA)

- This act was enacted by the Government of India to prevent the adulteration of food.
- The act has been amended several times, with over two hundred amendments made as per requirements.
- All food products manufactured in India or imported and sold in India must meet the requirements prescribed under this act.

Voluntary Product Certification

- Product certification highlights specific characteristics that differentiate a product from similar products. It supports the product's credibility and quality attributes.
- Certified products guarantee safety and quality while communicating their unique value.
- In India, there are voluntary grading and marking schemes such as the ISI mark of BIS and Agmark.
- **The Bureau of Indian Standards (BIS)** deals with the standardisation of various consumer goods, including food products, and runs a voluntary certification scheme known as the **ISI mark** for processed foods.
- **Agmark** is a voluntary certification scheme for agricultural products (raw and processed) aimed at safeguarding consumer health.

5 **Food Standards** The law sets out rules that cover the preparation, composition and labelling of food supplied for human consumption.

- To simplify compliance with different laws and rules for the food industry, the Indian Government passed the **Food Safety and Standards Act (FSSA)**[6] in 2006.
- The FSSA integrates various laws related to food safety under one umbrella.

ISI Mark AGMARK FSSAI Mark

Food Safety and Standards Act (FSSA), 2006

- The main objective of this act was to consolidate the laws relating to food.
- The **Food Safety and Standards Authority of India** was established to lay down science-based standards for food.
- The authority regulates the manufacture, storage, distribution, sale and import of food to ensure the availability of safe and wholesome food for human consumption.
- The act includes provisions for maintaining hygienic conditions in and around manufacturing premises. It addresses the assessment and management of risk factors related to human health in a scientific manner, which were not mentioned in the previous PFA.
- The FSSA reflects the international shift in food laws from compositional standards or vertical standards to safety or horizontal standards.

Functions of FSSAI

Food Safety and Standards Authority of India (FSSAI) has been mandated by the **Food Safety and Standards Act** (FSSA), 2006 for performing the following functions

- Framing of regulations to lay down the standards and guidelines for articles of food and the system of enforcing various standards.
- Laying down mechanisms and guidelines for the accreditation of certification bodies for certification of food safety management systems for food businesses and accreditation of laboratories, along with the notification of the accredited laboratories.
- To provide scientific advice and technical support to the Central Government and State Governments for framing policies and rules related to food safety and nutrition.
- Creating an information network across the country so that the public, consumers, panchayats etc., receive rapid, reliable and objective information about food safety and issues of concern.
- Providing training programmes for persons who are involved or intend to get involved in food businesses.
- Contributing to the development of international technical standards for food, sanitary and **phyto-sanitary**[7] standards.
- Promoting general awareness about food safety and food standards.

---

6 **FSSA** It is an act to consolidate the laws relating to food and to establish the Food Safety and Standards Authority of India for laying down science based standards for articles of food and to regulate their manufacture, storage, distribution, sale and import, to ensure availability of safe and wholesome food for human consumption and for matters connected therewith or incidental thereto.

7 **Phyto-sanitary** The word comes from the words "phyto" which means "plant" and "sanitary" which means "clean" or free from pests and diseases.

Prevention of Food Aduleration Act 1954

The Prevention of Food Adulteration Act 1954 **(PFA, 1954)** was enacted by the Government of India to prevent adulteration of food. The act has been amended over 200 times as per need. In addition to PFA, there are other orders or acts that help to ensure the quality of specific foods such as

- **Fruit and Vegetable Product Order** Specifications for fruit and vegetable products are laid down.
- **Meat Food Products Order** Processing of meat products is licensed under this order.
- **Vegetable Oil Products Order** Specifications for vanaspati, margarine and shortenings are laid down. All such acts have been consolidated under the Food Safety and Standards Act. All food products manufactured in India, or imported and sold in India have to meet the requirements prescribed under the Food Safety and Standards Act.

5.4 International Organisations and Agreements in the Area of Food Standards, Quality, Research and Trade

- Ensuring food safety and protecting consumers from dishonest practices has been a vital task for governments since ancient times. Several international organisations and agreements play a significant role in enhancing food safety, quality and security, as well as facilitating research and trade.
- The major organisations playing a key role include
  - Codex Alimentarius Commission (CAC)
  - International Organisation for Standardisation (ISO)
  - World Trade Organisation (WTO)

Codex Alimentarius Commission (CAC)

- The Codex Alimentarius Commission (CAC) is an inter-governmental body formed to establish international standards for protecting consumer health and facilitating food and agricultural trade.
- As of 2017, it is composed of **187 member** countries and one member organisation, the European Community. India is a member of CAC through the **Ministry of Health and Family Welfare.**
- CAC has become the most important international reference point for developments related to food standards.
- CAC has published a document called Codex Alimentarius, meaning **"Food Code"**, which is a collection of internationally adopted food standards.
- The published document includes standards, codes of practice, guidelines and other recommendations to protect consumers and ensure fair practices in food trade.
- Codex standards are adopted to help develop national standards in different countries around the world.

International Organisation for Standardisation (ISO)

- ISO is an independent **non-governmental** federation of national standards bodies.
- It brings together experts through its members to share knowledge and develop voluntary, consensus-based international standards.
- ISO's mission includes
  - Promoting the development of standardisation and related activities to facilitate the international exchange of goods and services.
  - Developing co-operation in the fields of intellectual, scientific, technological and economic activity.
- The work performed by ISO leads to international agreements that are published as international standards.

- ISO 9000 is an international reference for quality requirements, focusing on the **quality management of an organisation.**
- The adoption of ISO standards is voluntary for organisations.

Differences between Codex and ISO

Codex	ISO
Used to develop national regulations	Voluntary
Slow to change	Standards are reviewed every five years
Describe the minimal acceptable practices	Describe current standard industrial practices

World Trade Organisation (WTO)

- WTO is the sole global organisation mandated to deal with the rules of trade between nations and was formed in 1995.
- Its main objective is to help trade flow smoothly, freely, fairly and predictably by administering trade agreements, settling trade disputes and assisting countries with trade policy issues.
- The WTO Agreement covers goods, services and intellectual property.
- To enforce the adoption and implementation of standards, a strong Food Control System is needed.
- An effective Food Control System consists of
  - **Food Inspection** Helps to verify food quality standards and ensures that food items produced, handled, processed and stored comply with regulations.
  - **Food Inspectors** Appointed by the Government or Municipal Authorities to assess quality conformity to standards in laboratories.
  - **Analytical Capability** Requires a broad range of analytical capabilities for detecting food contaminants, environmental chemicals, bio-toxins, pathogenic bacteria, food-borne viruses and parasites.
  - **Accredited Laboratories** Well-equipped laboratories are necessary to carry out food analysis.
  - **Trained Personnel** Well-trained staff with knowledge of laboratory management and physical, chemical and microbiological analysis of food are required for testing food and food products.

Quick Test 2

1. What is the role of the Food Safety and Standards Authority of India (FSSAI)?
2. Name two voluntary certification schemes for food products in India.
3. What is the main objective of the Food Safety and Standards Act (FSSA) 2006?
4. What is the purpose of the Codex Alimentarius Commission (CAC)?
5. How does the World Trade Organisation (WTO) contribute to food trade?

5.5 Food Safety Management Systems

- The Food Safety and Management Systems is a **set of standards** established to direct and control food safety aspects. The issues related to food safety and quality have gone beyond the avoidance of food-borne pathogens, chemical toxicants and other hazards.
- A food hazard can come into the food at any stage of the food chain. To deal with these issues, adequate control throughout the food chain is essential. Food safety and quality can be ensured through

Good Manufacturing Practices (GMP)

- Part of quality assurance to ensure manufacturers take proactive steps to maintain product safety.
- Minimises or eliminates contamination and false labeling, ensuring consumers are not misled.
- Helps refine compliance and performance by manufacturers.

Good Handling Practices (GHP)

- Involves a comprehensive approach from the farm to the store or consumer to identify potential sources of risk.
- Aids in deciding steps and procedures to minimise contamination risks.
- Ensures appropriate hygiene practices are adopted by those handling food items.

Hazard Analysis Critical Control Point (HACCP)

- A management system addressing food safety through analysis and control of potential biological, chemical and physical hazards.
- Covers all stages from raw material production to consumption of the finished product.
- Provides assurance about food safety by evaluating each step in the process for potential hazards.
- These are several reasons to implement HACCP
  - It is a preventive approach to ensure food safety.
  - It enables detects hazards at any processing stage to maintain good quality products.
  - It enables efficient and cost-effective resource utilisation for food safety assurance.
  - It assigns primary responsibility for safe food to producers and suppliers through HACCP, GMP and GHP, essential for consumer protection and international trade.
  - It assures consistently good quality products.

5.6 Scope of Food Safety and Quality

Due to the Indian Food Safety and Standards Act of 2006, a major shift has been evident in food laws that seek to provide greater consumer protection by ensuring safety and wholesomeness of food at all stages of the food chain. The changing scenario has widened the scope and increased career options in this field of area.

- Professionals who take up careers in this field need to have adequate knowledge and expertise in Food Chemistry, Food Processing and Preservation, Food Analysis and Quality Control.
- A person must also be well versed in Food Microbiology, Food Laws and Sensory Evaluation.
- Professionals in the food industry may be employed with regulatory and public health agencies as food legislators, food safety officers and food analysts.
- Professionals can also be a part of voluntary agencies such as Agmark, BIS and in Quality Control Laboratories.
- Food Auditor positions can also be attained after undergoing training. Trained professionals are also required in quality-control units of large food industries.
- Self-employment and entrepreneurship are other available options for a professional.
- An individual can initiate entrepreneurship activities through analytical food laboratories, food safety consultancy and food safety and sanitation education.
- There are different placement options at various levels in both regulatory and health agencies.
- Integrated approaches are promoted in Home Science Curriculum mainly in the field of Food Science and Nutrition that impart the knowledge to improve safety and quality.

Thus, the courses in Food Science and Nutrition enable the development of skills that are necessary to understand and manage food safety hazards.

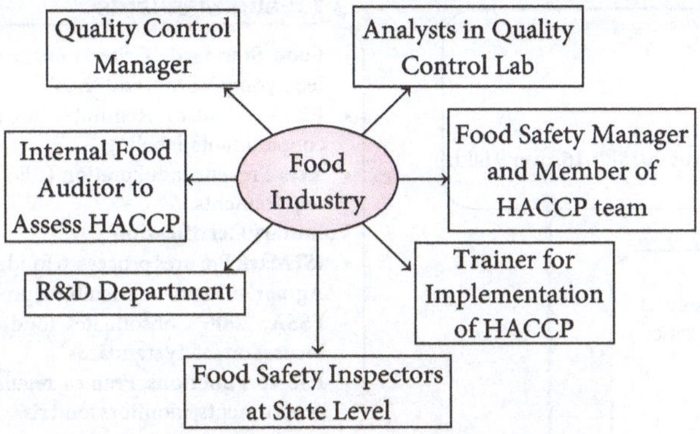

▲ *Job Opportunities in Food Industry*

Career Avenues

- Quality control laboratories in the food industry as analysts or at managerial level.
- Food testing laboratories in public and private sector-various positions including food inspectors and food testing.
- Specialist in HACCP
- Quality Certification such as ISO
- Research
- In voluntary organisations in various capacities.
- Food Auditors
- Teaching and Academics
- Scientific writers

Quick Test 3

1. What is the role of Good Manufacturing Practices (GMP) in food safety?
2. How does Hazard Analysis Critical Control Point (HACCP) ensure food safety?
3. What are the key areas of expertise required for professionals in food safety and quality?
4. Name two career options available for professionals in the food industry.

Mind Map

FOOD QUALITY AND FOOD SAFETY

1 Food Safety and Quality

Food and Health
- Food determines health, nutrition and productivity.
- **Unsafe food** Causes food-borne diseases
- **Food-borne Illnesses** Preventable but under-reported
- **Statistics** According to the National Family Health Survey 2015-2016, over 9 lakh children in India suffer from acute diarrhea.

Impact of Food-borne Illnesses
- Mortality
- Increased healthcare costs
- Economic loss (e.g., trade, tourism, unemployment, litigation)
- **Importance**
  Crucial for both home and large-scale food production

Historical Shift
- **Earlier Time** Food processed at home
- **Now a Days** Technological advancements and industrial processing

Factors Driving Change
- Larger incomes and better purchasing power.
- Increased consumer demand for functional foods.
- **Quality of Food** Includes raw and processed foods.
- **Public Health Concern** Needs proper management and assessment of safety.

2 Rising Importance of Food Quality

- **Multiple Handling** Increased contamination risk.
- Processed/raw foods (spices, oilseeds) are major health concerns.
- Risk assessment needed from production to distribution.
- New pathogens, global travel, and antibiotic resistance increase food-borne diseases.
- Pollution, pesticides, and additives raise food safety concerns.

Food Safety
- Refers to handling food to prevent illness.
- **Toxicity** Harmful substance potential.
- **Hazard** Agents (biological, chemical, physical) causing health risks.

Food-borne Illnesses
- **Food Infection** Caused by live pathogens (e.g., Salmonella).
- **Food Intoxication** Caused by toxins from bacteria (e.g., Staphylococcus aureus).

Microbial Pathogens
- New pathogens emerge due to global food systems and climate. (e.g., Norovirus, Rotavirus, Hepatitis E).

Contamination Vs. Adulteration
- **Contamination** Harmful substances in food.
- **Adulteration** Lowering food quality by adding inferior materials.

Food Quality
- Influenced by nutritional and sensory properties (taste, texture, colour).
- Ensured through standards and hygiene practices.

Maintaining Food Quality
- Quality raw materials, clean environments, proper storage, hygiene and good service practices.

3 Food Standards

- **Food Standards** Criteria ensuring food is safe for consumption (e.g., composition, additives).
- **FSSAI (India)** Regulates food standards, covers additives, contaminants, labeling.
- **Acts** Prevents adulteration (PFA Act, 1954) and sets food quality requirements.

Voluntary Certification
- **ISI Mark** Ensures processed food safety.
- **Agmark** Certifies agricultural products.
- **FSSA, 2006** Consolidates food laws, regulates food safety, and focuses on safety standards.
- **FSSAI Functions** Frames regulations, accredits bodies, advises governments, monitors food risks and promotes awareness.

4 International Organisations and Agreements

Role of International Organisations
- Enhance food safety, quality and security.
- Facilitate research and trade.

Key Organisations

Codex Alimentarius Commission (CAC)
- Sets international food standards.
- Protects consumer health and facilitates food trade.
- Published Codex Alimentarius (food code) with standards and guidelines.

International Organisation for Standardisation (ISO)
- Develops voluntary, consensus-based international standards.
- ISO 9000: Focuses on quality management systems.

World Trade Organisation (WTO)
- Regulates global trade, ensuring smooth, fair, and predictable trade.
- Covers goods, services and intellectual property.

5 Food Safety Management Systems

Food Safety Management Systems
- Set of standards to manage food safety across the food chain.
- Addresses food hazards (biological, chemical, physical) at every stage.

Good Manufacturing Practices (GMP)
- Ensures proactive steps to maintain food safety.
- Minimises contamination and false labeling.
- Improves compliance and performance.

Good Handling Practices (GHP)
- Comprehensive approach to identify and minimise contamination risks.
- Ensures hygiene practices from farm to consumer.

Hazard Analysis Critical Control Point (HACCP)
- System to control biological, chemical and physical hazards.
- Covers all stages from raw material to finished product.
- Preventive approach to ensure food safety and quality.

6 Scope of Food Safety and Quality

Indian Food Safety and Standards Act (2006)
- Major shift in food laws for greater consumer protection.
- Ensures safety and wholesomeness of food at all stages.

Career Opportunities
- **Required Expertise** Food Chemistry, processing, preservation, microbiology, laws, sensory evaluation.
- **Roles** Food legislators, safety officers, analysts, auditors, and quality control experts.
- Positions in regulatory bodies, public health agencies, Agmark, BIS and food industries.

Entrepreneurship
- Self-employment opportunities in food safety consultancy, analytical labs and education.

Career Avenues
- Quality control and food testing labs.
- HACCP specialists, food auditors, ISO certification.
- Teaching, research, scientific writers and voluntary organisations.

NCERT Folder

1. Explain why food safety and quality are of global concern.

Or Give an account of the factors that have made issues related to food, safety and quality of global concern. **Diksha App**

Or Give the significance of food, safety and food quality. **Diksha App**

Ans. Food safety and quality are of global concern because food-borne illnesses are a burden on public health and contribute significantly to the cost of health care. These illnesses are a preventable and underreported public health problem. Although anyone can get a food-borne illness, some people are at greater risk. For example,

- Children younger than age 5 have the highest incidence of infections from some food-borne pathogens which can be easily carried away and be transferable.
- People older than 50 years or those with reduced immunity are at greater risk for hospitalisations and death from intestinal pathogens commonly transmitted through unhygienic foods.

Food quality is an important aspect of manufacturing food. This is because consumers are susceptible to any form of contamination that may occur during the manufacturing process. Many consumers also rely on manufacturing and processing standards, particularly to know what ingredients are present, due to dietary, nutritional requirements or medical conditions like diabetes or allergies.

2. Explain the terms: Hazard, toxicity, contamination, food quality, adulteration.

Ans. **Hazard** A food hazard is a biological, chemical or physical agent in a food with the potential to cause adverse health effects.

Toxicity It is the capacity of a substance to produce harm or injury of any kind under any conditions.

Contamination It is the presence of harmful or objectionable foreign substances in food such as chemicals, micro-organisms, dilutants before/during or after processing or storage.

Food Quality The term food quality refers to attributes that influence a product's value to consumers. This includes both negative attributes such as spoilage, contamination, adulteration, food safety hazards as well as positive attributes such as colour, flavour, texture.

Adulteration Food adulteration is the process in which the quality of food is lowered either by the addition of inferior quality material or by extraction of valuable ingredient. It not only includes the intentional addition or substitution of the substances but biological and chemical contamination during the period of growth, storage, processing, transport and distribution of the food products.

3. What is Codex Alimentarius?

Ans. The Codex Alimentarius or 'Food Code' is a collection of internationally adopted food standards, guidelines, codes of practice adopted by the Codex Alimentarius Commission and related texts presented in a uniform manner. These food standards and related texts aim at protecting consumers' health and ensuring fair practices in the food trade. The publication of the Codex Alimentarius is intended to guide and promote the elaboration and establishment of definitions and requirements for foods to assist in their harmonisation and in doing so to facilitate international trade.

4. Discuss the significance of HACCP.

Ans. HACCP is so important because it

- Prioritises and controls potential hazards in food production.
- Controls major food risks, such as micro-biological, chemical and physical contaminants.
- Provides the framework to produce foods safely and to prove they were produced safely.
- Focuses on prevention and control of potential food safety hazards rather than inspection.
- Covers all types of potential food safety hazards whether they are naturally occurring in the food, contributed by the environment or generated by a mistake in the manufacturing process. Hazards such as Biological hazards (e.g. bacteria, viruses, etc.), Chemical hazards (e.g. pesticide residues, nitrates, etc.) and Physical hazards (e.g. metal, glass, etc.).
- It is important for consumer protection.

5. List the national and international food standards.

Ans. Following are the national food standards

- Voluntary product certification
- Food Safety and Standards Act (FSSA), 2006
- The Prevention of Food Adulteration Act, 1954 (PFA, 1954)
- Fruit and Vegetable Product Order
- Meat Food Products Order
- Vegetable Oil Products Order

Following are the international food standards

- Codex Alimentarius Commission (CAC)
- International Organisation for Standardisation (ISO)
- World Trade Organisation (WTO)

Exam Pattern Questions

Objective Type Questions

Multiple Choice Questions

1. What can lead to food-borne illnesses?
(a) Unsafe food
(b) Manufacturing practices
(c) Food
(d) Nutritious beverages

2. Why are food safety and quality important at large scale food production?
(a) Food is handled by many people
(b) Food undergoes several procedures
(c) Both (a) and (b)
(d) Food is not cooked at home

3. Food safety is of public health concern, globally. Choose the option which is an example of hazardous food. Competency Based Que
(a) Chalk powder in sugar (b) Lead in turmeric
(c) Cockroach in noodles (d) All of these

4. Choose the example of chemical hazard.
(a) Feathers (b) Pesticide residues
(c) Mice droppings (d) Worms

5. Which of the following is a visible biological hazard in food? CBSE SQP 2024
(a) Virus (b) Stones
(c) Protozoa (d) Caterpillars

6. Choose the correct pair of food hazard with its example. CBSE 2025
(a) Visible biological hazard : Bacteria
(b) Invisible microbiological hazard : Worms
(c) Chemical hazard : Bone fragments
(d) Physical hazard : Hair

7. Salmonella exists in the intestinal tract of animals raw milk and eggs but it can be destroyed by .... CBSE SQP 2020
(a) Heating (b) Cooling
(c) Refrigeration (d) Deep Freezing

8. Rahul ate a sandwich which appeared good and smelled pleasant. Within few hours he complained of severe stomachache, nausea and vomiting. This could be attributed to Competency Based Que; CBSE SQP, 2021
(a) Food adulteration (b) Food intoxication
(c) Food infestation (d) Food contamination

9. In how many minutes can Salmonella bacteria double their number? CBSE SQP Term I, 2021
(a) Every 10 minutes (b) Every 20 minutes
(c) Every 40 minutes (d) Every 5 minutes

10. Staphylococcus Aureus which is present in air, dust and water can cause. Diksha App
(a) Food poisoning (b) Food intoxication
(c) Food infection (d) Food adulteration

11. The presence of harmful or objectionable foreign sustances in food is called
(a) Adulteration (b) Toxicity
(c) Contamination (d) Hazard

12. Kiran bought 1 kg of tur dal from a local shopkeeper nearly. She found a no. of yellow coloured stones with dal. The presence of stone is called
(a) Contamination (b) Physical hazard
(c) Adulteration (d) Spoilage

13. Which of the following are the sources of Salmonella infection?
(a) Raw milk (b) Eggs
(c) Lentils (d) Both (a) and (b)

14. Agmark is a certification scheme for processed foods. Which type of foods contain Agmark? Competency Based Que
(a) Packaged foods (b) Agricultural products
(c) Ready to eat foods (d) None of these

15. Which of the following is not the function of FSSAI? CBSE SQP Term I, 2021

I. To establish international standards to protect the health of consumers.
II. Promote general awareness about food safety and food standards.
III. To promote the development of standardisation and related activities in the world.
IV. Provide training programmes for persons who are involved or intend to get involved in food businesses.

Choose the correct option
(a) I and II (b) II and IV (c) III and IV (d) I and III

16. Reflects international shift in food laws from vertical standards to horizontal standards.
(a) PFA (b) FSSA (c) ISO (d) FPO

17. Food colours and preservatives are examples of which type of hazard?

(a) Chemical hazard (b) Physical hazard
(c) Visible biological hazard (d) Microbiological hazard

18. If the food gets spoiled during transportation, then it shows a lack of control in which of the food safety management systems? **Competency Based Que; CBSE SQP 2024**

(a) ISO (b) GMP (c) GHP (d) GDP

19. Which of the following are voluntary grading and marking schemes in food standards?

(a) ISI mark and FSSAI (b) ISI mark and Agmark
(c) Agmark and Ecomark (d) FSSAI and BSI

20. Codex India is located at **CBSE SQP Term I, 2021**

(a) Ministry of Food Processing Industries
(b) Department of Agriculture and Co-operation
(c) Ministry of Health and Family Welfare
(d) Directorate General of Health

21. Which of the following is not the function of HACCP?

(a) Preventive approach to ensure food safety
(b) Enables only producers to utilise resources efficiently
(c) Assures consistently good quality products
(d) Detect hazards at any stage of processing or manufacturing of food

22. Match the organisation of food safety and quality given in List-I with its description in List-II? **CBSE 2025**

List I (Organisation)	List II (Description)
A. CAC	1. Worldwide non-governmental federation
B. ISO	2. Publishes 'Food Code' document
C. WTO	3. Voluntary Product Certification of India
D. BIS	4. Established in 1995 for administering trade agreements in the world

Codes

	A	B	C	D		A	B	C	D
(a)	4	3	2	1	(b)	3	4	1	2
(c)	2	1	4	3	(d)	3	2	4	1

Picture Based Question

23. Identify the type of food hazard given in the picture below

(a) Invisible chemical hazard
(b) Physical hazard
(c) Visible biological hazard
(d) Invisible microbiological hazard

Assertion-Reason Questions

Direction (Q. Nos. 24-25) Given below are two statements labelled as Assertion (A) and Reason (R). Read the statements and choose the correct option.

Codes

(a) Both A and R are true and R is the correct explanation of A.
(b) Both A and R are true, but R is not the correct explanation of A.
(c) A is true, but R is false.
(d) A is false, but R is true.

24. Assertion (A) Food quality refers to the texture of meal.
Reason (R) The WTO Agreement covers goods, services and intellectual property.

25. Assertion (A) New pathogens can be discovered in food with time.
Reason (R) Changes in human susceptibility, increased globalisation of food leads to transfer and emergence of pathogens in foods.

Cased Based Questions

26. Read the given passage and answer the following questions.

In 2014, FDA, the U.S. Centers for Disease Control and Prevention (CDC), Canadian health and regulatory officials and state and local officials investigated an outbreak of Salmonella Newport, Salmonella Hartford and Salmonella Oranienburg infections. The preliminary epidemiologic investigation identified chia seed powder as an item of interest. From this, the investigators began to narrow the focus by asking more specific questions.

Several case patients identified chia seeds or powder produced by a company in California. Investigators engaged with this business and learned that the product was manufactured in Canada. Laboratory testing by state partners isolated the outbreak strains from samples of leftover products collected from ill people's homes and from unopened retail samples. With increased sampling, more Salmonella serotypes were identified. A traceback investigation identified a Canadian manufacturer as a common supplier of organic sprouted chia powder used in these products. The products were exported to a company in California where they were re-packaged for further distribution and retail sale.

On 28th May, 2014, FDA, CDC and the California Department of Public Health warned consumers not to eat products that contained organic sprouted chia seed powder. The epidemiologic, laboratory and traceback investigations linked this international outbreak to a novel vehicle, organic sprouted chia seed powder.

(i) "Food preparation methods by the consumer or points of service can change the risk level of pathogen contamination and have led to novel food vehicles responsible for outbreaks". Based on the given statement choose which of the following is a common food-bacteria pair which is not harmful for human consumption.

(a) Curd – Lacobacillus casei
(b) Raw meat – Salmonella typhi
(c) Spinach – Escherichia coli
(d) Molluska – Norovirus

(ii) Such outbreaks can be prevented if

I. Proper precautions are taken
II. International and national food standards have been followed
III. HACCP is effectively applied
IV. Investigation is done

Codes

(a) I and II (b) II and III
(c) III and IV (d) I and IV

(iii) Given below are two statements labelled as Assertion (A) and Reason (R).

Assertion (A) The international outbreak was linked to a novel food vehicle, organic sprouted chia seed powder.

Reason (R) The manufacturer intentionally contaminated the food products with Salmonella.

Codes

(a) Both A and R are true and R is the correct explanation of A.
(b) Both A and R are true, but R is not the correct explanation of A.
(c) A is true, but R is false.
(d) A is false, but R is true.

(iv) Given below are two statements labelled as Assertion (A) and Reason (R).

Assertion (A) The investigation linked the outbreak of Salmonella infections to organic sprouted chia seed powder.

Reason (R) The preliminary epidemiologic investigation identified chia seed powder as an item of interest based on patient interviews.

Codes

(a) Both A and R are true and R is the correct explanation of A.
(b) Both A and R are true, but R is not the correct explanation of A.
(c) A is true, but R is false.
(d) A is false, but R is true.

27. Read the given passage and answer the following questions.

Factors that are important in the emergence of pathogens include human host, animal hosts and their interactions with humans, the pathogen itself and the environment including how food is produced, processed, handled and stored. For example, changes in host susceptibility due to malnutrition, age and other conditions can allow for the emergence of new infections in vulnerable populations. Genetic exchange or mutations in the organisms can create new strains with the potential to cause disease.

Exposure to new pathogens through changes in eating habits, climate, mass production, food processing and increased globalisation of the food supply can allow pathogens to emerge in new populations or new geographic areas.

(i) Which of the following does not contribute to 70 per cent of the viral cases?

(a) Rotavirus (b) Hepatitis E
(c) Norovirus (d) Malaria

(ii) One can get exposed to new pathogens through which of the following factors?

I. Climate **II. Mass production**
III. Eating habits **IV. Viral infections**

Choose the correct option

(a) I, II and III (b) II, III and IV
(c) I and II (d) III and IV

(iii) Given below are two statements labelled as Assertion (A) and Reason (R).

Assertion (A) It is essential to understand the terms contamination and adulteration in the context of food safety.

Reason (R) Understanding these terms helps in developing methods to detect the presence of pathogens in foods.

Codes

(a) Both A and R are true and R is the correct explanation for A.
(b) Both A and R are true, but R is not the correct explanation for A.
(c) A is true, but R is false.
(d) A is false, but R is true.

(iv) Given below are two statements labelled as Assertion (A) and Reason (R).

Assertion (A) Genetic exchange or mutations in organisms can create new strains with the potential to cause disease.

Reason (R) Mass production and food processing have no impact on the emergence of pathogens.

Codes

(a) Both A and R are true and R is the correct explanation for A.

(b) Both A and R are true, but R is not the correct explanation for A.

(c) A is true, but R is false.

(d) A is false, but R is true.

Answers

1. (a) Unsafe food
2. (c) Both (a) and (b)
3. (d) All of these
4. (b) Pesticide residues
5. (d) Caterpillars
6. (d) Physical hazard : Hair
7. (a) Heating
8. (b) Food intoxication
9. (b) Every 20 minutes
10. (b) Food intoxication
11. (c) Contamination
12. (b) Physical hazard
13. (d) Both (a) and (b)
14. (b) Agricultural products
15. (d) I and III
16. (b) FSSA
17. (a) Chemical hazard
18. (c) GHP
19. (b) ISI mark and Agmark
20. (c) Ministry of Health and Family Welfare
21. (b) Enables only producers to utilise resources efficiently
22. (c) 2 1 4 3
23. (c) Visible biological hazard
24. (d) A is false, but R is true.
25. (a) Both A and R are true and R is the correct explanation of A.
26. (i) (a) Curd-Lacobacillus casci
    (ii) (b) II and III
    (iii) (d) A is false, but R is true.
    (iv) (a) Both A and R are true and R is the correct explanation of A.
27. (i) (d) Malaria (ii) (a) I, II and III
    (iii) (b) Both A and R are true, but R is not the correct explanation for A.
    (iv) (c) A is true, but R is false.

Subjective Questions

Very Short Answer Type Questions

1. Exposure to new pathogens through chances in eating habits, climate, food processing, etc. can allow pathogens to emerge new populations of new geographic areas. Give two examples to justify the statement. **Competency Based Que; Diksha App**

Ans. The two examples that justify the given statement are as follows

(i) Genetic exchange or mutations in the organisms can create new strains with the potential to cause disease.

(ii) Norovirus, Rotavirus, hepatitis E contributing to about 70 per cent of cases.

2. Write down the factors responsible for the emergence of pathogens. **Diksha App**

Ans. Factors that are significant in the emergence of pathogens include

- Human host
- Animal hosts
- Pathogens interaction with humans
- Pathogen itself
- Environment, in which food is produced, processed, handled and stored.

3. What do you mean by food infection or poisoning?

Ans. The illness caused by food contaminated with bacteria, viruses, parasites or toxins led to food infection or poisoning.

4. Write any two ways by which Salmonella bacteria spreads. **CBSE 2023**

Ans. Two ways by which Salmonella bacteria spreads are as follows

- Cross-contamination could happen when raw meat/ poultry is cut on a chopping board and without cleaning, it is used for another food which does not involve any cooking such as salad.
- Inadequate cooking.

5. Define the term food standards.

Ans. It is generally defined as "The law sets out rules that cover the preparation, composition and labelling of food supplied for human consumption".

6. Differentiate between Food Infection and Food Intoxication. CBSE 2023

Ans. Difference between Food Infection and Food Intoxication are as follows

Food Infection	Food Intoxication
It is caused by eating contaminated food. Infectious organisms including bacteria, viruses and parasites or their toxins are the most common causes of food infection which multiply in the body and cause disease.	It occurs when food poisoning micro-organisms produce a toxin that triggers sickness when ingested.
For example, Salmonella exists in the intestinal tract of animals and raw milk and eggs are also sources.	For example, Staphylococcus Aureus and micro-organisms like it exist in air, dust and water.

7. What do you mean by Food Safety Management System?

Ans. The Food Safety and Management Systems is a set of standards established to direct and control food safety aspects.

8. Mention two adulterants commonly found in coffee.

Ans. Two adulterants commonly found in coffee are roasted chicory seed powder and tamarind seed powder.

9. Discuss the Prevention of Food Adulteration Act, 1954.

Ans. The Prevention of Food Adulteration Act, 1954 (PFA, 1954) was enacted by the Government of India to prevent adulteration of food. The act has been amended over 200 times as per need.

10. Mention the standard marks that you would look for while buying packets of baking powder and pure ghee.

Ans. The standard mark for baking powder is the certification mark 'ISI mark' given by BIS. The standard mark for pure ghee is the AGMARK certification mark.

11. Why good handling practices are essential to ensure food safety and quality?

Ans. Good handling practices indicate a comprehensive approach from the farm to the store or consumer, in order to identify potential sources of risk and indicates what steps and procedures are taken to minimise the risk of contamination. It ensures that all persons who handle food have good hygiene practices.

12. Apart from buying reputed brands from reputed shops, what four precautions would you adopt to buy unadulterated red chilly powder?

Ans. Precautions to be adopted to buy unadulterated black pepper/red chilly/coriander powder are

- Avoid buying loose powder if possible.
- Check the packets for standardisation labels like AGMARK and the logo of FSSAI.
- Read the labels on the packets carefully.
- Note any unusual changes in colour, texture or smell, if buying loose powder.

13. Difference between Codex and ISO. CBSE 2021 C

Ans. The differences between Codex and ISO are discussed below

	Codex	ISO
(i)	They are used to develop national regulations.	They are voluntary regulations.
(ii)	They are slow to change.	There standards are reviewed in every five years.
(iii)	They describe the minimal acceptable practices.	They describe current standard industrial practices.

14. Explain, the role of HACCP in ensuring food safety and quality. CBSE 2021 C

Ans. HACCP plays important role in ensuring food safety and quality. Some of these are

- It is a preventive approach to ensure food safety.
- It enables producers, processors, distributors and exporters to utilise resources efficiently and in a cost effective manner for assuring food safety.

15. Give full forms of the following international organisations dealing with food standards, quality and trade.

(a) CAC (b) ISO (c) WTO

Ans. (a) CAC : Codex Alimentarius Commission

(b) ISO : International Organisation for Standardisation

(c) WTO : World Trade Organisation

16. Various job options are available in food industry with respect to food safety and quality control. Get information on any four career avenues available in this field from your brother who has completed his Masters in Food Microbiology. CBSE 2024

Ans. Career avenues avilable in food industry with respect to food safety and quality control are as follows

(i) Quality control laboratories in food industry as analysts or at managerial level.

(ii) Specialist in HACCP

(iii) Food Auditors (iv) Scientific Writers.

17. Write down the mission of International Organisation for Standardisation (ISO).

Ans. The mission of International Organisation for Standardisation (ISO) is to

- Promote the development of standardisation and related activities in the world with a view to facilitate the international exchange of goods and services.
- To develop co-operation in the spheres of intellectual, scientific, technological and economic activity.

Short Answer Type Questions

1. Discuss about three types of hazards along with an example for each. **CBSE SQP 2024**

Or **"Hazards cause adverse effects on the health of consumers". With reference to the given statement discuss three types of food hazards.**

Ans. Hazards is the relative probability that harm of injury will result when substance is not used in a prescried manner and quantity. Hazards can be physical, chemical and biological causing harmful/adverse effects on the health of consumers.

The three types of hazards are given below

(i) **Physical Hazards** These are foreign materials not normally found in food. Examples include wood, stones, parts of pests or hair.

(ii) **Chemical Hazards** These involve chemicals or harmful substances that may be intentionally or unintentionally added to food. Examples include pesticides, chemical residues, toxic metals, polychlorinated biphenyls, preservatives and food colourings.

(iii) **Biological Hazards** These are living organisms that can cause contamination. Visible examples include flies and cockroaches, while invisible examples include bacteria, yeast and viruses.

2. List the factors that have contributed to the increasing incidence of microbial food-borne diseases.

Ans. The factors that have contributed to the increasing incidence of microbial food-borne diseases are

- **Changing Eating Habits** More people are consuming food prepared outside the home, increasing the risk of exposure to unsafe food handling and preparation practices.
- **Mass Production and Distribution** Large-scale food production and complex supply chains can lead to widespread contamination if safety measures are not strictly enforced throughout the process.
- **Increased Microbial Adaptation** Micro-organisms are evolving and adapting, leading to the emergence of new strains that may be more virulent or resistant to common food safety measures.
- **Globalisation and International Travel** Increased movement of people and food products across borders facilitates the spread of pathogens, allowing them to reach new populations and regions more easily.

3. Discuss the four levels of food standards which are well co-ordinated.

Ans. There are four major levels of standards which are well co-ordinated.

They are as follows

(i) **Company Standards** These are usually prepared by a company for its own use. These are the copies of national standards.

(ii) **National Standards** These are issued by the national standards body, Food Safety and Standards Authority of India (FSSAI).

(iii) **Regional Standards** Regional groups with similar geographical, climate, etc. have legislation standardisation bodies.

(iv) **International Standards** These are published by the International Organisation for Standardisation (ISO) and Codex Alimentarius Commission (CAC).

4. Suggest some tasks that should be undertaken by the food industry to ensure food safety.

Ans. The food industry can undertake following tasks to ensure food safety

- It may conduct hazard analysis test in order to identify hazards and finally removing them.
- It can also establish critical limits for each controlling point, procedures in order to maintain food making actions and to establish verification procedures in order to confirm the corrective steps taken.
- Extensive training should be given to the employees since they are also responsible for the right handling of food products.
- Distributors must ascertain the quality check of food articles.

5. (i) What is the full name of the comprehensive law that consolidated various old food laws in India? When was it enacted?

(ii) A food manufacturing company is establishing a Food Safety Management System. Describe two systems the company can use to ensure food safety and quality. **CBSE 2025**

Ans. (i) The full name of the law is the Food Safety and Standards Act. It was enacted in 2006 to unify and update India's food safety laws.

(ii) The two systems that a company can use to ensure food safety and quality are

- **HACCP (Hazard Analysis and Critical Control Points)** A system that identifies risks in food production and ensures they are controlled.
- **ISO 22000** An international standard focusing on safe food practices across the production process, from raw materials to packaging.

6. Which steps should be taken on the part of the customers to ensure food quality and safety?

Ans. On the part of consumers, following food quality and safety steps are to be performed

- Washing hands before handling food.

- Keeping raw material separate from the processed food.
- Consuming food article within the prescribed time.
- Analysing of the food ingredients according to their needs.
- Reading the labels on the food item carefully for manufacturing date, batch no., best before date, possible allergens present, etc.
- Checking the standardisation mark as per the food product e.g. ISI mark on processed foods, Agmark on agricultural products, etc.

7. What is food quality? What are its attributes? Diksha App

Ans. Food quality is a term that refers to the attributes that influence a product value to customers.

Food quality has both negative and positive attributes, which are as follows

Negative attributes

(i) contamination (ii) spoilage
(iii) adulteration (iv) safety hazards

Positive attributes

(i) colour (ii) flavour
(iii) texture

Besides, above mentioned attributes, safety is the preliminary attribute of food quality.

8. (i) "Food safety challenges have changed globally as well as in India, and Food Quality and Food Safety have gained tremendous importance". In this context, highlight two significant reasons of importance of Food Quality and Safety. CBSE 2025

(ii) Identify two common food-borne pathogens that can spread infection in healthy individuals.

Ans. (i) The two significant reasons of importance of Food Quality and Safety are

- Food quality ensures that the food we eat is nutritious and free from harmful substances, protecting our health and improving overall well-being.
- Food safety prevents contamination and food-borne diseases, ensuring the food is safe to consume and meeting global health standards.

(ii) The two common food-borne pathogens that can be spread infection in healthy individuals are

- **Salmonella** It is found in raw meat, eggs and dairy products and it can cause food poisoning.
- **E. coli** It is found in undercooked food or contaminated water, which can lead to stomach infections.

9. What are the points to be borne in mind by all food service providers to ensure food safety? Diksha App

Ans. Here are six points to ensure food safety by all food service providers

(i) Quality of Raw Materials Ensure that all raw materials and water used in food preparation meet safety and quality standards.

(ii) Cleanliness Maintain cleanliness in premises, personnel, equipment, and food preparation areas to prevent contamination.

(iii) Proper Storage Store food at appropriate temperatures to inhibit the growth of harmful micro-organisms.

(iv) Food Hygiene Follow strict food hygiene practices, including proper handwashing and sanitisation procedures for food handlers.

(v) Good Manufacturing Practices (GMP) Implement GMP to minimise the risk of contamination during food production.

(vi) Training Provide training for staff on food safety protocols and best practices to ensure compliance and awareness of food safety issues.

10. Mrs. Ramvati has started her own bread manufacturing unit. She wants to get her manufacturing unit certified by Government of India. CBSE 2023

(i) Name the new Food Safety Act implemented in India. Competency Based Que

(ii) Which year it was implemented?

Ans. (i) The new Food Safety Act implemented in India is Food Safety and Standards Act (FSSA). The main objective of this act was to consolidate the laws relating to food. The Food Safety and Standards Authority of India was established for laying down science-based standards for food and to regulate their manufacture, storage, distribution, sale and import, to ensure availability of safe and wholesome food for human consumption.

(ii) Food Safety and Standards Act (FSSA) was implemented in the year 2006.

11. Enumerate three roles of Codex Alimentarius Commission (CAC) in enhancing food safety. CBSE SQP 2024

Ans. Three roles of Codex Alimentarius Commission (CAC) in enhancing food safety are

(i) Establishing International Standards CAC sets global standards for food safety and quality to protect consumer health and ensure that food products are safet to eat.

(ii) Facilitating Trade By harmonising food safety standards, CAC helps streamline international trade, reducing barriers and fostering smoother exchanges between countries.

(iii) **Publishing Guidelines** CAC publishes comprehensive documents that include standards, codes of practice, and guidelines, which help protect consumers and promote fair practices in the global food trade. These resources guide countries in developing and implementing effective food safety regulations.

12. Give an account of the factors that are important for the emergence of pathogens.

Ans. The emergence of pathogens can be influenced by several key factors

(i) **Human Hosts** Changes in human demographics, behavior and health can impact susceptibility to infections, allowing pathogens to spread more easily.

(ii) **Animal Hosts** Interaction between humans and animals (zoonotic diseases) can facilitate the transfer of pathogens, especially in areas where wildlife and livestock are in close proximity.

(iii) **Pathogen Characteristics** Genetic mutations or exchanges among pathogens can lead to new strains with enhanced virulence or resistance to treatments, increasing their impact on human health.

(iv) **Environmental Conditions** Factors such as climate change, pollution, and urbanisation can create new habitats for pathogens, affecting their transmission dynamics.

(v) **Food Production and Processing** Mass production and globalisation of food supply chains can introduce pathogens into new regions and populations, especially if safety measures are inadequate.

(vi) **Global Travel** Increased international travel allows for the rapid spread of pathogens across geographic boundaries, making local outbreaks potentially global issues.

13. HACCP involves identification of food hazards during each stage in the food chain. CBSE 2024

(i) Give full form of HACCP.

(ii) Mention three reasons why implementing HACCP in food industry is important.

Ans. (i) HACCP stands for Hazard Analysis Critical Control Points.

(ii) Implementing HACCP in food industry is important because of the following reasons

(a) **Ensuring Food Safety** HACCP implementation identifies and controls hazards in food production, minimising the risk of contamination and food-borne illness.

(b) **Compliance with Regulations** Adhering to HACCP standards fulfills legal requirements, preventing penalties and legal consequences for non-compliance.

(c) **Enhancing Product Quality** HACCP improves product quality and consistency by identifying cirtical control points and implementing preventive measures, thus building consumer trust and protecting brand reputation.

Long Answer Type Questions

1. Identify four ways staphylococcus can illness in your family. Suggest any four ways to cook to prevent this infection. CBSE 2021 C

Ans. The four ways in which staphylococcus can illness in a family are

(i) From person to person as staphylococcus is present in the nasal passage, throat and on skin, hair of 50 per cent of healthy individuals.

(ii) Through contaminated objects (such as gym equipment, telephones, door knobs, television remote controls or elevator buttons).

(iii) By inhalation of infected droplets dispersed by sneezing or coughing.

(iv) From dirty fingers or hands when touched to food surface or places where food is kept.

Most important rules of personal hygiene while cooking food/rules to ensure that the cook has hygiene habits are

(i) Bathing daily, washing hands with anti-bacterial soap, especially after a visit to the washroom and before cooking.

(ii) Tie the hair or cover them with a cap.

(iii) Do not cook if suffering from any skin disease or communicable disease.

(iv) Keep nails trimmed and unpainted.

2. What is the full form of FSSA? When was it enacted? Why was there a need to enact it? What are the objectives of FSSA? Diksha App

Ans. The full form of FSSA is the Food Safety and Standards Act. It was enacted in 2006. It was elected to bring the different pieces of laws, rules and regulations related to food safety under one umbrella so that the food industry may adhere to these regulations.

The objectives of FSSA are as follows

(i) To consolidate the laws relating to food.

(ii) To lay down science based standards for food.

(iii) To regulate the manufacture, storage, distribution, sale and import and to ensure availability of safe and wholesome food for human consumption.

(iv) To provide maintenance of hygienic conditions and manufacturing premises along with the management of risk factors related to human health in a scientific manner.

(v) To reflect international shift in food laws from compositional standards to safety or horizontal standards.

3. Differentiate between contamination and cross contamination. **Diksha App**

Ans. Contamination Vs. Cross-Contamination

Basis	Contamination	Cross-Contamination
Definition	The presence of harmful substances or micro-organisms in food that can compromise safety.	The transfer of harmful micro-organisms or substances from one food or surface to another, often through direct or indirect contact.
Source	Can originate from various sources, including the environment (air, soil, water), food handlers or during processing and packaging.	Typically occurs when raw foods (especially meats) come into contact with ready-to-eat foods, often due to improper handling.
Types of Hazards	Includes biological (bacteria, viruses), chemical (pesticides, toxins) and physical hazards (foreign objects).	Mainly involves biological hazards, such as bacteria transferred from raw foods to cooked or ready-to-eat foods.
Process	Can happen at any stage of the food supply chain, from production to consumption.	Specifically involves the movement of contaminants between
Impact	Can lead to food-borne illnesses and health risks depending on the type and amount of contaminant present.	Increases the risk of food-borne illnesses by transferring
Examples	Presence of E. coli in lettuce due to contaminated water.	Using the same cutting board for raw chicken and vegetables without cleaning in between.

4. A food hazard can enter/come into the food at any stage of the food chain, therefore, adequate control throughout the food chain is essential. Explain three ways with two features of each to ensure food safety and quality. Also state two importance of FSSA, 2006. **CBSE SQP, 2020**

Or **A food hazard can enter into food at any stage of the food chain. How can food safety management systems exert a control over food safety and quality?** **Diksha App**

Ans. Food Safety Management Systems (FSMS) are essential frameworks designed to ensure food safety and quality at every stage of the food chain. They provide structured processes for identifying, evaluating, and controlling food safety hazards. Here's how FSMS exert control over food safety and quality

(i) **Preventive Approach** FSMS adopt a proactive stance by identifying potential hazards before they occur. By implementing preventive measures such as Good Manufacturing Practices (GMP) and Good Handling Practices (GHP), food businesses can minimise the risk of contamination and ensure that food remains safe throughout production and distribution.

(ii) **Hazard Analysis and Critical Control Points (HACCP)** HACCP is a cornerstone of many FSMS. It involves a systematic approach to identifying critical control points (CCPs) in the food production process where hazards can be prevented, eliminated or reduced to acceptable levels.

This involves

- Conducting hazard analyses to identify potential biological, chemical and physical hazards.
- Establishing critical limits for each CCP.
- Monitoring procedures to ensure that critical limits are met.

(iii) **Training and Education** Food safety management systems emphasise the importance of training for all personnel involved in food handling. Regular training sessions ensure that employees understand food safety protocols, hygiene practices and the significance of adhering to safety standards. Educated staff are less likely to engage in practices that compromise food safety.

(iv) **Documentation and Record Keeping** FSMS require detailed documentation of all processes, from raw material sourcing to final product distribution. This includes keeping records of inspections, training and monitoring activities. Documentation helps trace back any food safety issues to their source, facilitating quicker corrective actions and ensuring accountability.

(v) **Monitoring and Verification** Continuous monitoring of food safety practices is integral to FSMS. This involves regular inspections and testing to verify that safety measures are effective. Monitoring systems help detect deviations from established procedures, allowing for immediate corrective actions.

(vi) **Supplier Management** Effective FSMS include assessments of suppliers to ensure that they meet safety and quality standards. By implementing supplier verification programmes, businesses can mitigate risks associated with raw materials and ingredients. This also involves conducting audits and requiring certifications from suppliers.

(vii) **Continuous Improvement** FSMS encourage a culture of continuous improvement by regularly reviewing and updating safety protocols. Feedback mechanisms, including audits and incident reports, help identify areas for enhancement. This adaptability is crucial in addressing emerging food safety challenges.

5. What do you understand by the term 'Standardisation Mark' and on what basis are these marks given? Which three standardisation marks are commonly followed in India for food products and for which food products are they given?

Or **What are the two main Voluntary Product Certification Schemes in India?**

Ans. The term 'Standardisation Mark' refers to the marks given by agencies sponsored by the Government of India to products of acceptable quality to ensure good health and safety of consumers.

The standardisation marks are given after the marking agency ensures the quality of the products by conducting various tests on them.

Three standardisation marks commonly followed in India for food products are

(i) **ISI** This mark is given by Bureau of Indian Standards, earlier known as Indian Standards Institution (ISI). It is mandatory for a variety of items including packaged mineral water, various packaged milk products, etc.

(ii) **AGMARK** This mark is given by the Directorate of Marketing and Inspection of the Government of India. It is given for various agricultural and livestock products at natural and processed stages.

(iii) **FPO** This mark is given by the Food Safety and Standards Authority of India. It is mandatory for all packaged fruit products.

6. Why are food standards considered to be important? What are the different level of food standard that ensure supply of hygienic food as well as facilitate trade within and between the nations?

Ans. Importance of Food Standards are

(i) **Consumer Protection** Food standards ensure that food is safe, hygienic, and of good quality, protecting consumers from health hazards and unsafe products.

(ii) **Facilitation of Trade** Standardised food regulations help facilitate international trade by ensuring that food products meet universally accepted safety and quality criteria.

(iii) **Public Health** By maintaining food safety and quality, food standards contribute to the prevention of food-borne illnesses and promote overall public health.

(iv) **Consistency and Quality Control** They provide guidelines for manufacturers to follow, ensuring consistent quality and safety across food products.

Levels of Food Standards

(i) **Company Standards** Developed by individual companies for internal use, often based on national standards, to ensure compliance with safety and quality requirements.

(ii) **National Standards** Issued by national bodies such as the Food Safety and Standards Authority of India (FSSAI), these set the legal requirements for food safety and quality within a country.

(iii) **Regional Standards** Established by regional groups to address specific geographical and climatic conditions, ensuring that local food safety needs are met.

(iv) **International Standards** Formulated by organisations such as the Codex Alimentarius Commission (CAC) and the International Organisation for Standardisation (ISO), these standards provide a global framework for food safety and quality, aiding in international trade.

7. What is a food control system? What are the components of an effective food control system? **Diksha App**

Ans. A food control system is a comprehensive framework designed to ensure the safety, quality and integrity of food products throughout the food supply chain. It encompasses regulations, standards and practices aimed at protecting public health and ensuring that food is safe for consumption. The following components of an effective food control system are

(i) **Food Inspection** Regular inspections to verify compliance with safety and quality standards. Inspectors assess food production, handling, processing, and storage to ensure regulations are met.

(ii) **Trained Personnel** Well-trained food inspectors and laboratory staff are essential for conducting thorough evaluations and analyses, ensuring expertise in food safety protocols.

(iii) **Analytical Capability** A wide range of analytical techniques is required to detect food contaminants, including chemical residues, bio-toxins, pathogenic bacteria and food-borne viruses.

(iv) **Accredited Laboratories** Laboratories must be well-equipped and accredited to perform reliable food testing and analyses, contributing to accurate assessments of food safety.

(v) **Regulatory Framework** A robust set of regulations and guidelines must be established and enforced to maintain food safety standards, including laws related to food labeling, additives and contaminants.

(vi) **Public Awareness** Educating consumers about food safety practices and encouraging them to report food safety concerns can enhance the overall effectiveness of the food control system.

8. Mr. Rampal has started his own food processing unit for exporting the products. His friend has suggested him to implement HACCP. Competency Based Que; 2023

(i) What is HACCP?

(ii) Give reasons to implement HACCP.

(iii) State some other food safety management systems. Competency Based Que

Ans. (i) HACCP Hazard Analysis Critical Control Points is a management system in which food safety is addressed through the analysis and control of biological, chemical and physical hazards from raw material production, procurement and handling, to manufacturing, distribution and consumption of the finished product.

(ii) There are several reasons to implement HACCP

- It is a preventive approach to ensure food safety.
- It enables to detect hazards at any stage of processing or manufacturing in order to maintain good quality end product by taking up appropriate action at the stage where the problem arises.
- It enables producers, processors, distributors and exporters to utilise resources efficiently and in a cost effective manner for assuring food safety.

(iii) Some other food safety management systems are

- **Good Manufacturing Practices** (GMP) These are a part of quality assurance to ensure that manufacturers are taking proactive steps to maintain safety of their products. These practices enable to minimise or eliminate contamination and false labelling so that consumer is not misled and can buy those products which are safe.
- **Good Handling Practices** (GHP) These practices involve a comprehensive approach from the farm to the store or consumer so that potential sources of risk could be identified. It also helps in deciding what steps and procedures should be adopted to minimise the risk of contamination.

9. (i) Enumerate four factors which can lead to food deterioration or spoilage.

(ii) Mention any four traditional methods by which food is preserved from spoiling after harvesting or slaughtering.

Ans. (i) Four factors which can lead to food deterioration or spoilage are

- **Infestation by Insects** Pests can contaminate and damage food.
- **Improper Temperatures** Incorrect processing or storage temperatures promote spoilage.
- **Exposure to Light and Moisture** Excessive light, oxygen or moisture can lead to degradation.
- **Microbial Contamination** Bacteria, mold and yeast can cause food to spoil and become unsafe.

(ii) Four traditional methods by which food is preserved from spoiling after harvesting or slaughtering are

- **Sun Drying** It removes moisture to inhibit spoilage.
- **Controlled Fermentation** It uses beneficial micro-organisms to preserve food.
- **Salting/Pickling** Adds salt or acids to prevent microbial growth.
- **Candying** Coats food in sugar to deter spoilage.

10. What is the scope and career opportunities available in the field of food quality and safety?

Ans. Scope of Food Quality and Safety

The field of food quality and safety is expanding rapidly due to increased consumer awareness, globalisation of food supply chains and stricter food safety regulations. This sector plays a crucial role in ensuring public health, maintaining food standards and facilitating trade.

Career Opportunities

(i) **Quality Control Laboratories** Roles as analysts or managers in food quality control labs.

(ii) **Food Testing Laboratories** Positions for food inspectors and testing specialists in both public and private sectors.

(iii) **HACCP Specialist** Experts in Hazard Analysis Critical Control Point systems to ensure food safety.

(iv) **Food Auditors** Assessing compliance with food safety standards in various organisations.

(v) **Quality Certification** Opportunities in organisations providing certifications like ISO or Agmark.

(vi) **Academics and Teaching** Positions in educational institutions focusing on food science and safety.

(vii) **Research and Development** Roles in research institutions or industries focused on innovative food safety technologies.

SELF ASSESSMENT TEST

Objective Type Questions

1. Among various hazards .... are an important cause of food-borne illnesses.
   (a) physical (b) biological (c) chemical (d) biochemical
2. Choose the correct pair.
   (a) Physical hazard : Tiny pathogen
   (b) Visible hazard : Pesticides
   (c) Chemical hazard: Wood
   (d) Invisible hazard : Adulterants
3. Which of the following are the symptoms of Salmonella?
   (a) Abdominal cramps (b) Fever (c) Diarrhoea (d) All of these
4. Food Safety and Standards Authority of India was established for laying down ....
   (a) science-based standards
   (b) appropriate standards
   (c) hygiene-based standards
   (d) None of these
5. ISO 9000 deals with .... of an organisation.
   (a) quantity- management (b) safety management (c) voluntary standards (d) None of these

Very Short Answer Type Questions

6. What does the WTO agreement covers?
7. In which forms entrepreneurship can be taken up by an individual in the field of food quality management?

Short Answer Type Questions

8. What do you mean by food intoxication? Give an example.
9. Discuss the concept of food quality in detail.
10. What is the role played by the following orders related to food **Diksha App**
    (i) Fruit and Vegetable Product Order
    (ii) Meat Food Production Order
    (iii) Vegetable Oil Product Order
11. Discuss Voluntary Product Certification.

Long Answer Type Questions

12. Explain the role of International Organisation for Standardisation.
13. Discuss the scope of Food Quality Management as a field in detail.
14. Discuss the acts enacted with respect to Food Standards Regulations in India.
15. Unsafe food is a cause of a large number of diseases. Contaminated and adulterated food leads to a number of health problems. What was the initiative taken up by the Government of India to overcome the problem of adulteration? **Diksha App**
16. Explain the role played by international organisations in enhancing food safety, quality and securing and failitating reason and trade.
17. (i) State three differences between Codex and ISO.
    (ii) How does food get cross-contaminated? Name the micro-organism, which spreads through this.
    CBSE 2024 C

06
CHAPTER

Early Childhood Care and Education

Early Childhood Care and Education (ECCE) includes various processes that support development during these early years, encompassing education, physical care, social and emotional support and intellectual stimulation.

YOUR STUDY GOALS

YOUR PRACTICE GOAL

- Objective Type Questions (39 Qs ; MCQs, A-R, Matching, Case Based)
- Subjective Questions (15 VSAs, 14 SAs, 8 LAs)

6.1 Introduction

- **Early childhood** refers to the period from **birth to 8 years of life,** a crucial stage that significantly influences future growth and learning.
- ECCE involves essential components like health care and nutrition, all vital for a child's overall development and well-being.
- Family support and community involvement are critical in promoting healthy development, creating a nurturing environment for children.
- **United Nations Educational, Scientific and Cultural Organisation** (UNESCO) defines ECCE as more than just preparation for primary school; it focuses on the holistic development of a child's social, emotional, cognitive and physical needs. The goal of ECCE is to build a strong foundation for lifelong learning and well-being, equipping children for future challenges.

6.2 Significance of ECCE

- Early childhood care and education is a vital area of study for human development. A child begins learning at a very young age, recognising family members and familiar people.
- By around **8-12 months**, a baby demonstrates fear of unknown individuals, indicating their ability to distinguish familiar faces from strangers. This fear reflects the child's growing capacity for recognition.

- A one-year-old child typically forms a strong attachment to their primary caregiver[1], following them closely. Over time, the child develops a sense of security, understanding they will not be abandoned.
- Children are generally raised within a family setting during their early years. In cases where mothers work, alternative child care arrangements are made, often involving other female family members.
- In the past, a female household member, especially in joint families, was responsible for child care[2]. However, there is now an increasing demand for institutional child care options.

Institutional Care and ECCE

- Now-a days, however, there has been increasing need of institutional child care facilities. This is evident in the form of informal settings like neighborhood set up a crèches in her home for business purposes or more formal institutional centers.
- These crèches serve as substitutes for primary caregivers but do not necessarily provide essential experiences that enrich a child's learning and development.
- A child's activities and experiences typically increase around **3 years** of age, making it crucial to provide proper stimulation during this time. Early years are vital for learning, exploration and discovery of the environment.
- At this age, children can actively engage with their surroundings e.g., familiarising with sand, flowers, water etc. Through interactions with people and materials, they build up their vocabulary.
- ECCE creates a supportive atmosphere where children feel free to express their capabilities. Proper emotional nourishment fosters emotional stability, helping children adapt to various situations and reducing instability without burdening them.
- Learning experiences provided by pre-school are beneficial for young children. A child-centered approach and play-based methods make learning enjoyable and effective.
- In a quality pre-school environment, children learn from peers, including those from challenging circumstances.
- All children naturally learn at a young age, with or without formal education, but pre-school education[3] enhances their exposure to new environments and adults, prepares them for formal schooling, creates a positive learning atmosphere, and supports growth outside the home.

Importance of Institutional Care

- Many communities, particularly in remote areas, face resource limitations that prevent older children from attending school. This is often due to their responsibility for caring for younger siblings while parents work outside the home.
- This situation hinders the education of older children. Institutional care for younger siblings allows older children to focus on their studies, freeing them from childcare duties.
- Institutional services not only support learning but also provide nutrition and health care for young children, addressing their essential needs.
- These services contribute to community development by helping to raise the next generation effectively, ensuring a healthier future for society. Early Childhood Care and Education (ECCE) benefits not only individual children but also their families and communities in the process of child-rearing.
- According to the **National Curriculum Framework (NCF) 2005** Position Paper on Early Childhood Education published by NCERT, the basic objectives of ECCE include
  - Focusing on the holistic development of the child to help them realise and reach their potential.
  - Preparing children for school by equipping them with essential skills.
  - Providing support services for women and children, aiding in family stability and development.

1 Caregiver is a family member or helper who looks after a young child regularly.

2 Child Care refers to the care or guidance of a child by a person other than the child's parents or family.

3 Pre-school Education is the education imparted to young children, including learning through play.

6.3 Basic Concepts of ECCE

- Early childhood can be divided into two stages, i.e., from birth to 3 years and 3 to 8 years, based on the developmental changes children experience during these periods.
- Infancy is the stage between birth and one or two years, during which a child is completely dependent on adults for daily needs, typically their parents or primary caregivers.
- If the mother works outside the home, the infant may be cared for by a substitute caregiver, such as a family member or a hired person.
- Care for infants can take place at home, the caregiver's home, or in an institutional setting like a creche.
- Créche[4] refers to an institution specifically designed for the care of infants and young children when home care is unavailable.
- Day care[5] is care provided for children, including infants and pre-schoolers, in the absence of a primary caregiver at home. Both crèches and day care facilities operate as all-day programmes.
- To effectively manage these settings, teachers and helpers receive proper training to care for very young children, addressing their basic needs such as safety, feeding and language development.
- A **toddler** is a child aged between 2-3 years, a term derived from the characteristic jumpy walk of young children at this age.
- This stage signifies a readiness for children to explore environments beyond their families. Teachers in this context require special training as pre-school or nursery school educators.
- Some pre-chools are known as **Montessori schools**, which are based on the principles of early childhood education established by **Maria Montessori**.
- In India, the government supports pre-school education through **Anganwadis**, which operate under the Integrated Child Development Services (ICDS) and function in both rural and urban areas.

Other Concepts

- Under ECCE, it is essential to understand that young children have a unique approach to comprehend their surroundings. Developmental psychologist **Jean Piaget** emphasised that children interpret the world differently, necessitating a supportive environment for exploration.
- ECCE institutions must acknowledge the cultural context in which they operate, as young children are unable to grasp different perspectives and realities like older children or adults can. This understanding is crucial in educational and care arrangements.
- The guiding principles of ECCE, according to the NCF (2005), include
  - Play as the basis for learning, allowing children to engage actively in their education.
  - Art as the basis of education, fostering creativity and self-expression.
  - Recognition of the special features of children's thinking, valuing their unique cognitive processes.
  - Primacy of experience over expertise, emphasising the importance of experiential learning.
  - Experience of familiarity and challenge in everyday routines, promoting growth through balanced experiences.
  - Mix of formal and informal interactions, enhancing social and learning experiences.
  - Blend of textual and cultural sources, incorporating diverse materials into learning.
  - Use of local materials, arts and knowledge, making learning relevant to the child's environment.
  - Developmentally appropriate practices, ensuring flexibility and plurality in approaches to education.
  - Health, well-being and healthy habits, prioritising the overall well-being of children.

4 Créche refers to the care provided to infants and young children in the absence of a primary caregiver at home.
5 Day Care refers to the care provided to pre-schoolers and sometimes infants in the absence of a primary caregiver at home.

Quick Test 1

1. In which age group young child is able to recognise familiar and unfamiliar people?
2. What can be seen as a substitute for the primary caregiver?
3. Which teaching method is adopted for the young children?
4. Outline the principles of early childhood education.

6.4 Preparation for a Career in ECCE

Need for Training in ECCE

Children under 6 years of age have unique ways of understanding the world and their social relationships. They have specific developmental needs that require the attention of individuals who are professionally trained in early child development and care.

ECCE training would benefit parents by providing them with insights into how and why children behave as they do, in the following ways

- ECCE training helps parents understand the expected differences between children of the same age and recognises individual differences.
- Parents will come to realise that there is no need for competitive comparisons between children, even among siblings.
- Through this training, adults who interact with children will gain a scientific understanding of development and growth, leading to more realistic expectations and interactions with children.

Skills Required by ECCE Professionals

- For individuals pursuing careers in early childhood programmes, training and knowledge of childhood development are essential.
- Early child care professionals bear a greater responsibility for the well-being of multiple children.
- Parents focus on the care of their own child, while teachers and caregivers are accountable to families, institutions and society.
- ECCE professionals should
  - be committed to children's well-being and learning.
  - be knowledgeable about children's needs and challenges to support their growth and development.

Focus During Pre-school Years

- Less emphasis on physical care (cleaning, feeding) as children gain independence.
- Teachers should prioritise
  - Providing interesting and stimulating learning opportunities.
  - Offering diverse experiences: physical, language, social-emotional and other learning areas.
  - Enhancing creative expression and exploration.
- Young children require adult guidance for learning tasks.
- Adults can creatively arrange conditions for children's exploration and expression.

Lev Vygotsky's Perspective

- Children need concerned, caring and knowledgeable adults.
- Educators should focus on understanding children's capabilities rather than just general knowledge.

Optimal Learning Environment

- Activities should match children's abilities—neither too easy nor too difficult.
- Properly matched tasks help maintain children's interest and motivation.

Essential Skills

Some of the essential skills necessary for an early childhood professional are

- He/She must have an interest in children and their development.
- He/She must have knowledge about the needs and capabilities of young children.
- He/She must have the capacity and motivation for interacting with children.
- He/She must have the skills for creative and interesting activities with children in all areas of development.
- He/She must have enthusiasm for activities like story-telling, exploration, nature and social interaction.
- He/She must have the willingness and interest in answering children's queries.
- He/She must have the capacity for understanding individual differences.
- He/She must be energetic and prepared for physical activity for a considerably long period of time.

Eligibility Criteria

If an individual wants to prepare for a career in ECCE, then it is essential that

- He/She must have studied about children's development and basic principles of care.
- An undergraduate degree in a subject that has child/human development or child psychology as a part of the course.
- If an individual desires to enter into this field soon after schooling, there is an option of one-year diploma or open university educational courses in the field.
- Nursery Teacher Training is another course that offers training in ECCE.
- Other than degrees, an individual needs to be open and interactive with children.
- An individual should also be aware of the community and culture so that pre-school activities can be designed in the context of the culture and regional environment in which the child is growing up.
- The teacher also needs to be capable in administrative and management skills that are required for record keeping, accounting and report-writing so that the institutions can maintain proper records. This ensures that contact and interaction with the parent community is effective and productive.
- The teacher needs to be equipped with a good repertoire of skills in the arts. The skills of story-telling, dance, music and voice modulation are very beneficial when working with children.
- Training courses will offer several such sessions for the trainees, but it is essential that a person is deeply involved with and willing to interact with children in several different ways.

6.5 Scope of ECCE

The scope of Early Childhood Care and Education (ECCE) is very broad, offering numerous career options for trained educators and caregivers. He/She can work

- as a teacher in a nursery school.
- as a caregiver in a créche.
- as a member of a team working on programmes for young children.
- as a governmental/non-governmental professional, planning and promoting campaigns or services for young children.
- as an entrepreneur, setting up their own child care and education-related programme, either at home or in a separate space, requiring expertise in organisation and management.
- as a co-ordinator of a programme run by someone else or as a trainer of teachers in the same field.
- as a researcher or professional in the ECCE field.

Some commonly available services in ECCE include

- Créches
- Day care centers
- Nursery schools
- NGOs
- ICDS
- Training institutes

Career Avenue

- Teacher in nursery schools.
- Caregiver in day care centres and créches.
- Team members for programmes for young children.
- Professionals to plan and promote campaigns or services for young children organised by Governments or NGOs.
- Entrepreneur in child-related activities: camps, edu-picnics, activity clubs, pre-school education centers.
- Higher studies: a postgraduate diploma or degree in early childhood education, later doctoral degrees with research in the field.

Quick Test 2

1. Which organisation has published position paper on ECCE?
2. Who is an infant? Through which institution does the government support the pre-school education?
3. What qualities must a teacher have when working with children?
4. What are some commonly available services in the field of ECCE?

Mind Map

EARLY CHILDHOOD CARE AND EDUCATION

1 Introduction to ECCE

Early Childhood Definition
- **Age** Birth to 8 years.
- **Importance** Crucial for growth and learning.
- **Impact** Influences future development.

ECCE Components
- **Health Care and Nutrition** Key for development.
- **Family Support** Essential for nurturing growth.
- **Community Involvement** Encourages positive development.
- **UNESCO** Focus on holistic development (social, emotional, cognitive, physical).

Goal of ECCE
- Foundation for lifelong learning.
- Preparation for future challenges in life and education.

Significance of ECCE

Early Learning
- Begins with recognition of family and faces.
- Attachment to caregivers enhances emotional security.

Family Role
- Family care is primary.
- Alternative child care for working parents.
- Traditionally, female family members responsible for care.

Institutional Care Trends
- Need for crèches/centers.
- Stimulation from age 3 (exploration, vocabulary).
- Child-centered, play-based learning.
- Peer exposure enhances emotional growth.

2 Institutional Care and ECCE

Need for Institutional Care
- Crèches substitute for primary caregivers.
- Often lacks enriching learning experiences.

Supportive Learning Environment
- Children feel safe to express.
- Emotional nourishment promotes adaptability.

Pre-school Education Benefits
- Prepares for school.
- Fosters positive learning atmosphere.
- Encourages social skills through peer interactions.

Importance of Institutional Care

Impact on Older Children
- Older children focus on studies without child care duties.

Community Development
- Provides nutrition and healthcare.
- Contributes to community health.

ECCE Benefits
- Supports families in child-caring.

NCF Objectives
- Holistic development Realising potential.
- School readiness Equipping with skills.
- Family stability and support.

3 Basic Concepts of ECCE

Early Childhood Stages
- **Birth to 3 years Infancy** Dependent on caregivers.
- **3 to 8 years** Ready for exploration, independence grows.

Infancy (Birth to 2 Years)
- **Care options** Home, caregiver's home, or crèches/daycare.
- **Crèche** Childcare institution.
- **Daycare** Care when primary caregiver is absent.

Toddler (2-3 Years)
- Ready to explore beyond family.
- Montessori schools and Anganwadis support early learning.

Teacher Training

Training for teachers on safety, feeding and language development.

Other Concepts in ECCE

Piaget's Theory
- Children interpret the world differently
- Need support for exploration.

ECCE Guiding Principles (NCF 2005)
- Play-based learning and art for creativity.
- Experiential learning and cultural context.
- Developmentally appropriate practices.
- Focus on health and well-being.

4 Career Preparation in ECCE

Need for ECCE Training
- Children under 6 have unique development needs.
- Training helps parents to understand child behaviour and growth.

Skills Required by ECCE Professionals
- Knowledge of child development.
- Commitment to children's well-being and learning.
- Engage with children through creative, stimulating activities.

Focus During Pre-School Years
- Focus on learning opportunities, creative expression, and exploration.
- Guidance for learning tasks.

Vygotsky's Perspective
- Children need caring and knowledgeable adults.
- Focus on understanding children's capabilities.

Essential Skills
- Interest in children and development.
- Ability to interact and engage in creative activities.
- Energetic and willing to work physically with children.

Eligibility Criteria
- Degree in child development or related field.
- Nursery Teacher Training or diploma in ECCE.
- Skills in administration and arts (story-telling, music).

5 Career Options in ECCE

- Teacher in nursery schools.
- Caregiver in crèches and day care centers.
- Programme team member for children's development.
- Government/NGO professional planning campaigns or services for young children.
- **Entrepreneur** Set up child care or education programmes (e.g., camps, pre-schools).
- Programme co-ordinator or teacher trainer in ECCE.
- Researcher in the ECCE field.

Common Services in ECCE
- Crèches and Day care centers
- NGOs
- Nursery schools
- ICDS and Training institutes

Career Avenues
- Teacher, caregiver and team member for children's programmes.
- Entrepreneur in child-related activities.
- **Higher Studies** Post-graduate or doctoral degrees in ECCE.

NCERT Folder

1. What do you understand by the term, 'Early Childhood Care and Education'?

Ans. 'Early Childhood Care and Education' (ECCE) refers to a range of processes and mechanisms undertaken to sustain and support development of a young child. It encompasses physical, social, emotional, intellectual, stimulation, health care and development.

2. What are the different care arrangements young children may require?

Ans. The different care arrangements required by the young children includes pre-schools that offer more structured, stimulating and developmentally appropriate activities led by better-trained staff, and arrangements that are generally seen in the form of crèches which is a substitute for the primary caregiver.

3. What are some of the reasons why young children need a special informal programme before formal schooling?

Ans. Some of the reasons due to which young children need a special informal programme before formal schooling are as follows

- In most of the households, there is an absence of the primary caregiver these days. This absence can be substituted for by informal progammes like 'créche', which provide for a family care setting.
- Early childhood is a great time to actively engage with people and ask questions as the children become capable of it. Informal learning programmes can help curb a child's curiosity without over burdening them.
- The environment at a pre-school is very beneficial for a child as they learn very quickly with their peers.
- Pre-school education is child-centered and can provide a child with a good and healthy learning environment.

4. What is meant by a child-centred approach?

Ans. Child-centred approach is defined as placing the child at the national centre of the learning process in which they are active participants.

This approach involves giving children choices of learning activities, with the teacher acting as a facilitator of learning.

5. What is a créche and what services does this centre provide?

Ans. Créche refers to an institution designed for the care of infants and young children in the absence of home care.

The services provided by this centre includes care of very young children fulfilling their basic needs like their safety, feeding, toilet habits, language development, social and emotional needs and learning, etc.

6. List the skills an ECCE worker must have.

Ans. Some of the essential skills necessary for an early childhood professional are

- He/She must have an interest in children and their development.
- He/She must have knowledge about the needs and capabilities of young children.
- He/She must have the capacity and motivation for interacting with children.
- He/She must have the skills for creative and interesting activities with children in all areas of development.

7. Describe how we can prepare for a career in ECCE.

Ans. If we want to prepare for a career in ECCE then it is essential that

- He/She must have studied about children's development and basic principles of care.
- An undergraduate degree in a subject that has child/human development or child psychology as a part of the course.
- If an individual desire to enter into this field soon after schooling, there is an option of one year diploma or open university educational courses in the field.
- Nursery Teacher Training is another course that offers training in ECCE.
- Other than degrees, an individual needs to be open and interactive with children.
- An individual should also be aware of the community and culture so that pre-school activities can be designed in the context of culture and regional environment in which the child is growing up.

Exam Pattern Questions

Objective Type Questions

Multiple Choice Questions (MCQs)

1. Why Early Childhood Care And Education (ECCE) is an important area of study for human development?

(a) It aims at holistic development of a child
(b) It builds a strong foundation for lifelong learning and well-being
(c) The element of maladjustment is enhanced in this system.
(d) Both (a) and (b)

2. At which age the child can distinguish between the stranger and familiar people? CBSE SQP, 2021

(a) 6-8 months (b) 8-12 months
(c) 9-10 months (d) 10-12 months

3. In what way pre-school experiences help the children?

(a) Creates good-learning environment
(b) Prepare the young child for schooling
(c) Assist in child's growth and development
(d) All of the above

4. Which of the following approaches is the most suitable for a young child?

(a) Child-centred approach (b) Play way method
(c) Formal schooling (d) Both (a) and (b)

5. Which of the following are the commonly available services in the field of ECCE?

(a) Day care centres (b) Government organisations
(c) NGOs (d) All of these

6. Which is the key sector of ICDS to provide pre-school education in remote areas? CBSE SQP, 2021

(a) Anganwadis (b) Training institutes
(c) Créche (d) Day care centres

7. 'Young children have different ways of understanding the world and they need a supportive environment'. Name the psychologist who gave this theory. CBSE SQP, 2021

(a) Piaget (b) Maria Montessori
(c) Vygotsky (d) Sigmund Freud

8. Mrs. Verma wants to open up pre-school in her locality. Which guiding principles of ECCE should be considered by her? CBSE SQP, 2021

I. Blend of textual and cultural resources
II. Use of local materials
III. Focus only on nutritious meals
IV. Promoting difficult task

Choose the correct option

(a) I and II (b) II and IV (c) I and IV (d) II and III

9. Identify the desirable qualities in a caretaker working in an Anganwadi. CBSE 2025

I. Interest in children and their development
II. Unwilling to answer children's queries
III. Inability to understand individual difference
IV. Enthusiastic and energetic

Choose the correct option from the following

(a) I and IV (b) II and III
(c) I and III (d) II and IV

10. Sheena wants to work in famous play school of the town. What qualities she must possess? CBSE SQP, 2021

I. An interest in child
II. Health status of child
III. Skills for creative activities
IV. Cooking skills

Choose the correct option from the following

(a) I and II (b) II and III (c) II and IV (d) I and III

11. Which of the following is the most essential quality if one wishes to pursue a career in ECCE?

(a) Skills in arts
(b) Skills of storytelling and voice modulation
(c) A person's deep involvement with children
(d) A person's awareness of the community

12. Which of the following offers training in ECCE?

(a) ICDS (b) NCERT
(c) National Curriculum Framework (NCF)
(d) Nursery Teacher Training

13. Which of the following is NOT a career option in Early Childhood Care and Education (ECCE)?

(a) Nursery school teacher
(b) Entreprenuer in the field of child care and education
(c) Teachers' trainer
(d) A child doctor

14. Anita has just completed her schooling. She wants to be an early childhood professional. Suggest her a suitable course from the following which will help her in fulfilling her dream. CBSE SQP, 2021

(a) Diploma in Dietetics (b) Diploma in ECCE
(c) PG Diploma in ECCE (d) Diploma in HR

15. Where can an enterpreneur set up their child care and education related programme?

(a) At their home (b) At the child's home
(c) At a separate space (d) Both (a) and (c)

16. ‘To provide opportunities for a variety of experiences including physical, language, social-emotional and other learning experiences’.
Whose responsibility is mentioned in the statement above?
(a) Society’s (b) Parents’ (c) Teachers’ (d) A child’s

17. As per the NCF (2005), the basic objectives of ECCE are **CBSE 2023**
I. Holistic development of the child to enable him/her to realise the potential
II. Preparation for school
III. Preparation essential skills in ECCE professional
IV. Providing support services for women and children
Choose the correct option.
(a) I, II and III (b) I, II and IV
(c) I, III and IV (d) II, III and IV

18. Match the following.

List-I	List-II
A. Infancy	1. Child is in the age two-three years.
B. Toddler	2. Child is ready to experience for different experiences.
C. Pre-school child	3. Child is totally dependent on adults.

Codes

	A	B	C		A	B	C
(a)	1	2	3	(b)	2	3	1
(c)	3	2	1	(d)	1	3	2

19. The tell me why stage is .... **Diksha App**
(a) infancy (b) pre-schoolers
(c) middle childhood (d) adolescence

20. The children will be able to relate better with an adult of the same..... **Diksha App**
(a) community (b) gender
(c) family (d) peer group

21. Young children have a short attention span, hence one should not be ....
(a) prepared with several activities
(b) flexible
(c) adaptor
(d) focused on completing one plan

22. While looking for a play school teacher you would prefer someone who is .... **Diksha App**
(a) graduate
(b) post graduate
(c) counselor
(d) nursery teacher trained

23. After completing her postgraduation in .... field, Reena can work as a councilor/special. **Diksha App**
(a) Human Development
(b) Food and Nutrition
(c) Resource Management
(d) Community Extension and Development

24. Pre-schools which are based on the play method called ....
(a) Montessori school (b) Play school
(c) Nursery school (d) Pre-school

25. According to............... young children have different way of understanding the world.
(a) Vygotsky (b) Piaget
(c) Maria Montessori (d) Freud

26. Pre-school education is offered by the integrated child development services through the........
(a) Immunisation (b) Anganwadi
(c) Balwadi (d) Play school

27. .... has emphasised on the need for a concerned, caring and knowledgeable adult.
(a) Vygotsky (b) Piaget
(c) Maria Montessori (d) Freud

28. .... is an institutional setting designed for the care of Infants, in the absence of home care.
(a) Day care (b) Créche
(c) Pre-school (d) Play school

29. Montessori method of teaching focus on .... **Diksha App**
(a) self directed (b) chack and talk method
(c) online learning (d) demonstrative

30. The ideal adult: child ratio for a catch is 1:5 whereas for a play school it is.
(a) 1:20 (b) 1:30 (c) 1:10 (d) 1:15

31. ICDS along with providing supplementary nutrition, immunisation and health services also. **Diksha App**
(a) Non-formal education (b) Informal education
(c) Formal education (d) Structured curriculum

32. In a créche the main objective is to attend to the physical need of an infant’s where as a pre-school.
(a) Stimulating environment
(b) Food
(c) Toilet facility
(d) Adult supervision

33. Which of the following is not a career option in the field of ECCE? **Diksha App**
(a) Educated for children
(b) Caregiver
(c) Designing and merchandising
(d) Government and NGO related to women and child development

34. The Government of India offers pre-school education in urban and rural areas through .... **CBSE 2024**
(a) Crèches
(b) Montessori schools
(c) Day care centres
(d) Anganwadis

35. Match List-I with List-II. **CBSE 2024**

List I (Related to ECCE)	List II (Age)
A. Toddler	1. 8-12 months
B. Early childhood	2. Birth-6 years
C. Fear of unknown people	3. 2-3 years
D. Integrated Child Development Services (ICDS)	4. Birth-8 years

Codes

	A	B	C	D
(a)	4	2	1	3
(b)	1	3	2	4
(c)	3	1	4	2
(d)	3	4	1	2

36. Which of the following is the guiding principles of ECCE? **CBSE SQP 2024**
(a) Blend of modern and traditional sources
(b) Mix of formal and informal interactions
(c) Based on only informal interaction
(d) Use of expensive materials, arts and knowledge

Assertion-Reason Questions

Directions (Q. Nos. 37-38) In the questions given below, there are two statements marked as Assertion (A) and Reason (R). Read the statements and choose the correct option.

Codes
(a) Both A and R are true and R is the correct explanation of A.
(b) Both A and R are true, but R is not the correct explanation of A.
(c) A is true, but R is false.
(d) A is false, but R is true.

37. Assertion (A) 3 years old children are curious to learn more.
Reason (R) Satisfying a child's curiosity by providing an optimal learning environment is an essential consideration at this age. **CBSE SQP, 2021**

38. Assertion (A) ECCE incorporates ensuring physical, social, emotional, intellectual, health- related and education care and development.
Reason (R) It aims at holistic development of a child.

Case Based Questions

39. Read the given passage and answer the following questions.

A pre-school child is so called because he/she is now ready for experiencing some sort of environment beyond that of the family (extra-familial). Even for this programme, a teacher needs to be specially trained as a pre-school or nursery school teacher. Some pre-schools for young children are often called Montessori schools. These are schools based on the principles of early childhood education as outlined by a well-known educationist Maria Montessori.

(i) What kind of programmes are day care and crèche?
I. They are child care programmes.
II. They are educational programmes.
III. They are recreational training programmes.
IV. They are formal education programmes.
V. They are all-day programmes.
Choose the correct option.
(a) I and II
(b) II and III
(c) I, II and V
(d) II, III and IV

(ii) Pre-school teachers have many responsibilities towards the young children they deal with.
Which of the following is NOT one of the responsibilities of a pre-school teacher?
(a) To ensure that a child learns a language properly
(b) To ensure that a child has nutritious and healthy diet
(c) To ensure that a child's environment is neat and clean
(d) To ensure that a child receives proper education in future

(iii) What role has the government of India played in ensuring that young children receive proper pre-school education?
(a) It has affiliated several private pre-school institutions with the Integrated Child Development Services.
(b) It has offered pre-school education through several initiatives like the Anganwadis that operate in rural and urban areas.
(c) It has sponsored the pre-school education of many children through initiatives like the Anganwadis that operate in rural and urban areas.
(d) It has trained many educators through the ICDS, to operate and provide guidance in private institutions.

(iv) Given below are two statements labelled as Assertion (A) and Reason (R).

Assertion (A) A person is required to go through an adequate process of training and enroll in a proper educational programme to become an educator at a pre-school.

Reason (R) Proper training and education programme in a mandatory requirement in Montessori schools.

Codes

(a) Both A and R are true and R is the correct explanation of A.

(b) Both A and R are true, but R is not the correct explanation of A.

(c) A is true, but R is false.

(d) A is false, but R is true.

Answers

1. (d) Both (a) and (b)
2. (b) 8-12 months
3. (d) All of the above
4. (d) Both (a) and (b)
5. (d) All of these
6. (a) Anganwadis
7. (a) Piaget
8. (a) I and II
9. (a) I and IV
10. (d) I and III
11. (c) A person's deep involvement with children
12. (d) Nursery Teacher Training
13. (d) A child doctor
14. (b) Diploma in ECCE
15. (d) Both (a) and (c)
16. (c) Teachers'
17. (b) I, II and IV
18. (c) 3 2 1
19. (b) pre-schoolers
20. (b) gender
21. (d) focused on completing one plan.
22. (d) nursery teacher trained
23. (a) Human Development
24. (a) Montessori schools.
25. (b) Piaget
26. (b) Anganwadi
27. (a) Vygotsky
28. (b) Crèche
29. (a) self directed
30. (c) 1:10
31. (a) Non-formal education.
32. (a) Stimulating environment
33. (c) Designing and merchandising
34. (d) Anganwadis
35. (b) 1 3 2 4
36. (b) Mix of formal and informal interactions
37. (b) Both A and R are true, but R is not the correct explanation.
38. (a) Both A and R are true and R is the correct explanation of A.
39. (i) (c) I, II and V
    (ii) (d) To ensure that a child receives proper education in future
    (iii) (b) It has offered pre-school education through several initiatives like the anganwadis that operate in rural and urban areas.
    (iv) (b) Both A and R are true, but R is not the correct reason for A.

Subjective Questions

Very Short Answer Type Questions

1. What is the aim of Early Childhood Care And Education (ECCE)?

Ans. Early Childhood Care and Education (ECCE) aims at the holistic development of a child's social, emotional, cognitive and physical needs in order to build a strong foundation for life long learning.

2. Define day care as an institutional setup.

Ans. Day care is the care given to the children in the pre-school years. Crèche refers to an institution designed for the care of infants and young children in the absence of home care.

3. There is a need to focus on providing opportunities to young children by adults. Give reason. **Competency Based Que**

Ans. There is a need to focus on providing opportunities to young children because they have greater requirement for adult guidance.

4. After schooling, your elder sister completed her training in ECCE. Suggest two wage employment opportunities. **CBSE SQP, 2020**

Ans. Two wage employment opportunities are

(i) As a teacher in a nursery school.

(ii) As a caregiver in a créche.

5. What two skills should Sudha possess to work as an early child care professional? **CBSE SQP, 2020**

Ans. Sudha should posses the following two skills to work as an early childhood care professional

(i) She must have knowledge about the needs and capabilities of young children.

(ii) She must have the capacity for understanding individual differences.

6. "The learning and other experiences provided by a pre-school is considered beneficial for young children". With reference to the given statement discuss the relevance of pre-school experiences.

Ans. The learning provided in pre-school is beneficial for young children in following ways

- Enhance a child's exposure to new environments and other adults.
- Prepare them for proper schooling.
- Create a good learning environment.
- Assist in a child's growth outside of their home.

7. State the objectives of ECCE stated in the NCF 2005. **Diksha App**

Or **As per the National Curriculum Framework (NCF) 2005 Position Paper on Early Childhood Education, mention any two basic objectives of Early Childhood Care and Education (ECCE).** **CBSE SQP, 2024**

Ans. According to National Curriculum Framework (NCF) 2005, Position Paper on Early Childhood Education published by NCERT, the basic objectives of ECCE are discussed below

(i) It focuses on the holistic development of the child to enable him/her to realise and reach their potential.

(ii) It prepares the child for the school.

(iii) It provides support services for women and children.

8. Discuss the period of infancy in detail.

Ans. Infancy refers to the period between birth and one or two years. In this period, a child is totally dependent on adults that may be a mother, a father or any other primary caregiver for everyday needs. In case if the mother is working outside the home, then the infant is cared by the substitute caregiver that may be family member or a hired person.

9. Which four skills would you check before hiring an early childhood professional ? **CBSE 2021 C**

Ans. The four skills which should be checked before hiring an early childhood professional are

(i) He/She must have knowledge needs and capabilities of children.

(ii) He/She should be committed towards the children and their well-being.

(iii) He/She must have capacity for understanding individual difference.

(iv) He/She must have skill for creative and interesting activities.

10. Reena your classmate aspires to become a play school's teacher, guides her so that she can fulfill her dream. **Competency Based Que; Diksha App**

Ans. Reena, to fulfill your dream of becoming a play school teacher, focus on gaining knowledge about child development and effective teaching methods. Consider enrolling in a training programme that emphasises play-based learning and creativity. Building strong communication skills will help you connect with both children and parents. Lastly, be adaptable and open to new experiences, as this will enhance your ability to engage with young learners effectively.

11. List any two activities which a play school teacher can include in her curriculum to facilitate motor development. **Diksha App**

Ans. Here are two activities a play school teacher can include in her curriculum to facilitate motor development

(i) **Obstacle Course** Set up a simple obstacle course using soft mats, tunnels and small climbing structures. This encourages children to crawl, climb, and navigate through different challenges, enhancing their gross motor skills.

(ii) **Creative Movement and Dance** Incorporate music and rhythm into activities where children can dance, jump and move freely. This promotes co-ordination, balance and body awareness while allowing for self-expression.

12. Write the full form of ICDS and ECCE? **Diksha App**

Ans. ICDS stands for **Integrated Child Development Services,** and ECCE stands for **Early Childhood Care and Education.**

13. Differentiate between a créche and a day care centre. **Diksha App**

Ans. Difference between a créche and a day care centre

- A crèche specifically caters to infants and young children when home care is unavailable, often focusing on basic care needs.
- A day care centre serves a broader age range, including pre-schoolers and typically incorporates educational activities alongside care, providing a more structured environment for learning and development.

14. While planning activities for pre-schoolers it is important to have activities for a short duration of time why.

Ans. It's important to have activities for pre-schoolers that are of short duration because

- Short Attention Spans
- Engagement and Motivation
- Variety of Experiences
- Positive Learning Environment
- Adaptability

15. Fatima Bano wants to send her 3 years old child to a pre-school. Explain to her the six attributes that she should look for in a good pre-school. **Competency Based Que; CBSE 2023**

Ans. The qualities to look for in a good pre-school are

(i) School infrastructure (ii) Curriculum
(iii) Qualified and well-trained teaching staff
(iv) Child-Centred Quality Programme
(v) Safety and security standards
(vi) Activity based learning

Short Answer Type Questions

1. "The primary objective of Early Childhood Care and Education is the holistic development of the child and preparation for school". Justify this statement with the help of three examples each. **CBSE C 2021**

Ans. Early Childhood Care and Education helps in a child's overall growth, by

(i) exposing a child to an extra-familial environment.
(ii) providing a child with a supportive and congenial atmosphere where he/she feels free to express himself/herself.
(iii) providing proper emotional nourishment.

It also helps prepare a child for formal schooling, by

(i) creating a good learning environment.
(ii) helping them engage with their peers so that they could learn better.
(iii) providing them with an authoritative as well as compassionate figure of the 'teacher', away from their home.

2. Write down the expectations from an adult teacher of young children.

Ans. Some of the expectations from an adult teacher of young children are discussed below

- He/She must have studied about children's development and basic principles of care.
- An undergraduate degree in a subject that has child/human development or child psychology as a part of the course.
- If an individual desire to enter into this field soon after schooling, there is an option of one year diploma or open university educational courses in the field.
- Nursery Teacher Training is another course that offers training in ECCE.

3. Your friends want to become a pre-school teacher. Suggest her any four skills she need to have in order to become one. **Competency Based Que; Diksha App**

Ans. To become a pre-school teacher, my friend should have the following skills

(i) **Knowledge of Child Development** Understanding the developmental needs and capabilities of young children to support their growth effectively.

(ii) **Creativity in Activities** Ability to design and implement engaging and stimulating activities that promote learning across various domains, including physical, social-emotional and cognitive development.

(iii) **Effective Communication** Skills for interacting with children, parents and colleagues, ensuring clear and supportive communication.

(iv) **Flexibility and Adaptability** Being prepared to adjust lesson plans and activities based on the children's needs and interests, given their shorter attention spans.

4. Your niece is 8 months old, suggest eight criteria your sister needs to keep in mind while selecting a créche for her. Diksha App

Ans. (i) **Safety and Hygiene** The crèche should have a clean, safe environment with child-proofed spaces and proper sanitation practices.

(ii) **Qualified Staff** Caregivers should be trained in early childhood development and have experience with infants.

(iii) **Low Child-to-Caregiver Ratio** A smaller ratio ensures that each child receives adequate attention and care.

(iv) **Nutritional Standards** The crèche should provide healthy meals and snacks appropriate for infants, along with attention to dietary restrictions.

(v) **Developmentally Appropriate Activities** The programme should include activities that stimulate sensory, motor and social development suitable for infants.

(vi) **Communication with Parents** The crèche should maintain open lines of communication with parents, providing regular updates on the child's progress and daily activities.

(vii) **Flexible Hours** The facility should offer flexible hours that accommodate your sister's work schedule.

(viii) **Positive Reviews and Recommendations** Researching feedback from other parents and checking the crèche's reputation in the community can provide valuable insights.

5. Neena is a play school teacher, she has to play an activity for the children. Write any five points she should keep in her mind while doing the same. Competency Based Que; Diksha App

Or **Which four needs of young children are catered to in a day care centre/créche?** CBSE 2024 C

Ans. Neena should keep in mind while planning an activity for the children

(i) **Developmental Appropriateness** Ensure the activity is suitable for the children's age and developmental stage, fostering their physical, cognitive and social skills.

(ii) **Safety First** Choose materials and equipment that are safe and non-toxic and ensure the activity space is free from hazards.

(iii) **Engagement and Fun** Plan an activity that is interactive and enjoyable, capturing the children's interest and encouraging participation.

(iv) **Inclusivity** Consider the diverse needs and abilities of all children, adapting the activity to ensure everyone can participate and feel included.

(v) **Learning Objectives** Identify clear learning goals for the activity, focusing on skills such as co-operation, creativity or problem-solving and incorporate these into the play.

6. Early childhood is critical for the personality development of a child friendly environment. Diksha App

Ans. Here are points highlighting why early childhood is critical for personality development in a child-friendly environment

- **Foundation of Trust** A nurturing environment fosters secure attachments between children and caregivers, helping them develop trust and a sense of safety.
- **Social Skills Development** Interacting with peers in a supportive setting teaches children essential social skills, such as sharing, co-operation and empathy.
- **Emotional Regulation** A friendly environment encourages children to express their feelings and learn to manage their emotions, promoting emotional intelligence.
- **Encouragement of Exploration** A safe, stimulating space allows children to explore their surroundings, fostering curiosity and confidence in their abilities.
- **Positive Self-Concept** Supportive interactions and encouragement from caregivers help children develop a positive self-image and a sense of identity, which are crucial for healthy personality development.

7. Provide six reasons how a pre-school environment is beneficial for young children's development. CBSE 2025

Ans. Six reasons about a pre-school environment is beneficial for young children's development are

- It encourages social skills through interaction with peers.
- It develops communication abilities by improving language skills.
- It enhances emotional growth by teaching sharing and empathy.
- It builds cognitive skills with activities like puzzles and storytelling.
- It promotes physical development through play and movement.
- It prepares children for formal schooling by instilling discipline and routines.

8. Seema is a play school teacher, help her plan one activity for a class of 4 years old.
Competency Based Que; Diksha App

Ans. Here's a simple and engaging activity Seema can plan for her class of 4 years olds

- **Preparation** Create a list of items for the children to find outside, such as a leaf, a small stone, a flower or a twig. Ensure the items are safe and easily accessible.
- **Group Discussion** Before heading outside, gather the children and discuss what each item looks like. Show pictures or examples to help them recognise what to look for.
- **Exploration Time** Take the children outside and give them a set amount of time to search for the items on the list. Encourage them to work together and share their findings.
- **Sharing** Once the scavenger hunt is over, gather the children back in a circle and let each child share what they found. This promotes language development and boosts confidence.
- **Reflection** Conclude the activity by asking the children what they enjoyed the most and what they learned about nature, reinforcing their observation and communication skills.

9. ECCE is the need of the hour. List find factors responsible for this in contemporary time. **Diksha App**

Ans. Here are five factors responsible for the increased need for Early Childhood Care and Education (ECCE) in contemporary times

(i) **Changing Family Dynamics** With more parents working outside the home, there's a greater need for reliable child care options that support working families.

(ii) **Increased Awareness of Developmental Importance** Growing recognition of the critical role early childhood experiences play in lifelong learning and development has led to heightened demand for quality ECCE programmes.

(iii) **Educational Policy Support** Governments and organisations are increasingly advocating for ECCE as part of national education strategies, emphasising its importance for social and economic development.

(iv) **Access to Quality Education** A focus on ensuring that all children have access to quality early education, particularly in underserved communities, is driving the expansion of ECCE services.

(v) **Holistic Development Emphasis** There's a growing understanding that early education should address not just academic skills but also social, emotional and physical development, leading to a broader demand for comprehensive ECCE programmes.

10. "The NEP lays a lot of impetus on Early Childhood Care and Education". **Competency Based Que**

(i) List any two factors which have led to the increase in significance of ECCE in the contemporary times.

(ii) State one contribution of each of the following in the field of ECCE **CBSE SQP 2024**

(a) Piaget (b) Vygotsky

(c) Maria Montessori

Ans. (i) Two factors which have led to the increase in significance of ECCE in the contemporary times are

- Breakdown of Traditional Joint Families Necessitates substitute care for young children.
- Increased working mothers requires reliable early childhood programmes to support working families and ensure quality care.

(ii)
- Piaget's contribution in the field of ECCE is to providing a stimulating environment where children explore and learn through their own experiences, supporting cognitive development through active interaction with their surroundings.
- Lev Vygostsky, a psychologist and educator, held that there is a great need for children to have a concerned, caring and knowledgeable adult. A kind, caring and knowledgeable adult is required for care of children.
- Maria Mostessori establishment of pre-schools for young children based on the principles of early childhood education as outlined by a well-known educationist Maria Montessori

11. Discuss the role of pre-school teacher in detail.

Ans. The role of ECCE teacher is discussed below

- For a teacher, it is not only important to be prepared with several activities but it is also essential that he/she must be adaptive and flexible with children rather than be selfish and focussed on completing one's own action plan.
- To be an effective teacher, it is often seen that a pre-school teacher has to quickly change his/her lesson plan, his/her strategies and techniques to deal with the needs of young children.
- Good preparation of a large repertoire of activities and skills is essential before an individual is starting his/her career with children.

12. (i) Distinguish between the view point of Jean Piaget and Vygotsky in context to ECCE.

(ii) State any two role of ECCE professional.

Ans. (i) Difference between the view point of Jean Piaget and Vygotsky in context to ECCE are as follows

Jean Piaget	Lev Vygotsky
Jean Piaget, tried to comprehend and explain that young children have different ways of understanding things around them. This is the reason due to which they need supportive environment so, that they can explore phenomenon in their own ways.	Lev Vygotsky, a psychologist and educator, held that there is a great need for children to have a concerned, caring and knowledgeable adult.
Another significant aspect is that ECCE institutions must realise the importance of the cultural context within which they work.	The pre-school educator must have knowledge about the child's capabilities rather than information about the world.

(ii) Two roles of ECCE professionals are

(a) Being committed towards the children, their well-being and learning and towards being knowledgeable about their needs and challenges for providing opportunities for their growth and development.

(b) Providing interesting and stimulating opportunities for children to learn new things and experience new phenomenon.

13. As per National Curriculum Framework (NCF) publication on ECCE, enlist any six guiding principles of ECCE. **CBSE 2023**

Ans. The guiding principles of ECCE, according to the NCF (2005) are

(i) Play as the basis for learning.

(ii) Art as the basis of education.

(iii) Recognition of the special features of children's thinking.

(iv) Primacy of experience rather than expertise, i.e., experiential learning is emphasised.

(v) Experience of familiarity and challenge in everyday routines.

(vi) Mix of formal and informal interactions.

14. State the objective of ECCE as stated in the NCF 2005. **Diksha App**

Ans. The objectives of Early Childhood Care and Education (ECCE) as stated in the National Curriculum Framework (NCF) 2005 include

- **Holistic Development** To promote the overall development of the child, helping them realise and reach their potential across various domains—cognitive, social, emotional and physical.
- **School Readiness** To prepare children for formal schooling by equipping them with essential skills and a positive attitude towards learning.
- **Support for Families** To provide support services for women and children, aiding in family stability and contributing to community development.

Long Answer Type Questions

1. Why there is a need for training in ECCE for parents? Discuss.

Ans. The need for raising awareness and providing training in Early Childhood Care and Education (ECCE) for parents is crucial for several reasons

- **Understanding Developmental Needs** Children under the age of six have unique ways of understanding the world, and their developmental needs differ significantly from older children. ECCE training helps parents recognise and cater to these needs, ensuring children receive the right care and attention for healthy growth.
- **Recognising Individual Differences** ECCE training equips parents with the knowledge to understand that children, even of the same age, can have different developmental trajectories. It helps parents avoid making competitive comparisons, promoting a more supportive environment where children's individuality is respected.
- **Improving Parental Expectations** With scientific insights into child development, parents can have more realistic expectations of their children. This leads to more positive and age-appropriate interactions, reducing frustration and fostering healthier parent-child relationships.
- **Enhanced Parenting Skills** ECCE training empowers parents with effective strategies for engaging with their children in developmentally appropriate ways. This helps build strong emotional bonds and promotes better social and cognitive skills in children.

2. Mr. Anil wants to open up an institution for children,

(a) Guide him about any four principles given by NCF (2005) to be kept in mind.

(b) Which four facilities must be included in the institution for children? **CBSE SQP, 2020**

Ans. (a) Four principles given by NCF (2005) to be kept in mind are

(i) Play as the basis for learning

(ii) Art as the basis of education

(iii) Mix of formal and informal interactions

(iv) use of local materials, arts and knowledge

(b) Four facilities that must be included in the institution for children are

(i) Recreational learning facilities including fun games that help in the child's education.

(ii) The institution must ensure proper safety and security of each and every child.

(iii) There should be proper sanitation in the institution including clean drinking water and a clean surrounding.

(iv) Above all, adequate medical facilities should also be made available in such an institution, since children are prone to hurting themselves during playing games and other physical activities.

3. You are opening a play school prepare a list of educational toys which you will required for facilitating holistic development of a child. **Diksha App**

Ans. Here's a list of educational toys that can facilitate the holistic development of children in a play school

- **Building Blocks** Promote fine motor skills, creativity and problem-solving as children stack and construct different shapes.
- **Puzzles** Enhance cognitive skills, hand-eye co-ordination and spatial awareness through various difficulty levels and themes.
- **Art Supplies** Include crayons, markers, paper and clay to encourage creativity, self-expression and fine motor development.
- **Musical Instruments** Simple instruments like tambourines, xylophones, and maracas foster auditory skills, rhythm and co-ordination.
- **Pretend Play Sets** Items like kitchen sets, doctor kits, or tool kits encourage imaginative play, social skills and emotional expression.
- **Sensory Bins** Filled with materials like rice, sand or water beads, these promote sensory exploration and fine motor skills.
- **Storybooks** Age-appropriate books support language development, imagination and literacy skills.
- **Shape Sorters** Help children learn shapes, colors and enhance fine motor skills through sorting and matching activities.
- **Stacking Toys** Toys like nesting cups or stacking rings promote hand-eye co-ordination, balance and spatial awareness.
- **Movement Toys** Items like balance beams, tunnels or soft climbing structures encourage gross motor development and physical activity.

4. Define ECCE and discuss its significance.

Ans. Definition of ECCE

Early Childhood Care and Education (ECCE) refers to the comprehensive care and education provided to children from birth to 8 years of age. This period is crucial as it lays the foundation for a child's future development in areas such as cognitive, emotional, social and physical growth.

Significance of ECCE

- **Holistic Development** ECCE is not just about preparing children for primary school but focuses on their overall development, including their social, emotional, cognitive and physical needs. This ensures a well-rounded foundation for lifelong learning and well-being.
- **Early Learning and Attachment** Children begin learning at a very young age, recognising family members and familiar faces. Early attachment to primary caregivers promotes a sense of security and emotional stability, essential for future learning.
- **Building a Secure Foundation** ECCE helps in the development of secure attachment bonds and a sense of trust in children, which are vital for their emotional and psychological well-being.
- **Parental and Community Involvement** The involvement of families and communities in early childhood development is crucial for creating a nurturing environment, enhancing the child's overall growth and social integration.
- **Meeting Increasing Demand for Childcare** With more working mothers, there has been a growing demand for institutional child care. ECCE ensures that children receive the necessary care and education, even when parental care is not always available.

5. Reema works at a daily care centre. She has to deal with children under 6 years of age. She also has to guide parents on how to know more about how and why children do the things in their way.

(i) Why is ECCE training necessary for the parents?

(ii) What skills are required by ECCE professionals?

(iii) Distinguish between the view point of Piaget and Vygotsky in context to ECCE. **Competency Based Que**

Ans. (i) ECCE training is necessary for parents in following ways

- ECCE training would help parents to know more about expected differences between children of same age and the individual differences.
- Parents should realise that there is no need to do competitive comparisons between children and even between siblings.

(ii) Skills which are required for ECCE professionals

For answer refer to Q.No.12(ii) of Short Answer Type Questions.

(iii) Difference between the view point of Jean Piaget and Vygotsky in context to ECCE

For Answer refer to Q.No.12(i) of Short Answer Type Questions.

6. Prepare a 10 points checklist which would enable your sister to find a child-friendly school ensuring holistic development of your niece.

Competency Based Que; Diksha App

Ans. Here's a 10-point checklist your sister can use to find a child-friendly school that ensures the holistic development of her niece

(i) **Qualified Staff** Verify that teachers have training in early childhood education and child development.

(ii) **Safe Environment** Ensu4re the school has child-proofed facilities with secure play areas and proper safety measures.

(iii) **Play-Based Curriculum** Check if the school emphasises play as a primary method of learning, encouraging exploration and creativity.

(iv) **Low Student-to-Teacher Ratio** Confirm a manageable ratio that allows for individual attention and support for each child.

(v) **Focus on Social and Emotional Development** Look for programmes that promote social skills, emotional regulation and conflict resolution.

(vi) **Diverse Learning Activities** Ensure a variety of activities that cater to different areas of development: cognitive, physical, social and creative.

(vii) **Parental Involvement** Check if the school encourages regular communication and involvement of parents in their child's education.

(viii) **Healthy Meals and Nutrition** Ensure that the school provides nutritious meals and snacks to support physical well-being.

(ix) **Access to Outdoor Play** Confirm that there are safe outdoor spaces for physical activity and exploration in nature.

(x) **Positive Reviews and Reputation** Research feedback from other parents and the school's reputation in the community for quality education and care.

7. Mention method of teaching focus on........

(i) self-directed oblique experiential learning

(ii) chalk and talk method

(iii) online learning for the demonstrator **Diksha App**

Ans. Here are the teaching methods focusing on the specified areas

(i) **Self-Directed Oblique Experiential Learning** This method emphasises learning through direct experience and exploration. Children are encouraged to pursue their interests, ask questions and engage in hands-on activities. The teacher acts as a facilitator, providing resources and guidance while allowing students to take charge of their own learning journey.

(ii) **Chalk and Talk Method** This traditional teaching method relies on direct instruction, where the teacher presents information verbally while using a chalkboard to illustrate key concepts. It is effective for delivering structured content but may not engage all learning styles, making it essential to complement with interactive activities.

(iii) **Online Learning for the Demonstrator** This method involves using digital platforms to provide instruction and demonstrations. Educators can utilise videos, interactive tools and virtual classrooms to reach a wider audience. This approach allows for flexibility and access to diverse resources, enhancing the learning experience for both teachers and students.

8. Explain the term self-directed learning with reference to ECCE. **Diksha App**

Ans. Self-directed learning in the context of Early Childhood Care and Education (ECCE) refers to the process where young children take initiative in their own learning, guided by their interests, curiosity and motivations. This approach encourages children to explore, ask questions and engage with materials at their own pace.

Key Aspects

- **Child-Centered Approach** Self-directed learning emphasises the child's role as an active participant in their education, allowing them to make choices about what and how they learn.
- **Exploration and Discovery** Children are encouraged to explore their environment, leading to hands-on experiences that promote critical thinking and problem-solving skills.
- **Development of Autonomy** By allowing children to take charge of their learning, they develop a sense of independence and confidence in their abilities.
- **Fostering Lifelong Learning** Self-directed learning lays the foundation for a love of learning, as children become accustomed to seeking out knowledge and skills on their own.
- **Supportive Environment** ECCE settings provide resources, guidance and a nurturing atmosphere that fosters self-directed learning, enabling children to pursue their interests while receiving appropriate support from educators.

SELF ASSESSMENT TEST

Objective Type Questions

1. Which of the following classroom scheduling practices would be developmentally appropriate for children of pre-school age?
   (a) Providing frequent variations in routine
   (b) Beginning each day with a half-hour circle time
   (c) Introducing new learning centers each week
   (d) Alternating physically active and quiet activities
2. In which of the following scenarios is an early childhood teacher acting primarily in his or her role as an advocate for children and families in the programme? **Competency Based Que**
   (a) A pre-school teacher collaborates with an agency in the community to organise a series of health and wellness events.
   (b) A pre-school teacher participates in a workshop about incorporating the arts into the early childhood curriculum.
   (c) A pre-school teacher regularly reads professional journals to stay informed about developments in the field.
   (d) A pre-school teacher maintains a folder for every student to track individuals' development in each of the major domains.

Very Short Answer Type Questions

3. Anganwadis in rural and urban areas are operated under which initiative?
4. Why is there a need for an ECCE teacher to be capable in administrative and management skills?
5. Mita is a three year old young child. Give any two characteristics seen in her.

Short Answer Type Questions

6. Differentiate between a toddler and pre-school child.
7. Which guiding principles must be followed in ECCE?
8. To which notions are the ECCE professionals committed to?
9. Why training is essential in ECCE? Give reasons.

Long Answer Type Questions

10. Who is a pre-school child? What are the expectations from a caregiver of the child?
11. Why ECCE is significant for human development? Discuss.

07

CHAPTER

This chapter focuses on the significance of support services for vulnerable populations, including children, youth and the elderly. It explores their specific vulnerabilities, the importance of providing appropriate care, and the preparation needed for careers in support services. Additionally, it examines the scope, management, and programmes designed to address their needs.

Management of Support Services, Institutions and Programmes for Children, Youth and Elderly

▼ **YOUR STUDY GOALS**

7.1 Introduction
7.2 Significance of Support Services
7.3 Basic Concepts
7.4 Vulnerability of Children
7.5 Vulnerability of Youth
7.6 Vulnerability of Elderly
7.7 Preparing for a Career in Support Services
7.8 Scope

▼ **YOUR PRACTICE GOAL**

- Objective Type Questions (23 Qs ; MCQs, A-R, Matching, Case Based)
- Subjective Questions (12 VSAs, 8 SAs, 7 LAs)

7.1 Introduction

- Family serves as the fundamental unit of society, focused on meeting the diverse needs of its members. Its composition varies, typically including parents, children and grandparents, with each household reflecting different life stages.
- Members rely on one another to fulfill specific needs; for instance, children need formal education, while older members require health care. Communities develop various structures like schools, hospitals and training centers to provide specialised services that cater to these needs.
- Through these resources, families can access support tailored to their individual circumstances, highlighting the interdependence between family and community.

7.2 Significance of Support Services

- A family is expected to meet the needs of its members, supported by social structures like schools and hospitals. However, many families in India struggle to fulfill basic needs or lack access to available services.

- Financial resources are a significant barrier, alongside issues of separation, where children, **youth**[1] and the **elderly**[2] find themselves alone and unable to cope. These challenges contribute to rising poverty levels in the nation, impacting individuals and families in multiple ways.
- As of 2011-12, 29.5 per cent of the population lived below the national poverty line, while less than 30 per cent have access to proper sanitation facilities.
- Given these circumstances, many families and individuals face significant challenges. It is essential for the state and society to take proactive measures to address these needs.
- The government, along with societal support, has a responsibility to ensure all citizens can lead decent lives, providing children and youth opportunities for holistic development in a nurturing environment.
- To tackle these issues, the government establishes institutions and programmes focused on children, youth and the elderly, while also supporting the private and NGO sectors.
- Some programmes target specific needs, while others take a holistic approach, addressing multiple needs simultaneously for a more significant societal impact. This integrated strategy ensures that individual needs are met effectively, fostering overall well-being.

7.3 Basic Concepts

- In our society, children, youth and the elderly are identified as **vulnerable**[3] groups. Vulnerability refers to those individuals or groups particularly susceptible to adverse circumstances.
- These **three segments** are considered vulnerable because unfulfilled needs can significantly impact their well-being. For instance, children require education and protection, youth need opportunities for development and guidance, while the elderly need care and support.
- If their specific needs are not addressed within a timely manner, these groups may face greater challenges and hardships, leading to increased risk and vulnerability. This highlights the importance of timely intervention and support to ensure their safety and development.

7.4 Vulnerability of Children

- Children are particularly vulnerable because childhood is a critical period of rapid development across various domains. Development in one area influences growth in others, emphasising the need for a holistic approach to their well-being.
- A child can thrive only when their needs for food, shelter, health care, love, nurturance and stimulation are adequately met. Adverse experiences during this formative stage can have long-lasting effects on development.
- While all children are vulnerable, some face greater challenges due to difficult circumstances that hinder their basic needs. In India, a significant portion of the child population struggles to fulfill these needs.
- Nearly two-thirds of children under five suffer from malnutrition, impacting their overall growth. Approximately three million children are homeless, living on the streets without shelter.
- Only one in three pre-school-aged children have access to early learning programmes and less than half of children aged 6 to 14 attend school.
- The dropout rate is concerning, with only about one-third of children enrolled in Class I reaching Class VIII.

---

1 **Youth** It refers to people belonging to the age group of 15-29 years.

2 **Elderly** In India, elderly refers to people belonging to the age group of 60 years and above.

3 **Vulnerable** It refers to people who are more affected and prone to adverse circumstances.

- Estimates indicate that around 17 million children are engaged in work, with the true numbers potentially reaching 44 million, according to the World Bank. These statistics illustrate the urgent need for intervention to support vulnerable children in India.

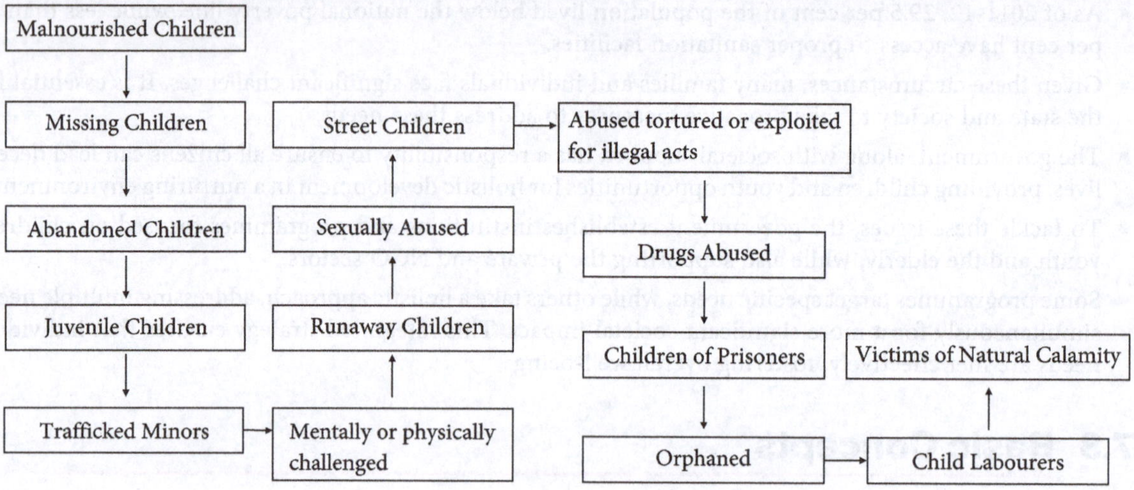

▲ *Vulnerability of Children*

Juvenile Justice Act for Child Protection

- Children in difficult circumstances require care and protection, but some may engage in illegal activities or anti-social behavior. The **Juvenile Justice** (Child Care and Protection) **Act, 2000** serves as the primary legal framework for addressing juvenile justice in India.
- This act categorises children into two groups
  - Those in conflict with the law.
  - Those in need of care and protection.
- Children in conflict with the law, often referred to as juvenile delinquents, have been apprehended by police for violating the law.
- The act supports juvenile delinquents in several ways. It promotes a special approach aimed at preventing and treating juvenile delinquency. Additionally, it provides a framework for the protection, treatment and rehabilitation of these children.
- In compliance with the Child Rights Convention, the act identifies children in need of care and protection, typically including those who
  - are without homes or means of sustenance, such as abandoned, street, runaway or missing children.
  - live with unfit guardians or in situations where they may face abuse or neglect.
  - are mentally or physically challenged, ill or unaware of the support available to them.
  - are victims of abuse, torture or exploitation for sexual purposes or illegal acts.
  - are vulnerable to drug abuse or trafficking.
  - have experienced armed conflict, civil unrest or natural disasters.
  - are likely to be exploited for profit, including abandoned or orphaned children, trafficked minors or those rescued from hazardous situations.

Institutions, Programmes and Initiatives for Children

Government has adopted several programmes and services which are operating in the country to meet the needs of vulnerable children. Some important initiatives and efforts taken up by the government and the non-governmental organisations are discussed below

Integrated Child Development Services (ICDS)

This scheme was launched on 2nd **October, 1975,** as a flagship programme by the Government of India. It is the world's largest early childhood programme, which aims to meet the health, nutrition, stimulation and early learning or educational needs of children below 6 years of age in an integrated manner to foster development. This programme also offers

- Health, nutrition and hygiene education to mothers.
- Non-formal pre-school education to children aged 3-6.
- Supplementary feeding for all children below 6 years.
- Growth monitoring and basic health care services such as immunisation and Vitamin A supplements to pregnant and nursing mothers.

I.C.D.S

ICDS covers more than 41 million children. These services are delivered in an integrated manner at the child-care centre known as **Anganwadi**[4].

SOS Children's Village

- SOS children's villages is an independent non-governmental social organisation that focuses on the **long-term care** of **orphaned** and **abandoned children** through a family-oriented approach. This organisation assists children by providing humanitarian and developmental aid while protecting their rights globally.
- SOS villages aim to offer family-based, long-term care for children who cannot grow up with their biological families. In each SOS home, a mother cares for 10-15 children, fostering relationships and helping them recover from trauma.
- Children grow up in a stable family environment, receiving individual support until they reach young adulthood. These SOS families live together, creating a supportive village atmosphere and are integrated into the local community, contributing to social life.
- The first Indian SOS village was established in **1964** and today the organisation cares for approximately 6,000 needy or abandoned children across 40 villages in the country. Additionally, SOS children's villages has provided immediate assistance through emergency relief programmes during times of unrest or natural disasters, such as the **Bhopal Gas Tragedy in 1984,** devastating cyclones and catastrophic earthquakes and tsunamis.

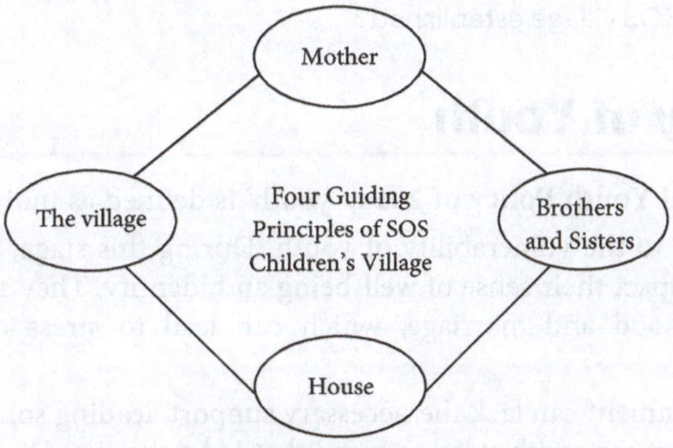

▲ *Principles of SOS children's*

4 **Anganwadi** Type of rural child-care centre in India.

Children's Homes run by the Government

These homes are supervised by the government for children from **3-18 years** who are in state custody for various reasons. There are three kinds of homes for children

(i) **Observation Homes** These are homes where children stay temporarily until the completion of an investigation to track down their parents and collect information on their family background.

(ii) **Special Homes** These are homes where juveniles, that is, children less than 18 years of age, who are found guilty of **violating the law,** are placed in custodial care.

(iii) **Juvenile or Children's Homes** These are homes where children whose families are untraceable, unfit, deceased or unwilling to take the child back reside. The government is responsible for providing them with room, board, education and vocational training.

These homes are generally run by the government in partnership with NGOs. Efforts are also made to help children develop skills that will enable them to become productive members of society.

Adoption

- Adoption refers to the process through which an adopted child becomes the lawful child of their adoptive parents, gaining all rights, privileges and responsibilities of a biological child. In India, child adoption is a prevalent practice that has evolved over time.
- Historically, adoption was often limited to within the family and governed by social and religious practices. Today, adoption beyond the family has been institutionalised and legalised.
- The Central and State Governments of India offer support and guidance through various policies and programmes to facilitate the adoption process. NGOs play a crucial role in delivering the necessary systems for adoption.
- To further strengthen adoption rules, the Government of India established the **Central Adoption Resource Agency (CARA)** on the advice of the Supreme Court. CARA sets guidelines for adoption to safeguard the welfare and rights of children.

Quick Test 1

1 What does it mean to be unable to meet the basic needs for life, health and efficiency?
2 Pervasive discrimination against girls and women is reflected in what areas?
3 When did the Juvenile Justice Act for Children's Protection come into effect?
4 When was the first SOS village established?

7.5 Vulnerability of Youth

- According to the **National Youth Policy of 2014,** 'youth' is defined as individuals aged 15-29 years.
- Several factors contribute to the vulnerability of youth. During this stage, individuals undergo many biological changes that impact their sense of well-being and identity. They also prepare for adult roles, such as earning a livelihood and marriage, which can lead to stress due to peer pressure and competition.
- A disturbed family environment can lack the necessary support, leading some adolescents to engage in substance abuse as a way to cope with stress, a trend that is on the rise. Health is also critical, as many youth face risks related to sexual and reproductive health, often lacking the knowledge needed to make informed choices.

- Certain groups within the youth category are particularly vulnerable including **rural and tribal youth, out-of-school youth, female adolescents, youth with disabilities** and those in difficult circumstances, such as victims of trafficking, orphans and street children.

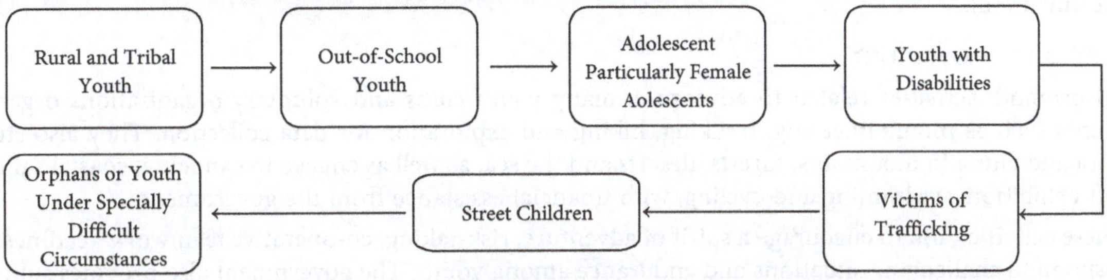

▲ *Youth are Vulnerable*

- For socially and economically productive youth, there is a need for appropriate education and training, gainful employment and opportunities for personal development. Additionally, they require shelter, a clean environment, quality health services, social protection and defense against exploitation.
- Youth should have suitable participation in decision-making bodies related to youth issues, as well as access to socio-economic and cultural matters, sports, physical education and recreational opportunities.

Youth Programmes in India

The Ministry of Youth Affairs and Sports adopted the **National Youth Policy in 2003**. Some of the schemes and programmes related to the welfare of youth are discussed below

The National Service Scheme (NSS)

This scheme aims at involving college students in social service and national development programmes like

- Construction and repair of roads, school buildings, village ponds and tanks.
- Activities related to environmental and ecological improvement, such as tree plantation, removal of weeds from lakes and digging pits.
- Activities related to hygiene and sanitation, family welfare, child-care, mass immunisation, vocational training in crafts, tailoring, knitting and organising co-operatives.
- NSS students also render assistance to local authorities for implementing various relief and rehabilitation programmes to meet the needs of the economically and socially weaker sections of the community.

The National Service Volunteer Scheme

- This scheme provides opportunities for students who have completed their first degree to engage full-time for one or two years in national development programmes, mainly through Nehru Yuva Kendras.
- These kendras are involved in various programmes, including adult education, establishment of youth clubs, organisation of work camps, youth leadership training, vocational training and promotion of rural sports and games.
- The **Nehru Yuva Kendras** also aim to assist non-student youth in rural areas towards development. They promote nationally accepted objectives such as self-reliance, secularism, socialism, democracy, national integration and the development of scientific temper.
- These objectives are achieved through activities like non-formal education, social service camps, development of sports activities, cultural and recreational programmes, vocational training and youth leadership training.

- Generally, these activities help non-student youth acquire literacy and numeracy skills for self-reliance, upgrade their functional capabilities and raise awareness of development opportunities.
- Thus, these activities enhance youth's functional efficiency, making them economically productive and socially useful.

Promotion of Adventure

- To promote activities related to adventure, many youth clubs and voluntary organisations organise events such as mountaineering, trekking, hiking and exploration for data collection. They also study flora and fauna in mountains, forests, deserts and the sea, as well as engage in canoeing, coastal sailing, raft exhibitions, swimming and cycling, with financial assistance from the government.
- These activities aim to encourage a spirit of adventure, risk-taking, co-operative teamwork, readiness to respond to challenging situations and endurance among youth. The government also provides support for the establishment and development of institutions to facilitate such activities.

Scouts and Guides

- The government provides financial assistance for training scouts and guides, as well as organising rallies and jamborees. The aim of scouts and guides is to develop the character of youth, helping them become good citizens by fostering loyalty, patriotism, and thoughtfulness for others.
- This programme promotes balanced physical and mental development while encouraging a desire for social service. The mission of scouts and guides is to contribute to building a better world where individuals are self-fulfilled and play a constructive role in society.

Commonwealth Youth Programme

- The Commonwealth Youth Programme aims to engage and empower youth to enhance their contribution to development. The programme encourages youth participation in the development processes of their countries while providing a forum for increased co-operation and understanding among commonwealth nations. India is a participant in this programme.
- As part of the initiative, three regional centers for advanced studies in youth work have been established in India, **Zambia** and **Guyana**. The **Asia Pacific Regional Centre** is located in Chandigarh, India.

Promotion of National Integration

- National integration remains a crucial issue in India. To address this, the government provides financial assistance to various voluntary agencies to organise visits for young people between states with distinct cultural differences.
- These initiatives aim to promote greater understanding of the country's historical and cultural heritage, as well as the challenges faced by people in different regions, including their social customs and environments. For example, camps and seminars are organised with the objective of fostering national integration.

7.6 Vulnerability of Elderly

- Older adults are generally considered one of the most vulnerable groups in the population. In many countries, a **senior citizen** is defined as someone aged 65 and above, while in India, this group includes those aged 60 and above.
- India has the second-largest population of senior citizens in the world, after China. According to the **Human Development Report of 2016,** elderly individuals will account for nearly 9 per cent of the total population.
- Some special features of the elderly population in India include
  - The majority (80 per cent) of elderly individuals live in rural areas, making it challenging for authorities to deliver services regularly.
  - There is a notable feminisation of the elderly population.

- The number of older-old persons, those aged 80 and above, is increasing.
- A significant percentage (30 per cent) of senior citizens live below the poverty line.

Reasons of Vulnerability of Elderly

The reasons that hold that elderly people are a vulnerable group are discussed below

- Health is a major concern for the elderly, who are more vulnerable to diseases due to decreased physiological reserves and defense mechanisms. The aging process can lead to disabilities such as low vision, deafness and loss of mobility, making self-care difficult.
- Social insecurity is prevalent as many elderly individuals find themselves alone, with children having moved away for marriage or work. This can lead to feelings of loneliness, isolation and being a burden on others. Financial dependence on younger generations may also contribute to their stress.
- In metropolitan areas, the fragmentation of traditional family networks and changing values impact support for the elderly. Factors like small family sizes, lack of time and high living costs reduce immediate and extended family support.
- Privacy, independence and materialism further hinder proper care for the elderly. As a result, many elderly individuals are left to care for themselves at a time when family support is crucial.
- Aging has become a significant social challenge, highlighting the need to address the economic and health needs of the elderly. Creating a supportive social environment that is sensitive to their emotional needs is essential.
- However, it is important to recognise that many elderly individuals lead fulfilling lives. In numerous families, they are respected and find personal fulfillment. Most elderly people aged 60 and above remain economically active, often engaged in sectors without a specific retirement age.
- Recognising the elderly as valuable human resources is vital and their experiences should be utilised for national development. The government must ensure a healthy and productive life for the elderly population. To support this, the **National Policy for Older Persons was adopted by the government in 1999.**

Some Programmes for the Elderly

Different types of programmes are implemented by the Government, Non-Governmental Organisations, Panchayati Raj Institutions and Local Bodies for the elderly. Some of these programmes are as follows

- Programmes catering to the basic needs of older persons particularly food, shelter and health care to the destitute elderly.
- Programmes to build and strengthen intergenerational relationships particularly between the younger and older persons.
- Programmes for encouraging active and productive ageing.
- Research, advocacy and awareness building programmes in the field of ageing.
- Old age homes to provide food, care and shelter.
- Respite care homes and continuous care homes for older persons who live in old age homes but are seriously ill and thus require continuous nursing care and respite.
- Multi-service Centres for older persons to provide day care, educational and entertainment opportunities, health care, companionship. Mobile medicare units to provide medical care to the older persons living in rural and isolated and backward areas.
- Day care centres for Alzheimer's Disease/Dementia patients to provide specialised day care.
- Help-lines and counseling centers for older persons.
- Mental health care and specialised care for the older persons to provide Mental Health Care Intervention programmes to the elderly.
- Disability and hearing aids for older persons.

- Physiotherapy clinics for older persons.
- **Awareness Generation Programmes** for older persons and caregivers like self-care, preventive health care, disease management, preparation for old age/healthy and productive ageing, inter-generational bonding.
- Training of caregivers to the older persons.
- Sensitising programmes for children, particularly in schools and colleges.
- **National Old Age Pension Scheme** (NOAPS) meant for old persons who are considered destitute. The beneficiaries should be above 65 years of age and they need to provide their proof of age and destitute status. The State Governments can add to the amount from their own resources.

7.7 Preparing for a Career in Support Services

A career in management of institutions and programmes for children, youth and elderly will need

- Improvement of the abilities and skills of a planner, manager, an evaluator and even an entrepreneur.
- Strong knowledge of the needs, characteristics and modes of care giving for the target group.

Following are some skills and abilities an individual will need to develop

People Skills

People skills[5] are required in running or working in an organisation to interact with people in different roles and from different backgrounds. Following are some of the groups with whom an individual may interact

- **Community** A programme or an institution for children will be successful if the community feels a sense of involvement and ownership with it. This generally happens when the programme is planned by involving people for whom it is meant from the start. Hence, there is a need for building links with the community and invoking community participation are the major aspects of the individual's work.
- **Private sector** The private sector financial institutions, companies and organisations have come forward to support innovative programmes and institutions. It is considered a positive step as the private sector is now able to discharge its social responsibilities.
- **Officials in the Government** An individual may have to interact with government officials for various purposes like funding and fulfilling legal requirements.
- **People within the Organisation** For the efficient and smooth functioning of an organisation, it is imperative that the people, i.e., both beneficiaries and personnel working therein, enjoy a balanced relationship with each other. Thus, maintaining cordial interpersonal relations in an organisation is a beneficial factor for the organisation and is also an important people skill an individual should develop if they wish to pursue a career in support services.

Administrative Skills

It refers to management skills required in working in or running an organisation. To run or manage an organisation or programme means properly **handling finance**, **recruiting personnel**, **renting space**, **buying equipment** and maintaining records and stocks. It is important for the individual to have a basic understanding of the issues involved in each of these areas.

For an individual who wasnts to start his/her new organisation for a specific needy target group, the following aspects must be considered

- Appropriate location.
- Who should it cater to suit the target beneficiaries.
- Services or combination of services to be provided.
- Finances to run the organisation.

5 **People Skills** It refers to interaction skills required in working in or running an organisation.

- Recruitment of staff with different skills.
- Knowledge base to handle various aspects of the programme, including handling formalities of registering the organisation, implementing the programme and improving the activities based on periodic evaluation and feedback.
- To have a strong vision about what he/she wants to achieve and how the organisation will contribute to meet the needs of the target group. Thus, strong passion is also a major requirement for work in this area.

Preparation for Career

The need for programmes and institutions for children, youth and the elderly, which provide quality services, will continue to remain a basic need of **civil society**. Steps that are essential in preparation for this career are

- Towards this career is to develop a knowledge base and understanding about children, youth and the elderly. It is appropriate for an individual to obtain an undergraduate degree in Home Science, Family and Community Sciences or Social Work. These degree programmes usually focus on these three vulnerable groups in the population.
- One can choose to enter the employment market after the undergraduate degree or opt to study further.
- Along with pursuing a programme of study through the conventional system, one can also explore opportunities provided by Open and Distance Learning in the country to pursue programmes that will equip an individual to work with the three vulnerable sections of society.
- The Indira Gandhi National Open University offers programmes like Certificate Programme in NGO Management and Diploma in Youth Development Work.
- There are other State Universities that offer programmes through distance mode education. One can explore the websites of IGNOU and State Open Universities for further details.

7.8 Scope

The scope in management of institutions and programmes for children, youth and elderly depends upon the type of programme chosen by an individual, as this field offers various possibilities. Some of the career avenues which one can opt for are discussed below

- One can set up one's own institution for services to any target group.
- One can be a manager in an established institution or programme.
- One can be a functionary at any level or cadre.
- One can be a researcher, consulting with, assessing or evaluating the existing programmes and institutions.

Career Avenue

- Set up your own institution for services to any target group.
- Be a manager in an established institution or a programme.
- Be a functionary at any level/cadre.
- Be a researcher consulting with/assessing/evaluating existing programmes and institutions.

Quick Test 2

1. What has become a major social challenge for elderly people?
2. Under the National Old Age Pension Scheme (NOAPS), what is the minimum age for beneficiaries?
3. What relationships are a major factor in the success of an organisation?

Mind Map

MANAGEMENT OF SUPPORT SERVICES, INSTITUTIONS AND PROGRAMMES FOR CHILDREN, YOUTH AND ELDERLY

1 Family and Community

Family as a Unit
- **Composition** Parents, children, grandparents.
- **Purpose** Meets diverse needs of its members.

Interdependence
- Children need education, older members need health care.
- Family members rely on each other.

Community Role
- Provides schools, hospitals, and training centers.
- Tailors support to family needs.

2 Significance of Support Services

Family Challenges
- Struggle to meet needs due to financial barriers and separation.

Poverty and Inequality
- 29.5% below poverty line.
- Low sanitation and maternal/infant mortality rates.
- Nutritional deficiencies (iodine).

Discrimination
- **Gender Bias** Poor outcomes for girls.

Government and Societal Role
- Programmes for children, youth and elderly.
- Integrated approach to meet multiple needs.

3 Vulnerability of Children and Support Systems

Children's Vulnerability
- Critical period of rapid development.
- Need for food, shelter, health care, love, nurturance and stimulation.
- Adverse experiences during childhood lead to long-lasting effects.

Challenges Faced by Children
- **Malnutrition** (2/3 of children under 5).
- **Homelessness** 3 million children on the streets.
- **Lack of Access to Education** only 1 in 3 children in early learning programmes.
- **Child labor** 17 million children engaged in work.

Juvenile Justice Act (2000)
- Categories of children
- In conflict with the law
- Need care and protection
- **Focus** Protection, treatment, rehabilitation with a child-friendly approach

4 Vulnerability of Youth and Support Systems

- Youth (ages 15-29) face stress from biological changes, peer pressure, family issues and substance abuse. Specific vulnerable groups include rural youth, female adolescents and orphans. They need education, training, healthcare and social protection.

Key Programmes
- **NSS** Involves students in social service and national development.
- **National Service Volunteer Scheme** Offers post-graduation youth full-time involvement in development activities.
- **Adventure Programmes** Encourages mountaineering and team-building.
- **Scouts and Guides** Focuses on character development and social service.
- **Commonwealth Youth Programme** Empowers youth for national development.
- **National Integration Promotion** Organises interstate visits and camps to promote unity.

5 Vulnerability of the Elderly and Support Systems

Vulnerability
- Elderly individuals (60+) face physical health issues, social insecurity and financial dependence. 80% live in rural areas, 30% live below the poverty line, and the population of older-old (80+) is growing.
- **Challenges** Aging causes health issues like poor vision and mobility loss. Social isolation is common due to smaller families, leading to loneliness and a lack of support.
- **Support Programmes** Mobile medicare units, day care centers, National Old Age Pension Scheme (NOAPS), multi-service centers and awareness programmes.

6 Preparing for a Career in Support Services

A career in support services for children, youth, and the elderly involves managing or establishing programmes that cater to these groups' needs. Key skills for success include

People Skills
- Interacting with community members, government officials, private sector partners, and organisational staff is crucial for effective programme planning and implementation.

Administrative Skills
- Basic knowledge in finance management, recruitment, equipment purchasing, and maintaining records is needed.
- For starting an organisation, factors like location, target group, services offered, staff recruitment, and finances must be carefully considered.

Steps for Career Preparation

Education
- Pursue undergraduate degrees in fields like Home Science, social work, or family and community sciences.

Further Studies
- Opt for specialised courses in NGO management, youth development, or similar fields, such as those offered by IGNOU and State Open Universities.

Passion and Vision
- A strong vision and passion for working with vulnerable populations, backed by knowledge and practical skills, are essential for success in this field.

7 Scope of Career in Support Services

- **Set up your Own Institution** Start a service organisation for a specific target group (children, youth, or elderly).
- **Manager in an Established Programmes** Take up managerial roles in existing institutions or programmes.
- **Functionary at any Level** Work in various positions or cadres within an organisation.
- **Researcher/Consultant** Assess, consult, or evaluate current programmes and institutions.

NCERT Folder

1. Why are children, youth and elderly 'vulnerable'?

Ans. Reasons responsible for the vulnerability of children are as follows

- Lack of fulfillment of basic needs (food, shelter, health, care and nurturance).
- Facing adverse experiences at a very young age.
- Facing exploitation at a very young age.
- Lack of proper education and guidance.

Reasons responsible for the vulnerability of youth are as follows

- During youth, an individual goes through many biological changes in her/his body which impact on the person's sense of well-being and identity.
- Peer pressure as well as the pressure to excel in an increasingly competitive world can also lead to stress and turmoil.
- Health is also an aspect is of critical importance. Youth faces significant risks related to sexual and reproductive health as many of them lack knowledge to make informed choices.

Reasons responsible for the vulnerability of the elderly are as follows

- Lack of financial resources.
- Prone to diseases due to decreased physiological reserves and defence mechanism.
- Social isolation and insecurity and feelings of loneliness.
- Lack of familial support.

2. Which types of programmes are appropriate for youth?

Ans. The types of programmes appropriate for youth are as follows

- The National Service Scheme (NSS)
- The National Service Volunteer Scheme
- Promotion of Adventure Programmes
- Scouts and Guides Programmes
- Commonwealth Youth Programme
- Promotion of National Integration

3. What are some of the concerns with respect to the elderly?

Ans. Some of the concerns with respect to the elderly are discussed below

- **Health Insecurity** Health is a major issue of concern for many individuals at this age. The elderly are more vulnerable to diseases due to decreased physiological reserves and defence mechanisms. Besides that, the aging process itself leads to many disabilities such as low vision and blindness resulting from cataracts, deafness resulting from nerve impairment, loss of mobility from arthritis and a general inability to care for oneself.
- **Social Insecurity** In this period, they find themselves alone because the children are likely to have moved away from the family due to marriage or to earn a living. Many elderly individuals may experience feelings of loneliness, isolation and a sense of being a burden on others. Many individuals are financially dependent on the younger generation which may add to their feeling of stress. This social isolation affects the living pattern of the aged people.
- **Lack of Family Support** Due to the fragmentation of the traditional family network, in metropolitan cities, the elderly face a lack of support time and care. Family members don't get adequate amount of time to care for the elderly, owing to their busy schedule.
  This leaves the elderly population along, to support and care for themselves.

4. Describe two programmes each for children, youth and elderly.

Ans. Several programmes and services, have been adopted by the Indian Government, that operate in the country to meet the needs of the vulnerable sections of the society. Some of them are as follows

Programmes for Children

(i) **Integrated Child Development Services** (ICDS) Launched on 2nd October, 1975, this is the world's largest early childhood programme. It aims to meet the health, nutritional, stimulation and early educational needs of children below six years of age to foster growth and development.

(ii) **SOS Children's Village** An independent non-government social organisation, this works on a familial approach to the long term care of orphaned and abandoned children. It provides humanitarian and development assistance to children in need and also protects their rights and interests.

Programmes for Youth

(i) **The National Service Scheme** (NSS) Aims at involving college youth in social serivce and national development programmes like

- Construction of helpful public buildings and spaces (schools, roads, village ponds, etc).

- Environmental and ecological improvement activities.
- Activities related to hygiene and sanitation, family welfare, child-care, mass immunisation, etc.
- Assistance to local authorities for implementation of relief and rehabilitation programmes.

(ii) **Commonwealth Youth Programme** works to engage and empower the youth to enhance their contribution to development. It aims at making the youth participate in the development processes of their respective countries and at providing a forum for increasing co-operatation and understanding among the commonwealth nations.

Programmes for the Elderly

(i) **National Old Age Pension Scheme** (NOAPS) is meant for old people who are considered destitute. Such elderly don't have any regular means of sustenance on their own or through financial support of the family. The beneficiaries of this scheme should be above 65 years of age and should provide their proff of age and destitute status in order to benefit from the scheme.

(ii) There are other programmes catering to the basic needs of the elderly, particularly food, shelter and health care to the destitute elderly.

5. What advice will you give to someone who is planning to set up her/his own institution for children/ youth/ elderly?

Ans. Following are the advice that can be given to someone who is planning to set up his/her own institution for children/youth/elderly are

- Appropriate location.
- Who should it cater to suit the target beneficiaries.
- Services or combination of services to be provided.
- Finances to run the organisation.
- Recruitment of staff with different skills.
- Knowledge base to handle various aspects of the programme including handling formalities of registering the organisation, implementing the programme, improving the activities based on periodic evaluation and feedback.
- To have a strong vision about what he/she wants to achieve and how the organisation will contribute to meet the needs of the target group.
- Thus, strong passion is also the major requirement for work in this area.

6. Describe the knowledge and skills you will need in order to pursue a career in management of institutions and programmes for children/ youth/ elderly.

Or **Discuss the steps which are essential for the preparation of career in the field of management of services for the children, youth and elderly.**

Ans. The skills and abilities that an individual will need in order to pursue a career in management of institutions and programmes for the vulnerable sections of the society can be divided into two broad categories

(i) **People Skills** It is required while working in or running an organisation so that one can interact with people in different roles and from different backgrounds. Some of the groups that an individual may interact with include

(a) **The Community** It is important for the community to feel a sense of involvement in a programme or organisation.

(b) **The Private Sector** The involvement of private companies and financial institutions is considered a positive step as it enables them to discharge their social responsibilities.

(c) **The Government Officials** For purposes like funding and legal requirements, an individual may have to interact with governmental officials.

(d) **The People within the Organisation** For the smooth functioning of an organisation, a balanced relationship between the beneficiaries and personnel is important.

(ii) **Administrative Skills** to run or manage an organisation or programme means to properly handle finance, to recruit personnel, to rend space, to buy equipment and to maintain records and stocks. Even though there may be other people dealing with these aspects, it is important for the individual to have a basic understanding of the issues involved in each of these aspects.

Exam Pattern Questions

Objective Type Questions

Multiple Choice Questions

1. As per the Juvenile Justice Act, which of the following children can be kept in special homes?

(a) Children in conflict with law (b) Neglected children
(c) Abused children (d) Disabled children

2. Which of the following constitutes a type of juvenile delinquency?

(a) Status Offence (b) Civil Offence
(c) Criminal Offence (d) Both (a) and (c)

3. When was the Integrated Child Development Services (ICDS) scheme launched?

(a) 1st October, 1974 (b) 2nd October, 1975
(c) 2nd October, 1976 (d) 1st October, 1977

4. Which of the following statement is not true with SOS children's villages?

(a) It is an independent non-governmental social organisation which works on a family approach to the long term care of orphaned and abandoned children.
(b) The SOS families live together forming a supportive village environment.
(c) In India, the first SOS village was set up in 1967.
(d) The SOS children's villages provides immediate assistance with emergency relief programmes.

5. In which year the first SOS village was set up in India and who were the beneficiaries? **CBSE SQP, 2021**

(a) 1954 and disabled children
(b) 1964 and abandoned children
(c) 1965 and special need children
(d) 1963 and juvenile delinquents

6. Name the agency which set up guidelines for adoption to safeguard the Welfare and Rights of children. **CBSE SQP, 2021**

(a) NARA (b) CARA
(c) CAPA (d) RACA

7. Which of the following are features of SOS children's home? **CBSE SQP 2024**

I. Grow with biological families
II. Supports till child becomes independent
III. Family-based long-term care to orphan children
IV. Government social organisation which has family approach

Choose the correct option

(a) I and II (b) II and III
(c) II and IV (d) I and IV

8. Mr. Ramesh found a 4 years old child near the railway station and handed over him to local police. Suggest the suitable option for the police for the time being, where the child should be sent. **Competency Based Que; CBSE SQP, 2021**

(a) Juvenile home (b) Special home
(c) Observation home (d) SOS village

9. Which of the following services are offered by ICDS? **CBSE SQP 2024**

I. Non-formal pre-school education
II. Supplementary feeding
III. Establishment of youth clubs
IV. Social defense and protection

Choose the correct option

(a) I and II (b) II and III
(c) II and IV (d) I and IV

10. 'The National Service Volunteer Scheme' provides opportunities to students to involve themselves, on a whole-time basis for a short period of one or two years, in programmes of national development.

Following are the programmes undertaken by them

I. Non-formal education through activities
II. Vocational training
III. Adult education
IV. Coastal sailing

Choose the correct option

(a) I and II (b) II and IV
(c) III and IV (d) I and IV

11. Which organisation enables the non-student youth of rural areas towards the development in the rural areas.

(a) Gandhi Yuva Kendras (b) Yuva Kendras
(c) Nehru Yuva Kendras (d) Civil Yuva Kendras

12. Which of the following is not a programme of NYKs?

(a) Education of adult
(b) Establishment of youth clubs
(c) Health care programmes for the Indian youth
(d) Vocational training

13. Which of the following programmes aims at providing a forum for increased understanding among the commonwealth countries?
(a) Commonwealth Adult Programme
(b) Commonwealth Youth Programme
(c) Commonwealth United
(d) Commonwealth of Countries

14. The elderly are vulnerable group due to various reasons. **CBSE SQP Term I, 2021**
Few reasons are
I. Decreased defence mechanism
II. Increased financial resources
III. Improved physiological reserves
IV. Nuclear family system
Choose the correct option
(a) I and II (b) II and III
(c) I and IV (d) II and IV

15. Mention the years in which 'National Policy for Older Person' and 'National Youth Policy' were adopted. **CBSE SQP Term I, 2021**
(a) Year 1999 and 2003 (b) Year 1998 and 2003
(c) Year 1999 and 2014 (d) Year 1998 and 2004

16. "Older people living in rural and isolated and backward areas need medical care".
Which of the following programmes operates for this purpose? **Competency Based Que**
(a) Day care centres (b) Mobile medicare units
(c) Respite homes (d) Multi-service centres

17. Mr. Anil is 80 years old, who is living in old age home and underwent heart surgery last week and he needs continuous nursing care. Which of the programme is suitable for him? **Competency Based Que; CBSE SQP, 2021**
(a) Mobile care unit (b) Respite homes
(c) Multi-units (d) Day care

18. Match the following. **CSBE 2024 C**

List-I (Initiatives for Children)		List-II (Features)	
A.	Special homes	1.	Adoption
B.	Observation homes	2.	Family based care for orphaned
C.	CARA	3.	Temporary home for missing children
D.	SOS Children's Village	4.	Custodial Care for Juveniles

Codes

	A	B	C	D		A	B	C	D
(a)	2	3	4	1	(b)	3	4	1	2
(c)	4	1	2	3	(d)	1	2	3	4

19. Match the following. **CBSE 2023**

List-I		List-II	
A.	National Youth Policy	1.	2014
B.	First SOS Children's Village	2.	2005
C.	National Curriculum Framework	3.	1964
D.	National Policy for Older Persons	4.	1999

Codes

	A	B	C	D		A	B	C	D
(a)	4	3	2	1	(b)	3	4	1	2
(c)	1	3	2	4	(d)	3	1	4	2

Assertion-Reason Question

Direction (Q. Nos. 20-21) Given below are two statements labelled as Assertion (A) and Reason (R). Select the most appropriate answer from the options given below.

Codes
(a) Both A and R are true and R is the correct explanation of A.
(b) Both A and R are true, but R is not the correct explanation of A.
(c) A is true, but R is false.
(d) A is false, but R is true.

20. **Assertion** (A) A programme or an institution for children will be successful if the community feels a sense of involvement and ownership with it.
Reason (R) While planning for such a programme people of management must be involved right from start. **CBSE SQP Term I, 2021**

21. **Assertion** (A) It is imperative for an individual to have people skills if they wish to pursue a career in support services.
Reason (R) The community feels a sense of participation and ownership of support service programmes.

Case Based Questions

22. Read the given passage and answer the following questions.
All children are vulnerable, but some are more vulnerable than others. These are the children who are living in such challenging conditions and difficult circumstances that their basic needs of food, health, care and nurturance are not met and this prevents them from developing their full potential. The needs of a large proportion of child population are not met. As nearly two-thirds of children under 5 years of age suffer from moderate and severe malnutrition. Malnutrition affects development in all areas. About 3 million children live on the streets without any shelter. Only one in three

children of the pre-school age has the opportunity to be in an early learning programme. Less than half of India's children between ages 6 and 14 years go to school. A little over one-third of all children who enroll in Standard I reach Standard VIII. The others drop out of school for one or other reason. 17 million children in India work, as per the official estimates. The actual numbers may be even more. According to the World Bank the number may be 44 million.

(i) Which of the following pairs is correctly matched based on the passage?

(a) Malnutrition : Only affects physical growth
(b) Early learning programmes : Accessible to most pre-school children
(c) Standard I to VIII : Many children do not complete this journey
(d) Children living on the streets : All have access to basic needs

(ii) Match the items in List I with their corresponding descriptions in List II.

List-I		List-II	
A.	Malnutrition	1.	Affects children's overall development
B.	Street children	2.	Lack basic shelter and safety
C.	Pre-school education	3.	Only a small proportion have access
D.	School dropout	4.	Affects the journey from Standard I to VIII

Codes

	A	B	C	D
(a)	4	3	2	1
(b)	3	2	1	4
(c)	3	2	4	1
(d)	1	2	3	4

(iii) Assertion (A) Many children in India are unable to complete their education.

Reason (R) Less than half of India's children between ages 6 and 14 go to school.

Codes

(a) Both A and R are true and R is the correct explanation for A.
(b) Both A and R are true, but R is not the correct explanation for A.
(c) A is true, but R is false.
(d) A is false, but R is true.

(iv) Assertion (A) A significant proportion of children under five years of age suffer from malnutrition.

Reason (R) Malnutrition does not have a significant impact on development.

Codes

(a) Both A and R are true and R is the correct explanation for A.
(b) Both A and R are true, but R is not the correct explanation for A.
(c) A is true, but R is false.
(d) A is false, but R is true.

23. Read the given passage and answer the following questions. **CBSE 2025**

Many families in our country are unable to meet even the basic needs of their members and/or access as well as utilise the various services provided by other structures of the society due to various reasons, one of them being lack of resources, especially financial. Further, many children, youth and elderly are separated from their families and are left to cope on their own. By themselves, they find it difficult to meet their own needs.

(i) In the context of institutes/programmes for vulnerable groups, choose the correct pair.

(a) CARA : Organising rallies
(b) Promotion of Adventure: Child Rights convention
(c) Observation Home : A kind of home for children
(d) Promotion of National Integration : Family- based care

(ii) Match the initiatives for children, youth and elderly given in List-I with their related year in List-II.

List-I (Initiatives)		List-II (Year)	
A.	SOS Children's Village	1.	2000, 2015
B.	National Youth Policy	2.	1999
C.	National Policy for Older Persons	3.	2003, 2014
D.	Juvenile Justice (Care and Protection of Children) Act	4.	1964

Codes

	A	B	C	D
(a)	4	3	2	1
(b)	3	4	1	2
(c)	2	1	4	3
(d)	3	1	2	4

(iii) Given below are two statements labelled as Assertion (A) and Reason (R).

Assertion (A) Within the broad category 'Youth', there are some groups who are especially vulnerable.

Reason (R) Rural and tribal youth are vulnerable groups.

Codes

(a) Both A and R are true and R is the correct explanation for A.
(b) Both A and R are true, but R is not the correct explanation for A.
(c) A is true, but R is false.
(d) A is false, but R is true.

(iv) **Given below are two statements labelled as Assertion (A) and Reason (R).**

Assertion (A) It is necessary to provide for the economic and health needs of the elderly to create a conducive social milieu.

Reason (R) In India, Senior Citizens constitute persons in the age group of 50 years and above.

Codes

(a) Both A and R are true and R is the correct explanation for A.

(b) Both A and R are true, but R is not the correct explanation for A.

(c) A is true, but R is false.

(d) A is false, but R is true.

Answers

1. (a) Children in conflict with law
2. (d) Both (a) and (c)
3. (b) 2nd October, 1975
4. (c) In India, the first SOS village was set up in 1967.
5. (b) 1964 and abandoned children
6. (b) CARA
7. (b) II and III
8. (c) Observation home
9. (a) I and II
10. (a) I and II
11. (c) Nehru Yuva Kendras
12. (c) Health care programmes for the Indian youth
13. (b) Commonwealth Youth Programme
14. (c) I and IV
15. (a) Year 1999 and 2003
16. (b) Mobile medicare units
17. (b) Respite homes
18. (c) 4 1 2 3
19. (c) 1 3 2 4
20. (c) A is true, but R is false.
21. (b) Both A and R are true, but R is not the correct explanation of A.
22. (i) (c) Standard I to VIII : Many children do not complete this journey.
    (ii) (d) 1 2 3 4
    (iii) (a) Both A and R are true and R is the correct explanation for A.
    (iv) (c) A is true, but R is false.
23. (i) (c) Observation Home : A kind of home for children
    (ii) (a) 4 3 2 1
    (iii) (b) Both A and R are true, but R is not the correct explanation for A.
    (iv) (c) A is true, but R is false.

Subjective Questions

Very Short Answer Type Questions

1. How can the government respond towards the poverty situation in India in an effective manner?

Ans. The government can respond towards the poverty situation in India in an effective manner by following these steps

- It can set up institutions.
- It can initiate programmes especially for the children, youth and the elderly.
- It can also provide support to the efforts of the private sector and the NGO sector.

2. To meet the needs of vulnerable children, the government has adopted many programmes. With reference to the given statement, discuss the Integrated Child Development Services (ICDS) in brief.

Competency Based Que

Ans. ICDS scheme was launched on 2nd October, 1975 as a flagship programme by the Government of India.

It is the world's largest early childhood programme which aims to meet the health, nutrition, stimulation and early learning or educational needs of children below 6 years of age in an integrated manner to foster development.

3. Discuss the concept of juvenile or children's home.

Ans. These are homes where children whose families are not traceable or are unfit or dead or simply unwilling to take the child back stay.

The government is responsible for providing them room, board, education and vocational training. These homes are generally run by government in partnership with NGOs.

4. Discuss the concept of adoption in brief.

Ans. Adoption refers to the process through which the adopted child becomes the lawful child of his/her adoptive parents with all the rights, privileges and responsibilities that are attached to a biological child.

5. What is meant by CARA? Highlight its one function to meet the need of vulnerable children. **CBSE 2024**

Ans. CARA refers to Central Adoption Resource Authority. It functions as the nodal body for adoption of Indian children and is mandated to monitor and regulate in-country and inter-country adoptions.

6. 'Youth should be encouraged to enroll with scouts and guides'. Support this statement with four reasons. **Competency Based Que; CBSE, SQP 2024**

Ans. Youth should be encouraged to enroll with scouts and guides because of the following reasons

(i) These programmes develops the character of boys and girls to make them good citizens by inculcating in them a spirit of loyalty, patriotism.

(ii) Scouts and guides develop a sense of thoughtfulness for others.

(iii) Scouts and guides promote balanced physical development.

(iv) They also foster mental growth by teaching problem-solving and leadership skills.

7. 'Youth is the period when the individual is preparing to take on adult roles'. Give four reasons why are youth considered vulnerable. **Competency Based Que; CBSE SQP 2024**

Ans. Youth are considered voluneable due to various factors such as

(i) Peer pressure can lead to risky behaviours.

(ii) Unsupportive family or friends may result in emotional instability.

(iii) Some adolescents might turn to alcohol and drugs for escape or acceptance.

(iv) Health issues, including mental health challenges, ……… their overall well-being and development during its critical period.

8. What is meant by NSS? Write its one aim in the development of youth in India? **CBSE 2024**

Ans. NSS stands for the National Service Scheme. It is a voluntary public service programme in India aimed at developing student's personality through community service. Aim of NSS in the development of youth in India is to foster social responsibility and leadership qualities among young people by actively engaging them in various community development activities.

9. List four common problems faced by the elderly population. **CBSE SQP 2024**

Ans. The elderly population commonly faces several challenges, including

(i) **Deteriorating Health** Reduced physiological reserves and defense mechanisms lead to increased vulnerability to illnesses.

(ii) **Weaker Defense Mechanisms** Aging weakness the immune system, making it harder to fight infections.

(iii) **Loneliness** Social isolation due to the loss of loved ones or limited social interactions can affect mental health.

(iv) **Financial Dependency** Many older adults rely on family or limited pensions, leading to financial insecurity and dependence on others for basic needs.

10. Discuss some special features related to the elderly population of India.

Ans. Some special features related to the elderly population of India

- Majority (80 per cent) of the elderly population are living in the rural areas. Thus, it becomes difficult for the authorities to deliver services at regular intervals.
- Feminisation of the elderly population.
- There is an increase in the number of the older-old persons above the age of 80 years.
- A large percentage (30 per cent) of the senior citizens is living below the poverty line.

11. What is the basic requirement for a career in management of institutions and programmes for the children, youth and elderly?

Ans. Two basic requirements for a career in management of institutions and programmes for children, youth and elderly are

- Improvement of the abilities and skills of a planner, manager, an evaluator and even an entrepreneur.
- Strong knowledge of the needs, characteristics and modes of care giving for the target group.

12. "There are different career options available in the management of institutions and programmes for children, youth and elderly". With reference to the given statement, discuss its scope.

Ans. With reference to the given statement there are different career options. These are

- One can set up one's own institution for services to any target group.
- One can be a manager in an established institution or a programme.
- One can be a functionary at any level or cadre.
- One can be a researcher consulting with or assessing or evaluating the existing programmes and institutions.

Short Answer Type Questions

1. Why were children's homes formed? Indicate the need of three kinds of children's homes. **CBSE SQP, 2020**

Ans. Children homes are formed for children from 18 years who are in state custody for various reasons.

The need of three kinds of children's homes are

(i) **Observation Homes** These are homes where children stay temporarily till the completion of an investigation to track down their parents and collect information on their family background.

(ii) **Special Homes** These are homes where juveniles that are children less than 18 years of age are found guilty in terms of violation of law are placed in custodial care.

(iii) **Juvenile or Children's Homes** These are homes where children whose families are not traceable or are unfit or dead or simply unwilling to take the child back stay.

2. (i) In which year the first SOS Children's Village was setup? **CBSE SQP 2023**

(ii) Explain features of SOS Children's Village.

Ans. (i) The first SOS Children's Village was set up in 1964. SOS is an independent non-governmental social organisation which works on a family approach to the long term care of orphaned and abandoned children.

(ii) Three features of SOS Children's Village are

(a) The SOS Children's Village provides humanitarian and developmental assistance to children in need and protects their interests and rights around the world.

(b) SOS helps children to experience relationships again and also helps them recover from traumatic experiences in a better way. In each SOS home, there is a mother who looks after 10-15 children.

(c) The SOS families live together forming a supportive village environment. They are integrated with the local community and contribute towards the social life.

(d) They grow up in a stable family environment and are supported individually until they become independent young adults.

3. What are the essential requirements for socially and economically productive youth? Discuss.

Ans. Appropriate education and training, profitable employment and adequate opportunities for personal development are few essential requirments for socially and economically productive youth.

They also required shelter, a clean environment and basic health services of quality, social defense and protection from all manner of exploitation. There is a need for suitable participation in decision-making bodies pertaining to youth issues, with socio-economic and cultural matters, access to sports, physical education, adventure and recreational opportunities being other requisites for them.

4. (i) Why are youth vulnerable? Give two reasons.

(ii) What is National Service Scheme?

(iii) Highlight any two activities taken up under National Service Scheme. **CBSE SQP 2022**

Ans. (i) Two reasons that makes the youth vulnerable are as follows

(a) Peer pressure as well as the pressure to excel in an increasingly competitive world can also lead to stress and turmoil. During youth, an individual goes through many biological changes in her/his body which impacts the person's sense of well-being and identity.

(b) A disturbed family environment fails to provide support to an individual; consequently, some adolescents may indulge in substance abuse (consumption of alcohol and drugs). Such behaviour for combating stress is on a rise. Health is also an aspect of critical importance. Youth faces significant risks related to sexual and reproductive health as many of them lack knowledge to make informed choices.

(ii) National Service Scheme aims at involving college students in social service and national development programmes.

(iii) Two types of activities undertaken under National Service Scheme are

(a) Activities related to environmental and ecological improvement like tree plantation, removal of weeds from lakes, digging pits.

(b) Activities related to hygiene and sanitation, family welfare, child-care, mass immunisation, vocational training in craft, tailoring, knitting and organising co-operatives.

5. Why were Nehru Yuva Kendras established and list any four programmes run under these Kendras? **CBSE SQP, 2020**

Ans. Nehru Yuva Kendras were established to provide opportunities to the students who have completed their first degree.

They can involve themselves on a full-time basis for a short period of one or two years in the programmes of national development through these Kendras.

Four programmes run under these Kendras are

(i) Adult education
(ii) Establishment of youth clubs
(iii) Organisation of work camps
(iv) Youth leadership training programmes

6. Few children of a village have become victims of a natural calamity and are without home. Besides these, which other four types of vulnerable children need care and protection? **CBSE 2025**

Ans. The other four types of vulnerable children, need care and protection are

- Orphans without parental support.
- Abandoned or neglected children.
- Children with disabilities or health issues.
- Victims of child labor or abuse.

7. Why are elderly vulnerable? Give any two reasons to support your answer. Name any two programmes operating in our country for elderly people. Also tell about two administrative skills required to work with organisations running for elderly people. **Competency Based Que; CBSE SQP, 2020**

Ans. Two reasons responsible for the vulnerability of the elderly are

(i) Lack of financial resources and familial support.
(ii) They are prone to diseases due to decreased physiological reserves and defence mechanism.

Two programmes operating in India for the elderly are

(i) National Policy for Older Persons (1999)
(ii) National Old Age Pension Scheme (NOAPS)

Two administrative skills required to work with organisations running for the elderly are

(i) Knowledge base to handle various aspects of a programme.
(ii) A strong vision about what an individual wants to achieve and how the organisation will contribute to meet the needs of the target group.

8. How are Respite Care Homes different from Mobile Medicare units in terms of services offered to the elderly? **CBSE SQP 2024, Competency Based Que**

Ans. Difference between Respire Care Homes and Mobile Medicare Units are

Respire Care Homes	Mobile Medicare Units
These are designed for elderly individuals in old age homes who are seriously ill and need continuous nursing care and respire.	These units provide medical care to elderly individuals living in rural, isolated and backward areas.
They focus an offering temporary relief and intensive care to manage severe illnesses or recovery periods.	They focus on bringing medical services directly to older people who may hot have easy access to healthcare facilities.
This is typically, a facility-based service providing a controlled environment for recovery and rest.	This is typically, a mobile service reaching remote areas to ensure healthcare accessibility.

Long Answer Type Questions

1. All children are vulnerable, but some children are more vulnerable than others. What can be its four reasons? In what four ways does SOS village help these children? **CBSE 2021 C**

Ans. Children are vulnerable but some children are more vulnerable. Reasons for this are

(i) Nearly two-thirds of children under 5 years of age suffer from moderate or severe malnutrition. Malnutrition affects development in all area.
(ii) About 3 million children live on the streets without any shelter.
(iii) Only one in three children of the pre-school age has the opportunity to be in an early learning programme.
(iv) Less than half of India's children between ages 6 and 14 years go to school.

SOS Children's Villages is an independent non-governmental social organisation which has pioneered a family approach to the long term care of orphaned and abandoned children. SOS helps children in following ways

For answer refer to Q. No. 2(ii) of Short Answer Type Questions.

2. Your neighbour's son recently started going to college for his undergraduation. He sees all his friends coming to college on bikes and in cars. He has to travel in public buses to reach college. All this has made him dislike going to college everyday. He keeps bringing up new excuses to skip college.

(i) Give reasons that are responsible for vulnerability of youth like this.
(ii) What can be done to overcome this vulnerability?
(iii) State a few youth programmes in India.

Competency Based Que

Ans. (i) For answer refer to Q. No. 4(i) of Short Answer Type Questions.

(ii) For socially and economically productive youth, there is a need for appropriate education and training, gainful employment and adequate opportunities for personal development and advancement. They also require shelter and a clean environment and basic health services of quality, social defense and protection from all manner of exploitation.

There is a need for suitable participation in decision-making bodies pertaining to youth issues, with socio-economic and cultural matters, access to sports, physical education, adventure and recreational opportunities being few other requisites for them.

(iii) Some of the schemes and programmes related to the welfare of youth are discussed below

- **The National Service Scheme** (NSS) This scheme aims at involving college students in social service and national development programmes like, construction and repair of roads, school buildings, village ponds, tanks. Activities related to environmental and ecological improvement like tree plantation, removal of weeds from lakes, digging pits.
- **The National Service Volunteer Scheme** This scheme provides opportunities to the students who have completed their first degree. They can involve themselves on a full-time basis for a short period of one or two years, in the programmes of national development mainly through Nehru Yuva Kendras.

3. Identify any four causes of youth being vulnerable in India. In what four ways does Nehru Yuva Kendras help these youth? CBSE 2021 C

Ans. Four causes of youth being vulnerable in India are

(i) Adolescents is the period in which an individual is trying to come to terms with many biological changes in her/ his body which have an impact on the person's sense of well-being and identity.

(ii) This is also the period when the individual is preparing to take on adult roles, two of the foremost being earning a livelihood and marriage, followed by raising a family.

(iii) Peer pressure and pressure to excel in an increasingly competitive world are other factors that can cause a lot of stress and turmoil.

(iv) When the family/environment is unable to provide positive support to the adolescent, some adolescents may consume alcohol and drugs.

Nehru Yuva Kendras help them offering them various programmes. Four such programmes are

(i) Adult education

(ii) Establishment of youth clubs

(iii) Organisation of work camps

(iv) Youth leadership training programmes

4. Discuss the National Service Volunteer Scheme in detail.

Ans. This scheme provides opportunities to the students who have completed their first degree.

They can involve themselves on a full-time basis for a short period of one or two years in the programmes of national development mainly through Nehru Yuva Kendras.

These Kendras are involved in programmes of

- Adult education
- Establishment of youth clubs
- Organisation of work camps
- Youth leadership training programmes
- Vocational training
- Promotion of rural sports and games, etc.

The Nehru Yuva Kendras also enable the non-student youth of rural areas towards the development in the rural areas. With the help of various activities, these Kendras also aim to popularise nationally accepted objectives like self-reliance, secularism, socialism, democracy, national integration and development of scientific temper.

These objectives are fulfilled through activities like non-formal education, social service camps, development of sports, activities for young people, cultural and recreational programmes, vocational training, youth leadership training programmes and promotion and establishment of youth clubs.

5. Discuss the youth programmes related to promotion of adventure and commonwealth youth programme.

Ans. The Ministry of Youth Affairs and Sports adopted the National Youth Policy in 2003. Under this policy some schemes and programmes related to the welfare of youth are run by the government.

- **Promotion of Adventure** Many youth clubs and voluntary organisations organise activities like mountaineering, trekking, hiking, exploration for collection of data, study of flora and fauna in the mountains, forests, deserts and sea, canoeing, coastal sailing, raft-exhibitions, swimming, cycling, etc., by using the financial assistance provided by the government for promotion of adventure.
  These activities are aimed at encouraging the spirit of adventure, risk-taking, co-operative team-work, capacity of ready and vital response to challenging situations and endurance among the youth. Government also provides assistance for establishment and development of institutions to facilitate such activities.
- **Commonwealth Youth Programme** India is participating in the Commonwealth Youth Programme which is aimed at making the youth participate in

development processes of their respective countries and to provide a forum for increasing co-operation and understanding among the Commonwealth countries. Under this programme, three regional centres for advanced studies in youth work have been set up in India, Zambia and Guyana. The Asia Pacific Regional Centre has been set up at Chandigarh, India.

6. Discuss some of the programmes for the elderly adopted by the Indian Government.

Ans. Some of the programmes, adopted by the Indian Government, for the elderly are as follows

- Programmes catering to the basic needs of older persons particularly food, shelter and health care to the destitute elderly.
- Programmes for encouraging active and productive ageing.
- Old age homes to provide food, care and shelter.
- Respite care homes and continuous care homes for older persons who live in old age homes but are seriously ill and thus require continuous nursing care and respite.
- Multi-service centres for older persons to provide day care, educational and entertainment opportunities, health care, companionship.
- Mobile medicare units to provide medical care to the older persons living in rural and isolated and backward areas.
- Day care centers for alzheimer's disease/dementia patients to provide specialised day care.

7. It is important to recognise the elderly as a human resource and their rich experience should be used for national development.

(i) To ensure a healthy and secure life for the elderly, which initiative was taken by the Government of India in the year 1999?

(ii) State three reasons why the elderly are considered to be a vulnerable group.

(iii) List any three facilities provided in multi-service centres for older persons. **CBSE 2024**

Ans. (i) In 1999, the Government of India launched the National Old Age Pension Scheme (NOAPS) to ensure a healthy and secure life for the elderly.

(ii) **Reasons of Vulnerability of Elderly**

The reasons that hold that elderly people are a vulnerable group are discussed below

(a) **Health Insecurity** Health is a major issue of concern for many individuals at this age. The elderly are more vulnerable to diseases due to decreased physiological reserves and defence mechanisms.

(b) **Social Insecurity** In this period, they find themselves alone because the children are likely to have moved away from the family due to marriage or to earn a living.

(c) **Lack of Family Support** Due to certain features of city life like small family size, lack of free time to care for the aged, limited living space, high cost of living, long working hours, etc. lead to reduced support within the immediate and extended family.

(iii) Facilities provided in multi-service centres for older persons are as follows

(a) **Daycare** Offering supervised care and support during daytime hours.

(b) **Educational and Entertainment Opportunities** Providing diverse activities and programmes tailored to older persons' interests.

(c) **Companionship** Creating a supportive community environment where older individuals can build relationships.

SELF ASSESSMENT TEST

Objective Type Question

1. Which age group is defined as juvenile delinquency?
   (a) Above 18 (b) Below 18 (c) Both (a) and (b) (d) None of these
2. What is the goal of the Juvenile Justice System?
   (a) To maintaining public safety (b) Skill development
   (c) Habilitation (d) All of these
3. A youth is considered a juvenile delinquent ....
   (a) as soon as they break the law.
   (b) when they are apprehended by the police.
   (c) when they are processed through the court and adjudicated.
   (d) All of the above

Very Short Answer Type Questions

4. State any two programmes organised by the government for youth to promote national integration.
5. What are the two categories of children as per the Juvenile Justice Act?
6. Name any two vulnerable groups.

Short Answer Type Questions

7. Discuss the role of Scouts and Guides programme for the youth.
8. National Integration is a crucial issue in Indian context. With reference to the given statement, discuss the promotion of National Integration Programme.

Long Answer Type Questions

9. How can an individual start his/her career in the field of management support services programmes for children, youth and elderly? Discuss in detail.
10. What are the groups with whom an individual preparing for a career in support services may interact?

08 CHAPTER

Design for Fabric and Apparel

This chapter explores the principles and elements of fabric and apparel design, focusing on how colour, texture, line, and proportion create both functional and aesthetically pleasing garments. It also highlights career opportunities in fashion, production and textile preservation, emphasising the importance of design in the textile industry.

YOUR STUDY GOALS

YOUR PRACTICE GOAL

- Objective Type Questions (29 Qs ; MCQs, A-R, Matching, Case Based)
- Subjective Questions (14 VSAs, 9 SAs, 8 LAs)

8.1 Introduction

- The term **design**[1] varies widely among contemporary designers, reflecting personal interpretations and diverse contexts. Many people, for instance, often equate design with high fashion and its accessories, overlooking its broader significance.
- In the realm of textiles, design is frequently linked to colour schemes and fabric prints. However, this perspective is quite narrow and does not capture the full essence of what design entails.
- Design is not merely about decoration; it inherently involves functionality and utility. Without a practical purpose, a fabric or object fails to meet the criteria of good design.
- A comprehensive understanding of design emphasises the importance of **harmony**[2] in form. This harmony arises from the interplay between aesthetics and the practical application of a product, which is vital for its success.
- The creativity and expression of designers play a significant role in shaping the meaning of design. True harmony can only be achieved when these elements are thoughtfully integrated with the object's usefulness.

1 **Design** It is associated with the colour scheme or the print on the fabric.

2 **Harmony** It is created when all elements of design come together to give a good and pleasing effect.

- In essence, design represents the human ability to conceive, plan, and create products that serve both individual and collective purposes. This capability highlights the multifaceted nature of design beyond simple visual appeal.
- A well-executed design considers price, colour and the overall service provided by the product.

Basic Concepts of Design

- Design is fundamentally a planned arrangement aimed at creating a desired object or fabric. It encompasses both functionality and aesthetic appeal, resulting in an outcome that satisfies visual and practical needs.
- There are two primary aspects of design **structural and applied.**

(i) **Structural Design**[3] It focuses on the intrinsic form of an object, while applied design deals with enhancements added on top of this basic structure.

- It involves the fundamental processing of fibers, the types of yarns used, and the various weaving or knitting techniques. It also considers when color is introduced in the production process.
- It refer to the basic cut or **silhouette**[4] of the garments.

(ii) **Applied Design**[5] It refers to the decorative elements superimposed on the basic structure. Techniques like dyeing, printing, and embroidery can significantly alter the fabric's appearance and enhance its value.

- This category also includes trims and notions, such as fasteners, which contribute to the final product's overall appeal and functionality.
- Like architecture, painting, and sculpture, fabric and dress design are considered forms of art. Thus, they adhere to the same fundamental principles of artistic expression.
- The two main factors of design are elements and principles.
- **Elements of Design**[6] It consist of the fundamental tools of art, including colour, **texture**[7], line, shape, form and pattern.
- **Principles of Design** It involve the manipulation of these elements to achieve harmony, balance, rhythm, proportion and emphasis. These principles are essential for creating cohesive and aesthetically pleasing designs.

8.2 Elements of Design I : Colour

- Colours surround us in various forms and play a significant role in fashion. They are crucial to all textile materials, whether for apparel, household items or commercial and institutional use.
- Often, a product's identity is closely linked to its colour, making it a defining characteristic. Everyone has personal favorites, which can influence their preferences and choices.
- **Colour**[8] also serves as a reflection of seasons, events and the collective spirit of people. It carries emotional and cultural significance, shaping how we perceive and connect with the world around us.
- The choice of colours is influenced by a variety of factors, including culture, traditions, climate and specific occasions. Personal reasons also play a significant role in individual colour preferences.
- Designers meticulously select fabric colours to convey a specific message or theme. This careful consideration ensures that the chosen colours resonate with the intended audience and context.
- Thus, colour is an important element of fashion.

---

3 **Structural Design** These are intrinsic parts of materials created through manipulation of fabrications, colour or texture.
4 **Silhouette** The dark shape and outline of someone or something visible in restricted light against a brighter background.
5 **Applied Design** It is that part of the design which has been superimposed on the basic structure, like dyeing, printing, etc.
6 **Elements of Design** Refer to the tools of the art, including colour, texture, line and shape.
7 **Texture** It refers to the sensory impression of sight and touch.
8 **Colour** It reflects seasons, events, and the spirit of people and is part of fashion.

Colour Theory

Colour can be defined as the reflection of light striking the surface of an object. When the visible light rays strike the retina and stimulate the nerve cells of the eye, **two things** happen

(i) The light rays are reflected, which results in the visual sensation that is referred to as a colour.

(ii) The nerves send a message to the brain, which produces a specific sensation, and we see colour.

Thus, the colour that is finally seen is dependent on the wavelength or the combination of the wavelengths of the light source. When all light rays are reflected, the object appears white; when no light rays are reflected, the object appears black.

- Light rays of short wavelengths are classified as receding or restful colours. This group includes green, blue-green, blue and purple.
- Light rays of long wavelengths are categorised as advancing or stimulating colours, which include red, orange and yellow.
- Colours can be perceived in varying intensities, as light consists of different wavelengths.
- Colours have three key aspects: hue, value and intensity (or chroma). These aspects are essential for understanding and describing colour.

Understanding Colour

- The study of colour is fundamentally dependent on light, which is a form of radiant energy. Light is part of the electromagnetic radiation spectrum.
- Sunlight is the primary source of radiant energy reaching Earth, transmitted through light waves.
- When light falls on raindrops, it is scattered, producing the spectrum of seven colours known as VIBGYOR: Violet, Indigo, Blue, Green, Yellow, Orange and Red.
- Thus, sunlight consists of these seven visible colours, in addition to ultraviolet and infrared rays.

Hue

Hue[9] is the common name of the colour. The **spectrum**[10] specifies the seven colours as **VIBGYOR**[11]. Colours can be understood from a design point of view for which Munsell's Colour Wheel is helpful. This divides colours as follows

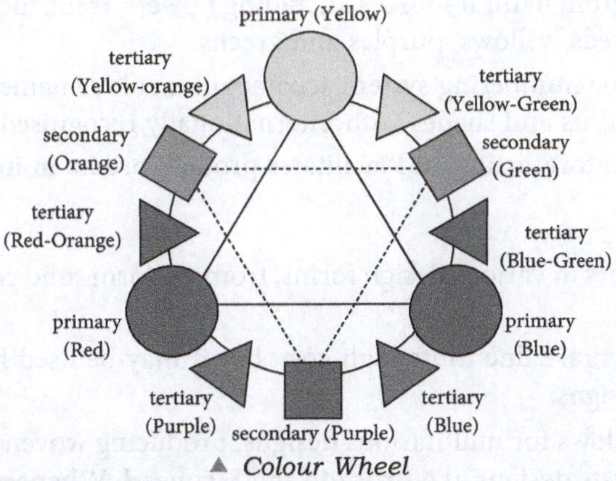

▲ *Colour Wheel*

- **Primary Colours** Primary colours are those colours which cannot be produced by mixing any other colour. These are red, yellow and blue.
- **Secondary Colours** These colours are made by mixing two primary colours, for example, orange, green and purple.

---

9 **Hue** The common name for colour.

10 **Spectrum** A continuous sequence of the VIBGYOR colours.

11 **VIBGYOR** It refers to the colours: Violet, Indigo, Blue, Green, Yellow, Orange and Red.

- **Tertiary or Intermediate Colours** These colours are made by mixing one primary and one secondary colour. Such colours include red-orange, yellow-orange, yellow-green, blue-green, blue-purple and red-purple.
- **Neutral Colours** This category includes the colours not mentioned in the above three categories, such as white, black, grey, silver and metallics. These are also called **achromatics**, i.e., colours without colour.
- The common colour wheel shows colours in their purest form and fullest intensity.

Value

- **Value**[12] describes the **lightness or darkness** of a hue, known as tint or shade. White has the maximum value, while black has the least.
- The value of colours is judged using a Grey Scale and Value Chart, which ranges from 0 to 10. Here, 0 represents black, 10 represents white, and 5 is the mid-value grey.
- According to this scale, a hue that approaches white is considered a tint, while one that approaches black is a shade. The Grey Scale also helps assess the equivalent value of any hue.

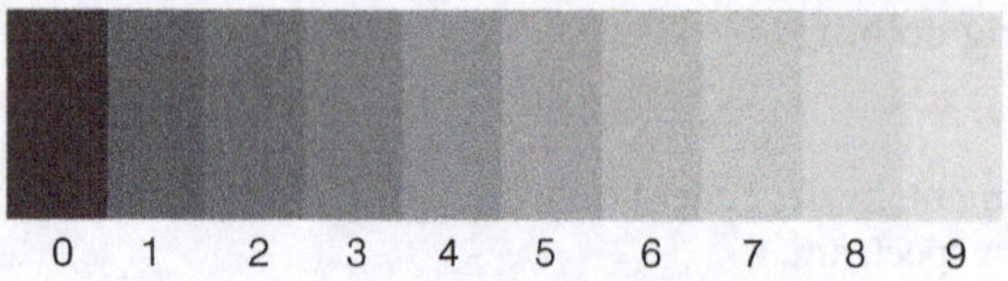

▲ *Grey Scale*

Chroma or Intensity

- It refers to the brightness or purity of a colour. Dullness occurs when a colour is blended with its opposite on the colour wheel.

Recognising Colour

- A person with normal eyesight can distinguish between different values and intensities of hues, giving them specific names, such as brick red, blood-red and ruby-red.
- Colour names are derived from natural sources, including flowers, trees, foods and minerals. Each group showcases variations like reds, yellows, purples and greens.
- In the textile trade, a unique numbering system accompanies colour names. **The Pantone Shade Card** displays all possible hues, tints and shades with internationally recognised code numbers.
- This system aids in fashion forecasting and facilitates product orders in international markets.

Colour in Fabrics

- Fabrics can showcase colours in various design forms, from uniform solid colours to patterns that follow the yarn interlacing.
- Dyeing at the fibre stage is rare due to its high cost, but it may be used for manufactured fibres that require multi-coloured designs.
- Dyeing at the yarn stage allows for multifarious designs, producing woven patterns like stripes, checks, and plaids, as well as intricate designs like **Brocade** and **Jacquard**. When yarns are tie-dyed, it results in beautiful Ikat patterns.
- Fabric dyeing is the most common method, used for creating both simple solid colours and designed materials through techniques like tie and batik. At the fabric stage, colour can be applied through painting, printing, embroidery, and patching in various shapes and forms.
- Textile designers must understand the dyeing properties of different fibres and fabrics, choosing the appropriate stage and technique of colour application based on the final product's requirements.

12 **Value** It describes the shade/tint of a hue.

Colour Schemes or Colour Harmonies

There are certain basic colour schemes used for combining colours. A colour scheme only suggests the hues that can be combined; the rest, including the values and intensities of the hue and the quantity to be used, are decided either by the designer or the consumer of the final product. The colour wheel is helpful for studying these colour schemes, which can be divided into two groups: **related and contrasting.**

Related schemes have at least one hue in common. These include

- **Monochromatic Harmony** This means a harmony based on one hue, which may be varied in value or intensity.
- **Achromatic Harmony** This scheme uses only neutrals, such as a combination of black and white.
- **Accented Neutral Harmony** This involves one hue combined with a neutral or achromatic colour.
- **Analogous Harmony** This refers to a colour combination using two or three hues that lie side by side on the colour wheel. Using four or more hues may create a jumble unless each is in very small quantity.

Contrasting schemes include

- **Complementary Harmony** This scheme uses two hues that lie directly opposite each other on the colour wheel.
- **Double Complementary** This consists of two pairs of complements, generally neighbours on the colour wheel.
- **Split Complementary Harmony** This is a **three-colour combination** using a hue, its complement (directly across on the colour wheel), and a neighbour. It may also use a hue and two neighbours of its complement.
- **Analogous Complementary** This is a combination of analogous and complementary schemes, selecting a complement for dominance within a group of neighbouring colours.
- **Triadic Harmony** This involves a combination of three hues that lie at equal distance from one another on the colour wheel.

Quick Test 1

1. What term relates to high fashion dresses, accessories, beauty, and the colour of fabrics?
2. Mention the two basic concepts of design.
3. A design consists of what?
4. What factors affect the choice of colour?

8.3 Elements of Design II : Texture

- Texture is the **sensory impression** of sight and touch. It refers to the tactile and visual qualities of the material, and each material has a different texture. The texture of a fabric can be described in terms of
  - **How it looks** shiny, dull, opaque, dense, transparent, translucent, glossy, etc.
  - **How it behaves** hangs limp, stiff, sticks out, clinging, flowing out, etc.
  - **How it feels** soft, crisp, harsh, grainy, smooth, rough, coarse, pebbly, etc.
- It is mainly the textile materials that bring texture into our daily life. The factors that determine the texture in textile materials can be summarised as follows
  - **Fibre Content** This includes fibre type, whether natural or man-made, its length and fineness, and its surface characteristics.
  - **Yarn Processing and Yarn Type** This includes the method of processing, twist inserted during processing, fineness of the yarn, and yarn type (simple, complex, novelty or textured).

- **Fabric Construction Technique** This includes weaving (type of weave and its compactness), knitting, felting, braiding, lace-making, etc.
- **Fabric Finishes** This includes stiffening (starching, sizing or gumming), ironing, calendaring, tentering, napping and fulling.
- **Surface Ornamentation** This includes tufting, flock printing, embroidery and stitched effects.

- The main purpose of texture in dress design is to create interest for the consumer and to enhance their desirable features. Textures used should have a good relationship with each other to achieve harmony. In dress, the texture should be appropriate to the figure, personal characteristics, silhouette or form of costume and occasion.

Line

- Line is defined as a mark that connects two points; it has a beginning and an end.
- It can also form the outline of an object, shape or form, helping to define the overall silhouette of a design.
- As an element of design, line indicates the shape of things, provides movement and determines direction.
- Line and shape are two important elements of design that work together to create the pattern or plan of every design.
- The decorative details on any article we see are a combination of lines and shapes, emphasising their inter-relationship in design.

Types of Line

There are two basic types of line

(i) **Straight Lines** This is a rigid, unbroken line that creates different effects depending on its direction. Straight lines can also express mood and have several sub-divisions

- **Vertical Lines** These stress up and down movement, emphasising height and giving a severe, dignified and reserved effect.
- **Horizontal Lines** These stress side-to-side movement and create an illusion of width. As they repeat the ground line, they give a stable and placid effect.
- **Oblique or Diagonal Lines** These can increase or decrease width and height depending on the degree and direction of the angle. They can create an active, startling, or dramatic effect.

(ii) **Curved Lines** The curved line has any degree of roundness and can be in the shape of a simple arc or a complicated freehand curve. The degree of roundness determines the type of curve. A slight degree of roundness is called a restrained curve, while a great degree of roundness gives a circular curve. Various objects are associated with these curves, such as parabola, scroll, meander, hairpin, whiplash, serpentine, figure of 8, ogee, etc. Curved lines also have sub-divisions

- **Long and Flowing Curved Lines** These appear most graceful and rhythmic.
- **Large Rounded Curved Lines** These lend a dramatic touch and tend to exaggerate size.
- **Tiny, Puffy Curved Lines** These are youthful and happy.

Line also expresses visual meaning and different traits. For example, straight lines indicate force, strength, and rigidity, whereas curved lines appear soft and graceful. If straight lines are more dominant in a fabric, the design effect is masculine. Curved lines give the impression of femininity and daintiness.

Shapes or Forms

- Lines are connected to make shapes or forms. Shapes can be two-dimensional, such as a drawing or a print on paper or fabric. They can also be **three-dimensional**, as an object that can be viewed from three or more sides, like a human body or the garments on it.
- Since shapes are formed by connecting lines, the characteristics of the lines used determine the characteristics of the shape. A shape made only by straight lines will differ from one made by curved lines. Different lines can be combined in various ways to create countless varieties of shapes.

There are four basic groups of shapes

(i) **Natural Shapes** These are shapes that mimic nature or common shapes of man-made objects.

(ii) **Stylised Shapes** These are simplified or modified natural shapes. They may have some distorted or exaggerated parts.

(iii) **Geometric Shapes** These shapes can be formed mathematically and give a similar impression. They can be created using rulers, compasses or other measuring instruments.

(iv) **Abstract Shapes** These are free-form shapes that do not resemble any specific object but may represent different things to different people based on personal associations.

- In a fabric, shape or form refers to the fall or drape of the material, the shape of ornamentation, patterns and motifs, and the type of placement or repeat, which contributes to the final pattern formation. It represents the silhouette, cut and final detailing in apparel.

Patterns

A pattern can be formed by grouping together one shape or a combination of two or more types of shapes. The shapes can also be arranged in a natural, stylised, geometric or abstract manner.

Quick Test 2

1. How do we get Ikat patterns?
2. What can a texture be made of?
3. What is a split complementary harmony?
4. How many types of basic lines are there?
5. Explain the term 'shape' in the context of fabric.

8.4 Principles of Design

A successful design greatly depends on the understanding principles of basic design. The rules that control how the elements of design are mixed appropriately are referred to as the principles of design.

The **principles of design**[13] are discussed below

Proportion

- **Proportion**[14] is the **relationship of the parts of the garments to** one another. A good design blends elements skillfully, making it unclear where one finishes and another begins, creating a pleasing relationship in size, colour, shape and texture.
- The principle often relies on the **golden mean**, represented by ratios like 3 : 5 : 8 or 5 : 8 : 13. In this ratio, the smaller part relates to the larger part and the whole in a harmonious way, visible in areas like waistlines and hemlines.

13 **Principles of Design** Elements of design are manipulated to create principles of design.

14 **Proportion** It is the relationship of parts of garments to one another.

- For example, In a skirt and blouse dress, the blouse represents 3, the skirt represents 5 and their combined effect represents 8. In a shirt-pant dress, the shirt represents 5 and the pant represents 8, creating a combined effect of 13.
- **Proportion of Colour** Different colours can be used for shirt and pant to create a pleasing proportion of colour, following the golden mean. This adds to the visual appeal of the outfit and helps create a balanced look.
- **Proportion of Texture** Using various textures in a dress can give the illusion of size, either increasing or decreasing the perceived size of the wearer. Heavy and bulky textures may appear overpowering on a thin person, while lighter textures may be more flattering.
- **Proportion of Shape and Form** The size and positioning of prints in a dress should correspond to the wearer's body size and shape.
- Width of the figure, length of legs.
- For example, a high-waist bodice in maternity clothes camouflages the fullness of the abdomen effectively. Equal division in a dress can make a person look shorter and wider, while unequal horizontal divisions can create a slimmer appearance.

Balance

- **Balance**[15] refers to the **proper distribution** of weight from the **central point** of a dress. It is essential for a good garment to achieve balance both vertically (from the center line) and horizontally (from top to bottom). This can be accomplished in three ways : **formal, informal and radial.**
- The elements of design-line, form, colour and texture-are all considered while creating balance in a dress.

Formal Balance

- An average human body is symmetrical, appearing similar on each side of a central vertical line. Each side has one arm, one eye and one leg, though slight differences may exist. Well-designed clothing can minimise noticeable differences, enhancing overall symmetry.
- For customers, **formal vertical balance** is often the least expensive and most expected type of design, commonly found in less expensive garments. This type of balance imparts a sense of stability, dignity and formality to the wearer, although it can sometimes feel monotonous.

Horizontal/Informal Balance

Horizontal balance is primarily used to address figure problems by employing various design elements. For instance, a dark hue can be used to create a slimming effect for larger sizes, contributing to a more balanced appearance.

Radial Balance

This type of balance can be created when the design details of a garment emerge or radiate from a central focus point. This is a complicated design and is used for novelty effect.

Emphasis

- The **emphasis**[16] or focal point of the garment is the area that first attracts customers. It enhances the garment's appeal through the use of colour, design lines, detailing or accessories.
- Emphasis creates interest by directing the customer's attention to a specific area of the garment. Fashion designers often focus on details that highlight the face, as it is considered the focal point of beauty in Indian society.

---

15 **Balance** The proper equalling of distribution of weight from the central point of a dress.
16 **Emphasis** It is the focal point of a garment.

- A beautifully embroidered yoke or a contrasting colour blouse can draw attention to the face, enhancing its prominence.
- For individuals with figure concerns, emphasis can be strategically used to highlight positive features. For example, a woman with a small waist can wear a bright, contrasting belt to accentuate that area. Conversely, a woman with larger hips may choose a hip belt or design details at the hip to draw attention to that part of her figure.
- Emphasis can be created through contrasting colours, unusual shapes, distinct lines and varied textures, adding visual interest to the garment.

Rhythm

Rhythm[17] can be defined as the **repetition of lines**, colours, other elements of design or details to create a pattern by which the eye can flow through the material or garment. It can be developed using lines, shapes, colours and textures in such a way that it gives visual unity.

It can be developed by the following ways

- **Repetition** of embroidery, laces, buttons, piping, colour, etc., at necklines, sleeves and hemlines.
- **Co-ordination** by gradual increase or decrease in size of motifs, lines, buttons, colours and textures.
- **Radiation** where eyes move in an organised way from a central point, for example, gathers in the waist, yolk or cuffs, etc.
- **Parallelism** where elements lie parallel to each other, for example, tucks in a yoke or knife pleats in a skirt. Bands of colour also create a rhythm effect in a dress.

Harmony

- Harmony or **unity** is created in a garment when all the elements of design come together to give a good harmonious effect. It is an important factor in producing marketable designs.
- Harmony by shape occurs when all the areas of a garment reflect the **same shape**. The collar, cuff and hem are curved, and if square pockets are given, they would interrupt the continuity of the design.
- Harmony by texture can be developed by using the right kind of texture for a garment when the garment is in several pieces, like in salwar, kurta and dupatta. With a cotton dupatta, a silk kurta and salwar will show a bad harmony.

Composition

- An artwork or concept created by the proper arrangement or placement of the elements of design and application of the principles in a given space is referred to as a composition.
- Good visual appeal is achieved by choosing two or three principles of design that best fit the requirements of the final artwork. It involves a play of elements of design in a given space.
- The composition can be 2-dimensional or 3-dimensional.

8.5 Preparing for a Career in Design

- The field of design for **fabric and apparel** has expanded into **two categories** of specialisations. Fabric is now used in various applications beyond apparel, while apparel incorporates materials other than fabric.
- Each application has specific requirements regarding appearance, sustainability and cost allocations. Fabric designers must have thorough knowledge of fibre characteristics, advantages, limitations and processing.
- Understanding dyeing properties of different fibres and fabrics is essential for fabric designers. They determine the stage and technique of colour application based on the final product's needs.

---

17 **Rhythm** The repetition of the elements of design to create a pleasing pattern.

- Fashion designers must also grasp the principles of design, which is crucial for their profession.
- Numerous institutes offer both long and short-term courses, including certificates, diplomas, associate and bachelor's degrees.
- Prospective students can choose courses based on their interests, considering the unique qualities of each degree programme.

8.6 Scope of Design

- The design industry is a popular, unique and dynamic sector that influences our lives both directly and indirectly.
- Working in textile or fabric design requires current knowledge of changing trends and styles. Designers must be able to produce fresh and innovative designs, often ahead of the fashion curve.
- Textile designs for apparel tend to change more rapidly compared to designs for furnishings.
- Textile designers conduct extensive research and produce designs for textile companies or fashion houses.
- They also have the option to work for design agencies or as freelancers, depending on their needs and desires.

Quick Test 3

1. What are two factors that determine texture?
2. What two points does a line connect?
3. What do various connecting lines create?
4. What type of degree, in addition to a certificate and a diploma, do many institutes offer for a career in designing?

Mind Map

DESIGN FOR FABRIC AND APPAREL

1 Basic Concepts of Design

Design Definition
- A planned creation balancing aesthetic and functional needs.

Types of Design
- **Structural Design** Focuses on form, fabric type and garment structure.
- **Applied Design** Involves decorative elements like dyeing, printing and trims.

Design Elements
- Colour, Texture, Line, Shape, Form, Pattern.

Design Principles
- Harmony, Balance, Rhythm, Proportion, Emphasis.

Importance
- Combines creativity with functionality.
- Considering factors like price and service.

2 Elements of Design

Colour
- **Importance** Defines identity, reflects emotions, influenced by culture and occasion.
- **Theory** Light reflection creates colour; primary (red, yellow, blue), secondary (orange, green, purple), tertiary (mixed primary + secondary).

Aspects
- **Hue** Colour name.
- **Value** Lightness/Darkness (tint = light, shade = dark).
- **Chroma** Brightness/Purity.

Schemes
- **Related** Monochromatic, Analogous.
- **Contrasting** Complementary, Triadic.

Texture
- **Definition** Visual and tactile quality of materials.
- **Factors** Fibre, yarn type, fabric construction, finishes.
- **Purpose** Adds interest and harmony in design.

Line
- **Definition** A mark connecting two points, defining shapes and direction.

Types
- **Straight** Vertical (height), Horizontal (width), Diagonal (dynamic).
- **Curved** Flowing, rounded (graceful, dramatic).
- **Effect** Straight = strength, Curved = softness.

Shapes
- **Definition** Formed by connecting lines, 2D or 3D.

Types
- **Natural** Mimic nature.
- **Stylised** Modified natural shapes.
- **Geometric** Mathematical.
- **Abstract** Free-form.

Patterns
- **Formation** Created by grouping shapes (natural, geometric, abstract).
- **Effect** Defines fabric design and garment silhouette.

3 Principles of Design

Proportion
- Relationship between parts (e.g., golden mean ratio).
- Affects size, colour, texture and shape balance.

Balance
- Weight distribution in design
- **Formal** Symmetrical
- **Informal** Figure-flattering
- **Radial** Central focus

Emphasis
- Focal point of attention, created by colour, texture, or accessories.

Rhythm
- Repetition of design elements (e.g., buttons, motifs) to create flow.

Harmony
- Unity of all elements working together (shape and texture).

Composition
- Arrangement of design elements to create visual appeal.

4 Preparing for a Career in Design

Fields of Specialisation
- **Fabric Design** Beyond apparel, fabrics are used in various applications.
- **Apparel Design** Includes materials other than fabric.

Key Knowledge Areas
- **Fibre Characteristics** Understand properties, advantages, limitations.
- **Dyeing Techniques** Know the dyeing properties of different fibres and fabrics.

Skills for Fashion Designers
- Grasp design principles for effective design creation.

Education

Courses Available at Institutes
- Certificates, diplomas, associate and bachelor's degrees.
- Choose programmes based on interest and specialisation.

5 Scope in Design

Industry Overview

The design industry is dynamic and influential, impacting our daily lives.

Textile and Fabric Design
- Requires knowledge of trends and the ability to create innovative designs.
- Apparel designs change faster than furnishings.

Work Opportunities
- **Textile Designers** Work for textile companies, fashion houses, design agencies, or as freelancers.

NCERT Folder

1. What do you understand by the term 'design'?

Ans. The word 'design' is used by people in a general sense who relate this with high fashion dresses, accessories, beauty colour of fabrics, its prints and so on. But design is not just a type of decoration. It has utility and appropriate function.

2. What are the factors that affect the texture of a fabric during its manufacture?

Or **Which four factors determine texture in textile material?** **CBSE SQP 2024**

Ans. The factors which determine the texture in textile materials are as follows

- **Fibre Content** It includes fibre type, whether natural or man-made, its length and fineness and its surface characteristics.
- **Yarn Processing and Yarn Type** It includes method of processing, twist inserted during processing, fineness of the yarn and yarn type (simple, complex and novelty or textured).
- **Fabric Construction Technique** It includes weaving (type of weave and its compactness), knitting, felting, braiding, lace-making, etc.
- **Fabric Finishes** It includes stiffening (starching, sizing or gumming), ironing, calendaring and tentering, napping, fulling.
- **Surface Ornamentation** It includes tufting, flock printing, embroidery and stitched effects.

3. How does the application of colour during the different stages of fabric manufacture affect the design in fabric?

Or **Ridhima wants to open a fabric construction unit suggest three ways of adding colour to the fabric during its production give one example of each.**

Competency Based Que; Diksha App

Ans. Ridhima can consider the following three ways to add colour to fabric during its production

(i) **Dyeing at the Fibre Stage** This method involves colouring the raw fibres before they are spun into yarn. It allows for uniform colour throughout the fabric.

Example Wool fibres can be dyed using acid dyes to achieve vibrant colours before being spun into yarn.

(ii) **Dyeing at the Yarn Stage** In this stage, yarn is dyed after it has been spun but before it is woven or knitted into fabric. This method can produce intricate patterns and effects.

Example Yarn can be dyed in a gradient (ombre) effect to create a visually appealing transition from one colour to another.

(iii) **Dyeing at the Fabric Stage** This involves applying colour to the fabric after it has been woven or knitted. Techniques like tie-dye, batik, or fabric painting can be used to add designs and colors.

Example Batik is a traditional technique where wax is applied to fabric before dyeing, creating unique patterns once the wax is removed.

4. What are the different types of lines and shapes? How do they create different effects and moods?

Ans. There are two broad categories of line

(i) **Straight Line** is a rigid unbroken line which creates different effects depending on its direction.
It has three sub-divisions.

(a) **Vertical lines** create a severe, dignified and reserved effect.

(b) **Horizontal lines** give a stable and placid effect.

(c) **Oblique/Diagonal lines** create an active, startling or dramatic effect.

(ii) **Curved Line** is a line which has any degree of roundness. It has three sub-divisions.

(a) **Long and flowing curved lines** appear most graceful and rhythmic.

(b) **Large rounded, curved lines** lend a dramatic touch and tend to exaggerate size.

(c) **Tiny, puffy curved lines** youthful and happy.

5. How do you achieve rhythm and harmony in dress?

Ans. In a dress, **rhythm** can be achieved in the following ways

- Repetition of embroidery laces, buttons piping, colour etc. at necklines, sleeves and hemlines.
- Cordation by gradual increase or decrease in size of motifs, lines, buttons, colours and textures.
- Radiation where eyes move in an organised way from a central point, for example, gathers in waist, yolk or cuffs etc.
- Parallelism where elements lie parallel to each other, for example, tucks in a yoke or knife pleats in a skirt. Bands of colour also create a rhythm effect in a dress.

In a dress, **harmony** can be achieved in the following ways

- Harmony is created in a garment when all the elements of design come together to give a good harmonious effect. It is an important factor in producing marketable designs.
- Harmony by shape occurs when all the areas of a garment reflect the same shape. The collar, cuff and hem are curved and if square pockets are given, they would interrupt the continuity of the design.
- **Harmony by texture** can be developed by using the right kind of texture for a garment when the garment is in several pieces like in salwar, kurta and dupatta. With a cotton dupatta, a silk kurta and salwar will show a bad harmony.

Exam Pattern Questions

Objective Type Questions

Multiple Choice Questions

1. In a comprehensive way design can be described as harmony in what?

(a) Form (b) Lines
(c) Pictures (d) None of these

2. Which of the following is the aspect of design?

(a) Structural design (b) Applied design
(c) Fabric design (d) Both (a) and (b)

3. Which of the following is not an advancing colour?

(a) Red (b) Yellow
(c) Orange (d) Blue-green

4. Which of the following is the aspect of colour?

(a) Hue (b) Value
(c) Intensity (d) All of these

5. Red yellow and blue are the .... colours. Diksha App

(a) secondary (b) territory
(c) primary (d) compound

6. What is the other name for 'achromatics'?

(a) Primary colours (b) Secondary colours
(c) Teritary colours (d) Neutral colours

7. Name the colour harmony/scheme where only neutral colours are used. CBSE 2023

(a) Split complementary (b) Monochromatic
(c) Achromatic (d) Triadic

8. Which of the following are colour names not derived from?

(a) Flowers (b) Trees
(c) Paints (d) Clothes

9. Rita has designed a frock for her six-years old daughter using light and dark pink colour, which indicates .... aspects of a colour. CBSE SQP

(a) chroma (b) value
(c) hue (d) intensity

10. Choose the correct option regarding accented neutral harmony?

(a) It is based on one hue.
(b) It uses only neutrals like black and white.
(c) It uses one hue and a neutral colour.
(d) It uses two hues lying directly opposite on the colour wheel.

11. At which of the following stage is dyeing the most common method?

(a) Fibre stage (b) Yarn stage
(c) Fabric stage (d) Production stage

12. "A combination of three hues that lie equidistant from one another on the colour wheel". Diksha App
What is being referred to in the above line?

(a) Analogous complementary harmony
(b) Double complementary harmony
(c) Triadic harmony
(d) Achromatic harmony

13. The main factors that determine the texture in textile material are .... Diksha App

(a) fibre content
(b) yarn processing and yarn type
(c) fabric construction techniques
(d) All of the above

14. The factors which determine the texture in textile materials can be summarised as

I. Fibre content **II. Principles of Design**
III. Yarn Type **IV. Colour of the yarn**

Choose the correct option

(a) I and II (b) II and III
(c) I and III (d) III and IV

15. Which of the following is a type of curved line?

(a) Vertical line (b) Horizontal line
(c) Oblique line (d) None of these

16. Which of the following is a principle of design?

(a) Textile (b) Form
(c) Colour (d) Harmony

17. Which line signify up and down movement emphasise height and give the effect of sliminess dignity and reverse. Diksha App

(a) Horizontal line (b) Vertical line
(c) Diagonal line (d) Curved line

18. Repetition of line colour other elements of design to create a pattern by which the eyes can flow through the material or article garment .... Diksha App

(a) proportion (b) flow
(c) rhythm (d) movement

19. **Which of the following is not a principle of design?** Diksha App

(a) Proportion (b) Balance
(c) Attractive (d) Emphasis

20. **What is used to correct figure problems using elements of design?**

(a) Formal balance
(b) Horizontal balance
(c) Harmony by texture
(d) Proportion of texture

21. **What is the focal point of a garment?**

(a) Composition (b) Emphasis
(c) Rhythm (d) Colour

22. **Proportion of Golden Mean with respect to garments size is respresented by the following ratios** CBSE 2023

I. 1 : 2 : 4 II. 2 : 4 : 10
III. 5 : 8 : 13 IV. 3 : 5 : 8

Choose the correct option.

(a) I and II (b) III and IV
(c) I and III (d) II and IV

23. **Match the Following.**

List-I	List-II
A. Primary colours	1. White, Black, Grey
B. Secondary colours	2. Blue-Green, Yellow-Green
C. Tertiary colours	3. Orange, Green and violet
D. Neutral colours	4. Red, Yellow and blue

Codes

	A	B	C	D		A	B	C	D
(a)	1	2	3	4	(b)	4	3	2	1
(c)	3	2	4	1	(d)	2	1	4	3

24. **Match colour harmony given in List I with its description in List II.** CBSE SQP 2024

List-I (Colour Harmony)	List-II (Description)
A. Monochromatic harmony	1. Two pairs of complementary
B. Achromatic harmony	2. Only neutrals
C. Double complementary harmony	3. Combination of three colours
D. Split complementary harmony	4. Single hue

Codes

	A	B	C	D		A	B	C	D
(a)	4	2	1	3	(b)	2	3	4	1
(c)	1	2	3	4	(d)	3	4	1	2

Assertion-Reason Questions

Direction (Q. Nos. 25-26) Given below are two statements labelled as Assertion (A) and Reason (R). Select the most appropriate answer from the options given below.

Codes

(a) Both A and R are true and R is the correct explanation of A.
(b) Both A and R are true, but R is not the correct explanation of A.
(c) A is true, but R is false.
(d) A is false, but R is true.

25. **Assertion** (A) A garment can make a person look tall, short, fat or thin.

Reason (R) Heavy and bulky textures appear overpowering on a thin and petite person.

26. **Assertion** (A) Horizontal lines, in a dress, create an illusion of width.

Reason (R) These lines give a stable and placid effect.

Picture Based Question

27. **Identify the picture**

0 1 2 3 4 5 6 7 8 9 10

(a) Colour scale (b) Black-white scale
(c) Hue scale (d) Grey scale

Case Based Questions

28. **Read the passage given below and answer the following questions.** CBSE SQP, 2020

Elements of design are the tools of the art. These are colour, texture and line, shape or form. Colour is all around us in many forms. The identity of the product is most often attributed to colour. Everyone responds to colour and has definite preferences. Colour reflects the season, events and the spirit of people. The choice is affected by culture, tradition, climate, season, occasion or purely personal reason. Colour is an important part of fashion. Designers carefully choose fabric colours to make a definite statement. Colour can be seen in fabrics in various design forms. Some fabrics may have one uniform solid colour, while the colour follows the yarn interlacing in others or may be coloured in other patterns.

(i) **Which word can be used for brightness of a colour?**

(a) Value (b) Intensity
(c) Hue (d) Complementary

(ii) **Which of the following pairs correctly matches an element of design with its description?**
(a) **Texture** Refers to the smoothness of a fabric
(b) **Shape** Defines the color preferences of individuals
(c) **Line** Represents seasonal changes in fashion
(d) **Colour** Influences cultural and personal choices

(iii) **Assertion** (A) Colour is an important part of fashion design.
Reason (R) Designers choose fabric colours to make a definite statement.
Codes
(a) Both A and R are true and R is the correct explanation of A.
(b) Both A and R are true, but R is not the correct explanation of A.
(c) A is true, but R is false.
(d) A is false, but R is true.

(iv) **Which of the following factors influence the choice of colour in design?**
(a) Only personal preferences
(b) Culture, tradition, climate, season and occasion
(c) The type of fabric only
(d) Only the event or season

29. Read the passage given below and answer the following questions.
Design industry is a vibrant, varied and dynamic creative sector the plays a powerful and important role in several areas of our lives. Working in textile or fabric design demands awareness of the changing trends and styles and an ability to produce designs that are fresh, current or even ahead of the fashion curve. Textile designs for apparel fashion tend to have a quicker turnaround than designs for furnishing. Textile designers work in industry-researching and producing designs for textiles companies or fashion houses-but they might also work for a design agency or as freelancers.

(i) **What is a person who can provide us consistent look and also adapt current trends, called?**
(a) Garment expert
(b) Fashion designer
(c) Garment merchandiser
(d) Interior decorator

(ii) **What is the dullness or brightness of any colour called?**
(a) Hue
(b) Value
(c) Intensity
(d) Spectrum

(iii) **Which of the following dress is an example of achromatic harmony?**
(a) White shirt
(b) Pink frock
(c) Black suit and colourful dupatta
(d) Red top and green skirt

(iv) **Which of the following is incorrect statement**
(a) Structural design depends on the basic cut of the garment.
(b) Applied design is super imposed on the fabric.
(c) VIBGYOR is a group of seven colours.
(d) Value is the common name of the colour.

Answers

1. (a) Form
2. (d) Both (a) and (b)
3. (d) Blue-green
4. (d) All of these
5. (c) primary
6. (d) Neutral colours
7. (c) Achromatic
8. (c) Paints
9. (b) value
10. (d) It uses two hues lying directly opposite on the colour wheel.
11. (c) Fabric stage
12. (c) Triadic harmony
13. (d) All of the above
14. (c) I and III
15. (d) None of these
16. (b) Form
17. (b) Vertical line
18. (c) rhythm
19. (c) Attractive
20. (b) Horizontal balance
21. (a) Composition
22. (b) III and IV
23. (b) 4 3 2 1
24. (a) 4 2 1 3
25. (b) Both A and R are true, but R is not the correct explanation of A.
26. (b) Both A and R are true, but R is not the correct explanation of A.
27. (d) Grey scale
28. (i) (b) Intensity
(ii) (d) Colour Influences cultural and personal choices
(iii) (a) Both A and R are true and R is the correct explanation of A.
(iv) (b) Culture, tradition, climate, season and occasion
29. (i) (b) Fashion designer
(ii) (c) Intensity
(iii) (a) White shirt
(iv) (d) Value is the common name of the colour.

Subjective Questions

Very Short Answer Type Questions

1. Differentiate between structural design and applied design. **CBSE 2024, Diksha App**

Ans. **Structural Design** and **Applied Design** are two fundamental aspects of design, particularly in textiles and apparel and they differ in their focus and execution

	Structural Design	Applied Design
Definition	This aspect pertains to the intrinsic form and construction of a fabric or garment.	This involves decorative elements added to the basic structure.
Focus	It emphasises the basic elements such as the type of fibres used, the yarn construction, and the methods of weaving or knitting.	It encompasses techniques like dyeing, printing, embroidery and embellishments that enhance the fabric's appearance.

2. Classify colour on the basis of Munsell's colour wheel. Provide an example of any one type of colour. **CBSE 2024**

Ans. Classification of colours on the basis of Munsell's colour wheel are as follows

- **Hue** Represents the pure colour of an object for example, Munsell Red (5R).
- **Value** Indicates the lightness or darkness of a colour. For example, Value 5 (middle grey).
- **Chroma** Refers to the purity of intensity of a colour. For example, Chroma 8 (high saturation in Munsell Blue, 5B).

3. By using different types of lines in various combinations on fabrics, name four basic groups of shapes which can be formed? **CBSE 2025**

Ans. By using different types of lines in various combinations on fabric, four basic groups of shapes that can be formed are

- **Straight Shapes like Rectangles and Squares** These are the fundamental building blocks, formed by straight edges in fabric and can be horizontal, vertical or diagonal.
- **Curved Shapes like Circles** These shapes are formed by flowing or rounded edges in fabric, creating smooth, non-linear forms.
- **Angular Shapes like Triangles** These are formed by the intersection of two or more straight lines, creating corners and points in fabric.
- **Combinations** These are shapes that are formed by combining the above three elements, creating complex and varied forms in fabric.

4. Renu wants to create a dress for herself using neutral colours. What is the other name for these colours? Also give three examples of neutral colours. **Competency Based Que; CBSE Term II, 2022**

Ans. Neutral colours includes the colours not mentioned in the above three categories, such as white, black, grey, silver and metallics. These are also called achromatics, meaning colours without colour.

5. What do you mean by value? How can you change the value of a hue? **Diksha App**

Ans. **Value** refers to the lightness or darkness of a hue. It describes how much light a color reflects, impacting its appearance.

You can change the value of a hue in two main ways

(i) **Tint** By adding white to the hue, you create a lighter version, increasing its value (e.g., adding white to red results in pink).

(ii) **Shade** By adding black to the hue, you create a darker version, decreasing its value (e.g., adding black to red results in burgundy).

6. Noori wants to create a clothing collection using contrasting colour scheme. What four different types of contrasting scheme she can apply? **Competency Based Que; CBSE SQP, 2021**

Ans. Four types of contrasting schemes are

(i) Complementary harmony

(ii) Double complementary harmony

(iii) Split complementary harmony

(iv) Analogous harmony

7. What is analogous harmony?

Ans. Analogous harmony refers to a colour combination using two or three hues that lie side by side on the colour wheel. Use of four or more hues may create a jumble unless each one is in very small quantity.

8. What do you mean by complementary colours. Give example. **Diksha App**

Ans. Complementary colours are pairs of colors that are opposite each other on the colour wheel. When used together, they create a strong contrast and can enhance each other's visual impact.

For example, red and green are complementary colours. In design, pairing a red dress with green accessories can create a vibrant and eye-catching look.

9. Why are fat people advised to wear vertical lines in clothing and thin people horizontal lines?

Ans. Fat people are advised to wear dresses with vertical lines as these lines create an illusion of height.

Thin people are advised to wear dresses with horizontal lines as these lines create an illusion of width.

10. Sushma wants to create dress using different shapes. Which four basic shapes she can create by using different types of lines? Competency Based Que; CBSE SQP, 2021

Ans. Sushma can create dress by using different types of lines

(i) Natural Shapes (ii) Stylised shapes
(iii) Geometric shapes (iv) Abstract shapes

11. Mrs. Gupta wants to open her own boutique. Name any four principles of design which would help her in designing clothes. Competency Based Que; CBSE, 2022

Ans. The principles of design which would help Mrs. Gupta are discussed below

(i) **Proportion** It is the relationship of the parts of the garments to one another.

(ii) **Balance** Balance is proper equalling of the distribution of weight from the central point of a dress.

(iii) **Emphasis** It creates interest by focusing the customers' attention or choice on a specific area of the garment.

(iv) **Rhythm** It can be defined as the repetition of lines, colours, other elements of design or details to create a pattern by which the eye can flow through the material or garment.

12. What are the effects of applying principle of balance in apparel design?

Ans. Following are the effects of applying principle of balance in apparel design

(i) Application of formal balance gives a feeling of stability, dignity and formality to the garment wearer but tends to get monotonous.

(ii) Application of horizontal balance is done to correct figure problems by using various elements of design, for example, dark hue for big size.

13. List down four qualities of a good design. Diksha App

Ans. Here are four qualities of a good design

(i) **Functionality** A good design serves its intended purpose effectively, ensuring that the product is practical and meets the needs of its users.

(ii) **Aesthetic Appeal** It possesses visual attractiveness, combining colours, shapes, and textures harmoniously to create an engaging and pleasing appearance.

(iii) **Durability** A quality design utilises materials and construction methods that ensure longevity and resilience, allowing the product to withstand wear and tear over time.

(iv) **User-Centricity** It considers the needs, preferences, and comfort of the end-users, ensuring that the design is intuitive and enhances the user experience.

14. What does yarn processing and yarn type include?

Ans. Yarn processing and yarn type include method of processing, twist inserted during processing, fineness of the yarn and yarn type (simple, complex, novelty or textured).

Short Answer Type Questions

1. Nikita is a fashion designer. She wants to design a saree blouse for herself using complementary colour scheme/harmony. Explain this colour scheme and also give one suitable example. Competency Based Que; CBSE, 2022

Ans. For answer refer to text under the heading 'Colour Schemes or Colour Harmonies' on page no. 171.

2. Give three tips on colour and design for selecting a shirt for a short and plump teenager.

Ans. The following points on colour and design should be kept in mind for selecting a shirt for a short and plump teenager

(i) The shirt should have thin vertical stripes to make the teenager appear tall and thin. Small checks or small prints may also be used.

(ii) Cool colours like green or blue should be used to minimise the body size.

(iii) Fine and clingy fabric like linen, crepe silk and satin should be the shirt's material to project an appearance of slimness.

3. Explain the effect of horizontal and diagonal line on the personality of a person. Diksha App

Ans. The use of horizontal and diagonal lines in design can significantly impact the perception of a person's personality and presence. Here's how each type of line affects personality

- **Horizontal Lines** Horizontal lines are associated with stability, calmness, and a sense of groundedness. They tend to convey a relaxed and balanced appearance.

  Personality Perception Clothing or designs featuring horizontal lines can give the impression of being approachable, friendly and secure. This can be beneficial in settings where a calm and trustworthy demeanor is desired, such as in business meetings or social gatherings.

- **Diagonal Lines** Diagonal lines create a sense of movement, energy and dynamism. They can make a design feel more active and engaging.

  Personality Perception Wearing clothing with diagonal lines can convey confidence, assertiveness, and a forward-thinking attitude. This type of line can make a person appear more adventurous and stylish, often attracting attention and suggesting a vibrant personality.

4. Write a short note on principle of proportion. Diksha App

Ans. The principle of **proportion** refers to the relationship between the various parts of a garment in relation to each other and to the whole design. It emphasises the importance of balance and harmony among different elements, such as size, color, shape and texture, to create a visually appealing garment.

Good proportion creates a pleasing relationship between different parts of an outfit, making it look cohesive. Designers often rely on the golden mean, a mathematical ratio (like 3:5:8), to guide them in achieving aesthetic balance. For example, in a dress, if the bodice represents 3 parts, the skirt may represent 5 parts, leading to a harmonious overall effect.

Proper proportion can enhance a wearer's appearance by flattering their body shape, emphasising positive features, and minimising any figure concerns. Thus, understanding and applying the principle of proportion is essential in fashion design to ensure that garments are not only beautiful but also functional and flattering.

5. (i) A fashion design team has been tasked with creating a new apparel collection inspired by the Golden Mean. Describe any three ways how they would integrate the principles of proportion into their design process, with a focus on Golden Mean.

(ii) They have been asked to use colour value 0 and 10 from & Grey Scale. What do these equivalent values represent? CBSE 2025

Ans. (i) The three ways by which a fashion design team would integrate the principles of proportion into their design process, with a focus on Golden Mean are

- **Balanced Garment Design** The team can use the Golden Ratio (1:1.618) to create well-proportioned clothing elements like sleeves and hemlines.
- **Pattern Placement** They can place prints, buttons or embroidery based on Golden Ratio points to enhance visual appeal.
- **Seam and Cut Lines** Proportional seam placements, inspired by the Golden Ratio, ensure the outfit looks harmoniously structured and elegant.

(ii) On the Grey Scale, colour value 0 means pure black and colour value 10 means pure white. These values show extreme ends of contrast.

6. What is the importance of texture of cloth in subduing body effects? Diksha App

Ans. The texture of cloth plays a significant role in influencing how a garment affects body appearance and perception. Here are some key points regarding its importance in subduing body effects

(i) **Visual Illusion** Different textures can create visual effects that either enhance or downplay certain body features. For example, smooth, shiny fabrics may highlight colours, while textured or matte fabrics can soften and obscure them.

(ii) **Proportion and Size** Heavier textures can add bulk, which may be flattering for some body types but overwhelming for others. Conversely, lighter, flowing textures can create a slimming effect and enhance movement, contributing to a more streamlined appearance.

(iii) **Comfort and Fit** The feel of a fabric against the skin affects how comfortable a garment is. Textures that are too rough may draw attention to certain areas, while soft textures can provide comfort and confidence, allowing the wearer to focus on their overall look rather than body concerns.

(iv) **Style and Context** The choice of texture can set the tone for a garment. For instance, softer textures may be more suitable for casual wear, while structured textures can convey formality. This contextual alignment helps in creating a harmonious look that aligns with the wearer's body shape.

7. You have bought a silk fabric to get a frock stitched for your younger sister. Illustrate three different ways to create 'Rhythm' in the frock.

Competency Based Que; CBSE SQP, 2020

Or **You are designing a frock for your younger sister how do you achieve rhythm in this?** Diksha App

Ans. To achieve rhythm in designing a frock for your younger sister, you can incorporate the following elements

(i) **Repetition of Patterns** Use a specific print or motif throughout the frock. For example, if you choose a floral pattern, repeat it in the bodice, skirt and sleeves. This creates a cohesive look that guides the eye through the design.

(ii) **Gradual Size Changes** You can create rhythm by varying the size of the motifs or patterns. Start with larger flowers at the top of the frock and gradually decrease their size towards the hem. This gradual change can give a flowing, dynamic feel to the design.

(iii) **Lines and Shapes** Incorporate lines, whether through stitching or design elements, that lead the eye from one part of the frock to another. For instance, use horizontal or vertical seams that draw attention and create movement.

(iv) **Color Co-ordination** Use a harmonious color scheme where the same colors appear in different areas of the frock. This could mean having a certain color in the bodice, waist and skirt, which ties the elements together and creates a rhythm that is pleasing to the eye.

8. Mandeep wants to buy a readymade pant and shirt. Explain two ways by which he can bring harmony in it. Competency Based Que; CBSE 2023

Or **What are the two ways to create harmony in garments?** Diksha App

Ans. The two ways by which Mandeep can bring harmony in it are

(i) Harmony by shape occurs when all the areas of a garment reflect the same shape. The collar, cuff and hem are curved and if square pockets are given, they would interrupt the continuity of the design.

(ii) Harmony by texture can be developed by using the right kind of texture for a garment when the garment is in several pieces like in salwar, kurta and dupatta. With a cotton dupatta, a silk kurta and salwar will show a bad harmony.

9. Ramesh/Rina has to wear a shirt and trousers, suggest three ways by which he/she can create harmony in it. Competency Based Que

Or **"The elements of design are considered while creating a balance in a dress". Compare formal balance with informal balance. Give three points.** CBSE SQP 2024

Ans. To create harmony in a shirt and trousers combination, consider these three ways

(i) **Texture Harmony** Ensure the textures of both the shirt and trousers are similar for a cohesive look, such as pairing a cotton shirt with cotton trousers.

(ii) **Shape Harmony** Use consistent lines and shapes throughout the outfit. Matching the prints, angles of lines, and shapes of elements like collars, cuffs, pockets, and hems helps maintain design continuity.

(iii) **Colour Harmony** Choose colours that blend well together, following a specific colour scheme or harmony, such as complementary or monochromatic tones, to create a balanced and pleasing appearance.

Or When comparing formal and informal balance in dress design, three main differences are

Formal Balance	Informal Balance
Achieved through symmetrical balance.	Achieved through asymmetrical balance.
Elements are identical on both sides of a central vertical line.	Elements are different on each side of a central vertical line.
Can appear monotonous due to repetition.	Appears dynamic and avoids monotony.

Long Answer Type Questions

1. While opening a fashion designing showroom, Reema wants to know the colour combination scheme so that she may have best collection of designer dresses. Guide her about the colour scheme that may help her create the best collection. Competency Based Que

Ans. Colour schemes that can help Reema create the best collection can be divided in two groups

Related Schemes

Related schemes have at least one hue in common. These are

- Monochromatic harmony which means a harmony based on one hue. This single hue may be varied in value and/or intensity.
- Achromatic harmony uses only neutrals such as a combination of black and white.
- Accented neutral utilises one hue and a neutral or an achromatic colour.
- Analogous harmony refers to a colour combination using two or three hues that lie side by side on the colour wheel. Use of four or more hues may create a jumble unless each one is in very small quantity.

Contrasting Schemes

Contrasting schemes can be explained in the following ways

- Complementary harmony refers to a harmony using two hues that lie directly opposite to one another on the colour wheel.
- Double complementary has two pairs of complements, generally neighbours on the colour wheel.
- Split complementary harmony is a three colour combination utilising a hue, its complement (directly across on the colour wheel) and neighbour. It may also use a hue and two neighbours of its complement.

- Analogous complementary is a combination of analogous and complementary schemes, a complement selected for dominance in a group of neighbouring colours.
- Triadic harmony is a combination of three hues that lie equidistant from one another on the colour wheel.

2. **(i) Suggest a suitable print and texture of a salwar kameez for a girl who is short in height.**
(ii) Briefly explain any four factors that you keep in mind while selecting colours for your dress. **CBSE 2021 C**

Ans. (i) • Vertical lines that give an illusion of height should be added to the salwar kameez.
• Textures that should be used is a fine and clingy fabric like linen, crepe silk and satin to give the appearance of taller and slimmer body.

(ii) Four factors to be kept in mind while selecting colours for a dress are
• It is important that the chosen colour highlights the appearance of the person and not focuses on the drawbacks.
• The shade or tint of the colour to be used should be considered as well.
• Proper chroma should be used.
• It should be ensured that the colours used maintain a proper harmony with each other.

3. **Anil is designing a bridal lehenga**
(i) How can be create rhythm in it? Suggest two ways, with examples.
(ii) Which colour scheme or colour harmony would he use if he wants to design the lehenga in a single hue?
(iii) Name any one technique that can enhance the texture of the lehenga through surface ornamentation. **CBSE 2024**

Ans. (i) Anil can create rhythm in bridal lehenga by incorporating the following techniques
• Repetition of embroidery laces, buttons piping, colour, etc. at necklines, sleeves and hemlines.
• Cordation by gradual increase of decrease in size of motifs, lines, buttons, colours and textures.

(ii) Monochromatic harmony colour scheme can be used to design lehenga in a single hue.

(iii) Technique of embroidery can be used to enhance the texture of the lehenga through surface ornamentation.

4. **Ms. Madhu wants to open a boutique. Help her to know about different kinds of shapes which should be considered while designing a dress.** **Competency Based Que**

Ans. Different kinds of shapes that Ms. Madhu should know about are as follows

(i) **Natural Shapes** These are the shapes that copy nature or common shapes of manmade objects.

(ii) **Stylised Shapes** These are simplified or modified natural shapes. They may have some distorted or exaggerated parts.

(iii) **Geometric Shapes** These are the shapes that can be formed mathematically or gives a similar impression. They can be formed using rulers, compasses or other measuring instruments.

(iv) **Abstract Shapes** are free-form. They do not resemble any specific object but, may represent different things to different people because of personal association.

5. **Your sister is creating a dress for a normal occasion. Explain her the way in which balance can be created in the dress.** **Competency Based Que; Diksha App**

Ans. To create balance in a dress for a normal occasion, your sister can consider the following

(i) **Vertical Balance** Ensure that the dress maintains symmetry along a central vertical line. This can be achieved by having equal design elements, such as sleeves or details, on both sides of the dress.
For example, if one side has a decorative feature, the other side should mirror it to maintain visual equilibrium.

(ii) **Horizontal Balance** This can be addressed by using various design elements. For instance, darker colours can create a slimming effect, helping to balance larger sizes. She can use horizontal lines or colour blocks to draw the eye across the body, creating a more balanced silhouette.

(iii) **Formal Vs. Informal Balance** Depending on the occasion, your sister can choose between formal balance (which is more symmetrical) and informal balance (which is more asymmetrical yet still visually pleasing). For a normal occasion, informal balance can allow for a bit of creativity while still appearing co-ordinated.

(iv) **Weight Distribution** Consider the weight of different fabrics and design elements. Heavier textures or embellishments should be balanced with lighter elements to avoid an overwhelming appearance on one side of the dress.

6. What do you mean by emphasis? How can emphasis be created in dress? Diksha App

Ans. Emphasis in design refers to the focal point or area in a garment that draws the viewer's attention. It's a way to highlight specific features of a dress, making it visually interesting and appealing.

How Emphasis Can Be Created in Dress

(i) **Colour Contrast** Using bold, contrasting colors in specific areas can attract attention. For example, a bright belt on a neutral dress can draw the eye to the waist.

(ii) **Unique Shapes or Lines** Incorporating unusual shapes or design lines, such as an asymmetrical hemline or unique collar, can create a focal point.

(iii) **Textural Variations** Combining different textures (e.g., smooth fabric with lace or embroidery) in one garment can highlight certain areas, like a textured bodice against a smooth skirt.

(iv) **Detailing and Embellishments** Adding decorative elements such as embroidery, beading or appliqués in strategic locations (like the neckline or sleeves) can enhance emphasis.

(v) **Accessories** Using statement accessories, like bold jewellery or a distinctive bag, can draw focus to specific parts of the outfit, such as the neckline or overall silhouette.

7. Your friend wants to pursue career in fashion designing field. Competency Based Que

(i) Tell her about the scope of this industry.

(ii) What are the requirements to become a fashion designer?

(iii) State the principles of design in brief.

Ans. (i) **Scope in Fashion Design** In today's modern world, design industry is a popular, unique and dynamic sector which directly or indirectly influences our lives. When working in textile or fabric design industries, these industries demand current knowledge of the changing trends and styles and also the ability to produce fresh, current or even ahead of the fashion curve designs. Textile designs for apparel fashion can have a quicker changing trait than designs for furnishing. Textile designers working in this industry conduct many researches and produce designs for textiles companies or fashion houses, but they can also work for a design agency or as freelancers as per their need and desires.

(ii) **Following are the requirements to become a fashion designer**

- The fabric designer must have a thorough knowledge of fibre characteristics, its advantages and limitations and its processing, which can help them achieve the desired results.
- The fabric designers must have a good knowledge of the dyeing properties of different fibres and fabrics.
- Based on the need of the final product or fabric, they decide the stage and technique of colour application.
- The fashion designers also understand the principles of design, which is very important for their profession.

(iii) For answer refer to Q. No. 11 of Very Short Answer Type Questions.

8. Write down any four career opportunities for a person with a fair for design what are the qualifications required for choosing a profession in this field? Diksha App

Ans. Here are four career opportunities for a person with a flair for design

(i) **Fashion Designer** A bachelor's degree in fashion design or a related field. Courses in textile science, pattern making and fashion illustration are beneficial. A strong portfolio showcasing design skills is essential.

(ii) **Textile Designer** A degree in textile design, fashion design, or fine arts. Knowledge of fabric properties, dyeing techniques and pattern design is crucial. Familiarity with design software is also helpful.

(iii) **Interior Designer** A degree in interior design or architecture. Accreditation from a recognised body, such as the National Council for Interior Design Qualification (NCIDQ), may be required. Strong understanding of space planning and colour theory is important.

(iv) **Graphic Designer** A degree in graphic design, visual communication, or a related field. Proficiency in design software (like Adobe Creative Suite) and a strong portfolio are essential. Skills in typography and layout design are also important.

SELF ASSESSMENT TEST

Objective Type Questions

1. What aspect of design is associated with trims and fasteners in garments?

(a) Structural design (b) Applied design (c) Architectural design (d) Functional design

2. Match the following **CBSE 2024 C**

	Aspects of Colour		Explanation
A.	Hue	1.	Darkness of colour
B.	Tint	2.	Brightness of colour
C.	Shade	3.	Common name of colour
D.	Intensity	4.	Lightness of colour

	A	B	C	D		A	B	C	D
(a)	1	3	2	4	(b)	3	4	1	2
(c)	4	3	2	1	(d)	2	1	4	3

3. What is the mid-value (grade 5) on the Grey Scale?

(a) Black (b) White (c) Grey or hue (d) Tint

4. What role do textile designers play in the colour application process?

(a) They manufacture the dyes used in production
(b) They determine when and how the colour is applied
(c) They ensure the fabric is cut correctly before dyeing
(d) They market the final textile product

Very Short Answer Type Questions

5. On which body parts do the divided sections under golden mean appear?

6. What does a 'line' indicate as an element of design?

7. While designing an outfit, what would you do when two contrasting elements meet?

Short Answer Type Questions

8. Your sister Vidya is tall and thin. Suggest five factors she should consider while deciding clothes like salwar kameez, skirt ans tops, jeans and shirt, etc., to be worn during the summer season.

Long Answer Type Questions

9. What do you understand by the 'colour theory'? Explain in brief.

10. Nayanika is wearing a plain saree with blouse, having heavy zari embroidery.

(i) State which principle of design has been created in the sari and blouse outfit. What effect does this principle of design have on the viewer? **Competency Based Que**

(ii) Describe any other three ways by which this principle of design can be created in garments.

09

CHAPTER

Fashion design and merchandising explore the creative and business aspects of the fashion industry, focusing on creating, marketing, and selling garments and accessories. This chapter delves into fashion fundamentals, the evolution of trends, merchandising strategies, and career opportunities in this dynamic field.

Fashion Design and Merchandising

▼ YOUR STUDY GOALS

▼ YOUR PRACTICE GOAL

- Objective Type Questions (26 Qs ; MCQs, A-R, Matching, Case Based)
- Subjective Questions (12 VSAs, 5 SAs, 10 LAs)

9.1 Introduction

- **Fashion design** is the art and application of design to create appealing clothing and accessories. It requires problem-solving to understand consumer needs and creatively express the designer's vision.
- **Fashion merchandising** involves **promoting** and **selling** apparel and accessories. It encompasses various aspects of the fashion[1] industry, including visual merchandising.
- Both fashion design and merchandising offer exciting career opportunities. India's rich textile history and recent developments in fashion design have opened up new prospects in garment and accessory design.
- The fashion industry fulfills both creative urges and materialistic needs. The origin of fashion merchandising traces back to the barter of products and crafts, leading to early trading practices.
- Over time, the trading system evolved to focus on what was available and saleable, simplifying the distribution process.
- The introduction of 'ready-to-wear' apparel in the 1920s led retailers to recognise the lucrative business potential of fashion garments.
- Fashion apparel quickly became a key merchandise type in department stores, increasing economic opportunities and leading to the emergence of fashion merchandising as a specialisation.

1 **Fashion** It refers to the style or styles most popular at a given time.

9.2 Significance of Fashion Design and Merchandising

- The fashion design and merchandising industry helps individuals understand how the fashion business operates. It involves all processes related to producing raw materials, apparel and accessories.
- This industry includes the retail stores that sell fashion merchandise to the public. It offers insights into textiles and the fibers used in their production.
- Fashion merchandising equips individuals to respond to what, why and when a **style** becomes fashionable.
- It also helps determine the suitability of styles for specific retail operations and the time required for their implementation.
- In essence, fashion merchandising incorporates planning, buying and selling in the fashion industry.

9.3 Basic Concepts

- The fashion industry is a vast business that employees millions of people across various fields. This includes design, manufacturing, distribution, marketing, retailing, advertising, communications, publishing and consulting.
- To grasp what 'fashion design' entails, individuals must understand the nature of fashion and how it operates in the market.
- Understanding the fundamentals of fashion is essential for recognising the relationships between fashion and the factors that influence the market.

Fashion Terminology

Some of the fashion terminologies are discussed below

- **Fashion** is defined as the style or styles most popular at a given time.
- Style refers to any particular look or characteristic in apparel or accessories. A style may come and go in fashion, but a particular style always remains.
- Fads are short-lived fashions that can come and go in a single season. They lack the design strength to hold consumers' attention for long. Examples include hot pants, baggy pants and unmatched buttons.
- Classic styles never become completely outdated; instead, they remain more or less accepted for an extended period of time. Classics are simple in design, which keeps them from being easily dated. Examples of classics include blazer jackets, polo shirts and the chanel suit.

9.4 Fashion Development

- A person must have knowledge of fashion fundamentals to understand how the fashion industry operates. The first step is to learn how the fashion business developed.
- The history of fashion aids designers in making decisions for present and future trends. It provides inspiration from past fashions that can be re-interpreted for today.
- Fashion is a relatively new concept; throughout ancient and medieval times, styles remained unchanged for centuries.
- During the Renaissance, Western civilisation began discovering various cultures, customs and costumes, which accelerated fashion changes.
- The availability of new fabrics and ideas fueled people's desire for more innovation in fashion.

France : The Centre of Fashion

- In the early 18th century, France began to dominate international fashion, with society divided into two classes: rich and poor. Fashionable clothing was primarily affordable for the wealthy.
- By the 18th century, members of **King Louis XIV's** court became **trendsetters**, establishing **Paris** as the **fashion capital of Europe**. French cities supplied the royal court with silk fabrics, ribbons and laces.
- Fashion at this time required painstaking hand sewing, with clothes custom-made to fit exact measurements. Support from the royal court and a flourishing silk industry solidified France's position as the fashion center.
- Couture[2] (kootour) referred to the art of dress-making. A male designer was called a **couturier**, while his female counterpart was a **couturiere**.
- The Industrial Revolution brought technological advancements in textile and apparel production, enabling the production of more fabrics in less time. Inventions like the spinning jenny and power looms spurred the growth of the American textile industry.
- The rise of trade and industry led to the emergence of a middle class with disposable income, which included spending on better clothing.
- The invention of the sewing machine transformed handicraft into an industry, democratising fashion and making it more accessible to everyone.
- In 1859, Isaac Singer developed the foot treadle for the sewing machine, freeing hands to guide fabric. Sewing machines were initially used to make Civil War uniforms.
- In 1849, Levi Strauss created long-wearing pants with pockets from tent and wagon cover fabric, which later became known as denims.
- The emergence of denims marked the beginning of clothing specifically made for laborers, with denim remaining unchanged for the past 150 years.
- By the 1880s, women began wearing separate skirts and blouses, signaling the start of ready-to-wear manufacturing for women.
- Ready-to-wear clothing allowed for easily adjustable lengths and waistlines, enabling the working class to diversify their wardrobes.
- By the 19th century, the general public gained access to affordable fashion through fairs and bazaars, where clothes were sold and buyers could bargain.
- As towns grew, general stores were established to meet local demands, leading to an increase in retail stores in cities.
- **Pret-a-porter (ready-to-wear)** clothing emerged in the 1960s as a radical alternative to couture, with factory-made clothing available in standardised sizes.
- The first French haute couturier to present a full pret-a-porter line was Yves Saint Laurent (YSL).

Fashion Evolution

- Fashion has evolved with time; this can be understood with the help of the fashion cycle.
- Fashion Cycle[3] The term fashion cycle is described as the way in which fashion changes or a period of time or life span during which the fashion exists. The stages of the fashion cycle include **introduction, rise, peak, decline** and then rejection of style. It is represented by a **bell-shaped curve** of time and sales. Stages of the fashion cycle are discussed below
  - **Introduction of a Style** After doing research, designers interpret their creative ideas into apparel and then present their new style to the public. New designs are created by changing the elements of design (colour, line, shape, fabric texture) and other details, as well as their relationships to one another.

---

2 Couture It refers to the art of dress-making.

3 Fashion Cycle It refers to the way in which fashion changes over a period of time.

- **Increase in Popularity** If a new style or fashion is purchased, worn and seen by a large number of people, its popularity levels will increase.
- **Peak of Popularity** When any kind of fashion is in high demand due to its popularity, many manufacturers try to produce replicas of that product to sell at different price levels.
- **Decline in Popularity** Mass production[4] of a certain fashion in the market leads to a decline in its popularity. This prompts fashion-conscious individuals to seek something new, resulting in declining styles being placed on sale racks in retail stores.
- **Rejection of a Style or Obsolescence[5]** In this last phase of the fashion cycle, some consumers move towards new fashion looks, which further leads to the beginning of a new fashion cycle.

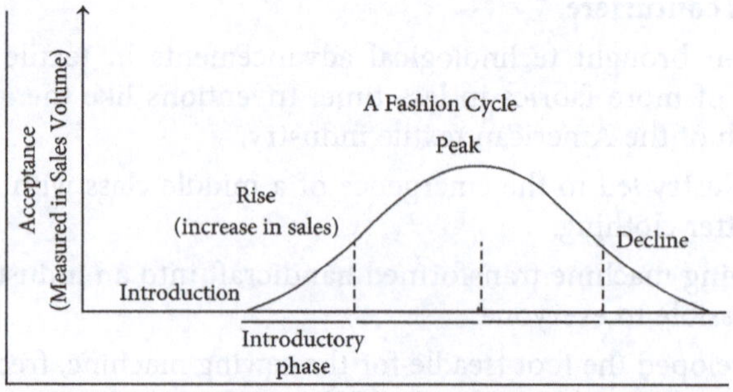

▲ *Stages of Fashion Cycle*

Quick Test 1

1. When did ready-to-wear apparel come into existence?
2. What is defined as the style or styles most popular at a given time?
3. What type of fashions can come and go in a single season?
4. When were the spinning jenny and powerlooms invented?
5. Describe the period of 'obsolescence'.

9.5 Fashion Merchandising

- Fashion merchandising refers to the planning needed to have the right merchandise at the right time, place, price and with the right sales promotion.
- Achieving maximum profits depends on meeting all these conditions through effective planning.
- A person who translates inspiration into design and uses technology to address planning, production, promotion and distribution in the fashion industry is known as a fashion merchandiser.
- Understanding fashion merchandising is essential for examining its role in manufacturing, buying, promoting and selling fashion items.

Role of Fashion Merchandiser

Manufacturing

- A fashion merchaniser suggests the types of fabrics to use in clothing production. A strong understanding of historical and socio-cultural fabric contexts helps realise the designer's vision. They apply knowledge about fabric and clothing construction to determine the best manufacturing methods, considering price and target market.

4 **Mass Production** It refers to the production of large quantities of a product by a mechanical process.
5 **Obsolescence** The state of being outdated.

Buying

- The buying process involves purchasing fashion items for presentation in stores. A fashion merchandiser understands the target market and conducts fashion trend analysis and forecasting.
- Their expertise in textiles and fabrics helps maintain accurate orders and supports designers in selecting appropriate materials.

Promoting

- For merchandisers working for designers, promoting products to stores that may buy in bulk is a key priority. They need creative minds and strong visual merchandising skills.
- Fashion shows are a crucial avenue for promotion, where designers' creations and visual effects are highlighted to attract potential buyers.
- Merchandisers also identify target markets for designer clothing, including children's clothing stores, department stores or discount retailers.

Selling

- The final component of fashion merchandising is selling fashion items to stores for retail. Knowledge of forecasting and market trends allows merchandisers to recommend production strategies.
- Creativity is essential, as they provide suggestions for item displays within stores. If working for a retail store, their responsibilities include buying and presenting fashion items effectively.

Levels of Merchandising

Retail Organisation Merchandising

- This specialised management function shifts fashion from a designer's showroom to the retail sales floor and finally to customers.
- Internal planning within the **retail organisation**[6] ensures that adequate merchandise is available at prices consumers are willing to pay, leading to profitable operations.

Buying Agency Merchandising

- This level provides consultancy services for buying goods. A buying agency acts as a procurement office for buyers.
- Selling through buying agencies is beneficial for exporters, as it helps them save costs and time. Buying agents identify vendors, negotiate costs and conduct quality inspections.
- They are responsible for maintaining quality control throughout the production process, ensuring that standards are met.

Export House Merchandising

In export houses, there are two types of merchandisers **buyer merchandisers** and **production merchandisers.**

- **Buyer Merchandisers** They act as a link between the buyer and the manufacturer, ensuring the product meets the buyer's requirements.
  Their responsibilities include sourcing, sampling and maintaining communication with the buyer.
- **Production Merchandisers** They connect production with buyer merchants, ensuring that production adheres to the buyer's schedule and requirements.
  Their role involves overseeing the production process to meet the buyer's expectations and deadlines.

6 **Retail Organisations** It refers to a system that outlines how certain activities are directed in order to achieve the goals of an organisation.

Other Concepts and Requirements in Fashion Merchandising

Target Market

This refers to the category of consumers targeted for selling a product. Understanding the target market allows the sales department to focus on customers most likely to purchase. It ensures the highest return on marketing and sales expenditures, which can be achieved through effective market segmentation.

Market Segmentation

- This strategy involves dividing a larger market into subsets of consumers with common needs and applications for the offered goods and services.
- Merchandisers need to interpret consumer demands and understand buying motivations in the market. Market can be segmented into different ways that are discussed below
- **Demographic Segmentation** This segmentation is based on population characteristics such as age, sex, occupation, education and income.
- **Geographic Segmentation** This type of segmentation is based on location, such as cities, states and regions. Climate differences significantly influence merchandise choices, particularly in clothing.
- **Psychographic Segmentation** This segmentation is based on lifestyle factors, including social activities, interests, leisure pursuits, needs and wants. Consumers with similar lifestyles can form a target market group.
- **Behavioural Segmentation** This segmentation is based on consumer opinions regarding specific products or services. It often involves ratings, usage or reviews, which help improve the service or product and differentiate it from competitors.

Merchandising Rights

- **Right Merchandise** The retailers must fill their stock with the merchandise as per the demands of the customers.
- **At Right Place** The location of setting up the merchandise is very important as it decides the accessibility of the product for the customers.
- **At Right Time** Most of the merchandise is seasonal in nature and it must be available when it is most required.
- **In Right Quantity** It basically means a profitable balance between volume of sales and amount of inventory.
- **Right Price** The merchandiser must present a price that is high enough to fulfill the store profit and low enough to meet the competition and customer's expectations.
- **With Right Promotion** Successful promotion helps to create a right balance between investment and the appeal created for the customers.

Quick Test 2

1. What is one of the specialised management functions within the fashion industry?
2. How many types of merchandisers are there in an export house?
3. What is the kind of market segmentation based on population?
4. What is the kind of market segmentation based on lifestyle?

Fashion Retail Organisations

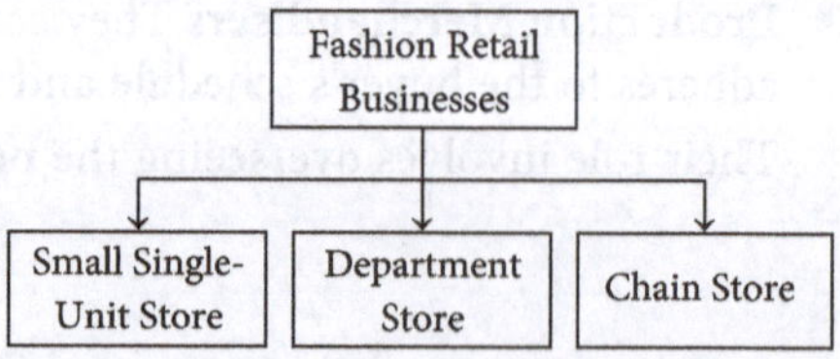

An organisational structure is a system that outlines how certain activities are directed in order to achieve the goals of an organisation. It gives a clear understanding of the authority and responsibility for each job to be done. Organisational systems with the difference in type of merchandise, size of retail firm and target customer.

Fashion retail businesses can be divided into different sectors

- **Small Single-Unit Store** It is also known as a neighbourhood store. These are generally owner and family oriented single stores.
- **Department Store** It consists of separate sections, known as departments, such as clothing, sporting goods, automotive supplies, health and beauty products and electronics equipment. Some of the department stores also sell food products.
- **Chain Stores** These are retail outlets that share a brand and central management. They usually have standardised business methods and practices.

Major Divisions

Some of the major divisions related to Fashion Retail Organisations are discussed below

- **Merchandising Division** This division deals with buying, merchandise planning and control, selling and fashion co-ordination.
- **Sales and Promotion Division** This division deals with advertising, visual merchandising, special events, publicity and public relations.
- **Finance and Control Division** This division deals with credit, account payable and inventory control.
- **Operational Division** This division deals with maintenance of facilities, stores, merchandise protection, personnel, customer service and receiving and marking of merchandise.
- **Personnel and Branch Store Division** This division may function separately if the store operations are very large.

9.6 Preparing for a Career

A career in fashion merchandising combines style with business sense; a flair for fashion will not bring success to any individual.

Skills Required

There are three primary and divergent skills that a fashion designer, merchandiser and marketer must hold in order to achieve success in this field.

- **Forecasting Ability** The ability to forecast fashion trends is essential. It requires knowledge of past and current trends and awareness of marketing impacts on fashion.
- **Analytical Ability** Fashion merchandisers and marketers must analyse the overall economy and their company's position. They need to understand how styles fit into consumer budgets to ensure profitability.
- **Communication Ability** Excellent communication skills are crucial. This includes negotiating prices with manufacturers and writing advertising copy, press releases and personalised letters to consumers.

Essential Qualifications

- **Degree Options** An associate or bachelor's degree in fashion design is needed. Many combine this with business, marketing or fashion merchandising for entrepreneurial goals.
- **Programme Duration** Certificate or diploma programmes in fashion merchandising can be completed in six months to one year, focusing on practical skills.
- **Master's Programme** A two-year master's programme includes liberal arts and courses in fashion and business, providing advanced knowledge.
- **Bachelor's Degree** A four-year bachelor's degree in fashion design or merchandising includes extensive liberal arts, fashion and business coursework, beneficial for long-term educational goals.

9.7 Scope of Fashion Designing and Merchandising

- People are more attracted to pursue a career in the field of fashion industry due to its well-paid income opportunities. The thought that one can succeed on their own further increases the motivation of the aspirants.
- In general, fashion designer professionals have innate artistic and creative qualities. They use creative and artistic talents to create unique design concepts for various fashion applications.
- Now-a-days, fashion designer professionals are in great demand in a variety of industries. There is a constant demand for fashion designers.
- Thus, most of the fashion aspirants channelise their talent in one specialised fashion area like interior designing, merchandise displays, clothing or apparel, theatre sets and many more. An individual may equip themselves with fresh ideas as per the changing market and fashion trends.
- Currently, there are various fashion design careers. Some of the popular fashion design careers one could opt for are as follows
  - **Visual Merchandise** Designers are mainly responsible for designing window displays, arranging store merchandise, creating props and accents, organising clothing placement, styling mannequins and spearheading marketing campaigns.
  - **Fashion Designers** These are professional designers who create designs for clothing and apparel. Some designers work with popular fashion designers while others manage their own fashion labels.
  - **Set Designers** These are primarily assigned to conceptualise designs which are required for movies, television and theatre productions. Their styles and designs are based in line with what the script or the director requires. Some of the set designers produce unique set designs for trade shows and museums.
  - **Interior Designers** The main aim to perfectly combine form with function. Their primary function is to introduce interior concepts that will increase the beauty, safety and functionality of a particular space or area.
  - Interior designers work in a variety of settings like retail stores, residential homes, offices, hospitals, hotels and many more.

Quick Test 3

1. What is another name for a neighbourhood store?
2. Which division deals with advertising and public relations?
3. Which ability of designers or merchandisers focuses on fashion trends?
4. Who is responsible for window displays or arranging store merchandise?

Mind Map

FASHION DESIGN AND MERCHANDISING

1 Introduction to Fashion Design and Merchandising

Fashion Design
- Art of creating clothing and accessories.
- Focus on problem-solving and creative expression.

Fashion Merchandising
- Involves promoting and selling apparel and accessories.
- Includes visual merchandising.

Career Opportunities
- Both fields offer exciting careers, especially with India's growing fashion industry.

History
- Originated from barter and trade.
- **1920s** Ready-to-wear apparel led to fashion merchandising becoming profitable.

2 Significance of Fashion Design and Merchandising

- **Understanding the Fashion Business** Covers processes from raw materials to finished apparel and accessories.
- **Retail Stores** Includes stores selling fashion merchandise and provides insights into textiles and fibers.
- **Fashion Merchandising** Focuses on why, when, and what styles become fashionable.
- Determines suitability of styles for retail operations and the time for implementation.

Core Functions
- Planning, buying, and selling are key in fashion merchandising.

3 Basic Concepts of Fashion Design and Merchandising

- **Fashion Industry Overview** Vast business with millions employed in areas like design, manufacturing, marketing and retailing.
- **Understanding Fashion Design** Essential to grasp fashion's nature and how it operates in the market.
- Recognising factors influencing the market and the relationships in fashion.

Fashion Terminology
- **Fashion** The most popular style at a given time.
- **Style** A distinctive look in apparel/ accessories, which may change over time but remains identifiable.
- **Fads** Short-lived trends, appearing in a season or two. (e.g., hot pants).
- **Classics** Timeless styles that remain accepted over time. (e.g., blazer jackets).

4 Fashion Development and Evolution

Fashion Development
- **Fashion Fundamentals** Understanding fashion history helps designers predict and create future trends.
- **Ancient and Medieval Fashion** Fashion remained unchanged for centuries until the Renaissance, when new cultures and costumes influenced fashion changes.
- **Fabric and Ideas** New fabric availability sparked a desire for innovation in fashion.
- **France** Fashion Centre
- **18th Century** France dominated fashion, especially with King Louis XIV's court setting trends.
- **Couture** Dress-making was a high art. Designers were called couturiers (male) and couturieres (female).
- **Industrial Revolution** Innovations like the spinning jenny and sewing machine revolutionised textile production, making fashion more accessible.
- **Denim** Levi Strauss created durable pants for laborers, marking the birth of denim as a workwear fabric.

5 Principles of Design

- **Fashion Merchandising** Ensures the right products are available at the right time, place, price, and with effective promotions to maximise profits.
- **Role of Fashion Merchandiser** Manufacturing, buying , promoting, selling.
- **Levels of Merchandising** Retail merchandising, buying agency and export house.

Market Segmentation
- Group of consumers based on needs.

Types
- **Demographic** Age, sex, income
- **Geographic** Location-based
- **Psychographic** Lifestyle and interests
- **Behavioural** Opinions, usage and feedback

Merchandising Rights
- **Right Merchandise** Meets customer needs
- **Right Place** Accessible to customers
- **Right Time** Seasonal availability
- **Right Quantity** Balanced inventory
- **Right Price** Competitive yet profitable pricing
- **Right Promotion** Effective promotional strategies

Fashion Retail Organisations
- A business that sells clothing and accessories to customers.
- **Type** Small stores, department stores, chain stores luxury brands.

6 Scope of Fashion Designing and Merchandising

- **Attraction** Fashion careers offer high income and self-success opportunities.
- **Creativity** Designers use artistic skills for unique fashion concepts.
- **High Demand** Fashion designers are sought after across industries.

Fashion Design Careers
- **Visual Merchandise Designers** Create displays and organise store merchandise.
- **Fashion Designers** Design clothing for brands or their own labels.
- **Set Designers** Design sets for TV, movies and events.
- **Interior Designers** Enhance functionality and beauty in spaces like homes and offices.

NCERT Folder

1. Outline the major developments in fashion.

Ans. The major developments in fashion are discussed below

- During the Renaissance, the Western civilisation made many cultural and custom discoveries. These discoveries led to the advancement in the field of fashion.
- The Industrial Revolution led to the emergence of technological advancements in textile and apparel production. Spinning jenny and power looms were invented during this period, which further gave rise to the American textile industry.
- The invention of sewing machine democratised fashion and made it accessible. In 1859, Issac Singer developed the foot treadle for the sewing machine which left an individual's hand free to guide the fabric and speeding the process.
- Long wearing jeans were invented in 1849 by Levi Strauss, which later became popular as Denims. The emergence of denims led to the beginning of clothes especially made for labourers.
- Women started wearing separate skirts and blouses in the 1880s, which eventually led to the manufacturing of ready-to-wear clothes for women.
- The general public got access to affordable fashion, by the 19th century, through fairs and bazaars, where both buyers and sellers could bargain.

2. Identify and explain the various stages of fashion cycle.

Or **Explain five stages of fashion cycle to your sister who wants to own a fashion industry.** **Diksha App**

Ans. (i) **Introduction of a Style** This is the first stage where designers create new styles based on research and their creative ideas. They present these styles to the public, showcasing new designs that often involve changes in color, fabric and shape.

(ii) **Increase in Popularity** Once a style is introduced, if people start buying and wearing it, its popularity will grow. This stage sees the style gaining visibility, often through media exposure, fashion shows and social influencers.

(iii) **Peak of Popularity** At this point, the style is at its height. Many manufacturers try to replicate the popular designs to meet the high demand. It's a critical stage where the fashion is widely accepted and sought after by consumers.

(iv) **Decline in Popularity** After the peak, the style begins to lose its appeal as it becomes overly common. Mass production leads to saturation in the market and fashion-conscious consumers start looking for something new, causing the style to go on sale.

(v) **Rejection of a Style (Obsolescence)** In this final stage, consumers completely move on to new trends, leaving the previous style behind. This shift paves the way for the introduction of new styles and the fashion cycle starts again.

3. What do you understand by the concept 'fashion merchandising'?

Ans. The concept fashion merchandising refers to the planning required to have the right merchandise, at the right time, at the right place, at the right price and with the right sales promotion.

4. Describe various levels of merchandising.

Or **Explain three levels of merchandising in fashion industry.** **CBSE SQP Term II, 2021-22**

Ans. In Fashion Industry, there are three levels of merchandising that are discussed below

(i) **Retail Organisation Merchandising** It is one of the specialised management functions within the fashion industry. Through this business, fashion is shifted from a designer's showroom to retail sales floor and into the hands of customers. This is achieved through the internal planning that takes place within a retail organisation. Thus, it ensures that adequate amount of merchandise can be sold at prices that the consumers are willing to pay to ensure a profitable operation.

(ii) **Buying Agency Merchandising** It provides services for goods buying consultancy. A buying agency acts as procurement (Purchase) office for the buyers. For exporters, selling through buying agencies is profitable as it helps them save cost and time. The buying agent is responsible to identify vendors, negotiate costs, check in-process quality and perform pre-shipment quality inspection. They also keep a regular control over the quality factor during the production process.

(iii) **Export House Merchandising** In an export house, there are two types of merchandisers i.e. buyer merchandiser and production merchandiser.

The buyer merchandisers generally act as a link between the buyer and the manufacturer. They ensure that the product is developed as per the requirements of the buyer. They possess the responsibility of sourcing, sampling and communication with the buyer. On the other hand, a production merchandiser acts as a link between production and buyer merchants. They possess the responsibility of ensuring that the production goes as per the schedule and requirements of the buyer.

5. 'To interpret consumer demand, one should understand target market and customer motivations'. Elaborate.

Ans. In order to understand and interpret consumer demands, it is imperative for an individual to understand target market and customer motivation if they wish to pursue a career in the field. Target market can be defined as a category of consumers one is targeting at for selling the product.

It is important to understand the target market as it will allow the sales department to focus upon those customers who are most likely to purchase the offering. Thus, it also ensures highest return for the marketing/sales expenditures.

A fashion merchandiser needs to interpret consumer demands. There is a need to understand what customers' buying motivations are in the market. A more active market helps the manufacturer to manufacture things according to the need of the consumer and it is the only thing which helps in increasing the sales. The consumer demand can be met through the market segmentation. Market segmentation is a strategy that involves dividing a larger market into subsets of consumers who have common needs and applications for the goods and services offered in the market. For example, consumers demand can be met on the basis of age or climate.

6. Enumerate the knowledge and skills that a fashion designer and merchandiser must possess.

Or **You want to become a fashion designer. Enumerate the knowledge and skills you must possess in order to succeed in this profession.**

Competency Based Que; Diksha App

Ans. Following are the skills that a fashion designer and merchandiser must possess are

(i) **Forecasting Ability** The ability to forecast fashion trends is an essential part of this career. This requires a thorough knowledge of past future trends, current future trends and an awareness of how the marketing of an item contributes to these fashion trends. Moreover, they must be able to keep well ahead of these fashion trends to capitalise on them in time.

(ii) **Analytical Ability** Fashion merchandisers and marketers must analyse the economy as a whole, that of their companies and how a particular style will fit into and affect a consumer's budget. They must understand a complex set of factors to ensure that they make a profit for their employees.

(iii) **Communication Ability** An individual must possess excellent communication skills. Through strong communication skills, fashion designers or merchandiser will must be able to negotiate prices with manufacturers and they can also sell their fashion to the people.

They also frequently write advertising copy, press releases and even personalised letters to consumers. Thus, all of this requires strong communication skills.

7. What advice would you give to your friend who wants to pursue fashion designing and merchandising as a career?

Ans. The most adequate advice for someone who wishes to pursue a career in fashion designing and merchandising is that they should get an associate or bachelor's degree in fashion design.

They can also combine a fashion design degree with a business, marketing or fashion merchandising degree, especially those who want to pursue their own business.

There are different degree programmes in fashion design and merchandising. One can earn a certificate, a diploma, an associate's or a bachelor's degree in this field.

An individual's choice depends upon a number of factors that includes the unique qualities of each degree programme.

- One can complete a certificate or diploma degree programmes in fashion merchandising in a period of six months to one year. These programmes are of short duration as the coursework will focus upon the actual job of fashion merchandising.
- Master's programme in Fashion Merchandising is of two-year duration that consists of a certain amount of liberal arts requirements with fashion and business courses.
- Bachelor's degree in Fashion Design or Merchandising is a four year programme that consist of a substantial amount of liberal arts requirements with fashion and business courses.

Exam Pattern Questions

Objective Type Questions

Multiple Choice Questions

1. Identify the style that is popular in the present or a set of trends that has been accepted by a wide audience.

(a) Style (b) Fad
(c) Fashion (d) Classic

2. Term used for the art of dress-making .... Diksha App

(a) creativity (b) creation
(c) couture (d) cartier

3. Who introduced the foot treadle for the sewing machine? CBSE 2021 C

(a) Isaac Singer (b) Levis Strauss
(c) King Louis XIV (d) Coco Chanel

4. Who introduced denim pants? CBSE 2021 C

(a) Isaac Singer (b) Levis Strauss
(c) King Louis XIV (d) Coco Chanel

5. Fashion acceptance or rejection is determined by whom?

(a) Consumers (b) Designers
(c) Retailers (d) Advertisers

6. What is the third phase of fashion cycle?

(a) Increase in fashion popularity
(b) Peak of fashion popularity
(c) Decline in fashion popularity
(d) Obsolescence

7. At which stage of the fashion cycle is a trend considered dull and boring because the market is saturated? Competency Based Que

(a) Increase in fashion popularity
(b) Peak of fashion popularity
(c) Decline in fashion popularity
(d) Obsolescence

8. Which of the following roles does a fashion merchandiser play in the process of manufacturing?

(a) He/She suggests inputs on the type of fabric used.
(b) He/She takes a designer's piece and taking things like price.
(c) He/She finds the best way to manufacture a product according to himself/herself.
(d) All of the above

9. Which stage of the fashion cycle involves manufacturers copying fashion and preparing adaptations of it at many price levels? CBSE 2023

(a) Decline in popularity (b) Increase in popularity
(c) Introduction of a style (d) Peak of popularity

10. It includes all the processes involved with producing raw material apparel and accessories and the retail store that sell fashion merchandise to the public. Diksha App

(a) Fashion retail and merchandising
(b) Fashion designing
(c) Textile engineering
(d) Retail management

11. What is basic objective of product promotion?

(a) Demonstrate the firm's social responsibility.
(b) Inform the public about the company's future.
(c) Enhance company morale and recruit employees.
(d) Persuade consumers to buy a good or service.

12. The category of target consumers for selling the products is known as .... Diksha App

(a) Choice customer (b) Target customer
(c) Target market (d) Preferred customers

13. Which merchandising right means a profitable balance between volume of sales and amount of inventory?

(a) Right Merchandise
(b) At Right Price
(c) In Right Quanity
(d) With Right Promotion

14. Retail outlet that share a brand and central management and usually have a standardised business method and practices. Competency Based Que, Diksha App

(a) Chain store
(b) Departmental store
(c) Small store
(d) Single-Unit store

15. Who acts as a link between production and buyer merchants?

(a) Buyer merchandisers
(b) Fashion designers
(c) Production merchandisers
(d) Retailers

16. **Which of the following is a sector of fashion retail businesses?**

(a) Small Single–Unit Store (b) Departmental Store
(c) Chain Store (d) All of these

17. **"The ability to predict the mood, behaviour and buying habits of the customer".**

Which of the following is described in the above statement? **Competency Based Que**

(a) Forecasting ability (b) Analytical ability
(c) Both (a) and (b) (d) None of these

18. **Varun is your brother's best friend. He is in Class XII. He wants to become a fashion designer. Which degree programme would you suggest for him?** **Competency Based Que**

(a) A Master's in Fashion Merchandising
(b) A Bachelor's in Fashion Merchandising
(c) A Bachelor's in Fashion Designing
(d) A Master's in Fashion Designing

19. **An individual who is mainly responsible for designing window displays, arranging store merchandising and clothing placements.**

Who is being referred to in the above statement? **Competency Based Que**

(a) Fashion designer
(b) Visual merchandising designer
(c) Set designer
(d) Interior designer

20. **The final component of fashion merchandising is ....** **Diksha App**

(a) manufacture (b) promoting
(c) selling (d) buying

21. **Which of the following are the stages of a fashion cycle?**

I. Introduction of a style II. Increase in popularity
III. Forecasting IV. Merchandising

Choose the correct option

(a) I and II (b) II and III (c) III and IV (d) I and IV

22. **Match the Following.**

List I	List II
A. Fads	1. Styles most popular at a given time.
B. Classic	2. Short lived fashions.
C. Style	3. Styles that never becomes completely out dates.
D. Fashion	4. Any particular look or charateristic in apparel or accessories.

Codes

	A	B	C	D		A	B	C	D
(a)	1	2	3	4	(b)	2	3	4	1
(c)	3	2	1	4	(d)	4	1	2	3

23. **Match List-I with List-II.**

List-I (Ways of market segmentation)	List-II (Basis of segmentation)
A. Demographic	1. Opinion on specific products or services
B. Psychographic	2. Regions, climate
C. Geographic	3. Similar lifestyles, interests
D. Behavioural	4. Age, population

Codes

	A	B	C	D		A	B	C	D
(a)	1	2	4	3	(b)	3	1	4	2
(c)	4	3	2	1	(d)	2	1	4	3

Assertion-Reason Questions

Directions (Q. Nos. 24-25) In the questions given below, there are two statements marked as Assertion (A) and Reason (R). Read the statements and choose the correct option.

Codes

(a) Both A and R are true and R is the correct explanation of A.
(b) Both A and R are true, but R is not the correct explanation of A.
(c) A is true, but R is false.
(d) A is false, but R is true.

24. **Assertion** (A) Fashion design and merchandising provides for very exciting career opportunities.

Reason (R) India has a very long and flourishing history of textile industries.

25. **Assertion** (A) A fashion merchandiser must possess appropriate knowledge regarding forecasting and market trends so that they can give recommendations accordingly.

Reason (R) A fashion designer has the responsibility of selling fashion items to stores.

Case Based Questions

26. **Read the given passage and answer the following questions.**

Due to the developments more fabrics were produced in less time. During this time spinning jenny and power looms were invented. This gave rise to development of American textile industry. Rapidly increasing trade and industry in return created a middle class with money to spend on the luxuries of life, including better clothing.

The invention of sewing machine turned the handicraft into an industry.

This democratised fashion and made it accessible for everyone. In 1859, Issac Singer developed the foot treadle for the sewing machine which left the hands free to guide the fabric. An early use for sewing machines was to make Civil War uniforms. In 1849, fabric intended for tents and wagon covers was used to make long wearing pants with pockets for tools by a young boy Levi Strauss. Later these became popular and were called denims. This was the beginning of clothes specially made for labourers. This is the only apparel that has remained same for the last nearly 150 years!

(i) 'In 1859, the foot treadle was invented'. Based on the above statement, choose the option that lists a benefit of foot treadle.

(a) It stopped time consumption.
(b) It radicalised the sewing industry.
(c) It reduced the time being consumed in sewing.
(d) All of the above

(ii) What kind of developments led to emergence of middle class?

I. Increase in trade **II. Luxuries of life**
III. Increase in industry **IV. New markets**

Choose the correct option

(a) I and II (b) II and III (c) I and III (d) II and IV

(iii) Given below are two statements labelled as Assertion (A) and Reason (R).

Assertion (A) More and more fabrics were produced in lesser time, during the period of Industrial Revolution.

Reason (R) The Industrial Revolution led to numerous technological advancement.

Codes

(a) Both A and R are true and R is the correct explanation of A.
(b) both A and R are true, but R is not the correct explanation of A.
(c) A is true, but R is false.
(d) A is false, but R is true.

(iv) Assertion (A) The invention of the sewing machine democratised fashion.

Reason (R) It made clothing production accessible to a wider population.

Codes

(a) Both A and R are true and R is the correct explanation of A.
(b) Both A and R are true, but R is not the correct explanation of A.
(c) A is true, but R is false.
(d) A is false, but R is true.

Answers

1. (c) Fashion
2. (c) couture
3. (a) Isaac Singer
4. (b) Levis Strauss
5. (a) Consumers
6. (b) Peak of fashion popularity
7. (c) Decline in fashion popularity
8. (d) All of the above
9. (d) Peak of popularity
10. (a) Fashion retail and merchandising
11. (d) Persuade consumers to buy a good or service.
12. (c) Target market
13. (c) In Right Quanity
14. (a) Chain store
15. (c) Production merchandisers
16. (d) All of these
17. (a) Forecasting ability
18. (c) A Bachelor's in Fashion Designing
19. (b) Visual merchandising designer
20. (c) selling
21. (a) I and II
22. (b) 2 3 4 1
23. (c) 4 3 2 1
24. (b) Both A and R are true, but R is not the correct explanation of A.
25. (c) A is true, but R is false.
26. (i) (c) It reduced the time being consumed in sewing.
(ii) (c) I and III
(iii) (a) Both A and R are true and R is the correct explanation of A.
(iv) (a) Both A and R are true and R is the correct explanation of A.

Subjective Questions

Very Short Answer Type Questions

1. Define 'Fashion Design'.

Ans. 'Fashion Design' is an art and application of design and aesthetics to create functional, yet appealing clothing and accessories.

2. The invention of sewing machine turned handicrafts into an industry. In which year and by whom was the foot treadle for the sewing maching invented? **CBSE Term II, 2022**

Ans. The invention of sewing maching converted the handicraft into an industry. The foot treadle for the sewing maching was developed in 1859 by Issac Singer. This helped in making the hands free to guide the fabric. Sewing machines brought a democracy to fashion and it became easy-to-access for everyone.

3. How does fashion industry helps an individual?

Ans. The fashion industry helps to satisfy both the creative urge and the materialistic needs of the people.

4. Explain fashion cycle in brief.

Ans. Fashion cycle is described as a way in which fashion changes or a period of time or life span during which the fashion exists.

5. Explain fashion merchandiser in brief.

Ans. A person who facilitates inspiration into design, who uses technology to conceptualise and address the planning, production, promotion and distribution of products in the fashion industry, to meet the needs and demands of a consumer is known as the fashion merchandiser.

6. Discuss the role of fashion merchandiser in the process of manufacturing.

Ans. In the process of manufacturing, a fashion merchandiser plays an important role by suggesting inputs on the types of fabrics used to make a piece of clothing.

A fashion merchandiser can apply his/her knowledge about fabric and clothing construction by taking up a designer's piece and trying to find the best way to manufacture the item and simultaneously, taking things like price and target market into consideration.

7. What do you understand by market segmentation?

Ans. Market segmentation refers to a strategy that involves dividing a larger market into subsets of consumers who have common needs and applications for the goods and services offered in the market.

8. What two roles Sudha will have as a fashion merchandiser in each of the following fields? **CBSE SQP Term II, 2021**

(i) In manufacturing (ii) In promoting

Ans. (i) As a manufacturer, Sudha will

(a) suggest inputs on the types of fabrics used to make a clothing.

(b) change a designer's vision into reality, through her historical and socio-cultural understanding.

(ii) As a promoter, Sudha will

(a) work for a designer and promote their product to stores that may want to buy in large quantities.

(b) seek out the target market for designer's clothings.

9. Discuss the level Buying Agency Merchandising.

Ans. For answer refer to Q. No. 4(ii) of NCERT folder.

10. Explain forecasting ability.

Ans. For answer refer to Q.No. 6(i) of NCERT folder.

11. What are the minimum requirements of fashion design?

Ans. Fashion design requires problem solving to understand the needs of the consumer and respond in a way that will meet their needs and creatively express the vision of the design.

12. List down the tasks involved to make fashion relatable to the customers.

Ans. There are following tasks involved to make fashion relatable to the customers

- Researching and predicting fashion trends.
- Directing and negotiating with suppliers, manufacturers and retailers.
- Determining a store's type of clientele.
- Pricing garments based on quality and affordability.
- Directing fashion photo shoots.

Short Answer Type Questions

1. What is the significance of fashion design and merchandising industry? **Diksha App**

Ans. The significance of fashion and merchandising can be understood with the help of following points

- Fashion design and merchandising industry will help an individual to understand how the fashion business works.
- It consists of all the processes involved with producing the raw material, apparel and accessories and the retail stores that sell fashion merchandise to the public.

- This industry is a part of fashion business, where one can learn about textiles or the fabrics and the fibers used to make them.
- Fashion merchandising equips an individual to first respond to what, why and when a style becomes a fashion.
- Then, it helps to determine its suitability for the particular retail operation and the time it will take. Thus, in a simple language, it encompasses 'planning, buying and selling' process.

2. Differentiate between demographic and geographic segmentation. Diksha App

Ans.

Basis	Demographic Segmentation	Geographic Segmentation
Definition	This type of segmentation divides the market based on characteristics of the population.	This segmentation divides the market based on geographic factors.
Criteria	Common criteria include age, gender, income level, education, occupation and family size.	It considers location, such as countries, regions, cities or even neighbourhoods. It can also include climate and urban Vs. rural distinctions.
Purpose	It helps businesses understand the needs and preferences of specific groups within the population, allowing for targeted marketing strategies.	Geographic segmentation helps businesses tailor their products and marketing strategies based on the geographical location of consumers, acknowledging that preferences can vary significantly based on where people live.

3. Explain three types of fashion retail organisations. CBSE Term II, 2022

Or **Mr. Sharma wants to expand his business of readymade clothing. Tell him about the different types of fashion retail organisations?** Competency Based Que; Diksha App

Ans. Fashion retail businesses can be divided into different sectors

(i) **Small Single-Unit Store** It is also known as a neighbourhood store. These are generally owner and family oriented single stores.

(ii) **Department Store** It consists of separate sections, known as departments, such as clothing, sporting goods, automotive supplies, health and beauty products and electronics equipment. Some of the department stores also sell food products.

(iii) **Chain Stores** These are retail outlets that share a brand and central management. They usually have standardised business methods and practices.

4. Nilesh wants to be a visual merchandise designer. CBSE SQP Term II, 2021

(i) What are the four merchandising rights he should be aware of? Competency Based Que

(ii) What two specific skills he must possess?

Ans. (i) For answer refer to text under the heading 'Merchandising Rights' on page no. 194.

(ii) For answer refer to text under the heading 'Skills Required' on page no. 195.

5. What is the need of merchandising from the perspective of the manufacturer? Diksha App

Ans.
- The buyer merchandiser plays the bridge between the manufacturer and buyer.
- They must be able to negotiate prices with manufacturers and sell their fashion choices to the public.
- The need of a merchandiser begins when enquiry of buyers comes for new orders.

Long Answer Type Questions

1. France's dominance over international fashion began in the early 18th century. Mention any two developments in fashion until the Industrial Revolution.

Ans. In the early 18th century, France began to dominate international fashion. Until the Industrial Revolution, people belonged to two classes i.e. rich and poor. Fashionable clothes could only be afforded by the rich people.

The two developments in fashion until the Industrial Revolution were

(i) The Industrial Revolution led to the emergence of technological advancements in textile and apparel production. Due to these developments, more fabrics were produced in less time. Spinning jenny and power looms were invented during

(ii) The invention of sewing machine converted the handicraft into an industry. This brought a democracy to fashion and it became easy-to-access for everyone.

2. Reema is a fashion designer and runs a fashion designing institute. CBSE 2024

(i) How will she explain the five stages of 'Fashion Cycle' to the new students pursing the course?

(ii) Draw a labelled 'Fashion Cycle' graph/diagram to be displayed in her institute. Competency Based Que

Ans. (i) For answer refer to Q. No. 2 of NCERT folder.

(ii) For answer refer to text under the heading 'Fashion Evolution' on page no. 191 and 192.

3. Discuss how market is segmented into different aspects in detail.

Or **"To interpret consumer demand one should understand target market and motivations'. What do you mean by target market? Describe four segments of target market.** **CBSE SQP 2024**

Or **Your best friend wants to choose a career of fashion merchandiser. Explain her the different types of market segments.** **Competency Based Que; Diksha App**

Or **(i) What do you understand by target market?**

(ii) In what four ways can the market be segmented? Explain in detail. **CBSE 2021 C**

Ans. Target Market is defined as category of consumers one is targeting at for selling the product. It is essential to understand the target market as this will allow the sales department to focus on that category of consumers who are 'most likely' to purchase the offering. It is also to insure the highest return for the marketing/sales expenditures.

Market segmentation is a strategy that involves dividing a larger market into subsets of consumers who have common needs and applications for the goods and services offered in the market.

Market can be segmented in various ways

- **Demographic Segmentation** is on the basis of population, age, sex, occupation, education and income.
- **Geographic Segmentation** is on the basis of cities, states and regions. Climate of various places may vary and it plays an important role as choice of merchandise, especially as selection of clothes is climate dependent.
- **Psychographic Segmentation** is on the basis of lifestyle like social activities, interests, leisure pursuits, needs and wants. People having similar lifestyles can make up a target market group.
- **Behavioural Segmentation** is on the basis of opinion on specific products or services. Many times rating of usage of products and services is done. This helps in improving the service/product and make it different from others.

4. Blazer jackets, hot pants, polo shirts and baggy pants are displayed in a fashion store for sale. **CBSE 2025**

(i) Classify and differentiate them as per fashion terms used in the fashion industry.

(ii) Which three career opportunities will be available to fashion design professionals in this fashion store? Mention any one role for each of them.

Ans. (i) The classification and differentiation of the garments such as, blazer jackets, hot pants, polo shirts and baggy pants as per fashion industry terms are

Garment	Category	Description
Blazer Jackets	Formal wear	These are tailored and structured jackets for business or formal events.
Hot Pants	Casual wear	These are very short and fitted shorts, which are popular for casual outings.
Polo Shirts	Semi-formal /Casual Wear	These are collared shirts, typically with buttons, suitable for semi-formal and casual settings.
Baggy Pants	Street wear	These are loose-fitting trousers, popular in urban and casual fashion.

(ii) The three career opportunities which are available to fashion design professionals in this fashion store and their role are

- **Fashion Designer** Creates new and trendy clothing designs for customers based on the latest fashion trends.
- **Merchandiser** Ensures the right products are available in the store, manages stock and displays clothes attractively for customers.
- **Stylist** Helps customers choose outfits that suit their style and preferences, providing a personalized shopping experience.

5. (i) Merchandising is done at which three levels? Explain in detail.

(ii) What two skills should a merchandiser possess, to be successful? **CBSE 2021 C**

Ans. (i) For answer refer to Q. No. 4 of NCERT folder.

(ii) For answer refer to Q. No. 6 of NCERT folder.

6. Anu is a fashion merchandiser who is working in a fashion house. She is involved with various activities including conversion of inspiration into design, use technology to conceptualise and address the planning and distribution of products in the fashion industry.

(i) Elaborate any four roles and responsibilities she will have in different phases of fashion merchandising.

(ii) How is small single unit store different from chain store? **Competency Based Que; CBSE SQP 2023**

(iii) Enumerate any two courses that Anu might have done to have a career in fashion merchandising.

Ans. (i) For answer refer to text under the heading 'Role of Fashion Merchancdiser' on page no. 192-193.

(ii) Small single unit store is different from chain store in a respect that it is also known as a neighbourhood store. These are generally owner and family oriented single stores whereas Chain stores are retail outlets that share a brand and central management. They usually have standardised business methods and practices.

(iii) Anu might have completed following two programme for a career in fashion merchandising. Completing a certificate or diploma degree programmes in fashion merchandising in a period of six months to one year. Master's programme in fashion merchandising are of two-years duration that consists of a certain amount of liberal arts requirements with fashion and business courses.

7. Your uncle wants to open a departmental store. Tell him about the major departments of stores. **Diksha App**

Ans.
- **Clothing and Apparel** This department offers a variety of clothing for men, women and children, including casual wear, formal wear and active wear. It may also include accessories like bags, belts and jewellry.
- **Health and Beauty Products** This section features cosmetics, skincare products, hair care items and personal hygiene products. It often includes fragrances and wellness products.
- **Home Goods and Kitchenware** This department provides items for home decoration, kitchen utensils, cookware, bedding and small appliances, catering to customers looking to enhance their living spaces.
- **Electronics** This section typically offers a range of electronic devices such as televisions, audio equipment, computers and accessories. It may also include cameras and other gadgets.
- **Sporting Goods** This department features sporting equipment, apparel for various sports and fitness accessories. It caters to active individuals and those looking to pursue hobbies related to fitness and sports.
- **Toys and Games** This section focuses on toys, games and educational materials for children, providing options for various age groups.
- **Food and Groceries** Some departmental stores include a grocery section that offers fresh produce, packaged foods and household essentials, making it convenient for shoppers.
- **Household Items** This department may include cleaning supplies, organisational products and other essentials needed for daily household management.

8. Hitika has joined as a visual merchandise designer in a reputed fashion store which deals with only ready-to-wear clothing lines. **CBSE 2024**

(i) List three job responsibilities which are expected of her to attract more customers.

(ii) Which terms are used in France for the following?

Ans. (i) Job responsibilities that are expected of her to attract more customers are as follows

(a) Designing eye-catching window displays and in-store displays to attract customers and showcase the latest ready-to-wear clothing lines effectively.

(b) Creating visually appealing product presentations and arrangements within the store to enhance the overall shopping experience and encourage sales.

(c) Collaborating with marketing teams to develop promotional materials and campaigns that highlight key fashion trends and drive customer engagement.

(ii) In France, the terms used for the following are
- Ready-to-wear clothing 'pret-a-porter'.
- Art of dress-making 'L'art de la couture'.

9. Jai and Shipra together have recently inaugurated their chain stores in the city. **Competency Based Que; CBSE 2024 C**

(a) Which type of designer would have been responsible for it has the beauty decoration and functionality of various workplaces of their chain stores?

(b) Name any four major departments within their chain stores.

(c) How is a small single unit store different from a chain store?

Ans. (a) Interior Designer

(b) The four major departments within the chain stores are as follows
(i) Sales and promotion division
(ii) Finance and control division
(iii) Operational division
(iv) Personnel and branch store

(c) A small unit store is a neighbourhood store, which is operated by either owner or a family whereas chain stores are the retail outlets that share a brand and central management. Chain stores usually have standardised business methods and practices.

10. Shweta wants to be an interior designer.

(i) Which functions will she need to perform in this profession?

(ii) Suggest to her two other career options related to fashion design. **Competency Based Que**

Ans. (i) The main objective of interior designers is to perfectly combine form with function. Their main function is to introduce interior concepts that will increase the beauty, safety and functionality of a particular space or area. Interior designers' works in variety of settings like retail stores, residential homes, offices, hospitals, hotels and many more.

(ii) For answer refer to text under the heading 'Scope of Fashion Designing and Merchandising' on page no. 196.

SELF ASSESSMENT TEST

Objective Type Questions

1. .... is more than just clothing.

   (a) Classic (b) Fads (c) Fashion (d) Style

2. Short lived fashion, that come and go in a single season is called **Diksha App**

   Or Sonakshi is a friend of yours. She constantly changes her style and does not stick to one fashion trend for long. Which of the following fashion is perfect for her? **Competency Based Que**

   (a) Style (b) Fad (c) Classic (d) Custom

3. What do you mean by classic or styles? **Diksha App**

   (a) That never becomes completely obsolete (b) That is not liked by customers

   (c) That is popular with high class society (d) That is changed frequently

4. .... is the inter face between an organisation and its customers.

   (a) Customer's satisfaction (b) Marketing

   (c) Fashion forecast (d) Product assortment

5. Identify the style that takes decades to move through the whole fashion cycle.

   (a) Classic (b) Modern (c) Traditional (d) Casual

Very Short Answer Type Questions

6. What does the second stage of fashion cycle signify. **Diksha App**
7. Write four functions of a fashion merchandiser. **Diksha App**
8. Describe sales and promotion division.

Short Answer Type Questions

9. Explain five merchandising rights. **Diksha App**
10. Explain the role of two types of merchandisers in an export house. **Diksha App**
11. Discuss Retail Organisation Merchandising.
12. Why is there a need for excellent communication skills in the field of fashion industry?
13. Discuss the scope of Fashion Designing and Merchandising.

Long Answer Type Questions

14. Discuss the varieties of career options available in Fashion Designing.
15. Discuss some of the major divisions related to Fashion Retail Organisations.

10

CHAPTER

This chapter explores the care and maintenance of fabrics, emphasising the importance of preserving their quality and functionality. It covers laundry processes, equipment, and techniques used in homes, hospitals and hospitality sectors, highlighting career opportunities in fabric management and care.

YOUR STUDY GOALS

10.1 Introduction
10.2 Basic Concepts
10.3 Institutions
10.4 Preparing for a Career
10.5 Scope

YOUR PRACTICE GOAL

- Objective Type Questions (30 Qs ; MCQs, A-R, Matching, Case Based)
- Subjective Questions (10 VSAs, 7 SAs, 8 LAs)

Care and Maintenance of Fabrics in Institutions

10.1 Introduction

- Fabrics play a significant role in daily life, used in apparel, household items, cars and various industries. Each fabric has specific characteristics that determine its usage and functionality. Maintaining these characteristics is crucial for the fabric's longevity and serviceability. Proper care enhances the lifespan of fabrics; the more care given, the longer they last.
- Care and maintenance of fabrics include two important aspects
  - Keeping the material free of physical damage and rectifying any damage that may occur.
  - Retaining or refreshing the fabric's appearance by removing stains and dirt to maintain its texture and visual characteristics.

10.2 Basic Concepts

- **Laundry**[1] is both a science and an art; it relies on scientific principles and techniques.
- It requires mastering skills to produce clean, fresh, and hygienic clothes that are aesthetically pleasing. Care and maintenance of fabrics depend on several factors

1 **Laundry** It refers to clothes, sheets, etc. that need washing.

- The fibre content of the fabric.
- The type of yarn and fabric construction techniques used.
- The finishes applied to the fabrics.
- The intended purpose of specific fabrics.

- The laundry process includes various steps such as stain removal, the role of water and the suitability of soaps and detergents.
- Other important aspects involve methods of **washing**[2], finishing treatments, ironing, pressing and folding.
- Common equipment required for fabric care and maintenance includes
  - Washing equipment for cleaning fabrics.
  - Drying equipment to remove moisture.
  - Ironing or pressing equipment for finishing the garments.

Washing Equipment

- A large amount of daily-use clothes are washed manually at home.
- Equipment required includes buckets, basins, bowls, and scrubbing boards and brushes.
- The washing method varies based on the type of fabric and degree of spoilage.
- Cotton, linen, and curtains are typically washed by rubbing with hands or on a scrubbing board.
- Excessively dirty clothes can be cleaned by rubbing with a brush or scrubbing board.
- Small, less dirty clothes can be cleaned by hand rubbing.
- Delicate items like silk with zari or expensive woollens should be dry cleaned.
- Due to busy schedules, many urban households now prefer **washing machines**[3] for daily laundry.

There are two types of washing machines available in the market. These are

- **Top Loading Washing Machines** Clothes are loaded from the top of the machine.
- **Front Loading Washing Machines** Clothes are loaded from the front side of the machine.

Models of Washing Machines

Washing machine are available in following models

- **Manually Operated Washing Machine** A non-electric machine where most work is done by the operator.

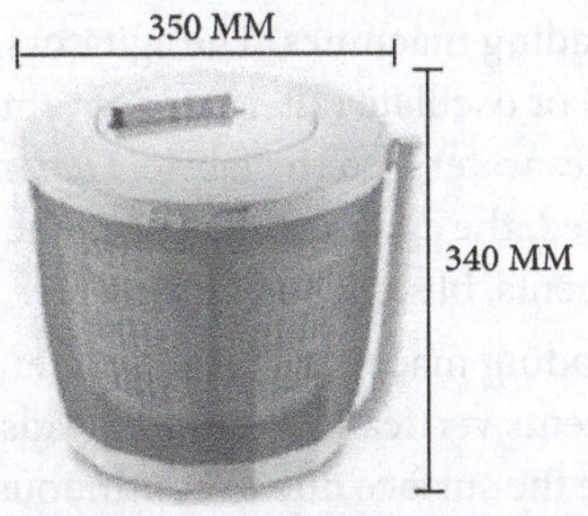

▲ *Manually Operated Washing Machine*

2 **Washing** It means an act of cleaning something using water and soap.
3 **Washing Machines** An electric machine for washing clothes.

- **Semi-Automatic Washing Machine** A machine contains two tubs for washing and drying; water is manually added.

▲ *Semi-Automatic Washing Machine*

- **Fully-Automatic Washing Machine** A machine has a single control setting for water filling, temperature, wash cycle, and rinses.

▲ *Fully-Automatic Washing Machine*

Following functions are performed by an automatic washing machine

(i) Filling of Water

(ii) **Controlling Water Level** The water level is controlled either automatically or manually in washing machine.

(iii) **Regulation of Temperature of Water** The washing machine has a button, dial or panel indication which permits selection of required temperature of the water. The temperature may be same or different for wash and rinse.

(iv) **Washing** The main principle of all washing machine is to keep the fabric in movement to get rid of all the dirt.

The main methods of washing in machine are

(a) **Agitation** It is used in top loading machines. The agitators have blades which may rotate (movement in one direction) or oscillate (alternate movement in two directions). This creates current in the tub which forces water into the fabric. Depending on the size of the machine and the type of fabrics to be washed, the agitators may be made of plastic, metal, bakelite, etc., which are not affected by any detergents, bleaches, softeners, etc.

(b) **Pulsation** It is used in top loading machine. The movement is caused by a vertical pulsator which has very rapid movements vertically. Pulsation leads to movement of fabric in both direction. Dirt particles leave the surface due to continuous pulsation.

(c) **Tumbling** This is only used in front loading machines. Washing takes place in a horizontally perforated cylinder. It revolves in a partially filled tub. With each revolution, the clothes are carried to top and then dropped in the wash water, i.e., the clothes move through the water, rather than water moving through the clothes.

(v) **Rinsing** It is an important phase in the wash cycle. If it is not properly done, the clothes may look dull and grey and have a harsh texture.

(vi) Water Extraction Water is drained out after the wash phase and after each rinse phase of the cycle. It can be done in the following three ways

(a) Spinning Spinning at speeds greater than 300 rpm generates a centrifugal force which in turn throws the water up and out. This water is pumped down the drain. It is important to avoid spinning to near dryness as it leads to wrinkles in a cloth, which are difficult to remove through ironing. The best speed is approximately 600-620 rpm.

(b) Bottom-Drain Machines with perforated tubs stop at the end of wash phase and then, at the end of rinse phase, drainage takes place through a hose pipe attached at the bottom. At the end of the drain period, the tub begins to spin which removes the remaining water from clothes.

(c) Combination Bottom-Drain and Spin Some machines drain through the bottom without stopping during the spin period. This system can remove the heavy dirt at the bottom and dirt suspended in water. This system provides the best water extraction method. The amount of water extracted from the clothes is due to the speed at which the tub spins.

Drying Equipment and Process

Drying in the open is the most common method of drying clothes. Driers, however, are used at commercial and institutional level. There are mainly two types of circulation systems in driers.

(i) Air of relatively low temperature is circulated at high velocity. Room air enters the drier from under the front panel. It passes over the source of heat and then passes through the clothes and leaves through an exhaust. In this way, the humidity and the temperature of the room stays normal.

(ii) Air of high temperature is circulated slowly. After the air enters the drier and passes over the heat source, it is drawn by a small fan through perforations at the top of the drier. Then it goes downward through the clothes and out through the exhaust. Since the movement of the air in this drier is slow, the relative humidity of the exhausted air is high.

Ironing and Hot Pressing

- Ironing is the process of smoothening out wrinkles in the clothes created during use or washing. Pressing helps to put creases in sleeves, trouser legs, and pleated skirts. The first known use of heated metal to 'iron' clothes was started in China.
- The electric iron was invented in 1882 by **Henry W. Seely**. Irons have smooth metal surfaces which can be heated. Most electric irons have an inbuilt thermostat which can adjust the temperature according to the texture of the fabric.

  There are different types of irons.

  - **Steam Iron** The iron may also have a system of producing steam while in use. Steam iron creates a smoother press and helps remove wrinkles on cotton and linen fabrics. Steam irons have a small water tub inside which produces steam to moisten clothes while pressing. These are more expensive than dry ones.
  - **Dry Irons** These are the most basic ones and are typically quite inexpensive. They are lightweight and have basic controls. When ironing clothes with a dry iron, we need to sprinkle a little amount of water on clothes to get the best press. The weight of the iron varies from 1.5-3.5 kgs.
  - **Charcoal Iron** It is like a metal box with a lid, in which live coal pieces are put to heat the iron. Heavier articles like curtains and bed covers can be pressed easily with this type of iron.
  - **Gas Iron** In a gas iron, a gas line carries fuel to the appliance which contains a burner to provide the heat. Other than charcoal iron, some dhobis also use gas irons which are cheaper to operate as compared to coal irons.

Dhobis

Individuals who collect materials from household for washing and ironing are known as **Dhobis**. They generally use charcoal iron. They also serve student hostels, small hotels and restaurants. They generally make use of specially marked places in town and cities for washing which are known as **Dhobi ghats**.

Commercial Laundry

- There are many laundries or dry cleaning[4] shops in cities. Customers bring articles for cleaning and return a few days later to collect the finished items.
- The customer may be an individual or an institution, such as students, hostels, or small hotels. Bigger laundries often have various centers or shops in different parts of a city.
- Some laundries provide transport services for materials to and from customers, especially for institutions like hostels, small hotels and restaurants. Commercial laundries are organised into different sections.
- Each section handles specific jobs, including washing, water extraction, drying, pressing, and ironing. Some laundries have separate sections for hospital and institutional work and another for individual and personal work.
- There may also be separate sections for dry cleaning, fiber-specific articles like woolens and silks, and special items like blankets and carpets. Some laundries have arrangements for dyeing and special finishes, such as zari polishing.
- Units for inspection, sorting of materials, and pre-treatments like mending and stain removal are also available. These laundries use larger equipment for washing and dry cleaning in large quantities.
- Washing machines in commercial laundries can handle 100 kg or more of load in one cycle. They are equipped with hydro-extractors[5], dryers, flatbed ironing equipment, roller ironing machines and folding tables.
- Commercial laundries follow a systematic record-keeping process. When an article is received from a customer, it is thoroughly checked for any damage and special care requirements are recorded.
- Customers receive an invoice detailing the kind and number of articles received, along with the delivery date. A system of code tags matching the invoice helps identify the specific items belonging to each customer.

Quick Test 1

1 What are the two types of washing machines available in the market?
2 Which washing machines require a permanent electricity and constant water supply?
3 What does the term 'pulsation' mean?
4 What types of equipment do commercial laundries have?

10.3 Institutions

- Large institutions like hospitals, hotels and prisons have their own laundry departments.
- These institutions require a constant flow of clean linen, working clothing or uniforms.
- Organised collection, laundering and timely delivery of processed material is essential for smooth operation.
- There are mainly two types of institutions with in-house laundry setups: **hotels and hospitals.**
- Hotels require a large quantity of bed linen and room furnishings.

4 **Dry-Cleaning** It means to clean clothes using chemicals instead of water.
5 **Hydro-Extractor** It works in centrifugal motion which gets rid of 60-70 per cent moisture while washing.

- Examples of furnishings include curtains, tablecloths, sofa covers and cushion covers.
- Hospitals require daily items such as aprons, caps, head dresses and masks.

Hospital Laundry

- The hospital laundry takes care of hygiene, cleanliness and **disinfection**[6].
- Many hospitals have started using disposable linen due to the threat of infection, which are destroyed by burning.
- Most of the articles in hospitals are made of cotton and are dyed (in colours specific to the hospital and department) with excellent wash-fast dyes. Only the blankets there are woolen.
- The daily laundry emphasises mainly on cleanliness of cotton materials.
- Stubborn stains may be neglected, and starching and whitening are also not done.
- Even the ironing and pressing may not be done to perfection.
- Sometimes repair and mending, and condemnation of unusable material are not done in hospital laundry.

Process of Laundry Functioning in Hospitals

- Collection of materials from Emergency, main OT, OPD, various specialised centers and wards of the hospitals.
- Transportation of these collected materials to the laundry plant.
- Unloading and sorting dirty linen like
  - Bed-linen-clean, mildly soiled and very soiled,
  - Doctor's dress and
  - Patient's dress,
  - Blankets.
- The clothes are washed in large washing machines (capacity of 100 kg per load).
- Hydro-extraction is done in centrifugal motion which gets rid of 60-70 per cent moisture.
- Drying, pressing, ironing, folding and stacking.
- Mending and segregation of condemned articles.
- Packing and distribution.

Laundry in Hospitality Sector

- For hotels and restaurants, aesthetics and final finish of the articles are of utmost importance.
- As compared to hospitals different fibers are used in hotels and restaurants, focusing on attractive and bright materials.
- Final finishing of laundered goods, including starching, ironing, pressing and perfect folding, is required.
- Hotels also provide personal laundry service for guests when needed.
- Some times small hotels may not have their own laundry service and rely on commercial laundries.
- Laundry work is much larger for hospitals than for hotels.
- Large hotels may have up to 400-500 rooms, while hospitals may have around or more than 2000 beds.
- Sheets in Operation Theatre, Maternity Ward and Labour Room may require more than 5 changes in a day.
- Linen requirement in stock is a minimum of 6 sets per bed.
- Blankets are not changed daily unless soiled.
- Apart from bed linen, tableclothes, curtains, and dresses of patients and doctors are also washed regularly.

---

6 **Disinfection** It means to clean something using a substance that kills bacteria.

- There is a system for keeping records of collection and disbursement of material to each department in commercial laundries.

Name of The Hospital
Receipt for Washable Linen

Receipt No. ....
Received From ....
Dated ....   Time ....

S.No.	Name of the Clothing	Qty.	Remarks
1.	Bed Sheet		
2.	Draw Sheet (White)		
3.	Draw Sheet (Green)		
4.	Patient's Kurta		
5.	Patient's Pajama		
6.	Doctor's Kurta		
7.	Doctor's Pajama		
8.	Doctor's Gown		
9.	Towel Split		
10.	Towel Hand		
11.	Face Mask		
12.	Baby Frocks		
13.	Blanket Big/Baby		
14.	Pillow Cover		
15.	Slings		
16.	Apron		
17.	Dirty Linen Bag		

▲ *Record Keeping for Laundry*

10.4 Preparing for a Career

The field of care and maintenance of fabrics is a technical field. The primary requirements to develop a career in this field are

- Knowledge of the **materials,** i.e. an individual must have the following knowledge about
  - The fibre content of the material.
  - Yarn and fabric production technique.
  - The colours and finishes of the material in terms of the effect of care required.
- Knowledge of the whole **process** involved.
- Knowledge of the **chemicals** and other reagents used in the process and their effect on the particular type of fabric.
- Working knowledge of the **machinery** requirements and its functioning.

Laundry Management Courses

- Management courses are short-term programmes that offer coaching and job placement assistance.
- They provide support for starting one's own business and opportunities for practical training with a stipend.
- Practical training is available in hi-tech laundry operations, offering job opportunities in airways, ships, railways, hotels and hi-tech hospitals.

- Each of these sectors has different types of equipment and specific requirements.
- Qualifications in textile science, textile chemistry, fabric and apparel are extremely beneficial for these jobs.
- These courses are offered as specialisations for graduate degrees by various institutions across the country that provide Home Science programmes.

10.5 Scope

Persons with specialisation in textile, clothing, fabric and apparel can venture into entrepreneurial activities.

- It provides much-needed help and support for the end users in **metropolitan areas,** especially when women work outside the homes.
- A large number of **nursing homes,** small hospitals, day care centers, etc., need such services on a regular basis.
- Hi-tech laundries of **railways**, **airways**, shipping lines, **hotels**, and **hospitals**, which have in-house programmes for care and maintenance of fabrics and textiles, need a large number of qualified professionals in this field.

Quick Test 2

1. What types of institutions have their own laundry departments?
2. The hospital laundry takes care of hygiene, cleanliness and what else?
3. What factors are essential for the final finishing of laundered goods in the hospitality sector?
4. What are two important requirements for developing a career in the care and maintenance of fabrics?

Mind Map

CARE AND MAINTENANCE OF FABRICS IN INSTITUTIONS

1 Introduction to Fabric Care

Importance of Fabrics
- Used in daily life (apparel, household items and cars, industries).
- Each fabric has specific characteristics for usage and functionality.

Fabric Longevity
- Maintaining fabric characteristics is key to longevity and service ability.
- Proper care increases fabric life span.

Key Aspects of Fabric Care

Prevent and Repair Damage
- Avoid physical damage.
- Repair any damage that occurs.

Refresh Appearance
- Remove stains and dirt.

2 Basic Concepts of Fabric Care

- **Laundry** Combines science and skill to clean and maintain fabric quality, based on fiber content and construction.

Washing Machines
- **Semi-Automatic** Two tubs, manual water filling.
- **Fully-Automatic** Single control for all functions.
- **Washing Methods** Agitation (top-loading), Pulsation (top-loading), Tumbling (front-loading).
- **Water Extraction** Spinning, Bottom-Drain, Combination.
- **Drying** Air circulation (low/high temperature) in commercial dryers.

Ironing and Pressing
- **Steam Iron** Moistens fabric while pressing.
- **Dry Iron** Basic pressing, requires water.
- **Charcoal/Gas Iron** For heavy fabrics.
- **Commercial Laundry** Large-scale laundries for individuals and institutions, offering washing, drying, pressing, and dry cleaning services.
- **Manual Washing Equipment** Buckets, basins, scrubbing boards; machines for daily use (top/front loading). Dry cleaning for delicate fabrics.

3 Institution Laundry Overview

Types of Institutions
- **Hotels** Focus on aesthetics, large linen requirements (bed linens, furnishings).
- **Hospitals** Hygiene-focused, daily laundry for cotton items (aprons, caps, etc.).

Hospital Laundry Process
- Collection from various hospital areas.
- Sorting (bed linen, doctor's/patient's clothes).
- Washing (large machines, 100 kg load).
- Hydro-extraction to remove moisture.
- Drying, Ironing, Folding.
- Mending, Packing and Distribution.

Hotel Laundry
- Focus on perfect finish (starching, ironing, folding).
- Smaller hotels may outsource laundry.
- **Key Differences** Hospitals have larger laundry volumes than hotels, with more frequent linen changes.

4 Preparing for a Career in Fabric Care

Knowledge of Materials
- Fiber content
- Yarn and fabric production
- Colors and finishes
- **Understanding the Entire Process** From care techniques to machinery and chemicals used.
- **Machinery Expertise** Knowledge of laundry equipment and its functions.

Laundry Management Courses
- **Short-Term Programmes** Offer job placement assistance and business startup support.
- **Practical Training** Opportunities in airlines, ships, railways, hotels and hospitals.
- **Specialised Qualifications** Textile science, chemistry, and fabric/apparel expertise are beneficial.
- **Offered by Institutions** Available as specialisations in Home Science programmes.

5 Scope in Fabric Care Field

- **Entrepreneurial Opportunities** Specialisation in textiles, clothing, fabric, and apparel opens doors for starting businesses.
- **Support for End Users** Especially in metropolitan areas, where working women need fabric care services.
- **High Demand in Institutions** Nursing homes, hospitals, day care centers require regular fabric care.
- **Hi-Tech Laundries** Railways, airways, shipping lines, hotels, and hospitals need qualified professionals for in-house fabric care programmes.

NCERT Folder

1. What are the two aspects of care and maintenance of fabrics? Diksha App

Or **Briefly explain the two aspects of care and maintenance of fabrics.** CBSE 2021 C

Ans. Two aspects of care and maintenance of fabrics are

(i) Keep the material free of physical damage and rectify any damage that may have occurred during its usage.

(ii) Retain the appearance by removing stains, dirt which help in retaining the textural and visual characterstics.

2. What are the factors which affect the process of cleaning of fabrics?

Ans. The factors that affect the process of cleaning of fabrics are

(i) The fibre content of the fabric.

(ii) Type of yarn and fabric construction techniques.

(iii) The finishes given to the fabrics.

(iv) The purpose for which they are used.

3. How are the different sections organised in commercial or institutional laundry?

Ans. In commercial or institutional laundry different sections are organised in the specific manner.

(i) Each section deals with a specific job like, washing, water extraction, drying, pressing and ironing.

(ii) Some laundries may have separate sections for dry-cleaning, for fibre specific articles like woolens, silks and synthetics and for special articles like blankets and carpets.

(iii) Some laundries also have arrangement for dyeing and special finishes like zari polishing.

(iv) Some laundries would have units for inspection, sorting out of materials and also taking care of pre-treatments like mending, repairing and stain removal.

(v) Some laundries also provide services of transport of material to and from the customer. They give this facility to the institutions like hostels, small hotels, restaurants and small hospitals and nursing homes.

(vi) Some commercial laundries also have a system of keeping record. When the article is received, it is checked and any damage or special care requirement is recorded.

4. What are the differences in processing laundry work in commercial laundries and hospital laundries? Diksha App

Ans. The processes adopted in laundry work for commercial laundries and hospital laundries are quite different.

Commercial Laundries	Hospital Laundries
Commercial laundries take care of bigger articles of household linen and some special articles.	It takes care of hygiene, cleanliness and disinfection. Now, a number of hospitals use disposables and destroy them by burning.
These are organised in different sections to deal with specific tasks–washing, water extracting, drying, pressing and ironing.	Most of the articles in hospitals are made of cotton and dyed with excellent wash-fast dyes.
There may be separate sections for dry cleaning, for special articles like blankets and carpets.	The blankets and woolen are washed, when required, not on a daily basis.
Some laundries have arrangements for dyeing, zari polishing, special treatment for silk sarees etc.	The daily laundry of hospital emphasises mainly on cleanliness of cotton materials.
Some laundries have units for inspection, sorting out of materials and taking care of pre- treatment like mending, repairing and stain removal.	Sometimes stubborn stains may not be taken notice of and finishings like starching and whitening are also not done.

Exam Pattern Questions

Objective Type Questions

Multiple Choice Questions

1. Care and maintenance of fabrics results in

(a) keeping the material free of physical damage
(b) rectifying the damage done during its use
(c) retaining the real appearance of the fabric
(d) All of the above

2. Care and maintenance requirements of different fabrics depend on .... **Diksha App**

(a) fibre content (b) colour
(c) size (d) None of these

3. A semi-automatic washing machine contain how many tub(s)?

(a) One (b) Two (c) Three (d) Four

4. A fully automatic machine should have ....

(a) singe tub (b) permanent electricity
(c) constant water supply (d) All of these

5. What is the main principle of a washing machine?

(a) To keep the fabric in movement
(b) To carry away the dirt
(c) To spin the clothes properly
(d) Both (a) and (b)

6. Soaking clothes for some time helps to .... dirt. **Diksha App**

(a) harden (b) fix
(c) settle (d) loosen

7. What in the washing machine has blades which may rotate and oscillate, producing current in the tub?

(a) Regulators (b) Agitators
(c) Cylinders (d) None of these

8. What leads to movement of fabric in both direction in washing machine which helps to leave the dirt particles?

(a) Tumbler (b) Pulsation
(c) Agitators (d) None of these

9. Agitation method used in ....

(a) front loading machines
(b) semi-automated machine
(c) manually operated machine
(d) top loading machines

10. Which method of washing is used in a front loading washing machine for clothes? **CBSE 2025**

(a) Tumbling (b) Agitation
(c) Spinning (d) Pulsation

11. Which of the following material is not suitable for making agitators in washing machines? **CBSE 2024**

(a) Plastic (b) Aluminium
(c) Bakelite (d) Iron

12. Which phase of the wash cycle if not done properly results in the clothes having a dull texture?

(a) Agitation (b) Tumbling
(c) Pulsation (d) Rinsing

13. Spinning in washing machines is meant to .... **CBSE 2021 C**

(a) dry the clothes
(b) rinse clothes
(c) extract water from clothes
(d) wash and dry clothes

14. The speed of the tub spin for water extraction may vary from.

(a) 33-110 rpm (b) 333-1100 rpm
(c) 3000-5000 rpm (d) None of these

15. Commercial laundries have the washing machine which have the capacity to handle how many kg or more load in one cycle?

(a) 50 (b) 75 (c) 100 (d) 150

16. In laundries of which institution is the hydro-extraction process adopted?

(a) Commercial (b) Local
(c) Hospitals (d) None of these

17. What capacity of washing machine would be suitable to handle a large load of clothes for washing in one cycle in a big hotel? **CBSE 2024**

(a) 100 kg (b) 5-10 kg
(c) 20-30 kg (d) 15 kg

18. How many times are bed linens in a maternity ward changed in a day?

(a) 1 time (b) 3 times (c) 5 times (d) 4 times

19. What type of irons are the most basic ones and are inexpensive?

(a) Charcoal (b) Steam
(c) Dry (d) Gas

20. Which of the following is NOT a typical service offered by a dhobi?

(a) Washing clothes (b) Ironing clothes
(c) Repairing torn clothes (d) Finishing clothes

21. **Which of the following is NOT an essential requirement for preparing for a career in the field of care and maintenance of fabrics?**

(a) Knowledge of the material
(b) Knowledge of the machines involved
(c) Knowledge of the chemicals
(d) None of the above

22. **For removing old blood stains on coloured cotton fabric, the most appropriate option** Diksha App

(a) Soak in salt water
(b) Soak in glycerin
(c) Soak in hot water
(d) Wash with soap and hot water

23. **Care and maintenance of the fabric depends on**

I. Fibre content
II. Fabric construction
III. Tie and Dye technique
IV. Brand of the fabric

Choose the correct option

(a) I and II (b) II and IV
(c) I and III (d) III and IV

24. **Care and maintenance of the fabric depends on** CBSE SQP

I. Fibre content
II. Fabric construction
III. Tie and Dye technique
IV. Brand of the fabric

Choose the correct option

(a) I and II (b) II and IV
(c) I and III (d) III and IV

25. **Identify the methods of washing clothes in a top-loading washing machine.** CBSE 2023

I. Research scholar II. Tumbling
III. Calendering IV. Pulsation

Choose the correct option

(a) I and II (b) I and IV
(c) II and IV (d) II and III

Assertion-Reason Questions

Directions (Q. Nos. 26-27) In the questions given below, there are two statements marked as Assertion (A) and Reason (R). Read the statements and choose the correct option.

Codes

(a) Both A and R are true and R is the correct explanation of A.
(b) Both A and R are true, but R is not the correct explanation of A.
(c) A is true, but R is false.
(d) A is false, but R is true.

26. **Assertion (A)** A semi-automatic washing machine is a better choice than a fully-automatic washing machine, for everyday use at home.

Reason (R) A semi-automatic washing machine saves both water and time.

27. **Assertion (A)** Disposable linens are used in most hospitals and they are destroyed by burning.

Reason (R) Burning is chosen because there is a high risk of infection on reuse.

Picture Based Question

28. **Identify the picture.**

(a) Front loading washing machine
(b) Manual operating washing machine
(c) Semi-automatic washing machine
(d) Fully-automatic washing machine

Case Based Questions

29. **Read the passage given below and answer the following questions.**

Care and maintenance of apparel and articles of household usage within the family may be done at different levels. Household laundry takes care of clothing and small articles of daily use. Bigger articles of household linen and some special articles are sent to commercial laundries. Sometimes services are hired of individual professionals who collect material from household for washing and/or ironing and finishing.

(i) **Select the option that lists the articles of clothing that would be sent to commercial laundries.**

I. Shirt II. Sofa covers
III. Trousers IV. Curtains
V. Bed sheets VI. Sarees

Codes

(a) I, III and IV (b) II, IV and V
(c) II, V and VI (d) I, III and V

(ii) **Given below are two statements labelled as Assertion (A) and Reason (R).**

Assertion (A) Dhobi and dhobi ghats are components of commercial laundry.

Reason (R) There are several different sections in a commercial industry that deals with different aspects of laundry.

Codes

(a) Both A and R are true and R is the correct explanation of A.
(b) Both A and R are true, but R is not the correct explanation of A.
(c) A is true, but R is false.
(d) A is false, but R is true.

(iii) Which of the following pairs correctly matches the type of laundry service with its description?

(a) Household laundry : Handles only large articles
(b) Commercial laundries : Takes care of clothing and daily use items
(c) Dhobis : Collects materials for washing and ironing
(d) Special articles : Managed solely by household members

(iv) Assertion (A) Some household articles require commercial laundering services.

Reason (R) These articles are too large or specialised for household care.

Codes

(a) Both A and R are true and R is the correct explanation of A.
(b) Both A and R are true, but R is not the correct explanation of A.
(c) A is true, but R is false.
(d) A is false, but R is true.

30. Read the passage given below and answer the following questions.

Institutional laundries are organised in different departments. Each part deals with a specific task, such as washing, drainage, drying, pressing. Some laundries may have separate sections for hospitals and institutions and for personal work of individuals. Most laundries have separate unit for inspection, sorting, segregation and pre-treatment for stubborn spots.

(i) After washing and rinsing, the process of removing water from clothes is known as ....

(a) Plusation
(b) Tumbling
(c) Agitation
(d) Water extraction

(ii) What tasks are typically performed in the inspection unit of a commercial laundry?

(a) Dyeing and zari polishing
(b) Mending, repairing and stain removal
(c) Water extraction and drying
(d) Washing and pressing

(iii) Which of the following is NOT typically a section in a commercial laundry?

(a) Washing
(b) Dyeing and special finishes
(c) Cooking
(d) Dry-cleaning

(iv) Which of the following options is correct?

(a) The amount of laundry work is more in hotels than in hospitals.
(b) Some washing machines drain water from the bottom without stopping and this is the best method of drainage.
(c) Aesthetic care, health, hygiene and disinfection of garments are taken care of in the washing house of the hospital.
(d) In the field of clothing care, practical training is not required to make a living.

Answers

1. (d) All of the above
2. (a) fibre content
3. (b) Two
4. (d) All of these
5. (d) Both (a) and (b)
6. (d) loosen
7. (b) Agitators
8. (c) Agitators
9. (d) top loading machines
10. (a) Tumbling
11. (d) Iron
12. (d) Rinsing
13. (c) extract water from clothes
14. (b) 333-1100 rpm
15. (c) 100
16. (a) Commercial
17. (c) 20-30 kg
18. (c) 5 times
19. (a) Charcoal
20. (c) Repairing torn clothes
21. (d) None of the above
22. (a) Soak in salt water
23. (a) I and II
24. (a) I and II
25. (c) II and IV
26. (a) Both A and R are true and R is the correct explanation of A.
27. (a) Both A and R are true and R is the correct explanation of A.
28. (c) Semi-automatic washing machine
29. (i) (b) II, IV and V
(ii) (b) Both A and R are true, but R is not the correct explanation of A

(iii) (c) Dhobis : Collects materials for washing and ironing

(iv) (a) Both A and R are true and R is the correct explanation of A.

30. (i) (d) Water extraction

(ii) (b) Mending, repairing and stain removal

(iii) (c) Cooking

(iv) (b) Some washing machines drain water from the bottom without stopping and this is the best method of drainage.

Subjective Questions

Very Short Answer Type Questions

1. What are the two aspects of care and maintenance of fabrics? **CBSE SQP 2024**

Ans. The two important aspects of care and maintenance of fabrics are

(i) **Preventing Physical Damage** This involves keeping the fabric free from tears, fraying, and other forms of physical wear. It includes handling fabrics with care during washing, drying, and storage to avoid damage.

(ii) **Maintaining Appearance** This aspect focuses on retaining or refreshing the fabric's visual characteristics, such as texture and colour. It includes regular cleaning to remove stains and dirt, ensuring that the fabric looks good and remains hygienic over time.

2. What is the principal of the agitator?

Ans. The principal of the agitator in a washing machine is to create movement that helps remove dirt and stains from fabrics. The agitator has blades or fins that rotate or oscillate, creating agitation within the wash tub. This movement forces water and detergent through the fabric, allowing them to penetrate and loosen dirt.

3. What are the equipment used for care and maintenance requirements of different fabrics. **CBSE 2024 C**

Ans. The equipment used for the care and maintenance of different fabrics includes

- **Washing Machines** Essential for cleaning fabrics, available in various types (top-loading, front-loading, semi-automatic, fully-automatic) depending on the needs.
- **Dryers** Used to remove moisture from washed fabrics, available in both commercial and residential settings.
- **Ironing Equipment** Includes electric irons (steam and dry), which smooth out wrinkles and creases in garments. Used in commercial settings for efficiently pressing large volumes of fabric or garments.

4. Give reason for the following

(i) Spinning to near dryness is avoided.

(ii) Agitators of washing machine should be made of bakelite.

Ans. (i) Spinning to near dryness is avoided because it can lead to wrinkling of a piece of clothing. Such wrinkles are difficult to remove.

(ii) Agitators of washing machine should be made of bakelite so that they are not affected by detergents, bleaches, softeners, etc.

5. Describe any three types of features of fully automatic washing machine.

Ans. Three features of fully-automatic machines are

(i) They have a single time setting of controls for each use i.e. water filling, temperature of water, wash cycle and number of rinses.

(ii) No further intervention of the operator is required.

(iii) Permanent electricity and constant water supply are needed.

6. Explain 'pulsation' as a method of washing clothes, to your mother.

Ans. **Pulsation** It is used in top loading machine. The movement is caused by a vertical pulsator which has very rapid movements vertically.

Pulsation leads to movement of fabric in both direction. Dirt particles leave the surface due to continuous pulsation.

7. What are the two types of institutions that have in-house laundry?

Ans. The two types of institutions that have in-house laundry are hotels and hospitals. Both of these institutions require a large quantum of bed linen, room furnishing equipments and different dresses for their employees.

For the smooth operations of these institutions, the in-house laundry is essential.

8. What type of knowledge is needed for an individual to care and maintain the fabrics properly?

Ans. The individual must have knowledge about

- The fibre content of the material.
- Yarn and fabric production technique.
- The colours and finishes of the material in terms of the effect of the care and maintenance required.

9. How will you remove tea stain from a cotton shirt? Diksha App

Ans. To remove a tea stain from a cotton shirt, follow these steps

- If the stain persists, soak the shirt in a solution of cold water and a bit of laundry detergent for about 30 minutes.
- Sleep in Glycerin until stain is removed.

10. Name two grease solvent which are used to remove stains from garments. Diksha App

Ans. Two common grease solvents used to remove stains from garments are

(i) **Dry Cleaning Solvent** Often referred to as perchloroethylene (perc), this solvent is used in dry cleaning processes to effectively dissolve grease and oil stains.

(ii) **Rubbing Alcohol (Isopropyl Alcohol)** This can also be used to treat grease stains, as it helps break down oil-based substances.

Short Answer Type Questions

1. Discuss the types of washing machine model available in the market? Diksha App

Ans. In the market, there are several types of washing machine models, each designed to cater to different needs and preferences. Here are the main types

- **Manually Operated Washing Machine** A non-electric machine where most of the work is done manually by the operator.Typically consists of a tub where clothes are manually agitated or scrubbed. Cost-effective and energy-efficient, ideal for areas without electricity.
- **Semi-Automatic Washing Machine** Consists of two tubs-one for washing and one for drying. Water must be manually added. Users need to manually switch between washing and rinsing cycles. More affordable than fully automatic machines and allows users to control the washing process.
- **Fully Automatic Washing Machine** Operates on a single control setting for washing, rinsing, and spinning without manual intervention. No futher involvement of the operator is needed here. These should be permanent electricity and constant water supply. Convenient and efficient; requires less user involvement as it handles all processes automatically.

2. Describe any two methods of water extraction from clothes. State the optimum speed of the spinning tub in a washing machine.

Or **Enlist the three methods of water extraction from clothes.** CBSE 2024 C

Ans. The two methods of water extraction from clothes are

(i) **Spinning** Spinning at speeds greater than 300 rpm generates a centrifugal force which in turn throws the water up and out. This water is pumped down the drain. It is important to avoid spinning to near dryness as it leads to wrinkles in a cloth, which are difficult to remove through ironing. The best speed is approximately 600-620 rpm.

(ii) **Bottom-Drain** Machines with perforated tubs stop at the end of wash phase and then, at the end of rinse phase, drainage takes place through a hose pipe attached at the bottom. At the end of the drain period, the tub begins to spin which removes the remaining water from clothes.

(iii) **Combination Bottom-Drain and Spin** Some machines drain through the bottom without stopping during the spin period. This system can remove the heavy dirt at the bottom and dirt suspended in water. This system provides the best water extraction method. The amount of water-extracted from the clothes is due to the speed at which the tub spins.

3. (i) How do the clothes get cleaned by agitation and tumbling methods in washing machines?

(ii) Which type of drier would you choose for your home? Why? CBSE 2021 C Diksha App

Or **What is the tumbling methods of Washing Machine?**

Ans. (i) In agitation method, creates current in the tub which forces water into the fabric and cleans the clothes.

In tumbling method, it causes the clothes to revolve in a front leading machine, which allows them to be carried through the water. Thus, it cleans clothes.

(ii) Although the best method of drying clothes at home is drying them in the open, a drier can be used for the same too.

The type of drier that should be used is the one in which air of lower temperature is circulated at high velocity. Such driers don't cause an increase in the humidity of the room, rather the humidity and temperature, after the use of such driers, of the room stays normal.

4. Most of the families have their own irons. Which type of irons are generally used?

Ans. Most of the families have their own irons. The family members generally use their irons to press their clothes of daily use. Both steam irons and dry irons are used for this purpose.

- Steam irons have a small water tub inside which produces steam to moisten clothes while pressing. It gives a smoother press and helps remove wrinkles on cotton and linen fabrics.

- Dry irons are the most basic ones and are light weight, having basic controls. While using it, we need to sprinkle a little amount of water on clothes to get the best press. These are quite inexpensive.

5. How is ironing different from hot pressing of clothes? Give any two differences. **CBSE 2025**

Ans. The two key differences between ironing and hot pressing of clothes are

- Ironing involves moving the heated iron back and forth over the fabric and applying pressure manually to remove wrinkles, while hot pressing relies on placing the garment between two heated plates and applying consistent pressure without movement.
- Ironing is generally used for day to day wrinkle removal from clothes, while hot pressing is often used in manufacturing processes or professional settings for precise shaping and finishing.

6. Why laundry is an art and science? Give any four differences between household and commercial laundry.

Or **'Laundry is both a science and an art'. Justify this statement.** **Diksha App**

Ans. Laundry is an art because its application requires mastering of some skills and it is a science because it is based on scientific principles and techniques.

Differences Between Household and Commercial Laundry

Basis	Household Laundry	Commercial Laundry
Scale of Operation	Typically handles small loads, washing clothes for a single household.	Handles large volumes of laundry, often catering to multiple customers, including institutions like hostels, hospitals and hotels.
Equipment	Uses basic washing equipment like buckets, basins, scrubbing boards, or home washing machines.	Uses industrial-sized washing machines, dryers, hydro-extractors, roller ironing machines and other large-scale equipment.
Process Complexity	The process is simpler and often done manually or using semi-automatic machines.	The process is highly systematic, involving various sections like sorting, washing, drying, pressing, and ironing, often with specialised sections for different types of fabrics and garments.
Customisation and Special Services	Usually involves standard washing and care with minimal customisation	Offers specialised services, including dry cleaning, stain removal, dyeing, zari polishing, and fabric-specific treatments like those for silks or woolens.

7. Differentiate between the laundry procedures of hotel and hospital laundries. **CBSE 2021 C**

Ans. The difference between hospital laundry and hotel laundry is given below

Hospital Laundry	Hotel Laundry
In hospitals articles made of cotton are dyed in colours specific to the hospital and department.	Different fibre is used in hotels and restaurants. Generally, materials which look attractive and bright are used.
Stubborn stains may be neglected and starching and whitening are also not done. Even ironing and pressing may not be done to perfection.	Final finishing of laundered goods, i.e. starching, ironing and correct and perfect folding are required.
Sometimes repair and mending and condemnation of unusable material are not done in hospital laundry.	Sometimes small hotels do not have their own laundry service, so they depend upon the commercial laundries from outside.

Long Answer Type Questions

1. (i) "The principle of all washing machines is to keep the fabric in movement in the washing solution to carry away the dirt".

(a) Discuss the three processes involved in the washing equipment of a commercial laundry.

(b) Which of the above process is used in front loading machines?

(ii) "The field of Care and Maintenance of Fabrics is a technical field and you want to work in hi- tech laundry".

(a) Present any three primary requirements you must possess for this.

(b) What qualifications are required for this role?

Ans. (i) (a) The three processes involved in the washing equipment of a commercial laundry are

- **Agitation** This process uses an agitator with blades that either rotate in one direction or oscillate back and forth. This movement creates currents in the tub, forcing water through the fabric to remove dirt.

- **Pulsation** A vertical pulsator generates rapid vertical movements, creating turbulence in the wash water.
- **Tumbling** In this method, clothes are washed in a horizontally placed, perforated cylinder that revolves. As the cylinder turns, clothes are lifted and then dropped into the wash water, ensuring thorough cleaning.

(b) The above process is used in front-loading machines is tumbling.

(ii) (a) Three primary requirements you must possess for working in hi-tech laundry are

- **Knowledge of Materials** Understanding different fabric types and their specific care needs.
- **Knowledge of Processes** Familiarity with various laundry processes and techniques, including washing, drying and pressing.
- **Knowledge of Chemicals** Awareness of the chemicals and reagents used in laundry and their effects on fabrics, ensuring appropriate usage for effective cleaning without damage.

(b) A short-term programme in laundry management or a similar course are required for this role. This training provides specialised knowledge and skills in managing laundry operations, understanding fabric care and operating hi-tech laundry equipment.

2. Explain the operation performed by the Automatic Washer.

Or **Mention six work operations which are performed by an automatie washing machine.** **CBSE 2025**

Ans. The operation performed by an automatic washer involves several key steps that streamline the laundry process. Here's an overview

- **Filling of Water** The washer automatically fills with water to a preset level based on the load size and type of fabric selected.
- **Controlling Water Level** Sensors monitor the water level, ensuring it remains at the optimal height for effective washing.
- **Regulation of Temperature** Users can select the desired water temperature for washing, which is controlled automatically during the cycle.
- **Washing** The machine agitates or tumbles the clothes, depending on the type of washer. This movement helps to remove dirt and stains as detergent mixes with the water.
- **Rinsing** After the washing cycle, the washer drains the soapy water and fills with fresh water for rinsing. This step ensures that all detergent and dirt residues are removed from the fabric.
- **Water Extraction** The washer spins the clothes at high speeds to extract excess water. This reduces drying time by removing 60-70 per cent of moisture.
- **Final Drain** After the spin cycle, the remaining water is drained from the tub, completing the washing process.
- **End of Cycle** The machine signals when the cycle is complete, allowing users to remove their clean laundry.

3. You are working in a hi-tech laundry of a hotel. **CBSE SQP, 2020**

(i) What four factors will you keep in mind before choosing the process of washing a fabric?

(ii) You are using a dryer to dry the washed fabric. Explain the two types of circulation system in a dryer. **Competency Based Que**

Or **Explain the types of circulation systems in driers.** **Diksha App**

Ans. (i) Four factors need to be kept in mind before choosing the process of washing

(a) The fibre content of the fabric.

(b) The yarn type and the fabric construction technique.

(c) The finish of the fabric.

(d) The purpose of use of the fabric.

(ii) Two types of circulation systems in dryer are

(a) **Air of relatively low temperature is circulated at high velocity** the air present in the room enters a drier from under the front panel, passes over the heat source and then through clothes and leaves through an exhaust and therefore the temperature and humidity of the room stays normal.

(b) **Air at high temperature is circulated slowly** In this, after the air enters the drier and passes over the heat source, it is drawn by a small fan through perforations at the top of the drier, then downwards through the clothes and out through the exhaust. Since the movement of the air in this drier is slow, the relative humidity of the exhausted air is high.

4. Sudha wants to get her heavy curtains washed from dhobi. Explain the process adopted by the dhobi. **Competency Based Que**

Ans. Local 'Dhobis' collect materials from household for washing and ironing. Sudha will gives her heavy curtains to a local dhobi for washing

The dhobi will adopt the following process

- First the dhobi will wash the curtains at 'Dhobighat'–the specially marked place for washing.
- He will then dry the heavy curtains in the open place. He won't use any driers.
- After drying, he will smoothen the curtains with charcoal iron. Charcoal iron is like a metal box with a lid, in which live coal pieces are put to heat the iron.
- With this heavy charcoal iron, he will smoothen the curtains nicely and then fold the curtains and pack it for delivery.

5. How is the laundry in hospitals different from a hotel? CBSE SQP, 2020-21

Ans. Hospitals are different from a hotel in following ways

In Hospitals	In Hospitality Sector
The hospital laundry takes care of hygiene, cleanliness and disinfection.	Aesthetics and final finish of the articles are the most important.
Many hospitals have started using disposables where there is a threat of infection, which are then destroyed by burning.	As compared to hospitals the articles here may be of different fibre contents.
Most of the articles in hospitals are of cotton and dyed (in colours specific to the hospital and department) with dyes which have excellent wash-fastness.	Final finishing of laundered goods i.e., starching, ironing pressing and correct and perfect folding, are emphasised.
The daily laundry thus emphasises mainly on cleanliness of cotton materials.	They also have to care of guests' personal laundry when required.
Even the ironing and pressing may not be done to perfection.	The smaller hotels may have link ups with commercial laundries from outside.
The quantum of work, especially for bed linen, is much larger for hospitals as compared to hotels. The larger hospitals may have to take care of 1,800-2,000 beds or even more.	The quantum of work, especially for bed linen, is much lesser in hotels. The big hotels may have up to 400-500 rooms.

6. Commercial laundries are organised in different section which deal with specific jobs.

(i) Make a list of any four jobs done in various sections for an entrepreneur who wants to set up his own commercial laundry.

(ii) What do you understand by the system of code tags in a commercial laundry? CBSE 2024

Ans. (i) The four jobs done in various sections for an entrepreneur in setting up commercial laundary are

(a) Commercial laundries take care of bigger articles of household linen and some special articles.

(b) These are organised in different sections to deal with specific tasks-washing, water extracting, drying, pressing and ironing.

(c) There may be separate sections for dry cleaning, for special articles like blankets and carpets.

(d) Some laundries have arrangements for dyeing, zari polishing, special treatment for silk sarees etc.

(ii) In a commercial laundry, the system of code tags involves attaching unique identification tags to each garment or item to track its progress throughout the laundry process, ensuring efficient sorting, washing, and return to the correct customer.

7. What are the primary requirements to develop a career in the field of care and maintenance of fabrics?

Ans. The primary requirements to develop a career in the field of care and maintenance of fabrics are

- **Knowledge of the Material** The individual must have knowledge about the fibre content, yarn and fabric production technique and the colours and finishes of the material.
- He or she must have knowledge of the whole process involved.
- He should have knowledge of the chemicals and other reagents used in the process and their effect on the particular types of fabric.
- He should have working knowledge of the machinery requirements and its functioning.

8. My friend Ritesh has completed a professional course in Textile Science. Mention the scope in this field.

Ans. The scope of this field are Competency Based Que

- Persons with specialisation in textile, clothing, fabric and apparel can venture into entrepreneurial activities.
- It provides move opportunities in metropolitan areas.
- He can work for nursing homes, small hospital which need such services on a regular basis.
- He can also join in hi-tech laundries of railways, airways, shipping lines, hotels and hospitals which have in-house programme for care and maintenance of fabrics.

SELF ASSESSMENT TEST

Objective Type Questions

1. What happens after the drain period in bottom-drain washing machines?
   (a) The tub begins to spin to remove remaining water from clothes
   (b) The machine starts a drying cycle
   (c) Detergent is added for another wash
   (d) The machine shuts down automatically
2. Which of the following is not a type of equipment required for care and maintenance of the fabrics?
   (a) Washing equipment (b) Ironing equipment (c) Drying equipment (d) Folding equipment
3. What does a hydro-extractor do?
   (a) Cleans the clothes to upto 60-70 per cent (b) gets rid of 60-70 per cent moisture
   (c) Helps in soaking a garment before cleaning it (d) Both (b) and (c)
4. In which type of iron, will you put coal pieces to heat?
   (a) Charcoal iron (b) Electric iron (c) Steam iron (d) Dry iron
5. You work in the laundry industry of a hotel. Your supervisor asks you to get the heavier articles, including curtains and bed covers, pressed. Which of the following methods would you select as the best suitable method for the given task?
   (a) Steam iron (b) Electric iron (c) Charcoal iron (d) Dry iron

Very Short Answer Type Questions

6. How do you regulate the temperature of water in a washing machine?
7. What are the two types of circulation system in driers?
8. Which types of institutions usually possess their own in-house laundries?

Short Answer Type Questions

9. Give a brief step-by-step process of laundry functionings in hospitals.
10. For what purposes the commercial laundries have separate sections? Give a brief idea about these different sections.
11. Discuss the precautions to keep in mind to use chemical to remove stains from clothes. **Diksha App**

Long Answer Type Questions

12. What are the four features of commercial laundry?
13. Which factors are neglected in hospital laundry?
14. Rahul has done courses in Textile Science. What are his scope for being a professional? **Competency Based Que**

11 CHAPTER

Hospitality Management

The chapter introduces the concept of hospitality management, emphasising its significance in providing comfortable, hygienic, and courteous services to guests. It explores the functioning of key departments like front office, housekeeping, and food and beverages while highlighting career opportunities and essential competencies required for success in this growing industry.

YOUR STUDY GOALS

YOUR PRACTICE GOAL

- Objective Type Questions (22 Qs ; MCQs, A-R, Matching, Case Based)
- Subjective Questions (7 VSAs, 9 SAs, 6 LAs)

11.1 Introduction

- Whenever someone visits a restaurant or hotel, they expect to be greeted and served well. If they are not treated well, it is unlikely they will revisit that place ever. India has the concept of **Atithi Devo Bhava**, meaning guests are equal to **God** and should be treated as such. This implies it is the prime responsibility of hosts to receive guests warmly and provide the best care services.
- In earlier times, people stayed with relatives, friends or at **dharamshalas** without any payment. Hosts took care of guests without expecting anything in return. With advancements in trade and commerce, paid hospitality services have become necessary. This shift reflects the evolution of hospitality in modern times.

Significance of Hospitality Management[1]

- The world has become a small place to live in due to globalisation.
- People can move within the country or internationally for various purposes.
- Reasons for travel include business, marketing, official purposes and study.

1 **Hospitality Management** Hospitality management is a broad field that involves overseeing the day-to-day administrative, operational and commercial activities of businesses in the hospitality industry.

- Others may travel for pilgrimages, healthcare (medical tourism), leisure or shopping.
- Some people travel to experience different cultures and see heritage monuments.
- Wildlife and natural beauty are also attractions for many travelers.
- Attractive advertisements for festivals encourage travel to various places.
- Events like the Pushkar and Kumbh melas, Dusshera in Mysore, and Ganapati in Mumbai attract visitors.
- Tourists prefer to stay and eat in safe and hygienic places during fairs and festivals.
- This creates a need for the hospitality industry to provide comforts similar to home.
- The main aim of the hospitality industry is to provide **"A Home Away From Home"**.
- Hospitality is one of the fastest-growing industries, emphasising the need for tourist comfort.

11.2 Basic Concepts

- **Hospitality** is the relationship between a guest and a host. The host receives the guest with goodwill, including friendly reception and entertainment. The basic concept of hospitality involves providing a place to stay, food and entertainment. Various establishments offer hospitality services, such as hotels, motels, lodges, resorts and furnished apartments.
  - A **hotel** provides accommodation, meals and services for travelers and tourists.
  - A **motel** offers hotel-like services with parking and rooms are accessible from an outdoor parking area.
  - A **lodge** offers rented accommodation primarily for sleeping, without food or other services.
  - A **resort** is known for leisure attractions, offering amenities, sports facilities and activities for a complete vacation experience.
  - **Furnished apartments** provide essential amenities needed by guests.
  - **Furnished camps** offer hospitality to people engaging in hiking and adventure sports.
  - Hospitality services are also integral to conventions, conferences, weddings and parties.
  - Other areas include theme parks, cruise lines, amusement parks, guest houses, hospitals and hostels.
  - Organisations providing hospitality typically have management departments.
  - Fundamental principles of hospitality management apply across all sectors, ensuring smooth and efficient functioning.

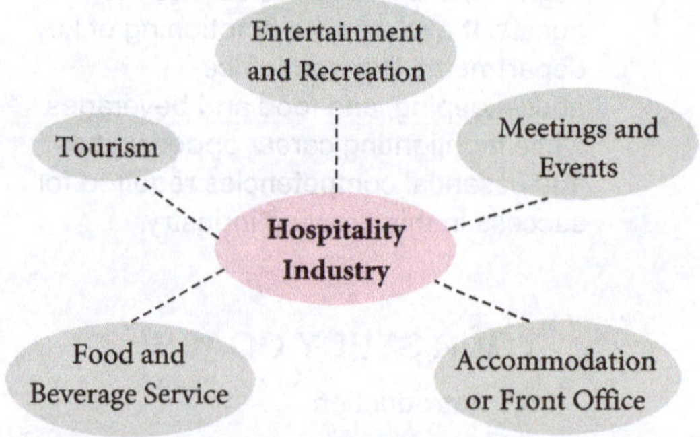

▲ *Departments/Sectors in Hospitality Industry*

Concept of Guest Cycle

To have a better understanding of the different departments, it is necessary to understand the concept of 'guest cycle'. Guest cycle refers to the distinct stages of interaction between the hotel and guests. On the basis of the stage of interaction and activities involved, the guest cycle is broadly classified into **four main stages** pre-arrival, arrival, stay and departure.

(i) **Pre-arrival Stage** The activities done in the pre-arrival stage include
  - Quoting rates for a guest.
  - Reserving a room as a part of the central reservation system or reservation department.

(ii) **Arrival Stage** In this stage, the guest actually arrives and registers or check-in.

(iii) **Occupancy** At this stage, various services are provided as per the guest's requirements, ensuring security of the guest and co-ordination of various guest services. To obtain and retain 'customer loyalty' is the priority of any service provider in the hospitality industry.

Thus, guest satisfaction is the main focus of service provider hotels, resorts etc., to ensure and encourage the guest to patronise and use the services of the establishment again.

(iv) **Departure** This is the final stage of the guest cycle where the guest is ready to leave/move out or 'check-out' of the accommodation.

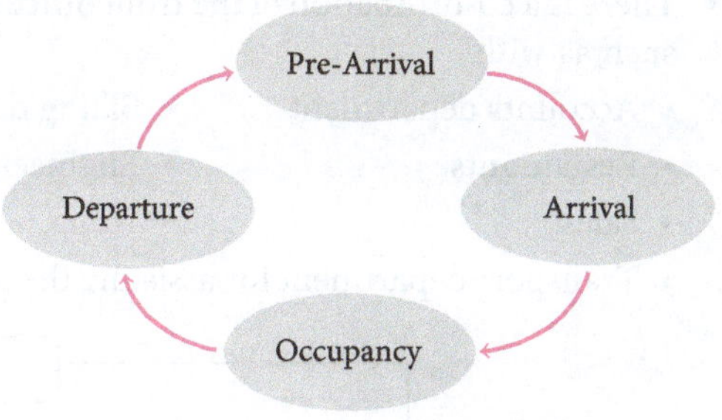

▲ *Stages of the Guest Cycle*

After the departure of a guest, the hotel or resort keeps a 'guest history' with it. Guest history is an up-to-date record of the room occupancy of the guest along with other information about the guest. It also includes feedback from the guest about his/her opinion about the services.

Quick Test 1

1. What is the primary responsibility of the host?
2. What is one purpose for people traveling from one place to another?
3. What is the main purpose of using advertisements by the hospitality industry?
4. The main aim of the hospitality industry is to provide what?
5. What type of establishment provides accommodation, meals and other services for travelers and tourists?

11.3 Departments Involved in Hospitality Management of An Organisation

Front Office

- **Front office**[2] is the main functionary that largely deals with the guest cycle. When a guest enters into a hotel, she/he first arrives at the front office and comes in contact with the staff of the hospitality industry.
- This interaction between the guest and the staff is very critical to develop a good relationship between the guest and the organisation and also in building a good image. Hence, the front office is the focal point of any hotel.
- The services offered by the staff
  - Welcoming guests
  - Meeting and greeting them
  - Organising reservation status of room availability
  - Registering guests and allocation of rooms
  - Maintaining records of check-in and check-out details
  - Porter services
  - Issuing room keys to guests
  - Passing messages to customers
  - Co-ordinating with other guest services
  - Providing in-house and external information to the guests
  - Preparing and settling their bills.
- No one likes to be greeted/served by a person who is expressionless and indifferent. Therefore, good manners are very important in the hospitality industry. The manner in which the services are offered plays a central role in the image building of the institution and ultimately determines the revenue generated.

2 **Front Office** Front office is the division of the company that has a direct contact with the clients.

- There is a co-ordination of the front office staff with various departments for providing services to guests such as with
  - Accounts department
  - Billing department
  - Room service department
  - Restaurants
  - Engineering service department
  - Stores
  - Sales
  - **Housekeeping**[3] departments
  - Transport department for assisting the guest with transport

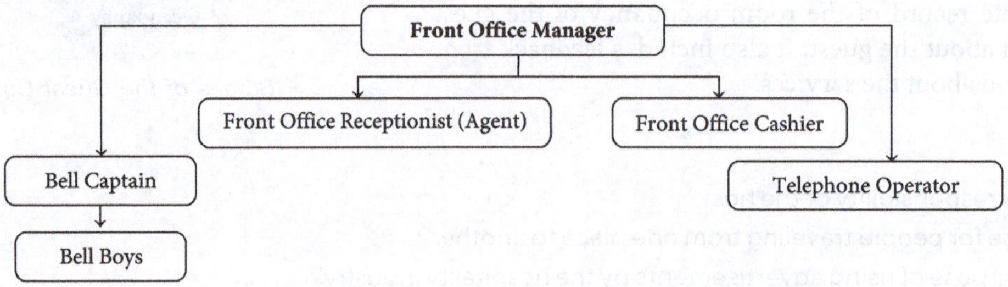

▲ *Organisation of the Front Office Department*

The services offered by different staff members under front office desk are given in table below.

Designations and functions/duties of various personnel in the front office.

Designation	Functions/Duties
Front Office Manager	Manages the front office, lobby and transport activities. Schedules staff shifts and duties, checks daily arrivals and co-ordinates with housekeeping and other departments.
Front Office Supervisor	Responsible for a shift. Greets all arrivals and ensures a quick and accurate rooming process. Checks room occupancy.
Front Office Cashier	Maintains guest bills and receives payments during check-out.
Telephone Operator/Information Assistant	Is responsible for provides information and communicates with in-house guests and visitors.
Assistant Manager Front Office	Organises and supervises the front office when the manager is absent, ensuring smooth operations.
Lobby Manager	Supervises and controls all uniformed services in the lobby area.
Receptionist (Front Office Agent)	Reserves, registers and assigns rooms to guests, providing information as needed during their stay.
Bell Captain	Supervises bellboys and manages all baggage movements during check-in and check-out.
Bell boy	Responsible for moving guests' baggage within and outside the room.
Doorman	Welcomes guests upon arrival and escorts them to the registration desk.

Housekeeping Department

- Providing a healthy environment is a major responsibility of the housekeeping department.
- This department maintains cleanliness and high standards of hygiene in the establishment.
- The aesthetics of the entire hotel or institution are also ensured by housekeeping.
- The quality of services provided influences guests' decisions to stay and return.
- Room decor, facilities, safety, cleanliness and hygiene are crucial in hotels.
- Many organisations hire housekeeping services on a contractual basis today.
- This creates opportunities for individuals to start their own enterprises.

3 **Housekeeping** The work or activity of cleaning and preparing rooms for customers.

- Housekeeping consultancy involves greater activities and challenges in a commercial setting.
- Maintaining numerous rooms and public areas is a complex and challenging task.
- The housekeeping department must provide the best services to clients.
- Planning and organising the department with various sections and trained staff is essential.

Functions of Housekeeping Department

The prime function of the housekeeping department is to maintain cleanliness and space hygiene. Thus, it is responsible for the following

- Cleaning of public areas and guestrooms.
- Supply, upkeep of laundry and exchange of various linen and uniforms.
- Internal flower arrangement and maintenance of external landscape or garden.
- Co-ordination and communication with other departments such as front office, restaurants, engineering, accounts, etc., through control desk.
- Pest control is also the responsibility of this department.

The housekeeping department is divided into different sections in order to perform these functions efficiently

- **Housekeeping control desk** passes on the information to housekeeping staff who are working in various parts of the hotel.
- **Housekeeping management** plans, organises, and controls all the activities of the housekeeping department.
- **Guestroom brigade** upkeeps and cleans the guestrooms.
- **Public area brigade** maintains cleanliness of foyer[4], lobby[5], front office and other common areas.
- **Linen and uniform room** Co-ordinates with laundry; responsible for providing clean linen to the entire establishment and uniform to all the staff.
- **Horticulture and flower arrangement team** maintains the landscape of the hotel and arranges flowers in rooms and at various places.
- **Lost and found section** deposits misplaced luggage of guests.

Staffing Pattern of Housekeeping Department

- Selecting appropriate manpower is crucial for smooth functioning of the housekeeping department.
- The organisational structure and hierarchy may vary from one hotel to another.
- It depends on the organisation to appoint different individuals for various posts.
- Some staff may also be assigned to 'multi- tasking' roles.
- The organisational chart of a housekeeping department illustrates the staff hierarchy in a hotel.
- This chart helps clarify roles and responsibilities within the department.

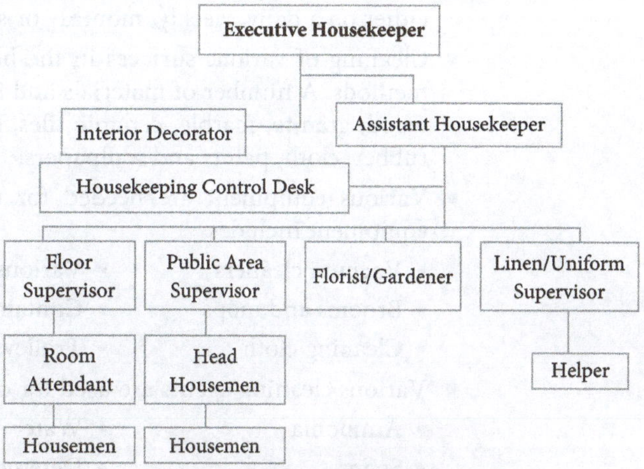

▲ *General Organisational Chart of a Housekeeping Department*

---

4 Foyer A large open area just inside the entrance of a public building such as a hotel, where people can wait and meet each other.

5 Lobby A corridor or hall connected with a larger room or series of rooms and used as a passageway or waiting room.

Responsibilities of the Housekeeping Department Personnel

- **Executive Housekeeper** He/She has the responsibility for managing the functioning of the department through judicious use of manpower, materials, money, time and other available resources. She/He checks schedules, cleanliness and all functioning of the housekeeping department.
- **Assistant Housekeeper** In a large hotel, there may be one assistant housekeeper for each shift of duty, i.e., day and night shifts. This person is responsible for preparing duty schedules and checking cleanliness and functioning of the workers.
- **Desk Control Supervisor** He/She is responsible for co-ordinating with the front office for information on the departure of guests, getting vacated rooms cleaned and handing over cleaned rooms. This desk should be manned 24 hours because guests and staff can contact this desk to receive or transmit information any time.
- **Floor Supervisor** Each floor has one supervisor who is responsible for cleanliness and maintenance of guest rooms, corridors, staircases and floor pantries.
- **Room Attendant** He/She does the actual cleaning of guest rooms and bathrooms. Housemen perform the heavy cleaning activities such as vacuuming, mopping, sweeping and shifting of furniture.
- **Public Area Supervisor** He/She is responsible for maintaining cleanliness of the public areas (main entrance, corridors, offices, banquet halls, restaurants, etc.). They get these works done through housemen.
- **Florist/Gardener** In case of a small hotel, there may be one gardener/florist. She/He maintains the garden and does flower arrangements in various areas of the hotel.
- **Linen Room/Uniform Room Supervisor** He/She is responsible for the supply, acquisition, storage, issue and cleanliness of the linen and uniforms required in various areas of the hotel.

Cleaning

It involves the following aspects

- Cleaning involves appropriate planning and having a good approach in selecting staff with practical housekeeping operational skills, correct cleaning procedures and the skill to do the task well under a qualified supervisor to ensure quality services.
- A good selection of specialised equipment, tools and cleaning solutions, along with knowledge of the latest technological applications, is an essential part of training. The cleaning activities are performed either on a daily, weekly, monthly or seasonal basis.
- Cleaning of various surfaces in the hotel is done with suitable tools, cleaning solutions and specific methods. A number of materials and finishes used for walls, floors, countertops and furniture include wood, granite, marble, ceramic tiles, stones, linoleum, plastic, vinyl, fibreglass, metals, leather, cane, rubber, cloth, paints and wallpapers.
- Various equipment are needed for maintaining good cleanliness in hotels. The commonly used equipment includes
  - Vacuum cleaners
  - Various types of brushes
  - Brooms and mops
  - Containers
  - Cleaning cloth
  - Trolleys to carry multiple equipment
- Various cleaning agents are used for cleaning different surfaces and materials, such as
  - Ammonia
  - Water
  - Vinegar
  - Soaps
  - Detergents
  - Washing soda
  - Abrasives
  - Polishes
  - Acids and other such liquids.

One should be very cautious while using these cleaning agents, as some strong agents may damage the surface while cleaning the material; hence, the choice of appropriate cleaning agents is important.

The Linen and Uniform Room

- The linen and uniform room is an integral part of the housekeeping department.
- If facilities are available, laundry may be done in the department; otherwise, it can be given to an outside agency.
- The linen room stores and maintains a large stock of bed linen, bath linen, linen for restaurants and uniforms for all staff members.

Flower Arrangement

- Flowers help enhance the aesthetic appeal of various interior spaces in a hotel.
- The hotel may contract florists to supply flower arrangements regularly.
- Alternatively, flower arrangements in various areas may be made by the housekeeping department.

Training for Environmental Conservation

- Many hotels train staff in environmental conservation and eco-friendly practices.
- Examples include using 100 per cent organic cotton bed sheets and chemical-free laundry cycles.
- Non-toxic, water-based, hypoallergenic and biodegradable agents are also promoted.
- Hotels often place cards in rooms urging the reuse of towels and promoting the saving of natural resources.
- Use of energy-efficient light bulbs in rooms can help save electricity.

Quick Test 2

1. Where does a guest first arrive when entering a hotel?
2. What is important in the hospitality industry?
3. What is a function of the lobby manager?
4. Which section of the housekeeping department provides information to the staff?

11.4 Food and Beverages Department

This is concerned with the sale of **food and beverages department**[6]. This department has many relevant service departments such as kitchen(s), banquets, restaurants, room service, stewarding and bars/coffee shops, etc.

Kitchen

- Kitchen is the place where food is prepared for guests. Large hotels have different sections in the kitchen for various aspects related to food preparations, such as
  - Butchery (to deal with raw meat)
  - Bakery and confectionery
  - Vegetable preparations
  - Soups section
  - Pantry
  - Hot range
- While in smaller hotels the kitchen would combine the sections. In large hotels there could be various staff or kitchen crew in the kitchen such as
- The executive chef (chef-de-cuisine) is the head of the kitchen who is responsible for planning, organising and controlling the kitchen operations.
  - Deputy chef comes after executive chef.
  - There are supervisors for some sections of the kitchen called 'chef-de-parties'.

6 **Food and Beverages Department** is responsible for maintaining the high quality of food and service, food costing, managing restaurant, bar, etc.

- Then, there are a number of cooks who make the common food dishes.
- The restaurant personnel co-ordinate closely with the kitchen for the supply of food orders to guests.

Kitchen Stewarding

- Kitchen stewarding is responsible for the storage, maintenance, cleanliness and issue of cutlery, crockery and glassware to the restaurant and kitchen.

  It is the responsibility of this department to maintain cleanliness in the kitchen and to wash the pots and pans used.
- This department may have an executive kitchen steward, kitchen steward, dishwasher, pot washer and utility workers to clean the kitchen.

  Those working in this department must have high standards of grooming, hygiene and sanitation, and good manners and basic etiquette.

Restaurant

- Each hotel is specialised in serving different varieties of food and beverages to the customers.

  Restaurant is a commercial facility that provides food and beverages to the customers.
- It has different utilities and arrangements for customers like dining tables, chairs and other required furniture with crockery, cutlery, linen and décor.

  The quality varies as suited to the objectives, concept and standards of the establishment.
- The restaurant has various staff members such as a restaurant manager who is the head of the restaurant responsible for overall functioning.

  The senior restaurant supervisor and head waiter lead a team of waiters/stewards who serve the food and the assistant waiter who clears the table.
- They keep a close watch that the standard of cleanliness, hygiene and service are maintained.

  They must always be smiling, courteous to the guests and possess good manners and etiquette.
- They should have thorough knowledge of the ways of serving the food.

Support Service Departments

- There are other departments in a hotel which provide support and are involved in the overall management and efficient functioning of the hotel. These departments are referred to as 'Back Office' departments such as
  - Finance and Accounts Department
  - Engineering Department
  - Human Resources Department
  - Sales and Marketing Departments
- Thus, a hotel consists of various departments which have complex relationships amongst them. Efficient management of man, material and other resources are required for the smooth functioning of the organisation.

Management Functions

Planning, organising, co-ordinating, staffing and directing, controlling and evaluating the use of resources in light of the goals of the institution are the important management functions.

11.5 Scope

- Every hotel has an organisational structure which has a hierarchy of top management, middle management, junior management, supervisors and operations staff. There are job opportunities at each of these levels in the hospitality industry.

  There are a number of reasons due to which hotels usually prefer youths for their staff
  - Youth have high energy to work for long hours, as compared to middle aged people.
  - They can also do overtime at the time of occasions and heavy work load.
  - They are better informed and have better competencies through advancement in education.
  - They are open to new ideas and latest technologies.
  - They have ambition for success and earn high monetary returns.
- Hospitality industry is fast growing, thus, there are ample opportunities for individuals to opt this field as career. It is important to note that the fundamentals of hospitality management are applicable to hostels and large hospitals also.

Essential Competencies Required to Work in Hospitality Industry

- There are some essential competencies which are required to work in hospitality industry such as
  - The staff needs to be well groomed, have good hygiene, orderliness, good manners and etiquettes besides a personality of smiling face.
  - An individual who wants to get recruited in the front office staff must possess cheerful attitude, self-discipline, courtesy, physical fitness and good communication skills along with self-confidence and multiple language skills.
  - The staff should have a clean and neatly ironed uniform, minimum accessories and well-groomed hair.
  - Nails should be clean and properly manicured.
  - The front office staff is expected to be seen at their best at all times. It is because this projects a good image not only of themselves but also of the establishments (hotels, restaurants and resorts, etc.).

In India, many institutes offer various courses in catering and hospitality management, starting from certificate to degree courses.

Career Opportunities

One can have various career opportunities in hospitality management. These are

- Positions in housekeeping departments at various hierarchical levels.
- Entrepreneurial opportunities in housekeeping.
- Positions in front office and reception/control desk in hotels.
- Entrepreneurial opportunities for supply of flower arrangements, etc.
- Specialised in theme-based events within the organisation.

Quick Test 3

1. Which department is concerned with the sale of food and beverages?
2. Bakery and confectionery are a section of what?
3. Who is the head of a restaurant?
4. Name one support service department.

Mind Map

HOSPITALITY MANAGEMENT

1 Introduction to Hospitality Management

- **Guest Treatment** Guests should be treated with respect, as per India's concept of Atithi Devo Bhava 'Guests are God'.
- **Historical Evolution** In the past, guests were hosted without payment; with time, paid hospitality services became essential.

Significance of Hospitality Management

- **Globalisation** The world is more connected, leading to increased travel for business, study, tourism and leisure.
- **Travel Purposes** Includes business, health care (medical tourism), leisure, cultural experiences, shopping and festivals.
- **Tourist Attractions** Festivals (e.g., Pushkar, Kumbh Mela), heritage monuments, wildlife, and natural beauty attract travelers.
- **Hospitality Industry's Role** Provides comfortable, hygienic accommodations, aiming to offer 'A Home Away From Home.'
- **Growth** Hospitality is one of the fastest-growing industries, focusing on tourist comfort.

2 Basic Concepts of Hospitality

- **Hospitality** The relationship between guest and host, providing accommodation, food and entertainment.
- **Types of Establishments** Hotels, motels, lodges, resorts, furnished apartments, camps, and more, each offering varying services.
- **Special Event Services** Includes hospitality for conventions, weddings, theme parks and more.
- **Hospitality Management** Ensures smooth operations in all sectors.

Guest Cycle

- **Pre-arrival** Quoting rates, room reservations.
- **Arrival** Guest checks in.
- **Occupancy** Providing services and ensuring guest satisfaction.
- **Departure** Guest checks out, and feedback is recorded in guest history.

3 Hospitality Management Departments

Front Office

- Handles guest check-ins, reservations and billing.
- Co-ordinates with other departments for guest services.

Housekeeping

- Manages cleanliness, hygiene, and aesthetics of the hotel.
- Includes tasks like room cleaning, linen management and flower arrangements.

Cleaning and Maintenance

- Uses specialised tools and agents for daily cleaning tasks, ensuring surfaces are properly maintained.

Linen and Uniform Room

- Stores and maintains bed linens, towels, and staff uniforms, handling laundry in-house or through outsourcing.

Flower Arrangement

- Manages the aesthetic appeal of the hotel with fresh flowers in public areas.

Environmental Conservation

- Promotes eco-friendly practices, like organic linens, chemical-free laundry and energy-efficient lighting.

4 Food and Beverages Department

- Responsible for the sale of food and drinks. Includes various service areas, like kitchens, restaurants, room service and bars.
- Key roles include kitchen steward, dishwasher, and utility workers, ensuring hygiene and cleanliness in the kitchen.

Restaurant

- A commercial facility serving food and beverages, with various staff like the restaurant manager, waiters and stewards.
- Staff must maintain high hygiene standards, be courteous, and possess proper etiquette.

Support Service Departments

Back office departments ensures the smooth running of the hotel includes

- Finance and Accounts
- Engineering
- Human Resources
- Sales and Marketing

Kitchen

- Food preparation area with different sections like butchery, bakery and soups.
- Large hotels have specialised roles such as executive chefs and kitchen supervisors.

Kitchen Stewarding

- Responsible for maintaining cleanliness, managing cutlery and washing kitchen utensils.

5 Scope of Hospitality Industry

- The hospitality industry has a hierarchical structure with opportunities at all levels, top management, middle management, junior management, supervisors and operations staff.
- With the industry's rapid growth, there are ample career opportunities, also extending to hostels and hospitals.

Essential Competencies

- Staff must be well-groomed, hygienic, orderly, and possess good manners and etiquette.
- Front office staff should have a cheerful attitude, self-discipline, physical fitness, communication skills and multi-language proficiency.
- Uniforms should be clean, and staff should maintain good personal grooming.

Career Opportunities

- Positions in housekeeping, front office and reception.
- Entrepreneurial opportunities like supplying flower arrangements and organising theme-based events.

Why Hotels Prefer Youth

- Youth are energetic, can work long hours, and are open to new ideas and technologies.
- They are ambitious, eager for success, and willing to earn high returns.

NCERT Folder

1. What is the importance of 'Front Office' in a hotel?

Ans. Front office is the first department of hotel which comes in guest contact, at the time of guest arrival and the last department when they depart from the hotel. It is important because of the following reasons

- The front office plays a major role in the guest cycle.
- It is the interaction between the front office staff and the guest that helps in building the image of the establishment as well as earning customer loyalty.
- The front office is responsible for co-ordinating with various departments for providing services to guests such as the transport, accounts, billing, room service, restaurants, engineering, stores, sales and housekeeping departments.

2. Write the responsibilities of any three members of the front office staff.

Ans. The responsibilities of any three members of the front office staff are as follows

Designations	Functions/Duties
Front Office Manager	Responsible for managing the front office, lobby, transport activities. Schedules shifts/staff rotations and duties of the staff in shifts, since all hotels work for 24 hours. Checks the arrivals of the day, the 'VIP', co-ordinates with housekeeping and other departments.
Front Office Supervisor	Is responsible for a shift. Meets and greets all arrivals, ensures accurate and speedy rooming procedure. She/He checks occupancy.
Telephone Operator/ Information Assistant	Is responsible for providing information and communicates with in-house guests check-out.

3. Write the responsibilities of any three members of the housekeeping department of a hotel.

Ans. The responsibilities of any three members of the housekeeping department of a hotel are as follows

(i) **Executive Housekeeper** This person has the responsibility for managing the functioning of the department through judicious use of manpower, materials, money, time and other available resources. She/He checks schedules, cleanliness and all functioning of the housekeeping department.

(ii) **Assistant Housekeeper** In a large hotel there may be one assistant housekeeper for each shift of duty i.e. day and night shifts. This person has the responsibility of preparing duty schedule and checking cleanliness and functioning of the workers.

(iii) **Desk Control Supervisor** She/He has the responsibility to co-ordinate with front office for information on departure of guests, gets vacated room cleaned and hands over clean rooms. Desk control supervisor has a duty of 24 hours, because guests and staff contact this desk to receive or transmit information any time.

4. Explain the meaning and functioning of restaurant and kitchen.

Ans. Kitchen is the place where food is prepared for guests.

Functions of Kitchen

- In large hotels, kitchen has many sections for various functions related to food preparations. For example, butchery (to deal with raw meat), bakery and confectionery, vegetable preparations, soups section, pantry, hot range and so on.
- In smaller hotels, the kitchen would combine the sections and all work is done in the same kitchen.
- There is various staff or kitchen crew in the large kitchens. The executive chef (chef-de-cuisine) is the head of the kitchen who is responsible for planning, organising and controlling the kitchen operations. Deputy chef comes after executive chef. There are supervisors for some sections of the kitchen called 'chef-de-parties'. After these personnel, there are a number of cooks who make the common food dishes.

Restaurant is a commercial facility that provides food and beverages to the customers.

Functions of Restaurant

- The restaurant has various staff members. A restaurant manager is the head of the restaurant who is responsible for overall functioning of the restaurant.
- The senior restaurant supervisor and head waiter lead a team of waiters/stewards who actually serve the food.
- The assistant waiter clears the table. They all keep a close watch that the standard of cleanliness, hygiene and service are maintained.

5. What are the different types of food services in a hotel?

Or **Your brother has recently joined the food and beverage department of a hotel. Briefly discuss any two service departments involved in the food and beverage department.** **Competency Based Que; CBSE Term II, 2022**

Ans. In a hotel, food and beverages department is concerned with the sale of food and beverages. This department has many relevant food service departments such as kitchen(s), banquets, restaurants, room service, stewarding and bars/coffee shops, etc.

Some of these are given below

- **Kitchen** It is the place where food is prepared for guests. There are different sections in the large kitchen for various functions related to food preparations. For example, butchery (to deal with raw meat), bakery and confectionery, vegetable preparations, soups section, pantry, hot range and so on. While in smaller hotels the kitchen would combine the sections.
  There is a staff or kitchen crew in the kitchen which consists of the executive chef (chef-de-cuisine), deputy chef, supervisors and a number of cooks.
- **Kitchen Stewarding** It is responsible for the storage, maintenance, cleanliness and issue of cutlery, crockery and glassware to the restaurant and kitchen. It is the responsibility of this department to maintain cleanliness in the kitchen and to wash the pots and pans used.
- **Restaurant** It is a commercial facility that provides food and beverages to the customers. It has different utilities and arrangements for customers like dining tables, chairs and other required furniture with crockery, cutlery, linen and decor, varying in quality as suited to the objectives, concept and standards of the establishment.

6. What are the management functions in relation to hotels?

Ans. Planning, organising, co-ordinating, staffing and directing, controlling and evaluating the use of resources in light of the goals of the institution are the important management functions.

7. State whether the following statements are True or False.

(a) Smile is the most enduring competency required of front office personnel.

(b) 'A suite' has two rooms, one serves as a living-cum-dining area and the other room has a bed.

(c) Housekeeping department provides food to the customers.

(d) Kitchen stewarding is concerned with the preparation of food.

(e) Controlling is the function of ensuring that the plans and objectives keep to the schedules and allocated budget.

Ans. (a) True (b) True (c) False (d) False (e) True

Exam Pattern Questions

Objective Type Questions

Multiple Choice Questions

1. 'Athithi Devo Bhava' is term used for which of the following?

(a) Tourists (b) Migrants
(c) Guests (d) All of these

2. In ancient times, people generally used to stay with which of the following?

(a) With relatives (b) With friends
(c) In 'dharmashalas' (d) All of these

3. The person who cleans the kitchen is ....

(a) utility worker (b) dish washer
(c) pot washer (d) kitchen steward

4. The term 'A Home Away From Home' is associated with ....

(a) migrants (b) pilgrims
(c) hospitality industry (d) Both (b) and (c)

5. What is the best definition of hospitality?

I. Service

II. Meeting the anticipation needs of our guests with kindness and goodwill

III. Businesses that provide services to people who are travelling

Select the correct option.

(a) Only I (b) II and III (c) Only II (d) III and IV

6. Motels are located on ....
(a) highways (b) roadways
(c) seaside (d) None of these

7. .... provide hospitality to people who go for hiking, undertake adventure sports etc. **CBSE 2023**
(a) Furnished apartments (b) Furnished camps
(c) Resort (d) Motel

8. Which of the following option does not fall under hospitality service?
(a) Hotel (b) Lodge
(c) Resort (d) Janta flats

9. The guest enters into the large hotel from its ....
(a) front office (b) reception
(c) lobby (d) restaurant

10. The person responsible for the landscapes and garden of the hotel is ....
(a) florist
(b) horticulturist
(c) housekeeping
(d) public area supervisor

11. Who does the actual cleaning of guest rooms and bathrooms in a hotel? **CBSE 2024**
(a) Bellboy (b) Doorman
(c) Room attendant (d) Floor supervisor

12. The linen and uniform room is an integral part of the housekeeping department. Who is responsible for maintaining the supply, acquisition, storage, issue and cleanliness of the linen and uniforms required in various parts of the hotel?
(a) Linen Room Supervisor
(b) Lobby Manager
(c) Bell Captain
(d) Executive Housekeeper

13. Which of the following thing should front office staff do to make the guest feel comfortable?
(a) Ask personal question (b) Laugh at the guest
(c) Talk with a smile (d) Stare the guest

14. A hotel has other departments referred to as 'back office' departments. Choose the department which comes under 'Back Office Department'.
(a) Food and Beverages Department
(b) Entertainment and Recreation
(c) Housekeeping Department
(d) Finance and Accounts

15. Mr. Mahajan's room geyser is not working. At which stage of the guest cycle will the hotel staff attend to his complaint? **CBSE 2021 C**
(a) Arrival (b) Departure
(c) Pre-arrival (d) Occupancy

16. Which of the following are sectors of hospitality industry?
I. Tourism II. Food and Beverage service
III. Clothing IV. Sports
Choose the correct option
(a) I and II (b) II and IV
(c) III and IV (d) II and III

17. Match the following **CBSE SQP 2024**

List I	List II
A. Hotel	1. Only loading
B. Motel	2. loading, meals and other services
C. Resort	3. Loding and parking near the room
D. Lodge	4. Loding with range of amenities

Codes

	A	B	C	D		A	B	C	D
(a)	1	2	3	4	(b)	2	3	4	1
(c)	1	3	4	2	(d)	4	3	2	1

18. Match the following

List I	List II
A. Guest Cycle	1. Finance and Account Department
B. Camp	2. Deputy Chief
C. Back Office	3. Arrival
D. Kitchen	4. Rafting

Codes

	A	B	C	D		A	B	C	D
(a)	3	4	1	2	(b)	1	2	3	4
(c)	1	3	4	2	(d)	4	3	2	1

Assertion-Reason Questions

Directions (Q. Nos. 19-20) In the questions given below, there are two statements marked as Assertion (A) and Reason (R). Read the statements and choose the correct option.

Codes
(a) Both A and R are true and R is the correct explanation of A.
(b) Both A and R are true, but R is not the correct explanation of A.
(c) A is true, but R is false.
(d) A is false, but R is true.

19. **Assertion** (A) The organisational structure of the hotel has a hierarchy of top management, middle management, junior management, supervisors and operations staff.
Reason (R) Hierarchy of management is necessary in hospitality industry to maintain the smooth functioning of an establishment.

20. **Assertion** (A) Housekeeping department is primarily responsible for providing a healthy environment to the customers.

Reason (R) The guest's decision to stay and repeatedly visit the hotel in future largely depends upon the quality of the services provided.

Case Based Questions

21. **Read the following passage and answer the questions that follow.**

Youth form the major part of workforce. Hotels prefer youth because they have high energy to work for long hours, as compared to middle aged people. They are better informed and have better competencies through advancement in education. They are open to new ideas and latest technologies. They have ambition for success and earn high monetary returns. Since hospitality industry is fast growing, there are ample opportunities for you to be absorbed in this field. The fundamentals of hospitality management are applicable to hostels and large hospitals also.

The essential competencies required to work in this industry are

The staff needs to be well groomed, have good hygiene, orderliness, good manners and etiquettes besides a smiling face. The cheerful attitude, self discipline, courtesy, physical fitness and good communication skills along with self-confidence and multiple language skills add to the possibility of ideal front office staff. Some of the other aspects to be kept in mind by the staff are a clean and neatly pressed uniform, minimum accessories and well groomed hair. Nails should be clean and properly manicured.

(i) Match the following competencies/qualities in the List I with their descriptions in the list II.

List I	List II
A. Well-groomed appearance	1. Maintaining clean nails and manicured hands
B. Good communication skills	2. Clean, pressed uniform and minimum accessories
C. Cheerful attitude	3. Ability to converse effectively and knowledge of multiple languages
D. Hygiene	4. Smiling demeanor and positive energy

Codes

	A	B	C	D		A	B	C	D
(a)	1	3	4	2	(b)	2	3	1	4
(c)	2	3	4	1	(d)	1	2	3	4

(ii) **Assertion** (A) Youth are generally preferred in the hospitality industry.

Reason (R) Youth are more energetic, open to new ideas, and better equipped with modern education and technology.

Codes

(a) Both A and R are true and R is the correct explanation of A.

(b) Both A and R are true, but R is not the correct explanation of A.

(c) A is true, but R is false.

(d) A is false, but R is true.

(iii) **Assertion** (A) Front office staff may not maintain a neat and clean appearance.

Reason (R) A well-groomed appearance creates a positive impression on guests and reflects professionalism.

Codes

(a) Both A and R are true and R is the correct explanation of A.

(b) Both A and R are true, but R is not the correct explanation of A.

(c) A is true, but R is false.

(d) A is false, but R is true.

(iv) Which of the following qualities do not match with the youth personality?

(a) Better informed

(b) Open to new ideas

(c) Lethargic and low energy in terms for success, ambition

(d) Aim for high monetary returns

22. **Read the following passage and answer the questions that follow.**

Cleaning is van integral part of any organisation/office /hotel, hence it involves planning and having a well organisation approach in selecting staff with practical house keeping operational skill with correct cleaning procedures and skill to do the task well under a qualified supervisor to ensure quality services .

(i) Which of the following hospitality service offer rented accommodation especially for sleeping and may not offer food and other services ?

(a) Hotel (b) Lodge (c) Motel (d) Camp

(ii) Which of the following is not included in stage of a guest cycle?

(a) Arrival (b) Departure (c) Pre-arrival (d) Tourism

(iii) Which of the following statement is incorrect?
(a) A hotel is a commercial establishment offering lodging, meals and other services to its guests.
(b) Smile is the most enduring competency required at front office personnel.
(c) Hospitality industry work on the idea of "A home away from work home" now days.
(d) Kitchen steward's work is related to cooking of food.

(iv) Which of the following can be used for environment conservationin hospitality sector?
I. Use of organic cotton sheets
II. Use of air conditioner
III. Excessive use of plastic
IV. Use of solor energy
(a) I and II (b) I and IV
(c) II and IV (d) III and IV

Answers

1. (c) Guests
2. (d) All of these
3. (d) kitchen steward
4. (c) hospitality industry
5. (c) Only II
6. (a) highways
7. (b) Furnished camps
8. (d) Janta flats
9. (a) front office
10. (a) florist
11. (c) Room attendant
12. (a) Linen Room Supervisor
13. (c) Talk with a smile
14. (d) Finance and Accounts
15. (d) Occupancy
16. (a) I and II
17. (b) 2 3 4 1
18. (a) 3 4 1 2
19. (a) Both A and R are true and R is the correct explanation of A.
20. (a) Both A and R are true and R is the correct explanation of A.
21. (i) (c) 2 3 4 1
(ii) (a) Both A and R are true and R is the correct explanation of A.
(iii) (d) A is false, but R is true.
(iv) (c) Lethargic and low energy in terms for success, ambition
22. (i) (b) Lodge
(ii) (d) Tourism
(iii) (d) Kitchen steward's work is related to cooking of food.
(iv) (b) I and IV

Subjective Questions

Very Short Answer Type Questions

1. What do you understand by the term tourist?

Ans. People who travel and stay temporarily in another place for a number of days are known as tourists. These people may visit various places within a country or across countries for excursion purpose and also for medical purpose (medical tourism).

2. State any three reasons due to which people move from one place to another.

Ans. People move from one place to another for many reasons and purposes. (Any three)

Three reasons for this movement are as follows

(i) People move for business purposes.
(ii) People move for marketing their products or for official purposes.
(iii) Many students leave their place just because to get enroll into good institution for study purpose.
(iv) People also move for pilgrimages, seeking health care (medical tourism), enjoying leisure time/vacation, visiting relatives or for shopping and so on.

3. Write the difference between a hotel and a motel. **CBSE Term II, 2022**

Ans. **Hotel** A hotel is an establishment providing accommodation, meals and other services for travellers and tourists.

Motel A motel is an establishment which provides services like hotel and parking and in which the rooms are usually accessible from an outdoor parking area.

4. Draw a diagram showing hospitality industry along with its various departments.

Ans. Diagram showing hospitality industry along with its various departments are as follows

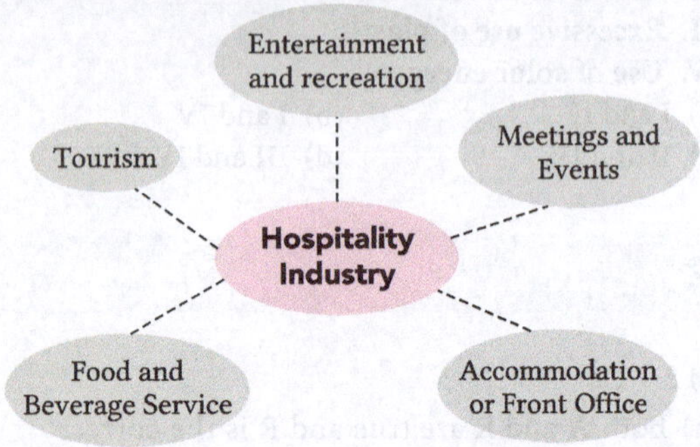

5. "The guest's decision to stay and repeatedly visit the hotel in future largely depends upon the quality of the services provided by housekeeping department of the hotel". Which four services are provided by this department? **CBSE SQP 2024**

Or **Enlist any four functions of housekeeping department.** **Competency Based Que; CBSE SQP, 2020**

Or **Enlist any four sections of housekeeping department.** **CBSE SQP**

Ans. Four services provided by housekeeping departments are

(i) **Cleaning Public Areas and Guestrooms** Ensuring cleanliness and hygiene throughout the hotel.

(ii) **Managing Laundry and Linen** Supplying and maintaining clean linens, towels and staff uniforms.

(iii) **Flower Arrangement and Garden Maintenance** Enhancing the hotel's ambiance with floral arrangements and well-kept landscapes.

(iv) **Co-ordination with Other Departments** Communicating with departments like front desk and maintenance to ensure seamless service, guest comfort and a pleasant stay experience.

6. You have been to a resort in your summer vacation. What are the four factors that will help you to decide whether you would like to go to the same resort in the future or not? **Competency Based Que; CBSE 2024 C**

Ans. The following factor will decide whether we would like to go to the same resort or not

(i) if we are greeted and served properly.

(ii) if we received warmth, and the best possible care and service in all respects including the affordable accommodation.

(iii) if we enjoyed the taste of the food offered by the resort services

(iv) if the resort maintains utmost quality in terms of hygiene and sanitation.

7. "Eco-friendly practices in hotels are crucial for reducing environmental impact, enhancing sustainability, and attracting environmentally conscious guests, ultimately leading to long-term cost savings and a positive brand image". Suggest four practices by which a hotel can ensure to be eco-friendly. **Competency Based Que, CBSE SQP 2024**

Ans. Four practices by which a hotel can ensure to be eco friendly are

(i) Using 100% organic cotton bed sheets minimises the use of harmful chemicals and supports sustainable agriculture.

(ii) Implementing a chemical-free laundry cycle with non-toxic, water-based, hypoallergenic, and biodegradable agents protects both the environment and guest health.

(iii) Placing cards in rooms encouraging towel reuse helps conserve water and energy.

(iv) Promoting the conservation of natural resources by saving water, electricity, and detergent used in laundering reduces overall consumption and waste.

Short Answer Type Questions

1. The phrase 'A home away from home' is often used in hospitality industry to denote that guests are provided with comforts and facilities similar to their homes. In this context, mention any four types of establishments who offer hospitality services. **CBSE 2024**

Ans. Establishments that offer hospitality services are as follows

(i) A **hotel** is an establishment providing accommodation, meals and other services for travellers and tourists.

(ii) A **hotel** is an establishment which provides services like hotel and parking and in which the rooms are usually accessible from an outdoor parking area.

(iii) A **lodge** offers rented accommodation especially for sleeping and may not offer food and other services.

(iv) A **resort** is known for its leisure attraction. It offers a broad range of amenities, sports facilities and leisure activities for ensuring a total vacation experience.

2. Enlist six features of Hospital laundry. **CBSE 2025**

Ans. The six features of Hospital laundry are

- It ensures the removal of germs and dirt from fabrics.
- It uses hot water to sanitize sheets and clothes.
- It has strong cleaning agents that are used for disinfection.
- It ensures clean and dirty laundry are kept apart to prevent contamination.

- It uses machines to dry items rapidly, meeting the hospital's immediate needs.
- It cleans staff uniforms regularly to maintain professional hygiene and safety standards.

3. Julia wants to set up her own small hotel. CBSE 2023

(i) She wants to make her employees understand the guest cycle first. Explain the four stages of guest cycle for her employees.

Or **Elaborate on the four stages of guest cycle.** CBSE SQP 2020

Or **Kartik's family has reserved a 3-night stay at a resort for their vacation.**

As the Front Office Manager, list down the actions to be taken during each stage of 'Guest cycle to ensure good hospitality services for Kartik's family. Which two staff members/personnel would assist the Front Office Manager in this work? CBSE 2025

(ii) List two environmental conservation and eco-friendly practices which she will ensure in her hotel. Competency Based Que

Ans. (i) On the basis of the stage of interaction and activities involved, the guest cycle is broadly classified into four main stages. These are pre arrival, arrival, stay and departure.

(a) **Pre-arrival Stage** The activities done in the pre-arrival stage include
- Quoting rates for a guest.
- Reserving a room as a part of central reservation system or reservation department.

(b) **Arrival** Stage In this stage the guest actually arrives and registers or checks-in.

(c) **Occupancy** At this stage various services are provided as per the guest's requirements, ensuring security of the guest and co-ordination of various guest services.

(d) **Departure** This is the final stage of the guest cycle where the guest is ready to leave/move out or 'check-out' of the accommodation.

The two staff members/ personnel, who assist the front office manager in this work are
- **Receptionist** Helps with check-in, check-out and guest inquiries.
- **Housekeeping Staff** Ensures clean and comfortable rooms and caters to guest needs.

(ii) Julia can encourage environment conservation in following ways

(a) By using 100 per cent organic cotton bed sheets, chemical-free laundry cycle and using agents which are non-toxic, water-based, hypoallergenic and biodegradable.

(b) Many hotels put cards in hotel rooms urging the reuse of towels, promoting the saving of natural resources like water, electricity, detergent used for laundering. Use of energy efficient light bulbs in rooms can help save electricity.

4. Ridhima joins front office staff of a large hotel where she gets to know about the various services provided by the staff. Competency Based Que

State the services given by the front office staff of the hotel.

Ans. After joining the front office staff of a large hotel, Ridhima gets to know about the services provided to guests by the staff. These services are as follows
- Welcoming guests
- Meeting and greeting them
- Organising reservation status of room availability
- Registering guests and allocation of rooms
- Maintaining records of check-in and check-out details
- Porter services
- Issuing room keys to guests
- Passing messages to customers
- Co-ordinating with other guest services
- Providing in-house and external information to the guests
- Preparing and settling their bills.

5. Shaurya has checked into a hotel. Which department's staff will first greet and welcome him? List any other three services provided by this department.

Competency Based Que; CBSE 2024

Ans. Shaurya will be greeted by staff of the front office department. Other services provided by this department include the following

For answer refer to Q. No. 4 of Short Answer Type Questions.

6. Explain the duties of the following

(i) Assistant Manager–Front Office
(ii) Bellboy
(iii) Public Area Supervisor
(iv) Room Attendant

Ans. (i) **Assistant Manager–Front Office** Organises and supervises the front office in the absence of front office manger and ensures smooth functioning of the front office.

(ii) **Bellboy** Responsible for shifting of baggage of guests, within and out of the room.

(iii) **Public Area Supervisor** She/He is responsible for maintaining cleanliness of the public areas (Main entrance, corridor, offices, banquet halls, restaurants, etc.). They get these works done through housemen.

(iv) **Room Attendant** She/He does actual cleaning of guest rooms and bathrooms. Housemen perform the heavy cleaning activities such as vacuuming, mopping, sweeping, shifting of furniture, etc.

7. The housekeeping department of a hotel is divided into several sections in order to function efficiently. Name any four of these sections. Mention any two duties of the executive housekeeper in the housekeeping department. **CBSE Term II, 2022**

Ans. The four sections of the housekeeping department are

(i) Floor supervisor (ii) Public Area supervisor

(iii) Florist (iv) Uniform supervisor

Two duties of the executive housekeeper are

(i) He has the responsibility for managing the functioning of the department through judicious use of manpower, materials, money, etc.

(ii) He checks schedules, cleanliness and all functioning of the housekeeping department.

8. Give one role of each of the following. **CBSE SQP**

(i) Assistant manager of front office

(ii) Chef-de-parties

(iii) Floor supervisor of housekeeping department

Ans. (i) Assistant manager of front office organises and supervises the front office in the absence of front office manager and ensures smooth functioning of the front office. He also handles guests while check-in and check-out, maintaining roster.

(ii) Chef-de-parties acts as supervisors for some sections of the kitchen.

(iii) Floor supervisor of housekeeping department is responsible for maintaining a particular floor or a wing. He is also responsible for cleanliness and maintenance of guest rooms, corridors and staircase and floor pantries.

9. What are the career opportunities available in the field of hospitality industry.

Ans. For answer refer to text under the heading 'Career Opportunities' on page no. 235.

Long Answer Type Questions

1. What do you understand by the term 'Hospitality'? Define the various establishments which offer hospitality services.

Ans. Hospitality is the relationship between a guest and a host, wherein the host receives the guest with some amount of goodwill, including the friendly reception or welcoming and entertainment of guests, visitors or strangers. The basic concept of hospitality is providing a place to stay, food, entertainment and other facilities to make the stay comfortable. There are various establishments that offer hospitality services.

- A **hotel** is an establishment providing accommodation, meals, and other services for travellers and tourists.
- A **motel** is an establishment which provides services like hotel and parking and in which the rooms are usually accessible from an outdoor parking area.
- A **lodge** offers rented accommodation especially for sleeping and may not offer food and other services.
- A **resort** is known for its leisure attraction. It offers a broad range of amenities, sports facilities and leisure activities for ensuring a total vacation experience.
- **Furnished apartments** provide all essential amenities needed by the guests.
- **Furnished camps** provide hospitality to people who go hiking, undertake adventure sports, etc.

2. Your brother has recently joined front office department of hotel. Tell him about four duties and responsibilities of each manager and supervisor of this department. **CBSE SQP Term II, 2021**

Ans. Four duties and responsibilities of front office manager are

(i) Responsible for managing the entire department, lobby, transport activities

(ii) Schedules shifts/staff rotation

(iii) Co-ordinating with housekeeping for VIP check-ins

(iv) Co-ordinating with sales department for any group or bulk check-ins

Four duties and responsibilities of front office supervisor are

(i) Manages each shift

(ii) Keeps a track of the occupancy

(iii) Briefing all the staff on the duty for that shift from the dept

(iv) Keeps a track on the check-ins and check-outs

3. Draw an organisational chart of a housekeeping department. What four responsibilities will Neeta perform if she joins this department? **CBSE SQP Term II, 2021**

Ans.

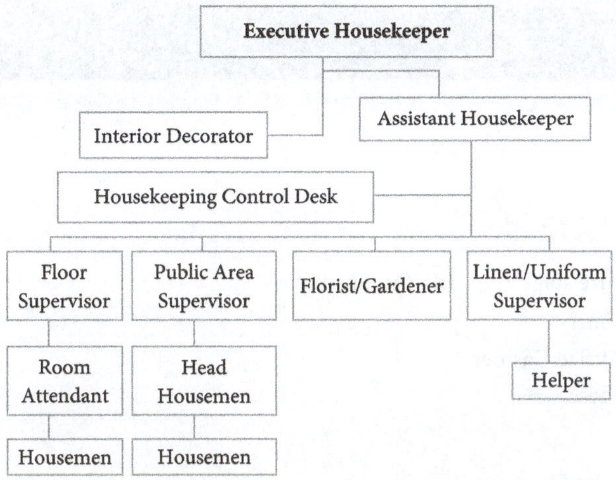

Four responsibilities of housekeeping department to be performed are

(i) Cleaning of public areas and guestrooms

(ii) Supply, upkeep of laundry and exchange of various linen

(iii) Internal flower arrangement and maintenance of external landscape or garden

(iv) Pest control

4. Suresh has got appointed as an assistant housekeeper. Who all will work under him? What responsibilities would he assign to each one of them?

Competency Based Que; CBSE 2021 C

Ans. An assistant housekeeper prepares duty schedule and checks cleanliness and functioning of the workers. Following people will work under Suresh and their responsibilities as assigned by Suresh will be

(i) **Desk Control Supervisor** has to co-ordinates with front office for information on departure of guests, gets vacated rooms cleaned and hands over cleaned rooms. This desk should be manned 24 hours, as guests and staff contact this desk to receive or transmit information any time.

(ii) **Floor Supervisor** is responsible for cleanliness and maintenance of guest rooms, corridors, and staircase and floor pantries.

(iii) **Room Attendant** will do actual cleaning of guest rooms and bath rooms. Housemen will perform the heavy cleaning activities such as vacuuming, mopping, sweeping, shifting of furniture.

(iv) **Public Area Supervisor** is responsible for maintaining cleanliness of the public areas (main entrance, corridor, offices, banquet halls, restaurants, etc.). They have to get work done through housemen.

(v) **Florist/Gardener** has to maintain garden and does flower arrangement in various parts of the hotel.

(vi) **Linen Room/Uniform Room Supervisor** is responsible for supply, acquisition, storage, issue and cleanliness of the linen and uniforms required in various parts of the hotel.

5. Mr. Kapoor is an executive housekeeper in the housekeeping department in a hotel. He explains his staff about their functions and duties. Explain about the functions of this department. **Competency Based Que**

Ans. Mr. Kapoor explains to his staff that the prime function of housekeeping department is to maintain cleanliness and space hygiene. The housekeeping department is divided into different sections in order to perform these functions efficiently

(i) **Housekeeping Control Desk** It passes on the information to housekeeping staff who are working in various parts of the hotel.

(ii) **Housekeeping Management** It plans, organises and controls all the activities of the housekeeping department.

(iii) **Guestroom Brigade** It upkeeps and cleans the guestrooms.

(iv) **Public Area Brigade** It maintains cleanliness of foyer, lobby, front office and other common areas.

(v) **Linen and Uniform Room** It co-ordinates with laundry; responsible for providing clean linen to entire establishment and uniform to all the staff.

(vi) **Horticulture and Flower Arrangement Team** It maintains landscape of the hotel and arranges flowers in rooms and at various places.

(vii) **Lost and Found Section** It deposits misplaced luggage of guests.

6. 'Fresh Cake and Cafe', a new bakery and coffee shop is opened in your city. Its Food and Beverage Department has the responsibility for the sale of food and beverages. Name any two service departments related to it. Describe four functions/roles of any one of these service departments. **CBSE 2025**

Ans. The two service departments in Fresh Cake and Cafe are

- **Marketing Department** Promotes the bakery and attracts customers.
- **Customer Service Department** Handles inquiries, resolves complaints and ensures satisfaction.

The four functions/roles of Marketing Department are

- **Advertising** Designs creative campaigns to showcase the menu and offers.
- **Social Media Management** Manages online presence to reach more people.
- **Market Research** Understands customer preferences and trends.
- **Event Planning** Organises special occasions like food festivals or celebrations.

SELF ASSESSMENT TEST

Objective Type Questions

1. In which stage of guest cycle a guest check-in a hotel?
   (a) Pre-arrival stage (b) Arrival stage (c) Departure stage (d) Occupancy
2. In a hotel bell captain and telephone operator work under whom?
   (a) Front Office Receptionist (b) Front Office Cashier
   (c) Front Office Manager (d) All of these
3. Match the following

	List I		List II
A.	Food and Beverage department	1.	Receptionist
B.	Front Office	2.	Accountant
C.	Housekeeping department	3.	Chef-de-partie
D.	Support service department	4.	Room attendant

   (a) A-3, B-1, C-4, D-2 (b) A-1, B-2, C-3, D-4 (c) A-2, B-3, C-1, D-4 (d) A-3, B-4, C-2, D-1
4. Who of the following is responsible for planning, organising and controlling the kitchen operations?
   (a) The deputy chef (b) The executive chef (c) Chef-de-cuisine (d) Both (b) and (c)
5. It is a commercial facility that provides food and beverages to the customers. It is equipped with dining tables, chairs and other required furniture with crockery, cutlery, etc.
   Which of the following institution of hospitality is described in the above description?
   (a) Lodge (b) Motel (c) Restaurant (d) Camps

Very Short Answer Type Questions

6. Enlist any three functions of a front office supervisor in a hotel.
7. Explain about three types of establishments which offer hospitality services to tourists.

Short Answer Type Questions

8. Being a lecturer of hotel management briefly explain about the importance and different stages of guest cycle.
9. In your hotel, there are various designations in front office and each has its assigned function/duty. Explain these in brief.

Long Answer Type Questions

10. What are back office departments? Explain the purpose of cleaning, linen and uniform room and flower arrangement.
11. Nishant wants to open his restaurant. In this context, define the restaurant. Describe the various designations and individuals handling the restaurant and their roles.
12. Why youth is form the major part of workforce in hospitality industry? Also mention essential competencies required to work in this industry.
13. Describe the scope of hospitality industry.

12

CHAPTER

Consumer Education and Protection involves informing and empowering consumers about their rights, responsibilities and available protections. It aims to enhance consumer awareness, help them make informed decisions, and safeguard them from unfair practices. Through education, consumers can better understand product quality, safety standards and ethical business practices.

▼ **YOUR STUDY GOALS**

12.1 Introduction
12.2 Significance of Consumer Education and Protection
12.3 Basic Concepts
12.4 Standardised Marks
12.5 Scope

▼ **YOUR PRACTICE GOAL**

– Objective Type Questions (33 Qs ; MCQs, A-R, Matching, Case Based)
Subjective Questions
– (15 VSAs, 9 SAs, 7 LAs)

Consumer Education and Protection

12.1 Introduction

- In our day-to-day life, we all purchase different varieties of goods and services to satisfy our needs and desires. This routine activity makes every human a natural consumer[1].
- However, some problems may arise after purchasing something or a service. These issues can lead to dissatisfaction and frustration with the buying experience.
- For example, even after paying for goods, the quality may not meet expectations for the price paid. Consumers often feel let down when they receive products that do not match their expected standards.
- Additionally, the quantity supplied might be less than what was promised. This discrepancy can lead to feelings of being cheated, as the consumer does not receive what they paid for.
- Sometimes, services paid for may fall short of what was advertised. Attractive promotions may create an image that does not align with the actual service provided.
- Such experiences can lead to feelings of frustration and being cheated by the manufacturer or service provider. Consumers may feel powerless when their expectations are not met.

1 **Consumer** A person who purchases goods and services for personal use.

- In these situations, consumers may take action to address the problem with the manufacturer or service provider. They might voice their concerns or seek corrective measures.
- However, it's uncertain whether they will be satisfied with the solution provided. Even if action is taken, the resolution may not meet the consumer's needs or expectations.
- Therefore, consumer education is important as it teaches us to be efficient and alert consumers. Being informed helps consumers to make better choices and advocate for their rights effectively.

12.2 Significance of Consumer Education and Protection

- The number of products being manufactured and sold are steadily increasing in both urban and rural markets. Consumers are now aware that manufacturers are responsible for supplying good quality products and if there is a problem, consumers have the right to redressal.
- **Manufacturers** can no longer take the consumers or customers for granted. Increasing number of consumers and volume of consumption of goods and services have made the manufacturers, suppliers or service providers realise that it is important to respect and satisfy the consumer, because consumer opinion determines the reputation of the company and its profits.
- India has made great efforts and transformed itself from an underdeveloped to a developing economy. This position has been attributed to industrialisation and globalisation. These economic changes have improved the standard of living along with increased purchasing power of consumers. The world has turned into a global village where global markets are facing many challenges. It is important that consumers should rise and give their global outlook for the progressive **global economy**.
- In order to ensure their welfare, consumers have to emerge as a progressive force. They have to understand the economic system and inter relationships of individuals with each other, with business and with government. It is necessary for today's consumer to be careful, alert and be well-informed. Thus, consumer education and protection have become important.
- Besides these, many foreign companies have been established in the country due to the liberal policy of the Indian Government. Today, a variety of products, made by multinationals that have established their manufacturing or assembly units in India or imported items, can be seen in many Indian stores. It is the outcome of globalisation.
- The establishment of these manufacturing or assembly units in India has both advantages and disadvantages. The advantage can be seen with the fact that Indian consumer has a variety of products to choose from and can look for better products with competitive pricing.
- The disadvantage of having a large range of products is that choosing the right product is now more difficult since one has to understand new technology, new products and new features. To make an informed decision one has to compare the price and quality, because consumers face problems such as malpractices, exploitation by unscrupulous sellers, misleading advertisements, making it important for each one of us to be wise consumers.

12.3 Basic Concepts

- A consumer is a person who is the final buyer of goods and services. They seek satisfaction for their personal needs and wants, from natural products to market offerings.
- Consumers are considered the primary component of a socio-economic system. Every human being, to some extent, desires a good standard of living.
- When purchasing power increases, consumers tend to buy products that offer comfort and satisfaction. These purchases often become symbols of prestige within society.
- This behavior contributes to an increasing number of **consumer footfalls**. As more people buy, more money flows into the market, driving the development and growth of the country's economy.

Important Terms Related to Consumer

There are other relevant terms related to consumer education and protection. These are as follows

- **Consumer Product** The term means any articles produced or distributed for sale to a consumer for personal or family use in one's home or in an institution, e.g. school, hospital, college, office, etc., or for business purposes.
- **Consumer Behaviour** It is a process through which the buyer makes decisions about purchasing goods or services.
- **Consumer Forum** A place or organisation where consumers can discuss consumer products or services and their advantages and disadvantages. Some forums work as advocacy groups that seek to protect consumers and help them address problems faced vis-a-vis consumer products.
- **Consumer Footfalls** This means the number of customers who visit any given space such as a store or a mall. Thus, with increasing consumption in a country, consumer footfalls are higher.

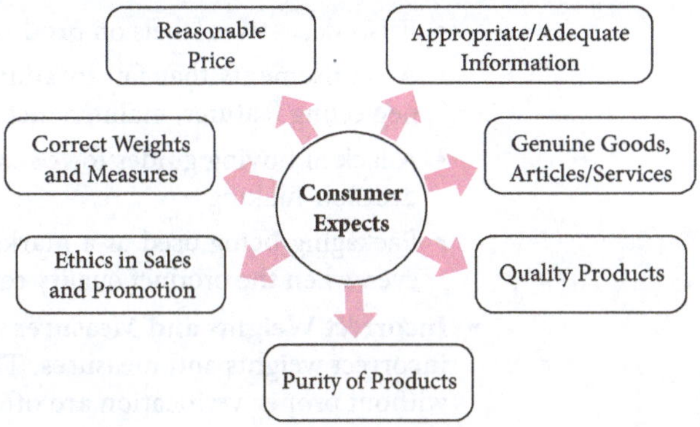

▲ *Consumers' Expectations while Purchasing Goods*

- The given figure explains that what a customer expects when she/he buys either a product or service.

Quick Test 1

1. What helps us become efficient and alert consumers?
2. Who ensures good quality products are supplied?
3. What is the process by which a buyer makes purchasing decisions?
4. What has the world turned into regarding global markets?

Consumer Problems

- Consumers often face problems in the marketplace due to unmet expectations by manufacturers or service providers.
- Some manufacturers may cheat consumers, leaving them uncertain about how to address issues.
- Many consumers lack knowledge about dealing with shoddy products and high prices.
- Issues such as adulteration and faulty weights and measures can arise when consumers are unaware of protection measures.
- Being aware of these problems is crucial to avoid being cheated.
- High levels of consumer awareness and protection are indicators of a country's development and progress.

Some of the major problems faced by consumers are

- **Substandard or Poor Quality Goods** A same product can be made by many manufacturers-multinationals, local Indian brands, or imported from outside. However, the quality of the product and the material used may differ significantly, making it difficult for a customer to identify an inferior quality product. Many consumers are unaware of quality standards.
- **Adulteration** Adulteration can be intentional or unintentional. It occurs when the quality of a substance is compromised by removing or adding something to the product. This is a serious issue as it exploits uninformed customers and can be injurious to their health and safety.
- **High Prices** Consumers expect fair and reasonable pricing for products. However, prices are influenced by government policy, availability, quality, delivery systems, market location, distribution methods, promotional costs and consumer demand for convenience. Some consumers mistakenly equate price with quality, leading to confusion, as products of the same quality may have different prices due to production costs and other factors.

- **Lack of Consumer Information** A lack of knowledge regarding consumer rights, responsibilities, and legislative protections can result in customers being cheated.
- Inadequate or wrong information given by manufacturers. This includes
  - False, deceptives labels on products. Labels with incomplete information
  - Advertisements that fail to address essential questions about the product's qualities or uses, often neglecting features, maintenance, and after-sales service.
  - A lack of buying guides for consumer durables[2] and non-durables[3], which would aid consumers in decision-making.
  - Packaging being used as a marketing tool, leading to impulsive purchases due to attractive designs, even when the product quality remains unchanged.
- **Incorrect Weights and Measures** Consumers may receive less quantity than what they paid for due to incorrect weights and measures. This exploitation can occur through deceptive practices, and weights without proper verification are often unreliable.
- **Spurious/Duplicate/Imitation Products** Customers may be misled by spurious products or imitations of well-known brands that use similar colors, packaging, and names. These products are typically of poor quality and can be unsafe.
- **Sales Promotion Schemes to Entice Consumers** The Indian market is flooded with products from both national and multinational brands competing for market share. They employ various sales promotion schemes like exchange offers and lucky draws, which can be deceptive. Consumers may feel pressured by these gimmicks, leading to misguided purchases.
- **Consumer Problems Regarding Services** Beyond product consumption, consumers often face grievances related to services from public utilities like electricity, water, banks and insurance companies. Poor after-sales service and unfulfilled promises are common issues.
- It is crucial for consumers to be informed and educated about their rights, responsibilities and protection mechanisms. Awareness can shield them from deceptive practices and clever marketing strategies. Consumer education and protection empower individuals to navigate market forces and understand relevant legislation and policies, ultimately fostering informed choices.

Eco-friendly Protection and Green Consumption The promotion of sustainability relates to both production and consumption. The green market offers eco-friendly products that generate less waste, utilise fewer raw materials and conserve resources.

The Consumer Protection Act (CPA) 1986

- The Consumer Protection Act[4] is a landmark legislation designed to protect consumer interests.
- Its main function is to safeguard consumers from fraudulent trade practices in the marketplace.
- It is based on the principle of **self-help**.

Six Consumer Rights[5] under the Consumer Protection Act

(i) Right to Safety	(ii) Right to Be Informed	(iii) Right to Choose
(iv) Right to Be Heard	(v) Right to Redressal	(vi) Right to Education

2 Consumer Durables Consumer durables are products that are intended to last for a long time. They are also known as durable goods. For example, automobiles, electronics like refrigerators.

3 Consumer non-durables These are the products that are consumed quickly or have a lifespan of less than three years. For example, food and beverages.

4 Consumer Protection Act The Consumer Protection Act, implemented in 1986, gives easy and fast compensation to consumer grievances.

5 Consumer Rights Empowers and protects consumer against market abuses and social injustices.

Implications of the Act

The Consumer Protection Act has two implications. These are as follows

- It allows consumers to file complaints with authorities for speedy redressal.
- Consumers can claim compensation for losses or injury due to manufacturer negligence.
- The act applies to all goods and services in the market unless specified by the Central Government.
- It empowers the consumer movement to be effective and people-oriented.

The Consumer Protection Act (CPA) 2019

- The CPA 2019 replaces the 30-year-old CPA 1986, tightening rules for consumer protection.
- Key highlights include the introduction of a central regulator, strict penalties for misleading advertisements and guidelines for e-commerce.

Consumer Rights

- These are rights designed to ensure that all consumers obtain goods and services of reasonable quality, at fair prices without any malpractices. Thus, consumer rights are a legal protection to the consumers. The six rights under the Consumer Protection Act are as follows

  (i) **Right to Safety** This right is very important for consumers. It refers to the right to be protected against hazardous effects that may be caused to the health or life of consumers. This right specifies that consumers have the right to be protected against products, production processes, and services that are hazardous to health or life.

  (ii) **Right to be Informed** This is the second right, which means the right to be informed about the quality, quantity, potency, purity, standard and price of goods and services. This right protects consumers against unfair trade practices.

  (iii) **Right to Choose** This right implies that every consumer has the right to have access to products of varying quality and quantities, prices, size and design, at competitive prices and to choose according to their needs and wants.

  (iv) **Right to be Heard** This right means that consumers' interests will receive due consideration at appropriate consumer forums. It also includes the right to be represented in various forums that help to ensure consumer welfare. To enable consumers to exercise this right, both the state and voluntary agencies are expected to set up such forums.

  (v) **Right to Seek Redressal** The act provides the right to seek redressal against unfair trade practices or unscrupulous exploitation to every consumer. It includes the right to fair settlement of genuine grievances and involves the right to receive compensation for faulty goods and services.

  (vi) **Right to Consumer Education** This right implies that every individual must have the right to acquire knowledge and skills in order to be an informed consumer, enabling them to make wise decisions while purchasing goods and hiring services. This right also suggests that consumers should be educated enough to solve problems themselves.

Quick Test 2

1 What can harm the health and safety of consumers?
2 What causes confusion for consumers in the marketplace?
3 How many rights are included in the Consumer Protection Act (CPA), 1986?
4 What principle is the Consumer Protection Act based on?

12.4 Standardised Marks

- **Standardised marks**[6] help ensure the **quality** and **purity** of products. These marks serve as symbols of assured quality for consumers. It is important for consumers to be aware of different standard marks and the products they cover.
- The government has provided some important standardised marks to protect consumers which are desailad follows

ISI Mark

- ISI is the certification mark of the Bureau of Indian Standards (BIS). It was previously known as the Indian Standards Institution (ISI). Licenses are issued to manufacturers whose goods meet the relevant standards. Food items covered under Indian standards include vegetables, fruits and meat products.
- Other food categories include spices and condiments, processed foods, cereal and soya products, candies and beverages. BIS standards also cover products like electrical goods, soaps, detergents, paints and paper. Some items under this scheme require **mandatory** certification.

▲ *ISI Mark*

AGMARK and Fruit Product Order (FPO)

- The Government of India has established standards for food products. AGMARK ensures the quality and reliability of agricultural products. Consumers should look for the AGMARK seal before purchasing any agricultural product.
- FPO sets statutory minimum standards for the quality of various fruits and vegetable products. FPO also regulates processing facilities for these products.
- Additionally, FPO establishes limits on metallic contaminants and preservatives in different fruit products.

▲ *FPO*

AGMARK

Wool Mark

- This standard mark signifies **quality for wool** or woolen garments. It is designed by the International Wool Secretariat.
- The mark indicates that the wool is pure. It ensures that the marked garment is made only of pure wool, without other fibers.

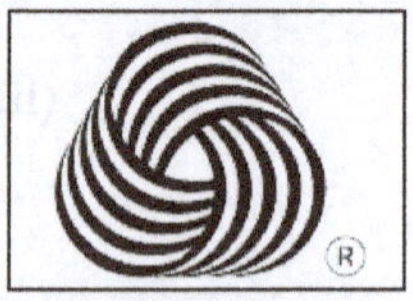

▲ *Wool Mark*

The Silk Mark

- The Silk Mark is a quality assurance label for pure silk. It guarantees the **authenticity of the silk.**
- The mark also serves as a brand for the generic promotion of pure silk. It ensures that the product is made of '100 per cent natural silk'.

▲ *Silk Mark*

Hallmark

- Hallmark is designed for precious metals like **platinum, silver** and **gold.** It indicates that articles made from these metals have been evaluated and tested.
- The testing is conducted at an official as saying and Hallmarking Centre. The hallmark certifies that the metal used meets national and international standards of fineness and purity.

▲ *Hallmark*

Ecomark Scheme

- BIS operates the Ecomark scheme for labeling **household** consumer **products.** Products covered include soaps, detergents, paper, packaging materials and plastic products.
- The logo for the Ecomark scheme is an earthen pot. The logo signifies that the product is environmentally friendly. Ecomark products do not produce hazardous waste, are biodegradable and can be recycled.

▲ *Ecomark*

6 Standardisation Marks Marks or symbols given to a product, which meets certain standards with respect to the quality in terms of material used, methods of manufacturing, labelling, packaging and performance.

FSSAI

- The Food Safety and Standards Authority of India (FSSAI) was established under the Food Safety and Standards Act, 2006. FSSAI lays down science-based standards for food articles.
- It regulates the manufacture, storage, distribution and sale of food products. The aim is to ensure the availability of safe food for human consumption.

▲ *FSSAI Mark*

Standardisation Marks

Standard Mark	Full Name	Agency Which Gives it	Items having this Marks
ISI	Indian Standard Institution	Bureau of Indian Standards (BIS)	Mandatory mineral water, Condensed milk, Milk powder etc Voluntary Biscuit, tea, coffee etc.
Agmark	Agricultural Marketing	Directorate of marketing and Inspection	Agricultural Product (raw and Processed) like flour, ghee, oil, besan etc.
FSSAI	Food Safety and Standards Authority of India	Ministry of Health and Family Welfare	All Food Product
Woolmark	Woolmark	International Wool Secretariat	Pure wool, woolen clothes, sweater blanket
Silk Mark	Silk Mark	Silk Mark Organisation of India (SMOI)	Pure Silk Products
Hallmark	Hallmark	Burear of Indian Standard (BIS)	Gold, Silver and Platinum Jewellery
Ecomark	Eco mark	Burear of Indian Standard (BIS)	Soap, Detergent, Paints, Paper, Cosmetics, Packing material

Protection Councils

- Apart from statutory, semi-government and non-government bodies like BIS and Directorate of Marketing and Inspection (DMI), Government of India, there are protection councils also.
- These protection councils are established by the Government of India at central and state levels.
- Many NGOs and voluntary consumer organisations focus on consumer education and protection.
- They create awareness by disseminating information through magazines, booklets and newsletters.
- Consumer organisations engage in activities like comparative testing of products.
- They raise awareness about harmful and unsafe products and facilitate product recalls.
- These organisations provide information about new legislative provisions for consumers.
- They offer legal advice, advocacy, and handle consumer grievances and complaints.
- Consumer organisations act as vigilance groups and organise public meetings.
- They maintain libraries and documentation centers to support consumer awareness and empowerment.
- Examples of consumer organisations in India include VOICE and CERC.
- International organisations are as follows
  - Consumer Reports by the US based Consumers Union.
  - Which by UK based Consumers Association.
  - Choice by Australian Consumers Association.

Consumer Responsibilities

Every human being has both rights and responsibilities. In order to exercise one's rights, it is necessary to be aware of one's duties. As consumers, we need to be mindful of our responsibilities.

Some important consumer responsibilities are as follows

- It is the responsibility of consumers to regularly update their knowledge of various laws and legislative provisions made by the government.
- Consumers should be honest in all their dealings and must pay for all their purchases.
- It is also the responsibility of consumers to conduct a market survey before making a purchase, to find out about different brands, features, etc., available in various shops and markets, and to compare prices. This will help them make a wise choice.
- Consumers should feel free to choose from the variety available according to their needs and requirements. It is the responsibility of the consumer to read all the information provided on the label or brochure while making a purchase.
- Consumers should buy only those products that have standardised marks to assure the quality of the products.
- Consumers should keep receipts and other relevant documents of purchase. These are proofs of purchase that may be needed if a consumer files complaints in case of problems, defects or malfunctioning products.
- In the case of purchasing services like insurance, credit cards or bank deposits, consumers should read and understand all terms and conditions, liabilities and service charges, and make an effort to clarify any unclear points with the representative.
- Consumers must have knowledge about various national and international consumer organisations regarding their activities and works. They should also understand the benefits of becoming a member of such organisations.

Skills Required for Career in Consumer Studies Field

If a person wants to be successful in the field of consumer studies, he/she needs knowledge about consumer protection mechanisms and redressal agencies. Besides these, the person also needs the following skills

- **Soft Skills Good communication** and interpersonal skills[7], an empathetic and understanding attitude, being a good listener, and being creative in developing programmes, advertisements, talks, etc., for consumer awareness.
- **Writing Skills** These are important for developing educational material for consumer education, reporting consumer tests of products, etc.
- **A willingness** to help fellow consumers and the public at large.
- Being a professional in this field, a person must have thorough knowledge about quality standards of various kinds of products, adulteration and detection of adulterants, as well as consumer protection laws, consumer rights and responsibilities.
- After pursuing graduate and postgraduate level courses, a person can choose several career options in the area of consumer education and protection. These programmes aim at creating an overall awareness and training on consumer affairs with special emphasis on consumer protection.
- To choose this as a career, a person has many options such as degree courses in B.Sc. Home Science or B.A. Home Science, B.Sc. Family Resource Management, B.Sc. Home Management, B.Sc. Resource Management, Bachelor of Business Administration (B.B.A.) or Bachelor of Business Studies (B.B.S.), etc.
- Different institutions have different names for this subject, such as Consumer Studies, Consumer Education, Consumer Behaviour and Consumer in the Market.

7 Interpersonal skills, also known as people skills, are the abilities and qualities that help people communicate and build relationships.

12.5 Scope

After getting training in the area of consumer education and protection, a person could develop his/her career in the following areas

- **Work in Government Organisations** A person can work in government organisations like the Bureau of Indian Standards, Directorate of Marketing and Inspection, and the Ministry of Consumer Affairs in various decision-making, managerial and technical positions.
- **Work in Voluntary Consumer Organisations** A person may have a career in a voluntary consumer organisation for product testing, creating consumer awareness, consumer education or empowerment, and publication of their magazine, etc.
- **Work in the Consumer Division of Corporate Houses** These houses deal with consumer complaints and suggestions or in customer relationship management and customer facilitation divisions, looking into creating customer databases and dealing with them on a one-to-one personal basis.
- **Work with Market Research Organisations** After working in such organisations, a person can work in areas of consumer behaviour, product reach, consumer acceptance of new products, and consumer feedback and suggestions.
- **Start Your Own Consumer Organisation** A person can also start his/her own consumer organisation and can deal with various issues related to consumers.
- **Work in National Consumer Helpline** By working in such organisations, a person can be a consumer counsellor or help people in getting redressal for their complaints, etc.
- **Work as Consultants to Consumer Clubs Being Run by Schools and Colleges** A person can work as a consultant in schools and colleges and can manage and plan their educative and outreach activities, take up teaching assignments in the area of consumer studies, etc. The person can also function as a freelance consultant for redressal guidance through consumer courts and other alternative redressal mechanisms.
- **Work with the Department of Audio-Visual Publicity as Content Developer** A person can work in such departments for their advertisements dealing with consumer awareness and education in the print and electronic media.
- **Work as an Analyst in Consumer Testing Laboratories** Being an analyst, the person can work for comparative evaluation of products.
- **Become Consumer Activists** Some people may also become consumer activists, and with legal training, can plead cases in Consumer Protection Courts.
- **Journalism Related to Consumer Affairs** Those who have excellent writing skills may take up journalism related to consumer affairs.
- Besides all these, those interested can work at junior level to assist individuals in financial management. With further training and experience, one can move into careers related to insurance, shares and financial portfolio management. For example, an interested person with some additional training can work at junior level to assist individuals in financial management. With further training and experience, a person can choose different career options related to insurance, shares, and financial portfolio management.

Quick Test 3

1. What are other mechanisms of consumer protection?
2. What does ISI stand for?
3. What type of product should consumers look for the AGMARK seal before purchasing?
4. Name the publication brought out by Delhi based consumer organisation?
5. Mention the consumer based publication launched by Australian Consumers Association.

Mind Map

CONSUMER EDUCATION AND PROTECTION

1 Introduction to Consumerism

- Every individual is a natural consumer, purchasing goods and services to meet their needs and desires.
- Problems can arise after purchasing goods or services, leading to dissatisfaction.

For example, Consumer education is crucial to help individuals make informed decisions, advocate for their rights, and address issues effectively.

2 Significance of Consumer Education and Protection

- **Growing Consumer Awareness** As the number of products and services increases, consumers are becoming more aware of their rights to good quality products and redressal if issues arise.
- **Manufacturer Accountability** Manufacturers and service providers can no longer take consumers for granted. Consumer satisfaction is essential for company reputation and profits.
- **Economic Growth and Globalisation** India's transformation to a developing economy has raised consumer purchasing power, but it also introduces challenges from global markets.
- **Consumer Empowerment** To ensure their welfare, consumers need to be well-informed, careful, and alert in navigating the economic system. Consumer education is vital in this process.
- **Impact of Globalisation** With the presence of multinational companies in India, consumers now have a wider range of products but face challenges in choosing the right one.
- **Challenges** The variety of products makes decision-making difficult due to misleading advertisements, exploitation, and malpractices by sellers. This emphasises the need for informed, wise consumers.

3 Basic Concepts in Consumer Education and Protection

- **Consumer** The final buyer of goods/services, seeking satisfaction for personal needs, driving economic growth.
- **Consumer Product** Goods for personal, family, or business use.
- **Consumer Behaviour** The decision-making process in purchasing goods/services.
- **Consumer Forum** A platform for consumers to discuss and advocate for their rights.
- **Consumer Footfalls** The number of customers visiting a place, indicating consumption and economic growth.

Major Consumer Problems

- **Substandard Goods** Poor quality products that exploit unaware consumers.
- **Adulteration** Contaminated products that pose health risks.
- **High Prices** Confusion between price and quality.
- **Lack of Information** Insufficient consumer knowledge leading to exploitation.
- **Incorrect Weights and Measures** Deceptive practices providing less than paid for.
- **Spurious Products** Fake products that mislead consumers.
- **Sales Promotion Deception** Misleading schemes influencing poor purchases.

The Consumer Protection Act (CPA)

- **CPA 1986** Provided redressal and compensation mechanisms.
- **CPA 2019** Strengthened protections with e-commerce regulations and penalties for misleading ads.

Consumer Rights Under CPA

- Right to Safety
- Right to Be Informed
- Right to Choose
- Right to Be Heard
- Right to Seek Redressal
- Right to Consumer Education

4 Standardised Marks for Consumer Protection

- **ISI Mark** Ensures product quality and safety (e.g., food, electrical goods).
- **AGMARK and FPO** Certifies agricultural and fruit products for quality.
- **Wool Mark** Guarantees pure wool products.
- **Silk Mark** Verifies 100% natural silk.
- **Hallmark** Ensures purity of precious metals.
- **Eco Mark** Indicates environmentally friendly products.
- **FSSAI** Regulates food safety and standards.

Protection Councils

- Government and NGO organisations protect consumers by raising awareness, handling complaints, and conducting product testing (e.g., VOICE, CERC).

Consumer Responsibilities

- Stay informed, conduct market research, read labels, choose products with standard marks and keep receipts.
- Understand service terms and conditions and support consumer organisations.

Skills for a Career in Consumer Studies

- Strong communication, writing and empathy skills.
- Knowledge of consumer protection laws and quality standards.
- Educational background in fields like Home Science, Business Admin, or Consumer Studies.

5 Career Opportunities in Consumer Education and Protection

- **Government Roles** Work in organisations like BIS or the Ministry of Consumer Affairs.
- **Voluntary Organisations** Engage in product testing and consumer awareness.
- **Corporate Sector** Handle consumer complaints, customer relationships and feedback.
- **Market Research** Analyse consumer behaviour and product acceptance.

- **Own Consumer Organisation** Start a business focused on consumer rights.
- **National Helplines** Assist in resolving consumer complaints.
- **Consulting in Schools** Advise on consumer education and awareness.
- **Publicity Content Development** Create consumer awareness campaigns.
- **Consumer Testing Labs** Analyse and evaluate products.
- **Consumer Activism** Advocate for consumer rights in legal forums.
- **Consumer Journalism** Write for publications on consumer issues.
- **Financial Management** Assist with financial planning and insurance.
- These offer varied career paths in consumer protection and education.

27. Six reasons about a pre-school environment is beneficial for young children's development are
- It encourages social skills through interaction with peers.
- It develops communication abilities by improving language skills.
- It enhances emotional growth by teaching sharing and empathy.
- It builds cognitive skills with activities like puzzles and storytelling.
- It promotes physical development through play and movement.
- It prepares children for formal schooling by instilling discipline and routines.

28. (i) Computer skills are vital for DCJ professionals as they help in data analysis, digital research, editing and efficient communication in today's technology-driven world.

(ii) Development Journalists can work in media reporting to highlight social issues and in community development projects to bring awareness and promote change.

(iii) The umbrella term for technologies like computer hardware, software and digital broadcast is Information and Communication Technology (ICT).

29. The six features of Hospital laundry are
- It ensures the removal of germs and dirt from fabrics.
- It uses hot water to sanitise sheets and clothes.
- It has strong cleaning agents that are used for disinfection.
- It ensures clean and dirty laundry are kept apart to prevent contamination.
- It uses machines to dry items rapidly, meeting the hospital's immediate needs.
- It cleans staff uniforms regularly to maintain professional hygiene and safety standards.

Or The six work operations which are performed by an automatic washing machine are
- **Filling Water** It automatically fills the drum with water as per the settings.
- **Washing Clothes** It rotates clothes to remove dirt with water and detergent.
- **Rinsing** It washes off detergent with clean water after the wash cycle.
- **Spinning** It spins clothes to remove excess water.
- **Drying** It partially dries clothes after spinning.
- **Heating Water** It heats water for better cleaning when required.

30. (i) A person with dentures should have a soft and easy-to-chew diet to avoid discomfort. The two examples of this diet are
- **Mashed Foods** Examples include mashed potatoes, cooked vegetables or pureed fruits.
- **Soft Dairy** Items like yogurt, paneer (cottage cheese), or milk-based puddings are suitable for easy consumption.

(ii) The two ways to feed a patient are
- **Oral Feeding** The patient is fed soft and easy-to-chew food directly using a spoon or feeding cup, ensuring small portions for easy swallowing.
- **Tube Feeding** A feeding tube is used to provide liquid nutrition directly to the stomach or intestine, suitable for patients unable to eat orally.

31. (i) A fruit and vegetable vendor deceive his customers using defective weights and measures by the following four ways
- Using tampered or damaged weighing scales.
- Adding extra weights hidden under the scale to mislead measurements.
- Not placing items properly on the scale for accurate weighing.
- Manipulating electronic scales to show incorrect readings.

(ii) As an alert consumer, the two responsibilities of the grandmother are
- Always check the accuracy of the weighing scales before buying.
- Demand fair practices and report fraud to authorities if the vendor cheats.

32. (i) The two significant reasons of importance of Food Quality and Safety are
- Food quality ensures that the food we eat is nutritious and free from harmful substances, protecting our health and improving overall well-being.
- Food safety prevents contamination and food-borne diseases, ensuring the food is safe to consume and meeting global health standards.

(ii) The two common food-borne pathogens that can be spread infection in healthy individuals are
- **Salmonella** It is found in raw meat, eggs and dairy products and it can cause food poisoning.
- **E. coli** It is found in undercooked food or contaminated water, which can lead to stomach infections.

Or (i) The full name of the law is the Food Safety and Standards Act. It was enacted in 2006 to unify and update India's food safety laws.

(ii) The two systems that a company can use to ensure food safety and quality are

- **HACCP (Hazard Analysis and Critical Control Points)** A system that identifies risks in food production and ensures they are controlled.
- **ISO 22000** An international standard focusing on safe food practices across the production process, from raw materials to packaging.

33. (i) The three ways by which a fashion design team would integrate the principles of proportion into their design process, with a focus on Golden Mean are

- **Balanced Garment Design** The team can use the Golden Ratio (1:1.618) to create well-proportioned clothing elements like sleeves and hemlines.
- **Pattern Placement** They can place prints, buttons or embroidery based on Golden Ratio points to enhance visual appeal.
- **Seam and Cut Lines** Proportional seam placements, inspired by the Golden Ratio, ensure the outfit looks harmoniously structured and elegant.

(ii) On the Grey Scale, colour value 0 means pure black and colour value 10 means pure white. These values show extreme ends of contrast.

34. As the Front Office Manager, the actions to be taken during each stage of 'Guest cycle' to ensure good hospitality services for Kartik's family are

- **Pre-Arrival** Ensure accurate reservations, confirm special requests and prepare a warm welcome.
- **Arrival** Greet the family, assist with check-in and provide a quick tour of resort facilities.
- **Stay** Address their needs, manage housekeeping and room service and ensure comfort throughout their stay.
- **Departure** Assist with check-out, confirm bill settlement and ask for feedback to improve services.

The two staff members/ personnel, who assist the front office manager in this work are

- **Receptionist** Helps with check-in, check-out and guest inquiries.
- **Housekeeping Staff** Ensures clean and comfortable rooms and caters to guest needs.

Or The two service departments in Fresh Cake and Cafe are

- **Marketing Department** Promotes the bakery and attracts customers.
- **Customer Service Department** Handles inquiries, resolves complaints and ensures satisfaction.

The four functions/roles of Marketing Department are

- **Advertising** Designs creative campaigns to showcase the menu and offers.
- **Social Media Management** Manages online presence to reach more people.
- **Market Research** Understands customer preferences and trends.
- **Event Planning** Organises special occasions like food festivals or celebrations.

35. (i) The classification and differentiation of the garments such as, blazer jackets, hot pants, polo shirts and baggy pants as per fashion industry terms are

Garment	Category	Description
Blazer Jackets	Formal wear	These are tailored and structured jackets for business or formal events.
Hot Pants	Casual wear	These are very short and fitted shorts, which are popular for casual outings.
Polo Shirts	Semi-formal/ Casual Wear	These are collared shirts, typically with buttons, suitable for semi-formal and casual settings.
Baggy Pants	Street wear	These are loose-fitting trousers, popular in urban and casual fashion.
Hot Pants	Casual wear	These are very short and fitted shorts, which are popular for casual outings.

(ii) The three career opportunities which are available to fashion design professionals in this fashion store and their role are

- **Fashion Designer** Creates new and trendy clothing designs for customers based on the latest fashion trends.
- **Merchandiser** Ensures the right products are available in the store, manages stock and displays clothes attractively for customers.
- **Stylist** Helps customers choose outfits that suit their style and preferences, providing a personalised shopping experience.